Ai Adobe
Illustrator
2020 release

CLASSROOM IN A BOOK®
The official training workbook from Adobe

Brian Wood

Adobe Illustrator Classroom in a Book® (2020 release)

Cover Illustration: Karan Singh, behance.net/madebykaran

ISBN-13: 978-0-13-641267-0
ISBN-10: 0-13-641267-X

1 2019

WHERE ARE THE LESSON FILES?

Purchase of this Classroom in a Book in any format gives you access to the lesson files you'll need to complete the exercises in the book.

1 Go to www.adobepress.com/IllustratorCIB2020.

2 Sign in or create a new account.

3 Click Submit.

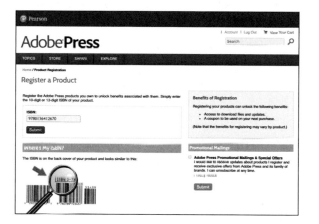

Note: If you encounter problems registering your product or accessing the lesson files or web edition, go to www.adobepress.com/support for assistance.

4 Answer the questions as proof of purchase.

5 The lesson files can be accessed through the Registered Products tab on your Account page.

6 Click the Access Bonus Content link below the title of your product to proceed to the download page. Click the lesson file links to download them to your computer.

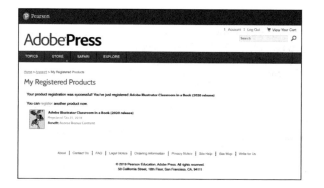

Note: If you purchased a digital product directly from www.adobepress.com or www.peachpit.com, your product will already be registered. However, you still need to follow the registration steps and answer the proof of purchase question before the Access Bonus Content link will appear under the product on your Registered Products tab.

CONTENTS

1 GETTING TO KNOW THE WORK AREA — 30

4 EDITING AND COMBINING SHAPES AND PATHS   112

5 TRANSFORMING ARTWORK   138

6 USING THE BASIC DRAWING TOOLS   166

7 DRAWING WITH THE PEN TOOL   184

8   USING COLOR TO ENHANCE SIGNAGE   210

GETTING STARTED

Adobe® Illustrator® is the industry-standard illustration application for print, multimedia, and online graphics. Whether you are a designer or a technical illustrator producing artwork for print publishing, an artist producing multimedia graphics, or a creator of web pages or online content, Adobe Illustrator offers you the tools you need to get professional-quality results.

About Classroom in a Book®

Adobe Illustrator Classroom in a Book® (2020 release) is part of the official training series for Adobe graphics and publishing software developed with the support of Adobe product experts. The features and exercises in this book are based on Illustrator (2020 release).

The lessons are designed so that you can learn at your own pace. If you're new to Adobe Illustrator, you'll learn the fundamentals you need to master to put the application to work. If you are an experienced user, you'll find that Classroom in a Book® also teaches some more advanced features, including tips and techniques for using the latest version of Adobe Illustrator.

Although each lesson provides step-by-step instructions for creating a specific project, there's room for exploration and experimentation. You can follow the book from start to finish or do only the lessons that correspond to your interests and needs. Each lesson concludes with a review section to quiz you on the main concepts covered.

Prerequisites

Before beginning to use *Adobe Illustrator Classroom in a Book® (2020 release)*, you should have working knowledge of your computer and its operating system. Make sure that you know how to use the mouse and standard menus and commands and also how to open, save, and close files. If you need to review these techniques, see the printed or online documentation for macOS or Windows.

Installing the program

● **Note:** When instructions differ by platform, macOS commands appear first and then the Windows commands, with the platform noted in parentheses. For example, "press Option (macOS) or Alt (Windows), and click away from the artwork."

Before you begin using *Adobe Illustrator Classroom in a Book® (2020 release)*, make sure that your system is set up correctly and that you've installed the required software and hardware.

You must purchase the Adobe Illustrator software separately. For complete instructions on installing the software, visit helpx.adobe.com/support/illustrator.html. You must install Illustrator from Adobe Creative Cloud onto your hard disk. Follow the on-screen instructions.

Fonts used in this book

The Classroom in a Book lesson files use fonts that are part of the Adobe Portfolio plan included with your Creative Cloud subscription, and trial Creative Cloud members have access to a selection of fonts from Adobe for web and desktop use.

For more information about fonts and installation, see the Adobe Illustrator Read Me file on the web at helpx.adobe.com/support/illustrator.html.

Online Content

Your purchase of this Classroom in a Book includes online materials provided by way of your Account page on adobepress.com. These include:

Lesson files

To work through the projects in this book, you will need to download the lesson files by following the instructions below.

Web Edition

The Web Edition is an online interactive version of the book providing an enhanced learning experience. Your Web Edition can be accessed from any device with a connection to the Internet and it contains:

- The complete text of the book
- Hours of instructional video keyed to the text
- Interactive quizzes

Accessing the lesson files and Web Edition

You must register your purchase on adobepress.com in order to access the online content:

1 Go to www.adobepress.com/IllustratorCIB2020

2 Sign in or create a new account.

3 Click Register.

4 Answer the question as proof of purchase.

5 The lesson files can be accessed from the Registered Products tab on your Account page. Click the Access Bonus Content link below the title of your product to proceed to the download page. Click the lesson file link(s) to download them to your computer.

The Web Edition can be accessed from the Digital Purchases tab on your Account page. Click the Launch link to access the product.

● **Note:** If you purchased a digital product directly from www.adobepress.com or www.peachpit.com, your product will already be registered. However, you still need to follow the registration steps and answer the proof of purchase question before the Access Bonus Content link will appear under the product on your Registered Products tab.

Restoring default preferences

● Note: If finding the preferences file proves difficult, please contact brian@ brianwoodtraining.com for assistance.

The preferences file controls how command settings appear on your screen when you open the Adobe Illustrator program. Each time you quit Adobe Illustrator, the position of the panels and certain command settings are recorded in different preference files. If you want to restore the tools and settings to their original default settings, you can delete the current Adobe Illustrator Prefs file. Adobe Illustrator creates a new preferences file, if one doesn't already exist, the next time you start the program and save a file.

You must restore the default preferences for Illustrator before you begin each lesson. This ensures that the tools function and the defaults are set exactly as described in this book. When you have finished the book, you can restore your saved settings, if you like.

To delete or save the current Illustrator preferences file

The preferences file is created after you quit the program the first time and is updated thereafter. *After launching Illustrator*, you can follow these steps:

1   Exit Adobe Illustrator.

2   Locate the file named Adobe Illustrator Prefs for macOS as follows:

   • <OSDisk>/Users/<username>/Library*/Preferences/
      Adobe Illustrator 24 Settings/en_US**/Adobe Illustrator Prefs

● Note: On Windows, the AppData folder is hidden by default. You will most likely need to enable Windows to show hidden files and folders. For instructions, refer to your Windows documentation.

3   Locate the file named Adobe Illustrator Prefs for Windows as follows:

   • <OSDisk>\Users\<username>\AppData\Roaming\Adobe\
      Adobe Illustrator 24 Settings\en_US**\x86 or x64\Adobe Illustrator Prefs

*On macOS, the Library folder is hidden by default. To access this folder, in the Finder press the Option key, and choose Library from the Go menu in the Finder.

**The folder name may be different depending on the language version you have installed.

▶ Tip: To quickly locate and delete the Adobe Illustrator preferences file each time you begin a new lesson, create a shortcut (Windows) or an alias (macOS) to the Adobe Illustrator 24 Settings folder.

For more information, refer to the Illustrator help: helpx.adobe.com/illustrator/using/setting-preferences.html

If you can't find the file, that's because either you haven't started Adobe Illustrator yet or you have moved the preferences file. The preferences file is created after you quit the program the first time and is updated thereafter.

4   Copy the file and save it to another folder on your hard disk (if you want to restore those preferences) or delete it.

5   Start Adobe Illustrator.

To restore saved preferences after completing the lessons

1 Exit Adobe Illustrator.

2 Delete the current preferences file. Find the original preferences file that you saved and move it to the Adobe Illustrator 24 (or other version number) Settings folder.

● **Note:** You can move the original preferences file rather than renaming it.

Additional resources

Adobe Illustrator Classroom in a Book® (2020 release) is not meant to replace documentation that comes with the program or to be a comprehensive reference for every feature. Only the commands and options used in the lessons are explained in this book. For comprehensive information about program features and tutorials, please refer to these resources:

Adobe Illustrator Tutorials: helpx.adobe.com/illustrator/tutorials.html (accessible in Illustrator by choosing Help > Illustrator Tutorials) is where you can find and browse tutorials on Adobe.com.

Adobe Illustrator Learn & Support: helpx.adobe.com/support/illustrator.html (accessible in Illustrator by choosing Help > Illustrator Help) is where you can find and browse tutorials, help, and support on Adobe.com.

Adobe Community: community.adobe.com lets you tap into peer-to-peer discussions, questions, and answers on Adobe products.

Adobe Create Magazine: create.adobe.com offers thoughtful articles on design and design issues, a gallery showcasing the work of top-notch designers, tutorials, and more.

Resources for educators: www.adobe.com/education and edex.adobe.com offer valuable information for instructors who teach classes on Adobe software. Find solutions for education at all levels, including free curricula that can be used to prepare for the Adobe Certified Associate exams.

Adobe Illustrator product home page: See www.adobe.com/products/illustrator.

Adobe Add-ons: exchange.adobe.com/creativecloud.html is a central resource for finding tools, services, extensions, code samples, and more to supplement and extend Adobe Creative Cloud.

Adobe Authorized Training Partners

Browse a wealth of courses offered worldwide by our Adobe Authorized Training Partners at learning.adobe.com/partner-finder.html.

WHAT'S NEW IN ADOBE ILLUSTRATOR (2020 RELEASE)

Adobe Illustrator (2020 release) has new and innovative features to help you produce artwork more efficiently for print, web, and digital video publication. The features and exercises in this book are based on Illustrator (2020 release). In this section, you'll learn about many of these new features.

Enhanced way of simplifying paths

If you have complex paths in your artwork and want to more easily edit them, use the Simplify feature to reduce the number of anchor points. With a path selected, choose Object > Path > Simplify. Streamlined options appear for simplifying a path. You can click the ellipses (...) to view more options in the Simplify dialog box.

Auto Spelling Check

Illustrator now includes an automatic way of checking spelling errors. With the Auto Spell Check feature enabled, spelling will be automatically verified as you type and all the misspelled words will be highlighted in the document. Do one of the following to enable this feature:

- Choose Edit > Spelling > Auto Spell Check.
- Right-click text and choose Spelling > Auto Spell Check.

Other enhancements

The following are other enhancements in Illustrator (2020 Release):

- **Enhanced file handling on remote networks:** Improved performance while performing file open and save operations with files on remote networks.

- **Reduction in file open issues:** Improved mechanism for avoiding and troubleshooting document corruption issues. In case the auto-recovery is not possible, Illustrator now shows an effective messaging that clearly states the file error(s) and troubleshooting steps for you to try.

- **Stability and other enhancements:** This release brings improved application performance, better stability, smoother workflows, and an enriched user experience.

- **Faster & quicker effects:** Applying blur, drop shadow, and inner/outer glow effects is now much faster and quicker.

- **Recoloring option:** The Recolor Artwork feature now supports freeform gradients.

- **Export in Background:** In Illustrator 2020, when you choose File > Export For Screens, the main part of the exporting process will run in the background, and you can resume work on other tasks. You will be notified when the export is complete.

- **Save in Background:** In Illustrator 2020, the save operation is now run in the background and you can continue working even when the save operation is in progress.

Adobe is committed to providing the best tools possible for your publishing needs. We hope you enjoy working with Illustrator (2020 release) as much as we do.

—*The Adobe Illustrator Classroom in a Book® (2020 release) team*

A QUICK TOUR OF ADOBE ILLUSTRATOR (2020 RELEASE)

Lesson overview

In this interactive demonstration of Adobe Illustrator (2020 release), you'll get an overview of the main features of the application.

 This lesson will take about 45 minutes to complete. To get the lesson files used in this chapter, download them from the web page for this book at www.adobepress.com/IllustratorCIB2020. For more information, see "Accessing the lesson files and Web Edition" in the Getting Started section at the beginning of this book.

In this demonstration of Adobe Illustrator, you'll be introduced to some key fundamentals for working in the application.

Starting the lesson

For the first lesson of this book, you'll get a quick tour of the most widely used tools and features in Adobe Illustrator, offering a sense of the many possibilities. Along the way, you'll create artwork for a clothing boutique. First, you'll open the final artwork to see what you will create in this lesson.

Note: If you have not already downloaded the project files for this lesson to your computer from your Account page, make sure to do so now. See "Getting Started" at the beginning of the book.

1 To ensure that the tools and panels function exactly as described in this lesson, delete or deactivate (by renaming) the Adobe Illustrator preferences file. See "Restoring default preferences" in the "Getting Started" section at the beginning of the book.

2 Start Adobe Illustrator.

Note: If a small window appears offering a "quick tour" after opening the document, you can close it.

3 Choose File > Open, or click Open in the Home screen that is showing. Open the L00_end.ai file in the Lessons > Lesson00 folder.

4 Choose View > Fit Artboard In Window to see an example of the artwork you'll create in this lesson. Leave the file open for reference, if you'd like.

Creating a new document

In Illustrator, you can start a new document using a series of preset options, depending on your needs. In this case, you will print the artwork you create as a postcard, so you will choose a preset from the Print presets to start.

1 Choose File > New.

Note: Learn more about creating and editing artboards in Lesson 5, "Transforming Artwork."

Note: The figures in this lesson are taken using Windows and may look slightly different from what you see, especially if you are using macOS.

2 In the New Document dialog box, select the Print preset category along the top of the dialog box.

Make sure the Letter document preset is selected.

In the Preset Details area on the right, change the following:

- Name (below Preset Details): **BoutiqueArt**
- Units (to the right of Width): **Inches**
- Width: **11 in**
- Height: **9 in**

3 Click Create, and a new, blank document opens.

4 Choose File > Save As. In the Save As dialog box, leave the name as BoutiqueArt.ai, and navigate to the Lessons > Lesson00 folder. Leave Adobe Illustrator (ai) chosen from the Format menu (macOS) or Adobe Illustrator (*.AI) chosen from the Save As Type menu (Windows) and then click Save.

5 In the Illustrator Options dialog box that appears, leave the Illustrator options at their default settings and then click OK.

6 Choose Window > Workspace > Essentials, make sure it's selected, and then choose Window > Workspace > Reset Essentials to reset the workspace.

Drawing a shape

Drawing shapes is the cornerstone of Illustrator, and you'll create many of them in the coming lessons. To start your project, you'll create a rectangle.

● **Note:** Learn more about creating and editing shapes in Lesson 3, "Using Shapes to Create Artwork for a Postcard."

1 Choose View > Fit Artboard In Window.

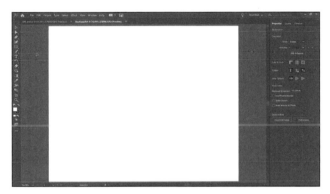

The white area you see is called the *artboard*, and it's where your printable artwork will go. Artboards are like pages in Adobe InDesign.

2 Select the Rectangle tool (▢) in the toolbar on the left. Move the pointer into the upper-left part of the artboard (see the red X in the figure). Press and drag down and to the right. When the gray measurement label next to the pointer shows a width of approximately 10 inches and a height of 7 inches, release the mouse button. The shape will be selected.

● **Note:** If you don't see the size of the rectangle as you draw it, make sure that Smart Guides are turned on by choosing View > Smart Guides. A checkmark next to the Smart Guides menu item means they are on.

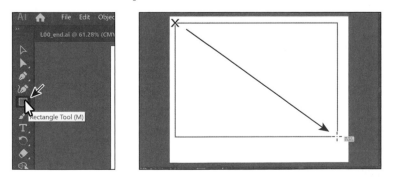

Editing shapes

● **Note:** Learn more about editing shapes in Lesson 3, "Using Shapes to Create Artwork for a Postcard," and Lesson 4, "Editing and Combining Shapes and Paths."

Most shapes are *live*, which means you can edit them without switching away from the tool you're drawing with. Next you'll resize the rectangle you just drew and round the corners using the Rectangle tool.

1   With the rectangle still selected, drag the bottom-middle point on the rectangle down until you see a height of approximately 8 inches in the gray measurement label next to the pointer.

2   Move the pointer over the blue circle in the center of the rectangle. When the pointer changes (◥▤), drag it into the approximate center of the artboard.

▶ **Tip:** You can also round all of the corners independently. You'll learn more about creating and editing Live Shapes in Lesson 3.

3   With the rectangle still selected, drag the upper-right corner widget (◉) toward the center of the rectangle. When the gray measurement label shows a value of approximately 0.7 in, release the mouse button to round all of the corners.

A lot of the different types of shapes in Illustrator have widgets, like the corner widgets, for editing properties such as the number of sides on a polygon, making ellipses into pie shapes, and more.

4   Choose File > Save to save the document.

Applying and editing color

Applying color to artwork is a common Illustrator task. Shapes you create can have a stroke (border) and can also be filled with a color. You can apply and edit *swatches*, which are the colors that come with each document by default, and create your own colors. In this section, you'll change the fill color of the selected rectangle.

● **Note:** Learn more about fill and stroke in Lesson 8, "Using Color to Enhance Signage."

1   With the rectangle still selected, click the Fill color box (☐) to the left of the word "Fill" in the Properties panel, to the right of the Document window. In the panel that opens, make sure that the Swatches option (▦) is selected at the top to show the default saved colors, called *swatches*. Move the pointer over an orange swatch, and when a tool tip appears ("C=0, M=50, Y=100, K=0"), click to apply the orange color to the *fill* of the shape.

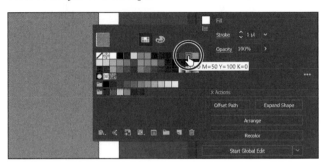

While you can use the default swatches, you can also create your own colors and save them as swatches to reuse them later.

2   With the Swatches panel still showing, double-click the orange swatch you just applied to the shape to edit the color.

3   In the Swatch Options dialog box, select Preview to see the change to the rectangle. Change the values to C=**9**, M=**7**, Y=**9**, K=**0** to make a light tan color. Click OK to save the change you made to the swatch.

● **Note:** Going forward, you'll find you need to hide panels such as the Fill color panel before you continue. You can press the Escape key to do this.

4   Press the Escape key to hide the Swatches panel.

Editing strokes

● **Note:** Learn more about working with strokes in Lesson 3.

A stroke is the outline (border) of artwork such as shapes and paths. There are a lot of appearance properties you can change for a stroke, including width, color, dashes, and more. In this section, you'll adjust the stroke of the rectangle.

1   With the rectangle still selected, click the Stroke color box () in the Properties panel. In the panel that appears, click the Color Mixer button () at the top to create a custom color.

    If you don't see CMYK sliders in the panel, choose CMYK from the panel menu (), which is circled in the figure.

2   Change the CMYK values to C=**80**, M=**39**, Y=**29**, and K=**3**.

3   To save the color you just created so you can use it again easily, click the Swatches button () at the top of the panel. Click the New Swatch button () at the bottom of the panel to save it as a swatch.

4   In the New Swatch dialog box that appears, deselect Add To My Library, if it isn't already deselected, and click OK.

    The blue color should now be showing in the Swatches panel as a saved swatch.

5   Click the word "Stroke" in the Properties panel to open the Stroke panel. Change the following options:

    • Stroke Weight: **3 pt**

    • Dashed Line: Selected

    • Dash: **3 pt** (Type **3** in the first dash field; then click the gap field to the right.)

Working with layers

Layers allow you to organize and more easily select artwork. Next, using the Layers panel, you'll start to organize your artwork.

● **Note:** Learn more about working with layers and the Layers panel in Lesson 10, "Organizing Your Artwork with Layers."

1   Choose Window > Layers to show the Layers panel to the right of the document.

2   Double-click the text "Layer 1" (the layer name) in the Layers panel. Type **Background**, and press Return or Enter to change the layer name.

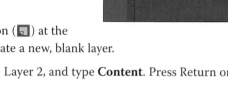

   Naming layers can be helpful when organizing content. Currently, the rectangle you created is on this layer.

3   Click the Create New Layer button (⬛) at the bottom of the Layers panel to create a new, blank layer.

4   Double-click the new layer name, Layer 2, and type **Content**. Press Return or Enter to change the layer name.

   By creating multiple layers in your artwork, you can control how overlapping objects are displayed. In the document, artwork on the Content layer will be on top of the artwork on the Background layer since the Content layer is above the Background layer in the Layers panel.

5   Click the eye icon (👁) in the visibility column to the left of the Background layer name to temporarily hide the rectangle on the Background layer.

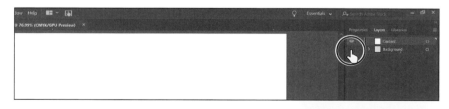

6   Click the Content layer to make sure it's selected in the Layers panel.

   Any new artwork will be added to the selected Content layer.

Working with type

● **Note:** Learn more about working with type in Lesson 9, "Adding Type to a Poster."

Next you'll add text to the project and change its formatting. You'll choose an Adobe font that requires an internet connection to activate. If you don't have an internet connection, you can simply choose another font that you already have installed.

1   Select the Type tool (T) in the toolbar on the left, and click in an empty area toward the bottom of the artboard. A text area will appear with the selected placeholder text, "Lorem ipsum." Type **Boutique**.

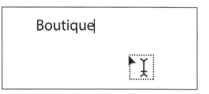

2   With the cursor still in the text, choose Select > All to select all of the text.

3   Click the Properties panel tab in the upper-right corner of the application window to show the panel. Click the Fill color box. In the panel that appears, make sure the Swatches button (■) is selected at the top of the panel, and click to select the blue swatch you created in a previous step. Press the Escape key to hide the panel.

4   In the Character section of the Properties panel, select the font size, and type **52**. Press Return or Enter to accept the size change.

    Next you'll apply an Adobe font, which requires an internet connection. If you don't have an internet connection or access to the Adobe fonts, you can choose any other font from the Font Family menu.

● **Note:** If a message appears in the font menu, you can click the X in the corner to close it.

5   Click the arrow to the right of the Font Family field in the Properties panel with the font name "Myriad Pro." In the menu that appears, click Find More to see a listing of Adobe fonts after they are initialized.

    The list of fonts you see may be different from the figure.

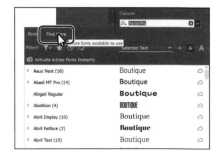

6 Scroll down in the menu to find the font named Montserrat. Click the arrow to the left of the Montserrat font name to show the font styles (circled in the following figure).

7 Click the Activate button (⌂) to the far right of the Montserrat Light font name to activate it.

8 Click OK in the dialog box that appears to activate the font.

9 Click the Show Activated Fonts button (🗀) to filter the font list and show the fonts you've activated. It may take some time for the font to be activated.

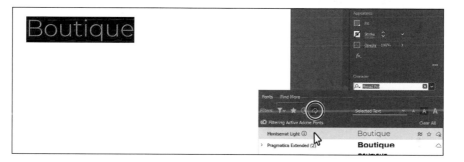

● **Note:** If you can't get the fonts to activate, you can go to the Creative Cloud desktop application and click the Fonts icon (*f*) in the upper-right to see what the issue may be, or simply choose a font you have on your system.

Move the pointer over the words "Montserrat Light" in the menu that appears to show a live preview of the selected text. Click Montserrat Light to apply it.

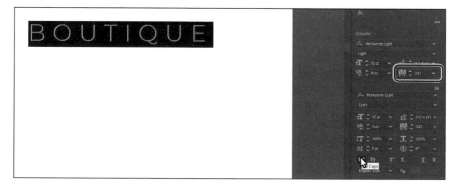

10 With the text selected, in the Properties panel on the right, change the Tracking (🆅🅰) value by selecting the value in the field and typing **300** (circled in the following figure). Press Return or Enter to accept the change.

11 Click More Options (•••) in the Character section to show more options. Click the All Caps option (TT) to make the text capitals.

12 Choose Select > Deselect and then choose File > Save.

Creating shapes using the Shape Builder tool

● **Note:** Learn more about working with the Shape Builder tool in Lesson 4.

The Shape Builder tool () is an interactive tool for creating complex shapes by merging and removing simpler shapes. Next you'll create the top of an acorn with several shapes using the Shape Builder tool to combine them.

1 Press and hold down on the Rectangle tool (▢) in the toolbar on the left. When a menu of tools appears, release the mouse button. Select the Ellipse tool (◯) in the menu that appears.

2 Above the text, drag to create an ellipse. See the figure for roughly how big to make it.

3 To zoom in to the shape, choose View > Zoom In three times.

4 Press the D key to apply the default color fill of white and a black stroke to the shape.

5 Click the Stroke color box in the Properties panel, and click the Color Mixer button (🎨) at the top of the panel to make a new color. Change the color values to C=**15**, M=**84**, Y=**76**, K=**4**. Press Return or Enter to hide the panel.

6 Change the stroke weight in the Properties panel to 2 by clicking the up arrow.

7 Press and hold on the Ellipse tool in the toolbar on the left, and select the Rectangle tool (▢). Drag to create a small rectangle on top of the ellipse. See the first part of the following figure.

● **Note:** If you don't see the corner widgets (◉) or it's difficult to drag one, you may need to zoom in closer. You can do that by choosing View > Zoom In.

8 To round the corners of the rectangle, drag any of the corner widgets (◉) toward the center of the shape.

9 Select the Selection tool (▶) in the toolbar on the left, and drag the ellipse so it is center-aligned with the rounded rectangle. A temporary vertical magenta guide may appear when they are aligned.

● **Note:** Don't worry if yours doesn't look like the figure. The goal is to understand how to create and edit the shapes. Besides, it's an acorn. They come in different shapes and sizes!

10 Drag across both shapes to select them (see the first part of the following figure).

11 Select the Shape Builder tool (🔧) in the toolbar on the left. Move the pointer to roughly where you see the red X in the middle part of the following figure. Press the Shift key, and drag across the two shapes to combine them. Release the mouse button and then the key.

Creating with the Curvature tool

With the Curvature tool (✏️), you can draw and edit paths quickly to create paths with smooth, refined curves and straight lines. In this section, you'll explore the Curvature tool while creating the final part for the acorn.

● **Note:** Learn more about working with the Curvature tool in Lesson 6.

1 Select the Curvature tool (✏️) in the toolbar on the left.

2 Move the pointer into a blank area, away from the top of the acorn you just created. Click and release to start drawing a shape (see the first part of the following figure). Move the pointer away (see the second part of the figure).

3 Click and release (see the first part of the following figure) to continue drawing a shape. Move the pointer away and notice the path curving in different ways as you move it.

Every time you click, you are creating what is called an *anchor point*. The anchor points you add control the shape of the path.

4   Move the pointer up and to the left, and when the path looks something like the figure, click and release to continue drawing the shape.

5   Move the pointer over where you first clicked. When the pointer shows a small circle next to it (🖋₀), click to close the path, creating a shape.

6   Move the pointer over the point on the left, and when the pointer looks like this ▶₀, double-click to make it a corner.

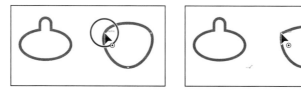

7   Do the same for the point on the right (the first anchor point you created). Move the pointer over the point, and double-click to make it a corner as well.

You now have all of the artwork you need to make the acorn.

Transforming artwork

● **Note:** Learn more about transforming artwork in Lesson 5.

In Illustrator, there are a number of ways to move, rotate, skew, scale, and more—in other words there are many ways of *transforming* artwork so you can get it just the way you want. Next you'll transform the acorn artwork.

1   Select the Selection tool (▶) in the toolbar on the left. Click the top of the acorn shape you created in a previous section.

▶ **Tip:** If you don't like how it erased, choose Edit > Undo Eraser and try again!

2   Select the Eraser tool (◆) in the toolbar on the left. Drag across the bottom of the artwork in a U shape to erase part of it. After releasing the mouse button, you will see the resulting shape.

3 Drag across any remaining artwork below the acorn top to erase it.

4 Select the Selection tool (➤), and drag the top of the acorn onto the bottom of the acorn, centering them as best you can (see the following acorn figure).

5 Click the Arrange button toward the bottom of the Properties panel to the right of the document and choose Bring To Front to bring the top of the acorn on top of the bottom.

6 Press Option (macOS) or Alt (Windows), and drag the right point on the box surrounding the shape to make it wider or narrower—whichever allows you to fit the top best. When it looks good, release the mouse button and then the key.

● **Note:** The figure shows making the top of the acorn a bit narrower. If you need to make yours wider, that's okay.

7 Drag across both acorn shapes to select them.

8 Click the Fill color box (☐) in the Properties panel on the right, and choose the None swatch (⊘) to remove the white fill color.

You'll see that the top shape of the acorn overlaps the bottom shape of the acorn. You can use the Shape Builder tool to fix that.

9 Select the Shape Builder tool (🔨) in the toolbar on the left. Move the pointer where you see the red X in the following figure. Drag across the top shapes to combine them. Make sure not to drag into the bottom shape.

● **Note:** If you make a mistake with the Shape Builder tool, choose Edit > Undo Merge and try again.

10 Leave the acorn shapes selected, and choose File > Save.

Working with symbols

● **Note:** Learn more about working with symbols in Lesson 14, "Creating Artwork for a T-Shirt."

A *symbol* is reusable art stored in the Symbols panel. Symbols are useful because they can help you save time and can save on file size as well. You will now create a symbol from the acorn artwork.

1 With the acorn shapes still selected, select the Selection tool (▶).

2 Choose Window > Symbols to open the Symbols panel. Click the New Symbol button (🔲) at the bottom of the panel to save the selected artwork as a symbol.

3 In the Symbol Options dialog box that appears, name the symbol **Acorn**, and click OK. If a warning dialog box appears, click OK.

The artwork now appears as a saved symbol in the Symbols panel, and the acorn on the artboard you used to create the symbol is now a symbol instance.

● **Note:** Your acorn symbol instances may be in different locations than those in the figure. That's okay. Also, the figure shows dragging the third symbol onto the artboard.

4 From the Symbols panel, drag the acorn symbol thumbnail onto the artboard *twice.* You'll arrange them later.

5 Click the X at the top of the Symbols panel group to close it.

6 With one of the acorns selected, move the pointer just off of a corner. When the rotate arrows appear, drag to rotate the acorn.

7 Click to select one of the other acorns and rotate it in the opposite direction.

8 Double-click the red path of one of the acorn instances on the artboard to enter isolation mode. In the dialog box that appears, click OK.

▶ **Tip:** You could have also clicked the Edit Symbol button in the Properties panel to the right of the document.

You can now edit the original acorn artwork and any changes you make will show in the three instances you dragged from the Symbols panel.

9 Click the stroke (border) of the bottom part of the acorn to select it.

10 Click the Stroke color box in the Properties panel, and click the Color Mixer button (⬛) at the top of the panel to make a new color. Change the color values to C=**2**, M=**44**, Y=**26**, K=**0**. After typing in the last value, press Return or Enter to make the change and also close the panel.

11 Click the Arrange button in the Properties panel and choose Send To Back to ensure that the bottom part of the acorn is behind the top part.

12 Double-click in an empty area of the Document window to exit isolation mode, and notice that the other acorns have changed as well.

Creating and editing gradients

Gradients are color blends of two or more colors that you can apply to the fill or stroke of artwork. Next you'll apply a gradient to the background shape.

● **Note:** Learn more about working with gradients in Lesson 11, "Gradients, Blends, and Patterns."

1 Choose View > Fit Artboard In Window.

2 Click the Layers panel tab in the upper-right corner of the application window to show the panel. Click in the Visibility column to the left of the Background layer name to show the rectangle on the Background layer.

3 With the Selection tool (▶) selected in the toolbar to the left, click in the rectangle in the background to select it.

4 Click the Properties panel tab in the upper-right corner of the application window to show the panel.

5 In the Properties panel, click the Fill color box and make sure the Swatches option () is selected. Select the white-to-black swatch with the tool tip "White, Black." Leave the panel with the swatches showing.

6 At the bottom of the panel, click the Gradient Options button to open the Gradient panel.

An arrow is pointing to the button in the previous figure. You can drag the Gradient panel by the title bar at the top to move it around.

7 In the Gradient panel, do the following:

- Click the Fill box to make sure you are editing the fill (circled in the figure).

- Double-click the little black color stop () on the right side of the gradient slider in the Gradient panel (it's circled in the figure).

- Click the Color button () in the panel that appears. Click the panel menu icon (), and choose CMYK.

- Change the CMYK color values to C=**9**, M=**7**, Y=**9**, K=**0**. Press Return or Enter after typing in the last value to make the change and hide the panel.

8 Click the Radial Gradient button () at the top of the Gradient panel to change the gradient to a circular gradient. Click the X at the top of the Gradient panel to close it.

9 Choose Object > Hide > Selection to hide the background shape temporarily. That way, you can focus on other artwork.

10 Click the Layers panel tab in the upper-right corner of the application window to show the Layers panel. Click the Content layer name so that any new artwork you add will be on the Content layer and above the content on the Background layer.

Placing an image in Illustrator

In Illustrator, you can place raster images, like JPEG files, Adobe Photoshop files, and other Illustrator files, and either link to them or embed them. Next you'll place an image of hand-drawn text.

1 Choose File > Place. In the Place dialog box, navigate to the Lessons > Lesson00 folder, and select the HandLettering.psd file. Make sure that the Link option in the dialog box is *not* selected, and click Place.

2 Move the loaded graphics cursor into the artboard. Click to place the hand-lettering image.

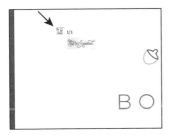

Using Image Trace

You can use Image Trace to convert raster images into vector artwork. Next you'll trace the hand-lettering Photoshop file you just placed.

1 With the Selection tool (▶) selected, click to select the hand-lettering image.

2 To trace the lettering so you can edit it as shapes in Illustrator, click the Properties panel tab to show the panel. Then, click the Image Trace button in the Properties panel, and choose Black And White Logo from the menu.

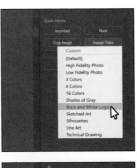

3 Click the Open The Image Trace Panel button (▣) in the Properties panel.

Note: Learn more about placing images in Lesson 15, "Using Illustrator with Other Adobe Applications."

Note: On macOS, if you don't see the Link option in the dialog box, click the Options button.

Note: Learn more about Image Trace in Lesson 3.

Note: The hand lettering was hand-drawn and a picture was taken of it. It was created by Danielle Fritz (www.behance.net/danielle_fritz).

4 In the Image Trace panel that opens, click the disclosure triangle to the left of Advanced (circled in the figure). Set the following options for a better trace:

- Paths: **25%**
- Corners: **0%**
- Noise: **25 px**
- Snap Curves To Lines: deselected
- Ignore White: selected

5 Close the Image Trace panel by clicking the small X at the top.

6 With the lettering still selected, click the Expand button in the Quick Actions section of the Properties panel to make the object a series of editable shapes that are grouped together.

7 With the lettering selected, click the Fill color box in the Properties panel. With the Swatches option (▦) selected at the top of the panel, click the blue color you created previously to apply it.

8 With the Selection tool, hold the Shift key and drag a corner of the text shapes to make them larger. The Shift key constrains the proportions as you scale. When you see a width of approximately 8.5 inches in the gray measurement label next to the pointer, release the mouse button and then the key.

Working with brushes

Brushes let you stylize the appearance of paths. You can apply brush strokes to existing paths, or you can use the Paintbrush tool (✏) to draw a path and apply a brush stroke simultaneously. Next you'll copy existing artwork from another Illustrator document and apply a brush to part of it.

● **Note:** Learn more about working with brushes in Lesson 12, "Using Brushes to Create a Poster."

1 Choose File > Open. In the Lessons > Lesson00 folder, select the Squirrel.ai file and click Open.

2 Choose View > Fit Artboard In Window.

3 To select and copy all of the squirrel artwork, choose Select > All On Active Artboard. To copy the artwork, choose Edit > Copy.

4 Choose File > Close to close the Squirrel.ai file, and return to the Boutique project.

5 Choose Edit > Paste.

6 Drag the squirrel artwork by one of the red paths, up toward the top of the artboard.

● **Note:** The lines in the tail of the squirrel and the squirrel artwork are separate objects. If you find that you only drag one, simply drag the other artwork into place.

7 Choose Select > Deselect to deselect all of the artwork. Click a lighter red path in the tail of the squirrel to select a group of paths. You can see what to select in the following figure.

8 Choose Window > Brush Libraries > Artistic > Artistic_Ink to open the Artistic_Ink collection of brushes in a separate panel.

9 Scroll down in the Artistic_Ink panel list. Move the pointer over a brush in the list, and you will see its name in a tool tip. Click the brush named "Marker" in the panel to apply it to the selected paths.

● **Note:** The brush you apply is an art brush, which means that it stretches artwork along the path. The brush artwork is scaled on the path based on the stroke (border) weight.

10 Click the X in the corner of the Artistic_Ink panel to close it.

11 With the Selection tool (▶) selected in the toolbar, press the Shift key, and click the red path of the squirrel artwork to select the paths in the tail and the squirrel.

12 Choose Object > Group to keep it all together.

Aligning artwork

● **Note:** Learn more about aligning artwork in Lesson 2, "Techniques for Selecting Artwork."

Illustrator makes it easy to align or distribute multiple objects relative to each other, the artboard, or a key object. In this section, you'll move all of the artwork into position and align some of it to the center of the artboard.

1 Choose Object > Show All to show all of the previously hidden artwork.

2 With the Selection tool (▶) selected, drag each object into position like you see in the figure. It doesn't have to match exactly.

Tip: You can also drag across the background rectangle and text to select them.

3 Click to select the background rectangle, press the Shift key, and click the BOUTIQUE text to select it as well.

4 Click the Align To Selection option (▦) in the Properties panel to the right of the document, and choose Align To Artboard from the menu.

Any content you apply an alignment to will now align to the edges of the artboard.

5 Click the Horizontal Align Center button (▣) to align the selected artwork to the horizontal center of the artboard.

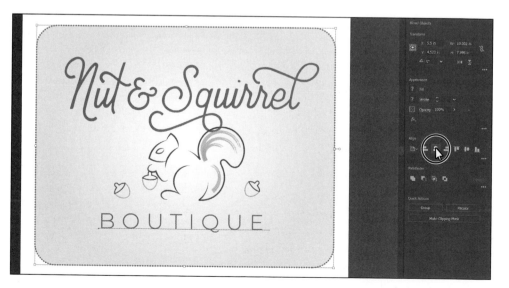

6 Choose Select > Deselect.

Working with effects

Effects alter the appearance of an object without changing the base object. Next you'll apply a subtle Drop Shadow effect to the Nut & Squirrel text.

● **Note:** Learn more about effects in Lesson 13, "Exploring Creative Uses of Effects and Graphic Styles."

1   With the Selection tool (▶), click the Nut & Squirrel text.

2   Click the Choose An Effect button (*fx*) in the Properties panel on the right, and choose Stylize > Drop Shadow.

3   In the Drop Shadow dialog box, select Preview to see your changes, then set the following options (if necessary):

   •   Mode: Multiply (the default setting)

   •   Opacity: **20%**

   •   X Offset and Y Offset: **0.05 in**

   •   Blur: **0**

4   Click OK.

5   Choose Select > Deselect.

6   Choose File > Save.

Presenting your document

In Illustrator, you can view your document in different ways. If you need to present your work to someone else, for instance, you can show the document in Presentation mode, which is what you'll do next.

1   Choose View > Presentation Mode.

   Everything but the active artboard is hidden from view. The area around the artboard is replaced by a solid color, usually black. If there were more artboards (like multiple pages in Adobe InDesign), you could press the right or left arrow key to navigate between them.

▶ **Tip:** Another way to show your document in Presentation mode is to click the Change Screen Mode (▣) button toward the bottom of the toolbar on the left and choose Presentation mode. You could also press Shift+F to turn on Presentation mode. To turn it off, press the Escape key.

2   Press the Escape key to exit Presentation mode.

3   Choose File > Save and then choose File > Close.

1 GETTING TO KNOW THE WORK AREA

Lesson overview

In this lesson, you'll explore the Illustrator workspace and learn how to do the following:

- Open an Adobe Illustrator file.

- Work with the toolbar.

- Work with panels.

- Reset and save your workspace.

- Use view options to change the display magnification.

- Navigate multiple artboards and documents.

- Explore document groups.

 This lesson will take about 45 minutes to complete. To get the lesson files used in this chapter, download them from the web page for this book at www.adobepress.com/IllustratorCIB2020. For more information, see "Accessing the lesson files and Web Edition" in the Getting Started section at the beginning of this book.

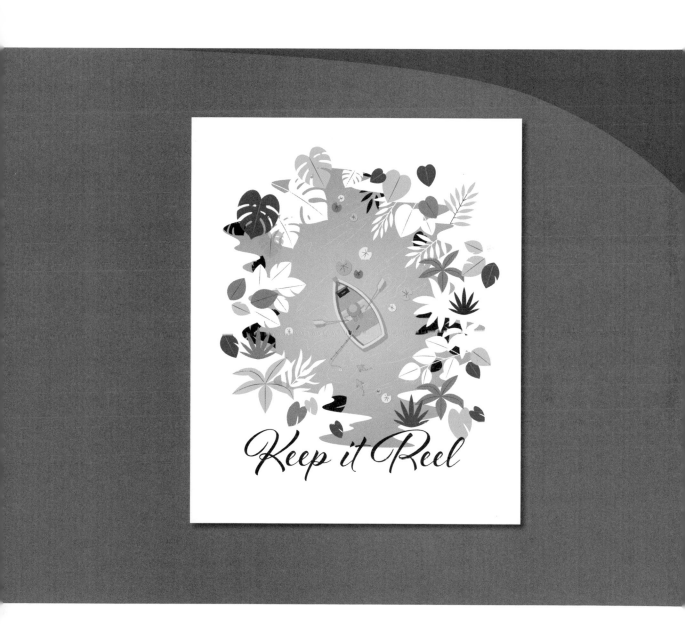

By learning how to navigate the workspace easily and efficiently, you'll be able to make the most of the extensive drawing, painting and editing capabilities of Adobe Illustrator. The workspace consists of the Application bar, menus, toolbar, Properties panel, Document window, and other default panels.

Introducing Adobe Illustrator

In Illustrator, you primarily create and work with vector graphics (sometimes called vector shapes or vector objects). *Vector graphics* are made up of lines and curves defined by mathematical objects called *vectors*. You can freely move or modify (resize) vector graphics without losing detail or clarity because they are resolution independent.

An example of vector artwork.

Editing vector artwork.

Vector graphics maintain crisp edges when they are resized, printed to a PostScript printer, saved in a PDF file, or imported into a vector-based graphics application. As a result, vector graphics are the best choice for artwork, such as logos, that will be used at various sizes and in various output media.

▶ **Tip:** To learn more about bitmap graphics, search for "Importing bitmap images" in Illustrator Help (Help > Illustrator Help).

Illustrator also allows you to incorporate *bitmap images*—technically called *raster images*—that are made up of a rectangular grid of picture elements (pixels). Each pixel is assigned a specific location and color value. Pictures you take on your phone camera are considered raster images. Raster images can be created and edited in a program like Adobe Photoshop.

Example of a raster image and a zoomed-in portion to show the pixels.

Opening an Illustrator file

In this first lesson, you'll begin exploring Illustrator by opening an art file. Before you begin, you'll restore the default preferences for Adobe Illustrator. This is something you will do at the start of each lesson in this book to ensure that the tools function and the defaults are set exactly as described in this lesson.

1   To delete or deactivate (by renaming) the Adobe Illustrator preferences file, see "Restoring default preferences" in the "Getting Started" section at the beginning of the book.

2   Double-click the Adobe Illustrator icon to launch Adobe Illustrator.

    With Illustrator open, you will see the Home screen showing resources for Illustrator, and more.

3   Choose File > Open or click the Open button in the Home screen. In the Lessons > Lesson01 folder on your hard disk, select the L1_start1.ai file, and click Open to open the poster design.

    You will use the L1_start1.ai file to practice navigating, zooming, and investigating an Illustrator document and the workspace. If a small window appears after opening the document offering a "quick tour," you can close it.

4   Choose Window > Workspace > Essentials, make sure it's selected, and then choose Window > Workspace > Reset Essentials to reset the workspace.

    The Reset Essentials command ensures that the workspace, which includes all of the tools and panels, is set to the default settings. You'll learn more about resetting the workspace in the section "Switching workspaces."

5   Choose View > Fit Artboard In Window.

    An artboard is the area that contains your printable artwork and is similar to a page in Adobe InDesign. This command fits the whole artboard into the Document window so you can see all of it.

● **Note:** If finding the preferences file proves difficult, please email me (brian@ brianwoodtraining.com) for assistance.

● **Note:** If you have not already downloaded the project files for this lesson to your computer from your Account page, make sure to do so now. See the "Getting Started" section at the beginning of the book.

Exploring the workspace

● **Note:** The screen captures in this lesson were taken using macOS and may look slightly different from what you see, especially if you are using Windows.

When Illustrator is fully launched and a file is open, the menus, Application bar, toolbar, and panels appear on the screen. The arrangement of these elements is called a *workspace*. When you first start Illustrator, you see the default workspace, which you can customize for the tasks you perform. You can create and save multiple workspaces—one for editing and another for viewing, for example—and switch between them as you work.

A. Application bar

B. Panels

C. Toolbar

D. Document window

E. Status bar

Below, the areas of the default workspace are described:

A. The **Application bar** across the top by default contains application controls, the Workspace Switcher, and Search. On Windows, the main menu bar items appear *inline* with the Application bar—see the following figure.

B. **Panels** help you monitor and modify your work. Certain panels are displayed by default in the panel dock on the right side of the workspace, and you can display any panel by choosing it from the Window menu.

C. The **toolbar** contains tools for creating and editing images, artwork, page elements, and more. Related tools are grouped together.

D. The **Document window** displays the file(s) you're working on.

E. The **Status bar** appears at the lower-left edge of the Document window. It displays information, zooming, and navigation controls.

Getting to know the toolbar

The toolbar on the left side of the workspace contains tools for selecting, drawing and painting, editing, and viewing, as well as the Fill and Stroke boxes, drawing modes, and screen modes. As you work through the lessons, you'll learn about the specific function of many of these tools.

1 Move the pointer over the Selection tool (▶) in the toolbar. Notice that the name (Selection Tool) and keyboard shortcut (V) are displayed in a tool tip.

▶ **Tip:** You can turn the tool tips on or off by choosing Illustrator > Preferences > General (macOS) or Edit > Preferences > General (Windows) and selecting or deselecting Show Tool Tips.

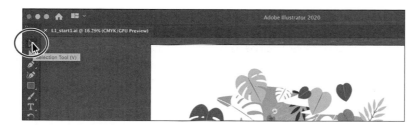

2 Move the pointer over the Direct Selection tool (▷). Press and hold until a tools menu appears, then release the mouse button. Click the Group Selection tool (▷⁺) in the menu to select it.

Any tool in the toolbar that displays a small triangle contains additional tools that can be selected in this way.

▶ **Tip:** You can also select hidden tools by pressing the Option key (macOS) or the Alt key (Windows) and clicking the tool in the toolbar. Each click selects the next hidden tool in the tool sequence.

3 Press and hold the Rectangle tool (▭) to reveal more tools. Click the arrow at the right edge of the hidden tools panel to separate the tools from the toolbar as a separate floating panel of tools, so you can access them easily.

4 Click the Close button (X) in the upper-left corner (macOS) or upper-right corner (Windows) of the floating tool panel to close it. The tools return to the toolbar.

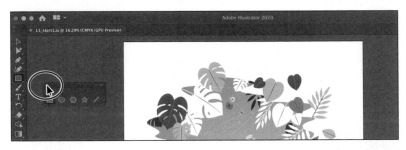

Next, you'll learn how to resize and float the toolbar. In the figures in this lesson, the toolbar is a single column by default. As I said before, you may initially see a double-column toolbar, depending on your screen resolution and workspace, and that's okay.

5 Click the double arrow in the upper-left corner of the toolbar to either expand the single column into two columns or collapse the two columns into one (depending on your screen resolution).

▶ **Tip:** You can click the double arrow at the top of the toolbar or double-click the title bar at the top of the toolbar to switch between two columns and one column.

When the toolbar is floating, be careful not to click the X or it will close! If you close it, choose Window > Toolbars > Basic to reopen it.

6 Click the same double arrow again to collapse (or expand) the toolbar.

7 Drag the toolbar into the workspace by the dark gray title bar at the top of the toolbar or by the dashed line beneath the title bar. The toolbar is now floating in the workspace.

8 Drag the toolbar to the left side of the Application window using either the solid bar at the top of the toolbar or the dashed line just below the solid bar.

When the pointer reaches the left edge, a translucent blue border, called the *drop zone*, appears. Release the mouse button to dock the toolbar neatly into the side of the workspace.

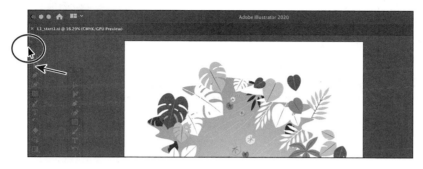

Finding more tools

In Illustrator, the default set of tools that appears in the toolbar does not include every available tool. As you make your way through this book, you'll explore other tools that you'll need to know how to access. In this section, you'll see how to access these other tools.

1 Click Edit Toolbar (●●●) at the bottom of the toolbar on the left.

► **Tip:** You can also toggle the display of the controls at the bottom of the toolbar in the menu that appears after clicking Edit Toolbar.

A panel appears that shows all of the available tools. The tools that appear dimmed (you can't select them) are already in the default toolbar. You can drag any of the remaining tools into the toolbar, where you can then select and use them.

2 Move the pointer over a tool that is dimmed, like the Selection tool, at the top of the tools list (you may need to scroll up).

The tool is highlighted in the toolbar. If you hover the pointer over a tool like the Ellipse tool, which is nested within the Rectangle tool, the Rectangle tool will highlight, showing you where it is.

3 Scroll in the list of tools until you see the Shaper tool (✐). To add it to the toolbar, drag the Shaper tool onto the Rectangle tool. When a highlight appears around the Rectangle tool and a plus (+) appears next to the pointer, release the mouse to add the Shaper tool.

4 Press the Escape key to hide the extra tools.

The Shaper tool will now be in the toolbar until you remove it or reset the toolbar. Next, you'll remove the Shaper tool. Later in the lessons, you will add tools to learn more about them.

▶ Tip: After clicking Edit Toolbar, you can reset the toolbar by clicking the panel menu icon (▤) and choosing Reset.

5 Click Edit Toolbar (▦) at the bottom of the toolbar again to show the panel of extra tools. Drag the Shaper tool onto the panel. When a minus shows next to the pointer (▸_), release the mouse to remove the Shaper tool from the toolbar.

Working with the Properties panel

When you start Illustrator for the first time and open a document, you'll see the Properties panel on the right side of the workspace. The Properties panel displays properties for the active document when nothing is selected. It also displays appearance properties for content you select. It's a panel you'll be using quite a bit; it puts all of the most commonly used options in one place.

1   Select the Selection tool (▶) in the toolbar, and look in the Properties panel on the right.

At the top of the Properties panel, you will see "No Selection." This is the *Selection Indicator*, which is a great place to see what type of content is selected (if any). With nothing selected in the document, the Properties panel shows the current document properties as well as program preferences.

2   Move the pointer into the green water shape in the artwork, and click to select it.

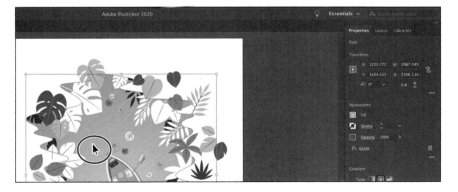

In the Properties panel, you should now see appearance options for the selected artwork, which is a path, as indicated by "Path" at the top of the panel. You can change the size, position, color, and much more for the selected artwork.

3 Click the underlined word "Opacity" in the Properties panel to open the Transparency panel.

Words that are underlined in the Properties panel will show more options when you click them.

4 Press Escape to hide the Transparency panel, if it's showing.

5 Choose Select > Deselect to deselect the path.

The Properties panel once again shows document properties and program preferences when nothing is selected.

Working with panels

Panels like the Properties panel give you quick access to many of the tools and options that make modifying artwork easier. All of the panels available in Illustrator are listed alphabetically in the Window menu. Next, you'll experiment with hiding, opening, and closing panels.

▶ **Tip:** To show a panel that is not currently visible, choose the panel name from the Window menu. A checkmark to the left of the panel name indicates that the panel is already open and in front of other panels in its panel group. If you choose a panel name that is already selected in the Window menu, the panel and its group either close or collapse.

1 Click the Layers panel tab to the right of the Properties panel tab.

The Layers panel is grouped with two other panels—the Properties panel and the Libraries panel. They are all part of the same panel group.

▶ **Tip:** To expand or collapse the panel dock, you can also double-click the panel dock title bar at the top.

2 Click the double arrow at the top of the dock to collapse the panels.

You can use this method of collapsing the panels to create a larger area for working on your document. You'll learn more about docking in the next section.

3 Drag the left edge of the docked panels to the right until the panel text disappears.

This hides the panel names and collapses the panel dock to icons only. To open a panel that is collapsed as an icon, you can click a panel icon.

4 Click the double arrow again to expand the panels.

5 Choose Window > Workspace > Reset Essentials to reset the workspace.

You'll learn more about resetting and switching workspaces in the section "Switching workspaces."

Moving and docking panels

Panels in Illustrator can be moved around in the workspace and organized to match your working needs. Next, you'll open a new panel and dock it with the default panels on the right side of the workspace.

1 Click the Window menu at the top of the screen to see all of the panels available in Illustrator. Choose Align from the Window menu to open the Align panel and the other panels grouped with it by default.

Panels you open that do not appear in the default workspace are free-floating. That means they are not docked and can be moved around. You can dock free-floating panels on the right or left side of the workspace.

2 Drag the Align panel group by the title bar above the panel names to move the group closer to the docked panels on the right.

Next, you'll dock the Align panel with the Properties panel group.

3 Drag the Align panel by the panel tab onto the Properties, Layers, and Libraries panel tabs on the right. When a blue highlight appears *around* the entire panel dock, release the mouse button to dock the panel in the group.

When dragging a panel to the dock on the right, if you see a blue line *above* the docked panel tabs before releasing, you'll create a new panel group rather than docking the panel with the existing panel group.

4 Click the X at the top of the Transform and Pathfinder panel group, which is free-floating, to close it.

Aside from adding panels to the dock on the right, you can also remove them.

5 Drag the Align panel by the panel tab, to the left, away from the dock of panels, and release the mouse button.

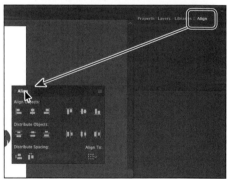

6 Click the X at the top of the Align panel to close it.

7 Click the Libraries panel tab on the right to show that panel, if the panel isn't already showing.

Scaling the Illustrator interface

When you launch Illustrator, it identifies your screen resolution and adjusts the application scale factor accordingly. You can scale the user interface of Illustrator based on your screen resolution to make the tools, text, and other UI elements easier to see.

Choose Illustrator > Preferences > User Interface (macOS) or Edit > Preferences > User Interface (Windows) and in the User Interface section of the Preferences dialog box, you can change the UI Scaling settings.

Switching workspaces

As you've seen, you can customize the parts of the default Essentials workspace, like the toolbar and panels. As you make changes, like opening and closing panels and changing their position (among other things), you can save that particular arrangement as a workspace—and switch between them while you work.

Illustrator comes with a host of other workspaces that are tailored to a variety of tasks. Next, you'll switch workspaces and learn about some new panels.

1   Click the workspace switcher in the Application bar above the docked panels to change the workspace. See the first part of the following figure.

▶ **Tip:** You can also choose Window > Workspace and choose a workspace.

You'll see a number of workspaces listed, each with a specific purpose, that will open panels and arrange the workspace according to each type of work.

2   Choose Layout from the workspace switcher menu to change workspaces.

▶ **Tip:** Press Tab to toggle between hiding and showing all panels. You can hide or show all panels at once, except for the toolbar, by pressing Shift+Tab to toggle between hiding and showing them.

You'll notice a few major changes in the workspace. One of the biggest is the Control panel, which is now docked at the top of the workspace, just above the Document window (it's circled in the following figure). Similar to the Properties panel, it offers quick access to options, commands, and other panels relevant to the currently selected content.

Also, notice all of the collapsed panel icons on the right side of the workspace. In workspaces, you can create groups of panels that are stacked on top of others. That way, a lot more panels are showing.

3 Choose Essentials from the workspace switcher above the docked panels to switch back to the Essentials workspace.

4 Choose Reset Essentials from the workspace switcher in the Application bar.

When you choose a previous workspace to switch to, it remembers any changes you made, like selecting the Libraries panel. To completely reset a workspace to its default settings, the Essentials workspace in this case, you'll want to reset it.

Saving a workspace

So far, you've reset the workspace and chosen a different workspace. You can also arrange the panels the way you like and save your own custom workspace. Next, you'll dock a new panel and create your own workspace.

1 Choose Window > Artboards to open the Artboards panel group.

▶ **Tip:** To delete workspaces you create, choose Window > Workspace > Manage Workspaces. Select the workspace name, and click the Delete Workspace button.

2 Drag the Artboards panel by the panel tab onto the Properties panel *tab* at the top of the docked panels on the right. When a blue highlight appears around the entire panel dock, release the mouse button to dock the Artboards panel and add it to the existing panel group.

▶ **Tip:** To change a saved workspace, reset the panels as you'd like them to appear and then choose Window > Workspace > New Workspace. In the New Workspace dialog box, name the workspace with a new, unused name. If you name a new workspace with a name that's already in use, a message appears in the dialog box warning that you will overwrite an existing workspace with the same name if you click OK.

3 Click the X at the top of the free-floating Asset Export panel to close it.

4 Choose Window > Workspace > New Workspace. Change its name to **My Workspace** in the New Workspace dialog box, and click OK.

Choosing Window > Workspace is just another method for choosing a workspace. The name of the workspace could be anything, as long as it makes sense to you. The workspace named "My Workspace" is now saved with Illustrator until you remove it.

5 Choose Window > Workspace > Essentials, and then choose Window > Workspace > Reset Essentials.

Notice that the panels return to their default positions.

6 Choose Window > Workspace > My Workspace. Toggle between the two workspaces using the Window > Workspace command, and return to the Essentials workspace before starting the next exercise.

Using panel and context menus

Most panels in Illustrator have more options available in a panel menu, found by clicking the panel menu icon (☰ or ☰) in the upper-right corner of a panel. These additional options can be used to change the panel display, add or change panel content, and more. Next, you'll change the display of the Swatches panel using its panel menu.

1 With the Selection tool (▶) selected in the toolbar on the left, click the green water shape in the background of the artwork again.

2 Click the Fill color box, to the left of the word "Fill," in the Properties panel.

3 In the panel that appears, called the Swatches panel, make sure that the Swatches option (▣) is selected. Click the panel menu icon (☰) in the upper-right corner, and choose Small List View from the panel menu.

This displays the swatch names, together with thumbnails. Because the options in the panel menu apply only to the active panel, only the Swatches panel view is affected.

4 Click the same panel menu icon (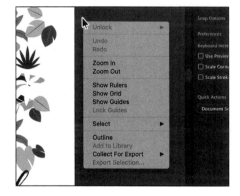) in the panel showing, and choose Small Thumbnail View to return the swatches to their original view.

In addition to the panel menus, context-sensitive menus display commands relevant to the active tool, selection, or panel. Usually the commands in a context menu are available in another part of the workspace, but using a context menu can save you time.

5 Choose Select > Deselect so the water shape is no longer selected.

▶ **Tip:** If you move the pointer over the tab or title bar for a panel and right-click, you can close a panel or a panel group from the context menu that appears.

6 Move the pointer over the dark gray area surrounding the artwork. Then, right-click to show a context menu with specific options.

The context-sensitive menu you see may contain different commands, depending on what the pointer is positioned over.

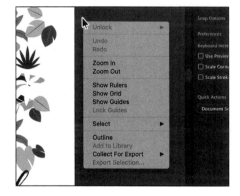

Adjusting the brightness of the user interface

As with Adobe InDesign and Adobe Photoshop, Illustrator supports a brightness adjustment for the application user interface. This is a program-wide preference setting that allows you to choose a brightness setting from four preset levels.

To edit the user-interface brightness, you can choose Illustrator > Preferences > User Interface (macOS) or Edit > Preferences > User Interface (Windows).

Changing the view of artwork

While working in files, it's likely that you'll need to change the magnification level and navigate between artboards. The magnification level, which can range from 3.13% to 64000%, is displayed in the title bar (or document tab) next to the filename and in the lower-left corner of the Document window.

There are a lot of ways to change the zoom level in Illustrator, and in this section you'll explore several of the most widely used methods.

Using view commands

View commands are found in the View menu and are an easy way to enlarge or reduce the view of artwork.

1 Choose View > Zoom In, twice, to enlarge the display of the artwork.

   Using the viewing tools and commands affects only the display of the artwork, not the actual size of the artwork. Each time you choose a Zoom option, the view of the artwork is resized to the closest preset zoom level. The preset zoom levels appear in a menu in the lower-left corner of the Document window, identified by a down arrow next to a percentage.

2 Click one of the fish in the water to select it. Choose View > Zoom In.

▶ **Tip:** The keyboard shortcut for the View > Zoom In command is Command and + (macOS) or Ctrl and + (Windows). You can zoom out using the keyboard shortcut Command and – (macOS) or Ctrl and – (Windows).

▶ **Tip:** Choose View > Actual Size to display the artwork at actual size.

If you have artwork selected, using the View > Zoom In view command will zoom in to what is selected.

3 Choose View > Fit Artboard In Window.

By choosing View > Fit Artboard In Window or by using the keyboard shortcut Command+0 (macOS) or Ctrl+0 (Windows), the entire artboard (page) is centered in the Document window.

4 Choose Select > Deselect so the fish is no longer selected.

Using the Zoom tool

In addition to the View menu options, you can use the Zoom tool (Q) to magnify and reduce the view of artwork to predefined magnification levels.

1 Select the Zoom tool (Q) in the toolbar and then move the pointer into the Document window.

Notice that a plus sign (+) appears at the center of the Zoom tool pointer.

2 Move the Zoom tool pointer over the text "Keep it Reel" and click once.

The artwork is displayed at a higher magnification, depending on your screen resolution. Notice that where you clicked is now in the center of the Document window.

3 Click two more times on the text. The view is increased again, and you'll notice that the area where you clicked is magnified.

4 With the Zoom tool still selected, hold down the Option (macOS) or Alt (Windows) key. A minus sign (–) appears at the center of the Zoom tool pointer. With the Option or Alt key pressed, click the artwork twice to reduce the view of the artwork.

Using the Zoom tool, you can also drag in the document to zoom in and out. By default, if your computer meets the system requirements for GPU performance and it's enabled, zooming is animated. To find out if your computer meets the system requirements, see the sidebar titled "GPU Performance" following this section.

5 Choose View > Fit Artboard In Window.

6 With the Zoom tool still selected, press and drag from the left side of the document to the right to zoom in. The zooming is animated. Drag from right to left to zoom out.

▶ **Tip:** With the Zoom tool selected, if you move the pointer into the Document window and press the mouse button for a few seconds, you can zoom in using the animated zoom. This will only work if your computer meets the system requirements for GPU Performance and it's enabled.

If your computer does not meet the system requirements for GPU Performance, you will instead draw a dotted rectangle, called a marquee, when dragging with the Zoom tool.

● **Note:** In certain versions of macOS, the keyboard shortcuts for the Zoom tool (🔍) open Spotlight or the Finder. If you decide to use these shortcuts in Illustrator, you may want to turn off or change those keyboard shortcuts in macOS System Preferences.

7 Choose View > Fit Artboard In Window to fit the artboard in the Document window.

The Zoom tool is used frequently during the editing process to enlarge and reduce the view of artwork. Because of this, Illustrator allows you to select the Zoom tool using the keyboard at any time without first deselecting any other tool you may be using.

- To access the Zoom tool using your keyboard, press spacebar+Command (macOS) or Ctrl+spacebar (Windows).

- To access the Zoom Out tool using your keyboard, press spacebar+Command+Option (macOS) or Ctrl+Alt+spacebar (Windows).

GPU Performance

The graphics processing unit (GPU), found on video cards and as part of display systems, is a specialized processor that can rapidly execute commands for manipulating and displaying images. GPU-accelerated computing offers faster performance across a broad range of design, animation, and video applications.

The GPU Performance feature in Illustrator has a preview mode called GPU Preview, which enables rendering of Illustrator artwork on the graphics processor.

This feature is available on compatible macOS and Windows computers. It is turned on by default for documents, and options can be accessed in Preferences by choosing Illustrator > Preferences > Performance (macOS) or Edit > Preferences > Performance (Windows).

To learn more about GPU Performance, visit helpx.adobe.com/illustrator/kb/gpu-performance-preview-improvements.html.

Panning in a document

In Illustrator, you can use the Hand tool (✋) to pan to different areas of a document. Using the Hand tool allows you to push the document around much like you would a piece of paper on your desk. This can be a useful way to move around in a document with a lot of artboards or when you are zoomed in. In this section, you'll access the Hand tool a few different ways.

1   Press and hold on the Zoom tool in the toolbar and select the Hand tool (✋).

2   Press and drag down in the Document window. As you drag, the artboard and artwork on it moves with the hand.

    As with the Zoom tool (🔍), you can select the Hand tool with a keyboard shortcut without first deselecting the active tool.

3   Click any other tool except the Type tool (T) in the toolbar, and move the pointer into the Document window. Hold down the spacebar on the keyboard to temporarily select the Hand tool, and then drag to bring the artwork back into the center of your view. Release the spacebar.

● **Note:** The spacebar shortcut for the Hand tool (✋) does not work when the Type tool (T) is active and the cursor is in text. To access the Hand tool when the cursor is in text, press the Option (macOS) or Alt (Windows) key.

4   Choose View > Fit Artboard In Window.

Viewing artwork

When you open a file, it is automatically displayed in Preview mode, which shows how the artwork will print. Illustrator offers other ways of viewing your artwork, such as outlined and rasterized. Next, you'll take a look at the different methods for viewing artwork and understand why you might view artwork each of these ways.

When you're working with large or complex illustrations, you may want to view only the outlines, or paths, of objects in your artwork so that the screen doesn't have to redraw the artwork each time you make a change. This is called Outline mode. Outline mode can also be helpful for selecting objects, as you will see in Lesson 2, "Techniques for Selecting Artwork."

1 Choose View > Outline.

   Only the outlines of objects are displayed. You can use this view to find and select objects that might not be visible in Preview mode.

▶ **Tip:** You can press Command+Y (macOS) or Ctrl+Y (Windows) to toggle between Preview and Outline modes.

2 With Outline mode still active, choose View > Preview (or GPU Preview) to see all the attributes of the artwork again.

3 Choose View > Overprint Preview to view any lines or shapes that are set to overprint.

   This view is helpful for those in the print industry who need to see how inks interact when set to overprint. Overprinting allows the color of artwork to print on top of the color of artwork underneath. For this example, the arms of the person in the boat are made semi-transparent or see-through when Overprint Preview is on.

● **Note:** When switching between viewing modes, visual changes may not be readily apparent. Zooming in and out (View > Zoom In and View > Zoom Out) may help you see the differences more easily.

4 Choose View > Pixel Preview.

   When you turn on Pixel preview, Overprint preview is turned off. Pixel preview can be used to see how the artwork will look when it is rasterized and viewed onscreen in a web browser. Note the "jagged" edge on some of the artwork. An arrow is pointing to it in the figure.

5 Choose 300% from the zoom level menu in the lower-left corner of the application window to more easily see the edges of the artwork.

6 Choose View > Pixel Preview to turn off Pixel preview.

7 Choose View > Fit Artboard In Window to make sure that the artboard is fit in the Document window, and leave the document open.

Navigating multiple artboards

● **Note:** Learn how to work more with artboards in Lesson 5, "Transforming Artwork."

As you may recall, artboards contain the printable artwork, similar to pages in Adobe InDesign. You can use artboards to crop areas for printing or placement purposes. Multiple artboards are useful for creating a variety of things, such as multi-page PDFs, printed pages with different sizes or different elements, independent elements for websites, video storyboards, or individual items for animation in Adobe Animate or Adobe After Effects. You can easily share content among designs, create multipage PDFs, and print multiple pages by creating more than one artboard.

Illustrator allows for up to 1000 artboards within a single file (depending on their size). Multiple artboards can be added when you initially create an Illustrator document, or you can add, remove, and edit artboards after the document is created. Next, you will learn how to efficiently navigate a document that contains multiple artboards.

1 Choose File > Open. In the Open dialog box, navigate to the Lessons > Lesson01 folder, and select the L1_start2.ai file on your hard disk. Click Open to open the file.

2 Choose View > Fit All In Window to fit all artboards in the Document window. Notice that there are two artboards in the document that contain the front cover and inside design for a thank you card.

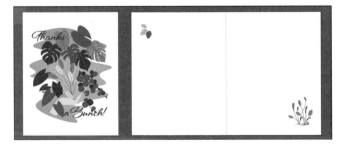

The artboards in a document can be arranged in any order, orientation, or artboard size—they can even overlap. Suppose that you want to create a four-page brochure. You can create different artboards for every page of the brochure, all with the same size and orientation. They can be arranged horizontally or vertically or in whatever way you like.

3 Select the Selection tool (▶) in the toolbar, and click to select the group of plants in the lower-right corner of the larger artboard on the right.

4 Choose View > Fit Artboard In Window.

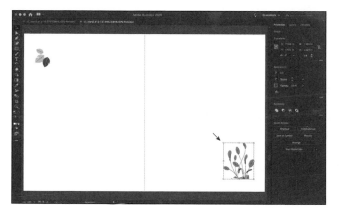

When you select artwork, it makes the artboard that the artwork is on the *active*, or selected, artboard. By choosing the Fit Artboard In Window command, the currently active artboard is fit into the Document window. The active artboard is identified in the Artboard Navigation menu in the Status bar in the lower-left corner of the Document window. Currently it's artboard 2.

5 Choose Select > Deselect to deselect the artwork.

6 Choose 1 from the Active Artboard menu in the Properties panel.

Notice the arrows to the right of the Artboard menu in the Properties panel. You can use these to navigate to the previous (◀) and next (▶) artboards. Those arrows plus a few others also appear in the status bar below the document.

7 Click the Next navigation button () in the Status bar below the document to view the next artboard (artboard 2) in the Document window.

The Artboard Navigation menu and navigation arrows always appear in the Status bar below the document, but they appear in the Properties panel only when not in Artboard Editing mode, the Selection tool is selected, and nothing is selected.

Using the Artboards panel

Another method for navigating multiple artboards is to use the Artboards panel. The Artboards panel lists all artboards currently in the document and allows you to navigate between artboards, rename artboards, add or delete artboards, edit artboard settings, and more. Next, you'll open the Artboards panel and navigate the document.

1 Choose Window > Artboards to open the Artboards panel.

2 Double-click the number 1 that appears to the left of the name "Artboard 1" in the Artboards panel. The artboard named Artboard 1 is now fit in the Document window.

● **Note:** Double-clicking the artboard name in the Artboards panel allows you to change the name of the artboard. Clicking the artboard icon (🖿 or 🖿) to the right of the artboard name in the panel allows you to edit artboard options.

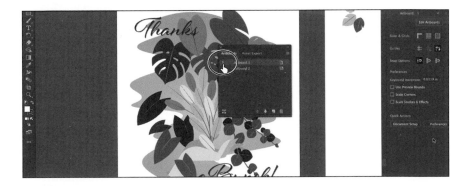

3 Double-click the number 2 to the left of the name "Artboard 2" in the Artboards panel to show the second artboard in the Document window.

4 Click the X at the top of the Artboards panel group to close it.

Zooming and panning with the Navigator panel

The Navigator panel is another way to navigate a document that has one or more artboards. This is useful when you need to see all artboards in the document in one window and to edit content in any of those artboards in a zoomed-in view. You can open the Navigator panel by choosing Window > Navigator. It is in a free-floating group in the workspace.

The Navigator panel can be used in several ways, including the following:

- The red box in the Navigator panel, called the *proxy view area*, indicates the area of the document that is being shown.

- Type in a zoom value or click the mountain icons to change the magnification of your artwork.

- Move the pointer inside the proxy view area of the Navigator panel. When the pointer becomes a hand (🖐), drag to pan to different parts of the artwork.

Arranging multiple documents

▶ **Tip:** On macOS if you prefer a free-form user interface, you can toggle the Application frame on and off by choosing Window > Application Frame. For the purposes of this lesson, ensure that it is toggled on.

In Illustrator, all the workspace elements, like the panels, Document window, and tools, are grouped in a single, integrated window, called the *Application frame*, that lets you treat the application as a single unit. When you move or resize the Application frame or any of its elements, all the elements within it respond to each other so none overlap.

When you open more than one document in Illustrator, the Document windows appear as tabs at the top of the Document window. You can arrange the open documents in other ways, such as side by side, so that you can easily compare or drag items from one document to another. You can also use the Window > Arrange menu to quickly display your open documents in a variety of configurations.

You should currently have two Illustrator files open: L1_start1.ai and L1_start2.ai. Each file has its own tab at the top of the Document window. These documents are considered a group of Document windows. You can create document groups to loosely associate files while they are open.

1 Click the L1_start1.ai document tab to show the L1_start1.ai document in the Document window.

● **Note:** Be careful to drag directly to the right! Otherwise, you could undock the Document window and create a new group. If that happens, choose Window > Arrange > Consolidate All Windows.

2 Drag the L1_start1.ai document tab directly to the right of the L1_start2.ai document tab. Release the mouse button to see the new tab order.

Dragging the document tabs allows you to change the order of the documents. This can be useful if you use the document shortcuts to navigate to the next or previous document.

▶ **Tip:** You can cycle between open documents by pressing Command+~ (next document) and Command+Shift+~ (previous document) (macOS) or by pressing Ctrl+F6 (next document) and Ctrl+Shift+F6 (previous document) (Windows).

To see both of the documents at the same time, maybe to drag artwork from one to the other, you can arrange the Document windows by cascading or tiling them. Cascading allows you to cascade (stack) different document groups. Tiling shows multiple Document windows at one time, in various arrangements. Next, you'll tile the open documents so that you can see both documents at one time.

3 Choose Window > Arrange > Tile.

The available space in the Application frame is divided between the documents.

4 Click in the Document window on the left to activate the document, and choose View > Fit Artboard In Window. Do the same for the Document window on the right.

With documents tiled, you can drag artwork between documents, which copies that artwork from one document to another.

To change the arrangement of the tiled windows, it's possible to drag document tabs to new positions. However, it's easier to use the Arrange Documents menu to quickly arrange open documents in a variety of configurations.

5 Click the Arrange Documents button (⊞▾) in the Application bar to display the Arrange Documents menu. Click the Consolidate All button (□) to bring the documents back together.

● **Note:** On Windows, menus appear in the Application bar.

▶ **Tip:** You can also choose Window > Arrange > Consolidate All Windows to return the two documents to tabs in the same group.

6 Click the Arrange Documents button (⊞▾) in the Application bar to display the Arrange Documents menu again. Click the 2-Up vertical button (□) in the Arrange Documents menu.

7 Click to select the L1_start1.ai tab, if it's not already selected. Then, click the Close button (X) on the L1_start1.ai document tab to close the document. If a dialog box appears asking you to save the document, click Don't Save (macOS) or No (Windows).

8 Choose File > Close to close the L1_start2.ai document without saving.

Finding resources for using Illustrator

For complete and up-to-date information about using Illustrator panels, tools, and other application features, visit the Adobe website. By choosing Help > Illustrator Help, you'll be connected to the Illustrator Learn & Support website, where you can search help documents, as well as other websites relevant to Illustrator users.

Data recovery

When you restart Illustrator after a program crash, you have the option of recovering work-in-progress files so that your hours of work are not wasted. The recovered files are opened with "[Recovered]" in the filename.

You can turn data recovery on and off as well as set options such as how often to save recovery data in the program preferences (Illustrator > Preferences > File Handling & Clipboard [macOS] or Edit > Preferences > File Handling & Clipboard [Windows]).

Review questions

1 Describe two ways to change the view of a document.

2 How do you select a tool in Illustrator?

3 How do you save panel locations and visibility preferences?

4 Describe a few ways to navigate between artboards in Illustrator.

5 How is arranging Document windows helpful?

Review answers

1 You can choose commands from the View menu to zoom in or out of a document or to fit it to your screen; you can also use the Zoom tool (Q) in the toolbar and click or drag over a document to enlarge or reduce the view. In addition, you can use keyboard shortcuts to magnify or reduce the display of artwork. You can also use the Navigator panel to scroll artwork or to change its magnification without using the Document window.

2 To select a tool, you can either click the tool in the toolbar or press the keyboard shortcut for that tool. For example, you can press V to select the Selection tool (▶) from the keyboard. Selected tools remain active until you click a different tool.

3 You can save panel locations and visibility preferences by choosing Window > Workspace > New Workspace to create custom work areas and to make it easier to find the controls you need.

4 To navigate between artboards in Illustrator, you can choose the artboard number from the Artboard Navigation menu at the lower left of the Document window; with nothing selected and while not in Artboard Editing mode, you can choose the artboard number from the Artboard Navigation menu or use the Active Artboard arrows in the Properties panel; you can use the Artboard Navigation arrows in the status bar in the lower left of the Document window to go to the first, previous, next, and last artboards; you can use the Artboards panel to navigate to artboards; or you can use the Navigator panel to drag the proxy view area to navigate between artboards.

5 Arranging Document windows allows you to tile windows or to cascade document groups (the process for cascading wasn't discussed in the lesson). This can be useful if you are working on multiple Illustrator files and you need to compare or share content between them.

2 TECHNIQUES FOR SELECTING ARTWORK

Lesson overview

In this lesson, you'll learn how to do the following:

- Differentiate between the various selection tools and use various selection techniques.

- Recognize Smart Guides.

- Save selections for future use.

- Hide and lock items.

- Use tools and commands to align shapes and points to each other and the artboard.

- Group and ungroup items.

- Work in Isolation mode.

 This lesson will take about 45 minutes to complete. To get the lesson files used in this chapter, download them from the web page for this book at www.adobepress.com/IllustratorCIB2020. For more information, see "Accessing the lesson files and Web Edition" in the Getting Started section at the beginning of this book.

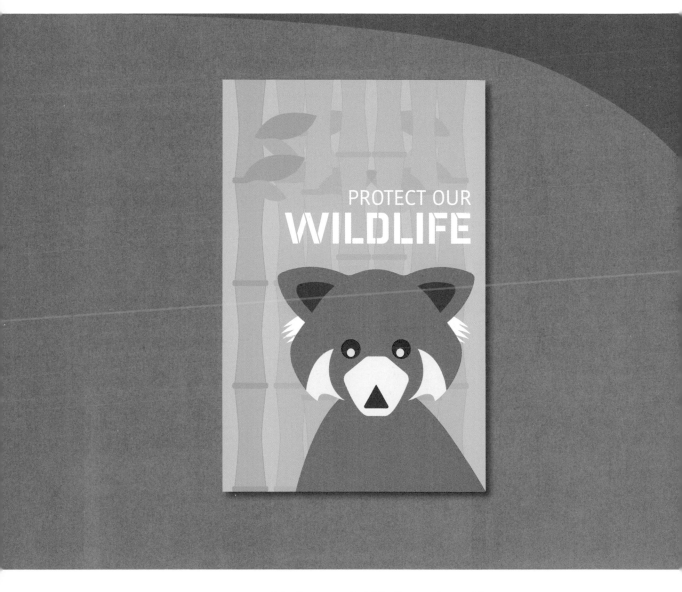

Selecting content in Adobe Illustrator is one of the more essential things you'll do. In this lesson, you'll learn how to locate and select objects using Selection tools; protect other objects by grouping, hiding, and locking them; align objects to each other and the artboard; and much more.

Starting the lesson

Creating, selecting, and editing are the cornerstones of working with artwork in Adobe Illustrator. In this lesson, you'll learn the fundamentals of selecting, aligning, and grouping artwork using different methods. You'll begin by resetting the preferences in Illustrator and opening the lesson file.

●**Note:** If you have not already downloaded the project files for this lesson to your computer from your Account page, make sure to do so now. See the "Getting Started" section at the beginning of the book.

1　To ensure that the tools function and the defaults are set exactly as described in this lesson, delete or deactivate (by renaming) the Adobe Illustrator preferences file. See "Restoring default preferences" in the "Getting Started" section at the beginning of the book.

2　Start Adobe Illustrator.

3　Choose File > Open. Locate the file named L2_end.ai, which is in the Lessons > Lesson02 folder that you copied onto your hard disk, and click Open.

This file contains the finished illustration that you'll create in this lesson.

4　Choose File > Open to open the L2_start.ai file in the Lessons > Lesson02 folder on your hard disk.

5　Choose File > Save As. In the Save As dialog box, name the file **WildlifePoster.ai**, and save it in the Lessons > Lesson02 folder.

Leave Adobe Illustrator (ai) chosen from the Format menu (macOS) or Adobe Illustrator (*.AI) chosen from the Save As Type menu (Windows), and click Save.

6　In the Illustrator Options dialog box, leave the Illustrator options at their default settings, and click OK.

7　To see all of the artwork, choose View > Fit All In Window.

8　Choose Window > Workspace > Essentials, make sure it's selected, and then choose Window > Workspace > Reset Essentials to reset the workspace.

Selecting objects

Whether you're creating artwork from scratch or editing existing artwork in Illustrator, you'll need to become familiar with selecting objects. It will help you to better understand what vector artwork is all about. There are many methods and tools for selecting and editing, and in this section, you'll explore the most widely used, which are the Selection (▶) and Direct Selection (▷) tools.

Using the Selection tool

The Selection tool (▶) lets you select, move, rotate, and resize objects. In this section, you'll become familiar with it.

1 Choose 2 Pieces from the Artboard Navigation menu in the lower left of the Document window.

This should fit the artboard on the right into the Document window. If the artboard doesn't fit in the window, you can choose View > Fit Artboard In Window.

2 Select the Selection tool (▶) in the toolbar on the left. Move the pointer over the different artwork on the artboards, but don't click.

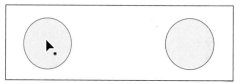

The icon that appears next to the pointer as it passes over objects (▶) indicates that there is artwork under the pointer that can be selected. When you hover over an object, that object is also outlined in a color, like blue in this instance.

3 Select the Zoom tool (🔍) in the toolbar, and click a few times on the beige ellipses to zoom in.

4 Select the Selection tool (▶) in the toolbar again and move the pointer over the edge of the beige ellipse on the left.

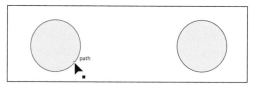

A word such as "path" or "anchor" may appear because Smart Guides are turned on by default (View > Smart Guides). *Smart Guides* are temporary snap-to guides that help you align, edit, and transform objects or artboards.

▶ **Tip:** You'll learn more about Smart Guides in Lesson 3, "Using Shapes to Create Artwork for a Postcard."

5 Click anywhere inside the ellipse on the left to select it. A bounding box with eight handles appears around the selected ellipse.

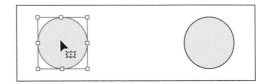

The *bounding box* can be used to make changes to content such as resizing or rotating. The bounding box also indicates that an item is selected and ready to be modified. The color of the bounding box indicates which layer the object is on. Layers are discussed more in Lesson 10, "Organizing Your Artwork with Layers."

6 Using the Selection tool, click in the ellipse on the right. Notice that the ellipse on the left is now deselected and only the ellipse on the right is selected.

7 Pressing the Shift key, click in the ellipse on the left to *add* it to the selection, and then release the key. Both ellipses are now selected, and a larger bounding box surrounds them.

8 Move the ellipses a short distance by pressing and dragging from inside either selected ellipse (in the beige color). Because both ellipses are selected, they move together.

As you drag, you may notice that magenta lines appear. These are called *alignment guides.* They are visible because Smart Guides are turned on (View > Smart Guides). As you drag, the objects align to other objects in the document. Also notice the measurement label (gray box) next to the pointer that shows the object's distance from its original position. Measurement labels also appear because Smart Guides are turned on.

9 Revert to the last saved version of the document by choosing File > Revert. In the dialog box that appears, click Revert.

Selecting and editing with the Direct Selection tool

As you draw, you create vector paths that are made up of anchor points and paths. Anchor points are used to control the shape of the path and work like pins holding a wire in place. A shape you create, like a simple square, is composed of at least four anchor points on the corners with paths connecting the anchor points.

One way to change the shape of a path or shape is by dragging its anchor points. The Direct Selection tool (▷) lets you select anchor points or paths within an object so they can be reshaped. Next, you'll become familiar with selecting anchor points using the Direct Selection tool to reshape a path.

1 Choose 2 from the Artboard menu in the Properties panel on the right.

2 Choose View > Fit Artboard In Window to make sure you see the whole artboard.

3 Select the Direct Selection tool (▷) in the toolbar on the left. Click inside one of the larger green bamboo shapes to see the anchor points.

Notice that the anchor points are all filled with a blue color, which means they are all selected.

4 Move the pointer directly over the upper-right anchor point.

With the Direct Selection tool selected, when the pointer is right over an anchor point, the word "anchor" appears. Also notice the little white box next to the pointer (▷). The small dot that appears in the center of the white box indicates that the cursor is positioned over an anchor point.

5 Click and release to select that anchor point, and then move the pointer away from it.

Notice that only the anchor point you selected is now filled with blue, indicating that it's selected. The other anchor points in the shape are now hollow (filled with white), indicating that they are not selected.

Note: The gray measurement label that appears as you drag the anchor point has the values dX and dY. *dX* indicates the distance that the pointer has moved along the x-axis (horizontally), and *dY* indicates the distance that the pointer has moved along the y-axis (vertically).

6 With the Direct Selection tool still selected, move the pointer over the selected anchor point and then drag it to edit the shape.

7 Try clicking another point on a corner of the shape. Notice that when you select the new point, the previous point is deselected.

8 Revert to the last saved version of the file by choosing File > Revert. In the dialog box that appears, click Revert.

Changing the size of anchor points, handles, and bounding box display

The anchor points, handles, and bounding box points may be difficult to see at times. In the Illustrator preferences, you can adjust the size of those features. By choosing Illustrator > Preferences > Selection & Anchor Display (macOS) or Edit > Preferences > Selection & Anchor Display (Windows), you can drag the Size slider to change the size.

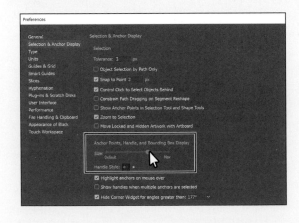

Selecting with a marquee

Another way to select content is by dragging across what you want to select (called a *marquee selection),* which is what you'll do next.

1 Select the Zoom tool (🔍) in the toolbar, and click the beige ellipses several times to zoom in closely.

2 Select the Selection tool (▶) in the toolbar on the left. Move the pointer above and to the left of the leftmost beige ellipse and then drag across both ellipses to create a marquee that overlaps at least part of them. Release the mouse button.

When dragging with the Selection tool (▶), you need to encompass only a small part of an object to select it.

3 Choose Select > Deselect, or click where there are no objects.

Now you'll use the Direct Selection tool to select multiple anchor points in the ellipses by dragging a marquee around anchor points.

4 Select the Direct Selection tool (▷) in the toolbar. Starting off the top left of the leftmost ellipse (see the first part of the following figure), drag across just the top edges of the two ellipses and then release the mouse button.

Only the top anchor points become selected. With the anchor points selected, you'll see little handles coming from the anchor points. Those are called *direction handles,* and they can be used to control the curve of the path.

In the next step, you'll drag one of the anchor points. Make sure you drag the square anchor point and not the round end of one of the handles.

5 Move the pointer over one of the selected anchor points at the top of an ellipse. When you see the word "anchor," drag it to see how they move together.

You can use this method when selecting points so that you don't have to click exactly on the anchor point that you want to select.

6 Revert to the last saved version of the file by choosing File > Revert. In the dialog box that appears, click Revert.

Hiding and locking objects

Selecting artwork may be more difficult when there are objects stacked one on another or when there are multiple objects in a small area. In this section, you'll learn a common way to make selecting objects easier by locking and hiding content. Next, you'll attempt to drag across artwork to select it.

1 Choose 1 Final Artwork from the artboard navigation menu in the lower left.

2 Choose View > Fit Artboard In Window.

3 With the Selection tool (▶) selected in the toolbar, move the pointer into the solid blue-green area to the left of the animal artwork (the "X" in the following figure) and then drag across part of the head of the animal to select it. Release the mouse button.

Notice that you dragged the large blue-green shape, rather than selecting the animal shapes.

4 Choose Edit > Undo Move.

5 With the large blue-green background shape still selected, choose Object > Lock > Selection, or press Command+2 (macOS) or Ctrl+2 (Windows).

Locking objects prevents you from selecting and editing them. You can unlock artwork by choosing Object > Unlock All.

6 Move the pointer into the solid blue-green area to the left of the animal artwork again and drag across all of the parts of the animal, this time selecting the whole thing.

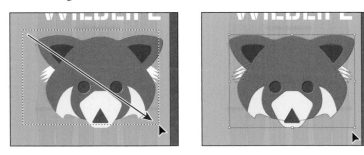

Next, you'll hide all of the shapes that make up the head of the animal, except for the eyes. You'll deselect the eyes and then hide the selected artwork.

7 Press the Shift key and click each eye shape, one at a time, to *remove* the eyes from the selection.

8 Choose Object > Hide > Selection, or press Command+3 (macOS) or Ctrl+3 (Windows).

The selected shapes are temporarily hidden so that you can more easily select other objects.

Selecting similar objects

You can also select artwork based on similar fill color, stroke color, stroke weight, and more, using the Select > Same command. The stroke of an object is the outline (border), and the stroke weight is the width of the stroke. Next, you'll select several objects with the same fill and stroke applied.

1 Choose View > Fit All In Window to see all of the artwork at once.

2 With the Selection tool (▶), click to select one of the larger green "bamboo" shapes on the right.

Tip: In Lesson 14, you'll learn about another method for selecting similar artwork using Global Edit.

3 Choose Select > Same > Stroke Color to select all objects on any artboard with the same stroke (border) color as the selected object.

All of the shapes with the same stroke (border) color are now selected. If you know that you may need to reselect a series of objects again, like the shapes you just selected, you can save that selection. Saved selections are a great way to easily make a selection later, and they are saved only with that document. You'll save the current selection next.

4 With the shapes still selected, choose Select > Save Selection. Name the selection **Bamboo** in the Save Selection dialog box, and click OK.

Now that you've saved it, you'll be able to choose this selection quickly and easily from the bottom of the Select menu when you need it.

5 Choose Select > Deselect.

Selecting in Outline mode

By default, Adobe Illustrator displays all artwork with their paint attributes, like fill and stroke (border), showing. However, you can view artwork in Outline mode to display artwork so that the appearance is removed and only outlines (or paths) are visible. Outline mode can be useful if you want to more easily select objects within a series of stacked objects.

1 Choose Object > Show All so you can see the artwork you previously hid.

2 Choose Select > Deselect so nothing is selected.

3 Choose View > Outline to view artwork as outlines.

4 With the Selection tool (▶), click within one of the eye shapes to select it.

In Outline mode, you *may* see a small X in the center of some of the shapes. If you click that X, you can select the shape.

You can't select the object by clicking the fill using this method. To select in Outline mode, you can click the edge of the object or drag a marquee across the shape to select it.

5 With the Selection tool selected, drag across both eye shapes to select them. Notice that the artwork behind the eyes (the bamboo) is not selected. That's because it was locked. Press the Up Arrow key several times to move both shapes up a little bit.

▶ **Tip:** You could have also clicked the edge of one of the shapes and then pressed the Shift key and clicked the edge of the other to select both.

6 Choose View > Preview (or GPU Preview) to see the painted artwork.

Aligning objects

Illustrator makes it easy to align or distribute multiple objects relative to each other, the artboard, or a key object. In this section, you'll explore the different options for aligning objects.

Aligning objects to each other

One type of alignment is aligning objects to each other. This can be useful if, for instance, you want to align the top edges of a series of selected shapes to each other. Next you'll align the green bamboo shapes to each other.

1 Choose Select > Bamboo to reselect the green shapes on the right artboard.

2 Click the Next Artboard button (▶) in the lower-left corner of the Document window to fit the artboard with the selected green shapes in the window.

3 Click the Horizontal Align Center button (▣) in the Properties panel on the right.

   Notice that all of the selected objects move to align to the horizontal center of the shapes.

4 Choose Edit > Undo Align to return the objects to their original positions. Leave the objects selected for the next section.

Aligning to a key object

A *key object* is an object that you want other objects to align to. This can be useful when you want to align a series of objects and one of them is already in the perfect position. You specify a key object by selecting all the objects you want to align, including the key object, and then clicking the key object again. Next, you'll align the green shapes using a key object.

● **Note:** The key object outline color is determined by the layer color that the object is on. You'll learn about layers in Lesson 10.

1   With the shapes still selected, click the leftmost shape with the Selection tool (▶). See the first part of the following figure.

    When selected, the key object has a thick outline indicating that other objects will align to it.

2   Click the Horizontal Align Center button (▤) in the Properties panel again. Leave the shapes selected for the next section.

Notice that all of the selected shapes moved to align to the horizontal center of the key object.

● **Note:** If you accidentally deselect some or all of the shapes, to reselect them, choose Select > Deselect, and then choose Select > Bamboo.

3   Click the key object (an arrow is pointing to it in the last part of the previous figure) to remove the blue outline, and leave *all* of the green shapes selected. The selected content will no longer align to the key object.

Distributing objects

Distributing objects using the Align panel enables you to select multiple objects and distribute the spacing between the centers or edges of those objects equally. Next, you will make the spacing between the green shapes even.

1   With the green shapes still selected, click More Options (▪▪▪) in the Align section of the Properties panel (circled in the figure). Click the Vertical Distribute Center button (▤) in the panel that appears.

Distributing moves all of the selected shapes so that their centers are spaced an equal distance apart.

2 Choose Edit > Undo Align.

3 With the shapes still selected, click the topmost shape of the selected shapes to make it the key object.

4 Click More Options (⚫⚫⚫) in the Align section of the Properties panel (circled in the following figure). Ensure that the Distribute Spacing value is 0 (zero) and then click the Vertical Distribute Space button (🖫).

Distribute Spacing distributes the spacing *between* selected objects, whereas the Distribute Objects alignments distribute the spacing between the *center* points of selected objects. The value you can set is a great way to set a *specific* distance between objects.

5 Choose Select > Deselect and then choose File > Save.

Aligning anchor points

Next you'll align two anchor points to each other using the Align options. As with setting a key object in the previous section, you can also set a key anchor point that other anchor points will align to.

1 Select the Direct Selection tool (▶), and click in the orange shape at the bottom of the current artboard to see all of the anchor points.

2 Click the lower-right corner point of the shape (see the first part of the following figure). Press the Shift key and click to select the lower-left point of the same shape to select both anchor points (second part of the following figure).

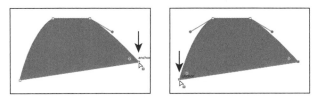

The last selected anchor point is the *key anchor point*. Other points will align to this point.

3 Click the Vertical Align Top button () in the Properties panel to the right of the document.

The first anchor point selected aligns to the second anchor point selected.

4 Choose Select > Deselect.

Aligning to the artboard

You can also align content to the active artboard (page) rather than to a selection or a key object. Aligning to the artboard aligns each selected object separately to the edges of the artboard. Next, you'll align the orange shape to the artboard that contains the final artwork.

1 Select the Selection tool (▶) and click the orange shape at the bottom of the right-hand artboard to select it.

2 Choose Edit > Cut to copy to the clipboard and remove it from the artboard.

3 Click the Previous artboard button (◀) in the lower-left corner of the Document window to navigate to the first (left) artboard in the document, which contains the final artwork.

4 Choose Edit > Paste to paste the shape in the center of the Document window.

5 Choose Window > Align to open the Align panel.

As of the writing of this book, there is no option in the Properties panel to align a single selected object to the artboard. That's why you're opening the Align panel.

6 Choose Show Options from the Align panel menu (▤) (circled in the following figure). If you see Hide Options in the menu, then you are all set.

7 Click the Align To button (▦) in the Align panel, and choose Align To Artboard in the menu that appears. Any content you align will now align to the artboard.

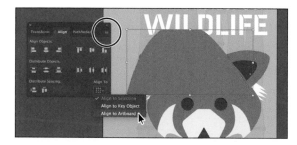

8 Click the Horizontal Align Right button (▤) and then click the Vertical Align Bottom button (▥) in the Align panel to align the orange shape to the horizontal right and vertical bottom of the artboard.

9 Choose Select > Deselect. Leave the Align panel open.

The orange shape will be on top of the other artwork. Later, you will put it behind the other animal artwork.

Working with groups

You can combine objects into a group so that the objects are treated as a single unit. This way, you can move or transform a number of objects without affecting their individual attributes or positions relative to each other. It can also make selecting artwork easier.

Grouping items

Next you'll select multiple objects and create a group from them.

1 Choose View > Fit All In Window to see both artboards.

2 Choose Select > Bamboo to select the green shapes on the right artboard.

3 Click the Group button in the Quick Actions section of the Properties panel on the right to group the selected artwork together.

▶ **Tip:** You can also choose Object > Group to group content.

4 Choose Select > Deselect.

5 With the Selection tool (▶) selected, click one of the shapes in the new group. Because they are grouped together, all are now selected.

6 Drag the bamboo group of shapes close to the top of the artboard on the left.

Next you'll align the bamboo group to the top of the artboard.

7 With the group still selected and Align To Artboard (▣˅) chosen from the Align To menu in the Align panel, click the Vertical Align Top button (▥).

8 Click the X at the top of the Align panel group to close it.

9 With the Selection tool selected, press the Shift key and then drag the lower-right corner of the bounding box down to the bottom of the artboard to make the bamboo shapes larger. When the pointer reaches the bottom of the artboard, release the mouse and then the key.

10 Choose Select > Deselect and then choose File > Save.

Editing a group in Isolation mode

Isolation mode lets you isolate groups so that you can easily select and edit specific objects or parts of objects without having to ungroup the objects. When in isolation mode, all objects outside of the isolated group are locked and dimmed so that they aren't affected by the edits you make. Next, you will edit a group using isolation mode.

1 With the Selection tool (▶), drag across the two green leaves on the right artboard to select them. Click the Group button at the bottom of the Properties panel to group them together.

2 Double-click one of the leaves to enter isolation mode.

● **Note:** You'll learn more about layers in Lesson 10.

Notice that the rest of the content in the document appears dimmed (you can't select it). At the top of the Document window, a gray bar appears with the words "Layer 1" and "<Group>." This indicates that you have isolated a group of objects that is on Layer 1, and they are now temporarily ungrouped.

3 Click to select the smaller leaf shape. Click the Fill color box in the Properties panel on the right, and making sure the Swatches option (▦) is selected in the panel that appears, click to select a different green color.

● **Note:** You'll need to hide the panel to continue. To do that, press the Escape key. I won't always tell you to hide these panels, so it's a good habit to get into.

When you enter isolation mode, groups are temporarily ungrouped. This enables you to edit objects in the group or to add new content without having to ungroup.

4 Double-click outside of the shapes within the group to exit isolation mode.

5 Click to select the leaf group, and leave it selected for the next section.

Notice that the leaves are once again grouped, and you can also now select other objects.

▶ **Tip:** To exit isolation mode, you can also click the gray arrow in the upper-left corner of the Document window, press the Escape key when in isolation mode, or double-click a blank area of the Document window.

Creating a nested group

Groups can also be *nested*—grouped within other objects or grouped to form larger groups. Nesting is a common technique and a great way to keep associated content together. In this section, you'll explore how to create a nested group.

● **Note:** If the bamboo leaves are behind the bamboo group, you can select the leaves and choose Object > Arrange > Bring To Front.

1 Drag the group of leaves onto the bamboo on the left artboard, and leave them selected. Shift-click the bamboo group to select it as well.

2 Click the Group button in the Properties panel.

   You have created a *nested group*—a group that is combined with other objects or groups to form a larger group.

3 Choose Select > Deselect.

4 With the Selection tool, click the leaves to select the nested group.

▶ **Tip:** Instead of either ungrouping a group or entering isolation mode to select the content within, you can select with the Group Selection tool (▷✢). Nested within the Direct Selection tool (▷) in the toolbar, the Group Selection tool lets you select an object within a group, a single group within multiple groups, or a set of groups within the artwork.

5 Double-click the leaves to enter Isolation mode.
   Click to select the leaves again, and notice that the leaf shapes are still grouped. This is a nested group.

6 Choose Edit > Copy and then Edit > Paste to paste a new group of leaves.

7 Drag them lower onto the bamboo.

8 Press the Escape key to exit isolation mode; then click a blank area of an artboard to deselect the objects.

Exploring object arrangement

As you create objects, Illustrator stacks them in order on the artboards, beginning with the first object created. This ordering of objects, called *stacking order*, determines how they display when they overlap. You can change the stacking order of objects in your artwork at any time, using either the Layers panel or the Arrange commands.

Arranging objects

Next you'll work with the Arrange commands to change how objects are stacked.

1   With the Selection tool (▶) selected, click the orange shape at the bottom of the artboard.

2   Click the Arrange button in the Properties panel. Choose Send To Back to send the shape behind all of the other shapes.

3   Click the Arrange button again, and choose Bring Forward as many times as necessary to bring the orange shape on top of the large blue-green background shape and other bamboo shapes. I chose it three times.

Selecting objects behind

When you stack objects on top of each other, sometimes it becomes difficult to select objects that are underneath. Next, you'll learn how to select an object that's part of a stack of objects.

1   Drag across both beige ellipses on the artboard on the right to select them.

2   Pressing the Shift key, drag a corner to make them smaller. When the measurement label shows a width of approximately 1.3 inches, release the mouse button and then the key.

3 Click away from the ellipses to deselect them, and then drag either of them on top of one of the dark eye shapes on the animal. Release the mouse button.

The ellipse disappears but is still selected. It went behind the dark circle (the eye) because it was created before the eye shape, which means it is lower in the stacking order.

4 With the ellipse still selected, click the Arrange button in the Properties panel, and choose Bring To Front. This brings the smaller ellipse to the front of the stack, making it the topmost object.

5 With the Selection tool (▶), select the other beige ellipse on the right artboard and then drag it onto the other eye shape on the left artboard.

This ellipse disappears like the other, but this time, you will deselect the ellipse and then reselect it using another method.

6 Choose View > Zoom In a few times.

7 Choose Select > Deselect.

Because it is behind the larger eye shape, you can no longer see the smaller beige ellipse.

● **Note:** To select the hidden beige ellipse, make sure that you click where the ellipse and the eye overlap. Otherwise, you won't be able to select the beige ellipse.

▶ **Tip:** To see where the beige ellipse is, you can choose View > Outline. When you see it, you can choose View > Preview (or GPU Preview) and attempt to make the selection.

8 With the pointer over the location of the beige ellipse you just deselected, the one behind the eye shape, hold down the Command (macOS) or Ctrl (Windows) key, and click until the smaller ellipse is selected again (this may take several clicks).

9 Click the Arrange button in the Properties panel, and choose Bring To Front to bring the ellipse on top of the eye.

10 Choose View > Fit Artboard In Window.

11 Choose File > Save and then File > Close.

Review questions

1 How can you select an object that has no fill?

2 Explain how you can select an item in a group without ungrouping.

3 Of the two Selection tools (Selection [▶] and Direct Selection [▷]), which allows you to edit the individual anchor points of an object?

4 What should you do after creating a selection that you are going to use repeatedly?

5 To align objects to the artboard, what do you need to first change in the Properties panel or Align panel before you choose an alignment option?

6 Sometimes you are unable to select an object because it is underneath another object. Explain two ways to get around this issue.

Review answers

1 You can select an object that has no fill by clicking the stroke or by dragging a marquee across any part of the object.

2 You can double-click the group with the Selection tool selected to enter isolation mode, edit the shapes as needed, and then exit isolation mode by pressing the Escape key or by double-clicking outside of the group. Read Lesson 10, "Organizing Your Artwork with Layers," to see how you can use layers to make complex selections. Also, using the Group Selection tool (▷⁺), you can click once to select an individual item within a group (not discussed in the lesson). Click again to add the next grouped items to the selection.

3 Using the Direct Selection tool (▷), you can select one or more individual anchor points to change the shape of an object.

4 For any selection that you anticipate using again, choose Select > Save Selection. Name the selection so that you can reselect it at any time from the Select menu.

5 To align objects to an artboard, first select the Align To Artboard option.

6 If your access to an object is blocked, you can choose Object > Hide > Selection to hide the blocking object. The object is not deleted. It is just hidden in the same position until you choose Object > Show All. You can also use the Selection tool (▶) to select an object that's behind other objects by pressing the Command (macOS) or Ctrl (Windows) key and then clicking the overlapping objects until the object you want to select is selected.

3 USING SHAPES TO CREATE ARTWORK FOR A POSTCARD

Lesson overview

In this lesson, you'll learn how to do the following:

- Create a new document.

- Use tools and commands to create a variety of shapes.

- Understand live shapes.

- Create rounded corners.

- Work with drawing modes.

- Use Image Trace to create shapes.

- Simplify paths.

 This lesson will take about 60 minutes to complete. To get the lesson files used in this chapter, download them from the web page for this book at www.adobepress.com/IllustratorCIB2020. For more information, see "Accessing the lesson files and Web Edition" in the Getting Started section at the beginning of this book.

Basic shapes are essential to creating Illustrator artwork. In this lesson, you'll create a new document and then create and edit a series of shapes using the shape tools for a postcard.

Starting the lesson

In this lesson, you'll explore the different methods for creating artwork using the shape tools and other methods to add artwork to a postcard for a farmers market.

● **Note:** If you have not already downloaded the project files for this lesson to your computer from your Account page, make sure to do so now. See the "Getting Started" section at the beginning of the book.

1 To ensure that the tools function and the defaults are set exactly as described in this lesson, delete or deactivate (by renaming) the Adobe Illustrator preferences file. See "Restoring default preferences" in the "Getting Started" section at the beginning of the book.

2 Start Adobe Illustrator.

3 Choose File > Open. Locate the file named L3_end.ai, which is in the Lessons > Lesson03 folder that you copied onto your hard disk, and click Open.

This file contains the finished illustrations that you'll create in this lesson.

4 Choose View > Fit All In Window; leave the file open for reference, or choose File > Close.

Creating a new document

To start, you'll create a new document for the postcard that you'll add artwork to.

1 Choose Window > Workspace > Essentials (if it's not already selected). Choose Window > Workspace > Reset Essentials to reset the Essentials workspace.

2 Choose File > New to create a new, untitled document. In the New Document dialog box, change the following options:

- Select the **Print** category at the top of the dialog box.

You can set up a document for different kinds of output, such as print, web, video, and more, by choosing a category. For example, if you are designing a web page mock-up, you can select the Web category and select a document preset (size). The document will be set with the units in pixels, the color mode as RGB, and the raster effects to Screen (72 ppi)—all optimal settings for a web document.

- Select the Letter document preset, if it isn't already selected.

On the right, in the Preset Details area, change the following:

- Name: Change it from Untitled-1 to **Postcard**.

The name will become the name of the Illustrator file when you save it later.

- Units: Choose **Inches** from the units menu to the right of the Width field.
- Width: Click in the Width field and type **6**.
- Height: Click in the Height field and type **4.25**.
- Orientation: Landscape ().
- Artboards: **1** (the default setting).

You'll learn about the Bleed option shortly. At the bottom of the Preset Details section on the right side of the New Document dialog box, you will also see Advanced Options and More Settings (you may need to scroll to see it). They contain more settings for document creation that you can explore on your own.

3 Click Create to create a new document.

With the document open in Illustrator, now you'll save it.

4 Choose File > Save As. In the Save As dialog box, ensure that the name of the file is Postcard.ai, and save it in the Lessons > Lesson03 folder. Leave Adobe Illustrator (ai) chosen from the Format menu (macOS) or Adobe Illustrator (*.AI) chosen from the Save As Type menu (Windows), and click Save.

Adobe Illustrator (.ai) is called a native format. That means it preserves all Illustrator data so you can edit everything later.

▶ **Tip:** If you want to learn more about these options, search for "Save artwork" in Illustrator Help (Help > Illustrator Help).

5 In the Illustrator Options dialog box that appears, leave the options at their default settings, and click OK.

The Illustrator Options dialog box is full of options for saving the Illustrator document, from specifying a version for saving to embedding any files that are linked to the document.

6 Click the Document Setup button in the Properties panel (Window > Properties).

The Document Setup dialog box is where you can change document options like units, bleeds, and more after a document is created. You will typically add bleed to artboards for printed artwork that needs to be printed all the way to the edge of the paper. *Bleed* is the term used for the area that extends beyond the edge of the printed page, and it ensures that no white edges show up on the final trimmed page.

7 In the Bleed section of the Document Setup dialog box, change the value in the Top field to **0.125 in**, either by clicking the Up Arrow button to the left of the field once or by typing the value, which should make all four fields change. Click OK.

The red line that appears around the artboard indicates the bleed area.

8 Choose View > Fit Artboard In Window to fit the artboard (page) in the Document window.

Working with basic shapes

In the first part of this lesson, you'll create a series of basic shapes, such as rectangles, ellipses, rounded rectangles, polygons, and more. Shapes you create are composed of *anchor points* with paths connecting the anchor points. A basic square, for instance, is composed of four anchor points on the corners with paths connecting those anchor points (see the upper figure at right). A shape is referred to as a *closed path* because the ends of the path are connected.

Examples of closed paths.

A path can also be open with distinct anchor points on each end, called end points (see the lower figure at right). Both open and closed paths can be filled with color, gradients, and patterns.

Examples of open paths.

Creating rectangles

You'll start this lesson by creating a bowl from a few rectangles that will contain some fruit. You'll explore creating rectangles using two distinct methods.

1   Select the Rectangle tool (⬜) in the toolbar on the left.

2   Move the pointer into the artboard. Press the mouse button and drag down and to the right to create a rectangle that is taller than it is wider. Release the mouse button. Don't worry about the size right now. You'll adjust it shortly.

As you drag to create shapes, the tool tip that appears next to the pointer is called the measurement label and is part of Smart Guides (View > Smart Guides). It shows the width and height of the shape as you draw.

3   Move the pointer over the small blue dot in the center of the rectangle (called the *center point widget*). When the pointer changes (▶⊞), drag the shape into the bottom half of the artboard, roughly centered horizontally.

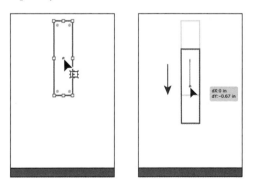

4 With the Rectangle tool still selected, click anywhere in the document to open the Rectangle dialog box. Change the Width to **1** inch and the Height to **0.1** inches. Click OK to create a new rectangle.

Creating a rectangle by clicking is useful when you know the size of the shape you need. For most of the drawing tools, you can either draw with the tool or click to create a shape of a specific size.

● **Note:** Since the rectangle is small, it may be challenging to drag from the center point. As you go through the lessons, you'll zoom in and out to make selections easier.

5 Move the pointer over the center point widget and drag the rectangle below the first rectangle.

You'll move both shapes into their final positions shortly.

Editing the rectangles

All of the shape tools, except for the Star tool and Flare tool, create Live Shapes. *Live Shapes* have attributes such as width, height, rotation, and corner radius that are editable later, without having to switch from the drawing tool you are using, and are retained even if you scale or rotate the shape.

With two rectangles created, you'll make some changes to the first.

1 Select the Selection tool (▶) in the toolbar.

2 Click in the first rectangle you created to select it. Move the pointer over the middle point on the top of the rectangle. Drag up to make it taller. As you drag, press the Option (macOS) or Alt (Windows) key to resize the top and bottom together. When you see a height of approximately 3 inches in the measurement label (the gray tool tip next to the pointer), release the mouse button and then the key.

3 To rotate the rectangle, move the pointer just off of a corner on the shape. When you see rotate arrows (↰), drag clockwise to rotate the shape. As you drag, press the Shift key to constrain the rotation to increments of 45 degrees.

When an angle of 270 shows in the measurement label, release the mouse button and then the key. Leave the shape selected.

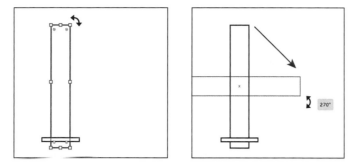

4   In the Transform section of the Properties panel on the right, make sure Constrain Width And Height Proportions to the right of Width (W:) and Height (H:) is *deselected* (it looks like this: ⬚). Select the Height (H:) value and type **0.75**. Press Return or Enter to accept the change.

The Constrain Width And Height Proportions setting is useful when you change either the height or the width and you want the other value to change proportionally. The options in the Transform section of the Properties panel are useful for transforming selected shapes and other artwork in precise ways. You'll learn more about those options in Lesson 5.

By default, shapes are filled with a white color and have a black stroke (border). Next, you'll change the color of the larger rectangle.

5   Click the Fill color box in the Properties panel on the right. In the panel that opens, make sure that the Swatches option (⬚) is selected at the top. Select a brown color to fill the rectangle. I chose a brown with a tool tip that shows "C=50, M=50, Y=60, K=25" when you hover the pointer over the color.

6 Press the Escape key to hide the Swatches panel before moving on.

7 Click the Stroke color box in the Properties panel, make sure that the Swatches option () is selected, and select None to remove the stroke from the rectangle. Press the Escape key to hide the Swatches panel before moving on.

8 Choose Select > Deselect and then choose File > Save to save the file.

Rounding corners

You can round all of the corners of a rectangle or individual corners, using several methods. In this section, you'll round all the corners of the smaller rectangle.

1 Click the smaller rectangle to select it.

2 Choose View > Zoom In as many times as necessary until you see the Live Corners widgets (⊙) in each corner of the rectangle.

If you are zoomed out far enough, the Live Corners widgets are hidden on the shape.

● **Note:** If you drag until you see a red arc, in the next step, the value won't change when you click the up arrow since the maximum is already achieved.

3 Drag any of the Live Corners widgets (⊙) in the rectangle toward the center to round the corners a little.

The more you drag toward the center, the more rounded the corners become. If you drag a Live Corners widget far enough, a red arc appears on the shape, indicating you've reached the maximum corner radius.

▶ **Tip:** You can also double-click a Live Corners widget in a shape to open the Transform panel as a free-floating panel.

4 In the Properties panel to the right, click More Options (•••) in the Transform section to show more options. Ensure that Link Corner Radius Values is on (🔗) (an arrow is pointing to it in the figure), and click the up arrow for any of the Radius values as many times as you can until the value no longer increases (the maximum radius value is achieved). If necessary, click in another field or press the Tab key to see the change to all corners.

Aside from changing the corner radius values, you can also change the corner type. You can choose between Round (default), Inverted Round, and Chamfer.

5   With the options still showing in the Properties panel, click the corner type for each of the bottom corners and choose Chamfer.

6   Press the Escape key to close the options panel.

 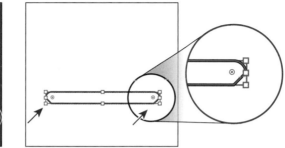

7   Click the Fill color box in the Properties panel on the right. In the panel that opens, make sure that the Swatches option (■) is selected at the top. Select a darker brown color to fill the rectangle.

8   Click the Stroke color box in the Properties panel, make sure that the Swatches option (■) is selected, and select None to remove the stroke from the rectangle.

9   Choose Select > Deselect.

Rounding individual corners

Next, you'll explore rounding the individual corners of a rectangle.

1   Choose View > Fit Artboard In Window.

2   Click the larger rectangle to select it and show the Live Corners widgets (◉) in the corners of the shape.

3   Select the Direct Selection tool (▷). With the shape still selected, double-click the lower-left Live Corners widget (◉). In the Corners dialog box, click the up arrow for the Radius value until the value stops changing (the maximum value is reached). Click OK.

▶ **Tip:** You can Option-click (macOS) or Alt-click (Windows) a Live Corners widget in a shape to cycle through the different corner types.

Notice that only that one corner changed. The Corners dialog box allows you to also set an extra option called Rounding for setting absolute versus relative rounding (see the previous figure). Absolute (⌐) means the rounded corner is exactly the radius value. Relative (⋀) makes the radius value based on the angle of the corner point.

4 Click the lower-right Live Corners widget (⊙) to select just that one Live Corners widget. See the first part of the following figure.

5 Drag that widget (⊙) to round the corner until you see the red color on the path, indicating that the corner is as round as it can get.

6 Select the Selection tool in the toolbar and drag the larger rectangle so that it touches the smaller rectangle and is aligned horizontally with the smaller rectangle. A magenta line will appear in the center of both shapes when they are aligned.

7 Choose Select > Deselect and then choose File > Save.

Drawing on a grid for alignment

The grid appears behind your artwork in the illustration window. It does not print.

- To show or hide the grid, choose View > Show Grid or View > Hide Grid.

- To snap objects to gridlines, choose View > Snap To Grid, select the object you want to move, and drag it to the desired location.

  When the object's boundaries come within 2 pixels of a gridline, it snaps to the point.

Note: If you choose View > Pixel Preview, Snap To Grid changes to Snap To Pixel.

- To specify the spacing between gridlines, grid style (lines or dots), grid color, or whether grids appear in the front or back of artwork, choose Edit > Preferences > Guides & Grid (Windows) or Illustrator > Preferences > Guides & Grid (macOS).

—From Illustrator Help

Creating and editing ellipses

Next, you'll create a few ellipses with the Ellipse tool (◯) to create a pear. The Ellipse tool can be used to create ellipses and circles.

1 Press and hold the mouse button on the Rectangle tool (▢) in the toolbar, and select the Ellipse tool (◯).

2 Move the pointer above the bowl, on the left side of the artboard. Drag to make an ellipse that has an approximate width of 0.6 inches and height of 0.75 inches.

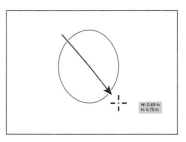

After creating an ellipse, with the Ellipse tool still selected, you can move the shape by dragging from the center widget, transform the shape, and also drag the pie widget to create a pie shape.

3 With the Ellipse tool still selected, move the pointer just below the edge of the ellipse, aligned with the center of it. A magenta guide will appear when the pointer is aligned with the horizontal center (see the first part of the following figure). To draw the shape from the center, press the Option (macOS) or Alt (Windows) key and drag to create a circle that has an approximate width and height of 1 inch. As you drag the pointer, you can tell it's a perfect circle when a magenta crosshairs appears.

4 To keep the shapes together, select the Selection tool (▶) and drag across both shapes to select them. Click the Group button in the Quick Actions section of the Properties panel to the right.

Grouping treats content like a single object, which makes it easier to move the currently selected artwork. You'll group other content you create going forward for the same reason.

5 Click the Fill color box in the Properties panel on the right. In the panel that opens, make sure that the Swatches option (▦) is selected at the top. Select a green color to fill the shapes in the group.

6 Choose Select > Deselect and then choose File > Save.

Creating and editing circles

Next, you'll create three perfect circles with the Ellipse tool (⬭) to create an apple. For one of those circles, you'll explore the Live Shapes feature that allows you to create a pie shape.

1 Select the Ellipse tool (⬭), and, to the right of the pear, press and drag to begin drawing an ellipse. As you drag, press the Shift key to create a perfect circle. When the width and height are both roughly 0.7 inches, release the mouse button and then the Shift key.

Without switching to the Selection tool, you can reposition and modify an ellipse with the Ellipse tool, which is what you'll do next.

2 With the Ellipse tool selected, move the pointer over the center point of the circle. To make a copy of the circle, press Option (macOS) or Alt (Windows) and drag to the right a little. Release the mouse button and then the key when the circles overlap a bit.

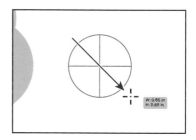

You'll create one more circle by drawing it. This new circle needs to be as wide as the two circles you already have, so you'll align the circle with them as you draw it.

3 Move the pointer over the left edge of the left-most circle. When you see "anchor" next to the pointer, press and drag to the right to draw a circle. As you drag, press the Shift key. When it's as wide as the two circles, a magenta Smart Guide appears on the right edge. Release the mouse button and then the key.

 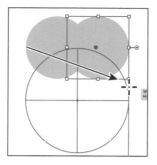

▶ **Tip:** To reset a pie shape back to an ellipse, double-click either pie widget.

4   With the ellipse selected, drag the pie widget (─⊙) off the right side of the ellipse, counterclockwise around the top of the ellipse—don't worry about how far.

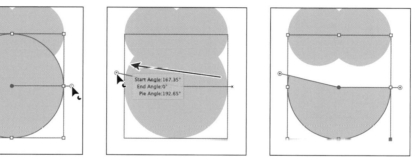

Dragging the pie widget allows you to create a pie shape. After dragging the widget initially and releasing the mouse button, you will then see a second widget. The widget you dragged controls the start angle. The widget that now appears on the right side of the ellipse controls the end angle.

5   In the Properties panel to the right, click More Options (•••) in the Transform section to show more options. Choose 180° from the Pie Start Angle menu. Press the Escape key to hide the panel.

6 Move the pointer over what *was* the center of the ellipse, and drag the ellipse up over the two smaller circles. When it's aligned horizontally and vertically centered with the two circles, magenta alignment guides and the word "intersect" will most likely appear next to the pointer.

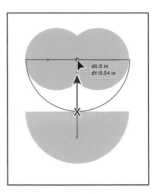

7 Select the Selection tool in the toolbar. Drag across all three circles to select them. Click the Fill color in the Properties panel, and make sure that the Swatches option (▦) is selected in the panel that appears. Select a red color with a tool tip of "C=15 M=100 Y=90 K=10."

Later in this lesson, you'll create an orange. You'll create a copy of the half circle from the apple as a starting point.

8 Click in an empty area of the artboard to deselect. To make a copy of the half circle, press Option (macOS) or Alt (Windows) and drag it into an empty area of the artboard. Release the mouse button and then the key.

Changing stroke width and alignment

So far in this lesson, you have mostly edited the fill of shapes but haven't done too much with the strokes aside from remove them. Strokes are visible outlines or borders of an object or path. You can easily change the color of a stroke or the weight of a stroke to make it thinner or thicker. You'll do that next.

1 With the Selection tool (▶) selected, click the smaller rectangle that is the bottom of the bowl.

2 Choose View > Zoom In a few times.

3 Click the word "Stroke" in the Properties panel to open the Stroke panel. In the Stroke panel, change the stroke weight of the selected rectangle to **2**. Click the Align Stroke To Inside button () to align the stroke to the inside edge of the rectangle.

● **Note:** You may notice in the selected artwork that you only see the corner points of the bounding box. It depends on the zoom level of your document.

● **Note:** You can also open the Stroke panel by choosing Window > Stroke, but you may need to choose Show Options from the panel menu (▤).

Aligning a stroke to the inside of a shape can be a great way to ensure that the stroke doesn't overlap the shape above.

4 Click the Stroke color box in the Properties panel, make sure that the Swatches option (▦) is selected, and select a lighter brown color.

5 Choose Select > Deselect.

Creating a polygon

Using the Polygon tool (⬡), you can create shapes with multiple straight sides. By default, the Polygon tool draws hexagons (a six-sided shape), and all shapes are drawn from the center. Polygons are also Live Shapes, which means attributes such as size, rotation, number of sides, and more remain editable after you create them. Now you'll create a polygon to make a series of leaves using the Polygon tool (⬡).

1 Choose View > Fit Artboard In Window to fit the artboard in the Document window.

2 Press and hold down the mouse button on the Ellipse tool (◯) in the toolbar, and select the Polygon tool (⬡).

3 Choose View > Smart Guides to turn them off.

4 Move the pointer in a blank area of the artboard. Drag to the right to begin drawing a polygon, but *don't release the mouse button yet.* Press the Down Arrow key once to reduce the number of sides on the polygon to five, and don't release the mouse button yet. Hold down the Shift key to straighten the shape. Release the mouse button and then the key. Leave the shape selected.

Notice that you didn't see the gray measurement label (the tool tip) since it's part of the Smart Guides that you turned off. The magenta alignment guides are also not showing, since the shape is not snapping to other content on the artboard. Smart Guides can be useful in certain situations, such as when more precision is necessary—maybe you want to know how large the shape is—and can be toggled on and off when needed.

5   To change the fill color, click the Fill color box in the Properties panel, and make sure that the Swatches option (▦) is selected in the panel that appears. Select a green color with a tool tip of "C=85 M=10 Y=100 K=10."

6   Click the Stroke color box in the Properties panel, make sure that the Swatches option (▦) is selected, and select None to remove the stroke from the shape.

7   Choose View > Smart Guides to turn them back on.

8   With the Polygon tool still selected, drag the side widget (◇) on the right side of the bounding box down to change the number of sides to 6.

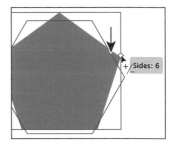

This widget is a feature of "live" shapes. You can still edit certain properties after the shape has been created.

Editing the polygon

Now you'll edit the polygon and create a leaf from it.

1   To rotate the polygon, move the pointer just off a corner of the bounding box around the shape. When the pointer changes to a rotate arrow (↻), press and drag counter-clockwise. As you drag, press the Shift key to constrain the rotation to 45 degrees. When you see an angle of 90 in the measurement label next to the pointer, release the mouse button and then the key.

2   To change the size of the polygon, move the pointer over a corner and drag. As you drag, press the Shift key to change the width and height proportionally (together).

When the measurement label shows a height of approximately 0.65 inches, release the mouse button and then the key. Depending on how big your polygon was to start, you will make it either larger or smaller in this step to match the width we suggest.

3   In the Transform section of the Properties panel on the right, make sure Constrain Width And Height Proportions to the right of Width (W:) and Height (H:) is *deselected* (it looks like this: ▧), so you can change the values independently. Select the Width (W:) value and type **0.35**. Press Return or Enter to accept the change.

With the leaf shape (polygon) now created, you'll round some of the corners to make it look a little more natural.

4   With the polygon selected, to zoom in to it, choose View > Zoom In a few times.

If you look at the polygon right now, with the Selection tool (▶) selected, you'll see a single Live Corners widget (◉) in the shape. If you were to drag that widget, all of the corners would be rounded. In this instance, you'll use the Direct Selection tool to round some of them.

5   Select the Direct Selection tool (▷) in the toolbar. You should now see Live Corners widgets in each corner. You'll select and change four of the corners. Click the Live Corners widget (◉) with an arrow pointing to it in the second part of the figure. Press the Shift key and click the three other widgets marked in the figure to select all four. Release the Shift key.

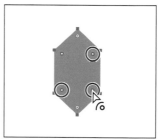

You can tell that the widgets are now selected because they have a more filled appearance.

6   Drag one of the selected Live Corners widgets toward the center of the shape. Keep dragging past the center until you see the red lines indicating that you can't round them any more.

Creating a star

Next you'll use the Star tool (⭐) to create a few stars that will become flowers. The Star tool currently doesn't create Live Shapes, which means editing the star after the fact can be more difficult. When drawing with the Star tool, you'll use keyboard modifiers to get the number of points you want and to change the radius of the arms of the star (the length of the arms). Here are the keyboard modifiers you'll use in this section when drawing the star:

- **Arrow keys:** Pressing the Up Arrow or Down Arrow key adds or removes arms from the star, respectively, as you draw it.
- **Shift:** This straightens the star (constrains it).
- **Command (macOS) or Ctrl (Windows):** Pressing this key and dragging while creating a star allows you to change the radius of the arms of the star (make the arms longer or shorter).

Next you'll create a star. This will take a few keyboard commands, so *don't release the mouse button* until you are told.

1   Press and hold down the mouse button on the Polygon tool (⬡) in the toolbar, and select the Star tool (⭐). Move the pointer to the right of the leaf.

▶ **Tip:** You can also click in the Document window with the Star tool (⭐) and edit the options in the Star dialog box instead of drawing it.

2   Press and drag to the right to create a star shape. Notice that as pointer moves, the star changes size and rotates freely. Drag until the measurement label shows a width of about 1 inch and then stop dragging. *Don't release the mouse button!*

3   Press the Down Arrow key once to decrease the number of points on the star to four. *Don't release the mouse button!*

4   Press Command (macOS) or Ctrl (Windows), and continue to drag a little toward the center of the star. This keeps the inner radius constant, making the arms shorter. Drag until the star looks something like the figure and then stop dragging, *without releasing the mouse button.* Release Command or Ctrl but *not the mouse button.*

5   Press the Shift key. When the star straightens out, release the mouse button and then the key.

Editing the star

With the star created, next you'll transform and copy the star.

1   Select the Selection tool (▶), press the Shift key, and drag a corner of star bounding box toward the center. When the star has a width of approximately 0.4 inches, release the mouse button and then the key.

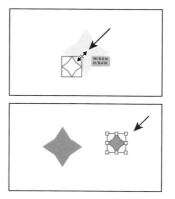

2   Select the Star tool (☆). Press the Shift key and draw a star that's a little smaller than the first. Release the mouse button and then the key.

Notice that the new star has the same basic settings as the first star you drew.

3   To rotate the star, in the Transform section of the Properties panel, change the Rotate value by selecting the value and typing in **45**. Press Return or Enter. To scale the star, make sure Constrain Width And Height Proportions to the right of Width (W:) and Height (H:) is *selected* (it looks like this: ▯). Select the Height (H:) value and type **0.14**. Press Return or Enter to accept the change.

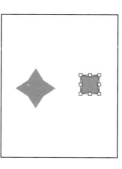

4   Select the Selection tool (▶) and drag the smaller star into the center of the larger star.

5   Change the fill color of the smaller star in the Properties panel to a yellow.

6   Click in an empty area of the artboard to deselect, then click the larger star and change the fill color to white.

7   Drag across the star shapes to select them and then click the Group button in the Properties panel to group them together.

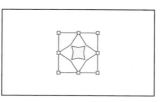

8   Choose File > Save.

Drawing lines

Next you'll create lines and line segments, known as *open paths*, with the Line Segment tool. Lines created with the Line Segment tool are Live Lines, and similar to Live Shapes, they have many editable attributes after they are drawn.

1 Press and hold on the Star tool (⭐) in the toolbar, and select the Line Segment tool (╱). To the right of the bowl, press and drag up to draw a line. As you drag, press the Shift key to constrain the line to 45 degrees. Notice the length and angle in the measurement label next to the pointer as you drag. Drag until the line is around 2 inches in length.

2 With the new line selected, move the pointer just off the top end. When the pointer changes to a rotate arrow (↶), press and drag down until you see an angle of 0 (zero) in the measurement label next to the pointer. That will make the line horizontal.

Lines rotate around their center point by default. The angle of the line can also be changed in the Properties panel.

3 Select the Selection tool (▶) in the toolbar, and drag the line from the center point to just below the bowl. When it is touching the bottom of the bowl and it is aligned horizontally with the bowl—you'll see a vertical alignment guide when the line is aligned with the bowl—release the mouse button.

This line represents a table that the bowl is sitting on, so make sure the line touches the bottom of the bowl.

4 With the line selected, change the stroke weight to **2 pt** in the Properties panel to the right of the document.

5 Click the Stroke color box in the Properties panel, and make sure that the Swatches option (▦) is selected in the panel that appears. Select a brown color with a tool tip of "C=35, M=60, Y=80, K=25."

6 To change the length of the line from the center, move the pointer over one of the ends, press Option (macOS) or Alt (Windows), and drag away from the center. Drag until the line is 4 inches in length, release the mouse button and then the key.

If you drag a line in the same trajectory as the original path, you will see the words "Line Extension" and "on" appear at opposite ends of the line. These appear because the Smart Guides are turned on. You can drag a line to make it longer or shorter without changing the angle.

7 Drag across the two rectangles for the bowl and the line beneath. Click the Group button in the Properties panel to keep the artwork together.

Converting raster images to editable vector using Image Trace

In this part of the lesson, you'll learn how to work with the Image Trace command. Image Trace converts a raster image, like a picture from Adobe Photoshop, into editable vector artwork. This can be useful for turning something you drew on paper, for instance, into vector art, or tracing raster logos, tracing a pattern or texture, and much more. In this section, you'll trace a picture of a lemon to get shapes you could then edit.

1 Choose File > Place. In the Place dialog box, select the lemon.jpg file in the Lessons > Lesson03 folder on your hard disk, leave all options at their defaults, and click Place.

2 Click in an empty part of the artboard to place the image.

3 To center the selected image in the Document window (since it's large), choose View > Zoom Out.

4 With the image selected, click the Image Trace button in the Properties panel to the right of the document, and choose Low Fidelity Photo.

● **Note:** You can also choose Object > Image Trace > Make, with raster content selected, or begin tracing from the Image Trace panel (Window > Image Trace).

▶ **Tip:** Use Adobe Capture on your device to photograph any object, design, or shape and convert it into vector shapes in a few simple steps. Store the resulting vectors in your Creative Cloud libraries, and access them or refine them in Illustrator or Photoshop. Adobe Capture is currently available for iOS (iPhone and iPad) and Android.

This converts the image into an image tracing object. That means you can't edit the vector content yet, but you can change the tracing settings or even the original placed image and then see the updates.

5   Choose Silhouettes from the Preset menu that's showing in the Properties panel.

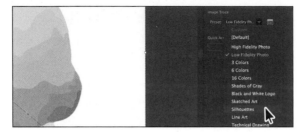

The Silhouettes preset will trace the image, forcing the resulting vector content to turn black. An image tracing object is made up of the original source image and the tracing result, which is the vector artwork. By default, only the tracing result is visible. However, you can change the display of both the original image and the tracing result to best suit your needs.

▶ **Tip:** The Image Trace panel can also be opened by choosing Window > Image Trace.

6   Click the Open The Image Trace Panel button (▣) in the Properties panel.

The buttons along the top of the Image Trace panel are saved settings for converting the image to grayscale, black and white, and more. Below the buttons at the top of the Image Trace panel, you will see the Preset menu. This is the same menu as in the Properties panel. The Mode menu allows you to change the color mode of resulting artwork (color, grayscale, or black and white). The Palette menu is also useful for limiting the color palette or for assigning colors from a color group.

▶ **Tip:** You can deselect Preview at the bottom of the Image Trace panel when modifying values so Illustrator won't apply the trace settings to what you are tracing every time you make a change.

7   In the Image Trace panel, click the triangle to the left of the Advanced options to reveal them. Change the following options in the Image Trace panel, using the values as a starting point:

   • Threshold: **206**
   • Paths: **20%**
   • Corners: **50%** (the default setting)
   • Noise: **100 px**

8   Close the Image Trace panel.

9 With the lemon tracing object still selected, click the Expand button in the Properties panel.

The lemon is no longer an image tracing object but is composed of shapes and paths that are grouped together.

Cleaning up traced artwork

Since the lemon image has been converted to shapes using the Image Trace command, you can now refine the shapes to make the lemon look better.

1 With the lemon artwork selected, click the Ungroup button in the Properties panel to break apart the different shapes and edit them separately.

2 Deselect the artwork by choosing Select > Deselect.

3 Click the extra shape that was traced. Use the figure as a guide. Press Delete or Backspace to remove it.

4 Click in the lemon shape to select it. To change the color, click the Fill color box in the Properties panel on the right. In the panel that opens, make sure that the Swatches option (▦) is selected at the top. Select a yellow color to fill the lemon.

To make the edges a little bit smoother, you'll apply the Simplify command. The Simplify command reduces the number of anchor points that the path is made of without affecting the overall shape too much.

5 With the lemon selected, choose Object > Path > Simplify.

6 In the Simplify options that appear, by default, the Reduce Anchor Point slider is set to an auto-simplified value. Drag the slider to the right to add a few more points.

You can drag the slider to reduce the anchor points and further simplify the path. The position and value of the slider specifies how closely the simplified path matches the curves of the original path. The closer the slider is to the minimum value on the left, the fewer the anchor points there are, but the path will most likely start to look different. The closer the slider is to the maximum value on the right, the closer the precision to the original curve is.

7 Click More Options (⋯) to open a dialog box with more options.

8 In the dialog box that opens, make sure Preview is selected to see the changes happen. You can see the original number of anchor points (Original) of the lemon and the number of anchor points after applying the Simplify command (New). Drag the Simplify Curve slider all the way to the right (Maximum). This is a great starting point and the artwork will look like it did before you applied the Simplify command. Drag the slider to the left until you see New: 5. You'll need to drag a little, and release to see the New value change.

For the Angle Threshold, if the angle of a corner point is less than the angle threshold, the corner point is not changed. This option helps keep corners sharp, even if the value for Curve Precision is low.

9 Click OK.

10 To scale the lemon, pressing the Shift key, drag a corner to make it smaller. When you see a width of the approximately 1.2 inches in the tool tip, release the mouse button and then the key.

11 Drag the lemon into an empty area of the artboard.

Working with drawing modes

▶ **Tip:** You can cycle through the drawing modes by pressing Shift+D.

Illustrator has three different drawing modes available that are found at the bottom of the toolbar: Draw Normal, Draw Behind, and Draw Inside. Drawing modes allow you to draw shapes in different ways. The three drawing modes are as follows:

- **Draw Normal mode:** You start every document by drawing shapes in Normal mode, which stacks shapes on top of each other.

- **Draw Behind mode:** This mode allows you to draw behind all artwork on a selected layer if no artwork is selected. If artwork is selected, the new object is drawn directly beneath the selected object.

- **Draw Inside mode:** This mode lets you draw objects or place images inside other objects, including live text, automatically creating a clipping mask of the selected object. You'll learn more about masks in Lesson 15.

Placing artwork

Next you'll place artwork from another Illustrator document that contains text shapes and artwork you will use to create another piece of fruit.

1   Choose File > Open. In the Open dialog box, select the artwork.ai file in the Lessons > Lesson03 folder on your hard disk, and click Open.

2   Select the Selection tool (▶) in the toolbar. To select all of the content, choose Select > All On Active Artboard. Choose Edit > Copy.

3   Click the Postcard.ai tab to return to the postcard document.

4   Choose View > Fit Artboard In Window.

5   Choose Edit > Paste to paste the "FARM FRESH" text and part of the artwork for an orange.

6   Choose Select > Deselect.

Tip: The orange group is made of a circle drawn with the Ellipse tool, a star drawn with the Star tool, and a series of lines drawn with the Line Segment tool.

Using Draw Inside mode

Now you'll add the artwork of the orange you copied from the artwork.ai file to the inside of the red half-circle using the Draw Inside drawing mode. This can be useful if you want to hide (*mask*) part of the artwork.

1   Click the red half-circle copy you made earlier when creating the apple.

2   Click the Fill color box in the Properties panel on the right. In the panel that opens, make sure that the Swatches option (▦) is selected at the top. Select an orange color to fill the shape. I chose the color with the tool tip "C=0, M=50, Y=100, K=0."

3   With the orange half-circle selected, choose Draw Inside from the Drawing Modes menu (▣), near the bottom of the toolbar.

Note: If the toolbar you see is displayed as a double column, you will see all three of the drawing modes as buttons toward the bottom of the toolbar.

This button is active when a single object is selected (path, compound path, or text), and it allows you to draw within the selected object only. Notice that the orange shape has a dotted open rectangle around it, indicating that if you draw, paste, or place content, it will be inside the shape.

4   Choose Select > Deselect.

Notice that the orange shape still has the dotted open rectangle around it, indicating that Draw Inside mode is still active. You can draw, place, or paste content into a shape with Draw Inside mode active. The shape you are about to add content inside of does not need to be selected.

5 Select the Selection tool (▶), and click the artwork that is the inside of the orange you pasted to select it. Choose Edit > Cut to cut the selected artwork from the artboard.

6 Choose Edit > Paste.

The artwork is pasted within the orange shape.

▶ **Tip:** You can separate the artwork again by choosing Object > Clipping Mask > Release. This will make two objects, stacked one on another.

7 Click the Drawing Modes button (▣) toward the bottom of the toolbar. Choose Draw Normal.

When you are finished adding content inside a shape, you can choose Draw Normal so that any new content you create will be drawn normally (stacked rather than drawn inside).

8 Choose Select > Deselect.

Editing content drawn inside

Next you'll edit the orange artwork inside of the shape to see how you can later edit content inside.

1 With the Selection tool (▶) selected, click to select the orange artwork you pasted. Notice that it selects the half-circle shape instead.

The half-circle shape is now a mask, also called a *clipping path*. The half-circle shape and the orange pasted artwork together make a *clip group* and are now treated as a single object. If you look at the top of the Properties panel, you will see Clip Group. As with other groups, if you would like to edit the clipping path (the object that contains the content drawn inside of it) or the content inside, you can double-click the Clip Group object.

2 With the Clip Group selected, click the Isolate Mask button in the Properties panel to enter isolation mode and be able to select the clipping path (half-circle shape) or the orange pasted artwork within.

3 Click the orange pasted artwork within the map boundaries, and drag it to be more centered in the half-circle.

4 Press the Escape key to exit isolation mode.

5 Choose Select > Deselect and then choose File > Save.

Working with Draw Behind mode

Throughout this lesson, you've been working in the default Draw Normal mode. Next, you'll draw a rectangle that will cover the artboard and go behind the rest of the content using Draw Behind mode.

1 Click the Drawing Modes button () at the bottom of the toolbar, and choose Draw Behind.

As long as this drawing mode is selected, every shape you create using the different methods you've learned will be created behind the other shapes on the page. The Draw Behind mode also affects placed content (File > Place).

Note: If the toolbar you see is displayed as a double column, you will see all three of the drawing modes as buttons toward the bottom of the toolbar.

2 Press and hold down the mouse button on the Line Segment tool (╱) in the toolbar, and select the Rectangle tool (▭).

3 Move the pointer off the upper-left corner of the artboard where the red bleed guides meet. Press and drag to the lower-right corner of the red bleed guides.

4 With the new rectangle selected, click the Fill color box in the Properties panel. Make sure that the Swatches option (▦) is selected and then change the fill color to a gray color with the tool tip "C=0, M=0, Y=0, K=20."

5 Press the Escape key to hide the panel.

6 Choose Object > Lock > Selection to lock the rectangle so it can't be accidentally moved.

Finishing up

To finish the postcard, you'll move the artwork into position on the artboard, rotate some, and make copies.

1 Choose View > Fit Artboard In Window to see the entire artboard, if necessary.

2 Select the Selection tool (▶) and click one of the red shapes in the apple. Press the Shift key and click the remaining two shapes, then release the key. Click the Group button in the Properties panel to group the apple shapes together.

3 Drag each piece of fruit and the text into position.

4 Make copies of the fruit and leaf artwork. To do so, click each piece of artwork and choose Edit > Copy and then Edit > Paste.

5 To rotate a group, you can move the pointer just off a corner of the selected artwork and drag when you see the rotate arrows (↶).

● **Note:** If you don't see the Arrange button in the Properties panel, you can also choose Object > Arrange and choose an arrangement option.

6 To bring artwork in front of other artwork, click the artwork to select it. Click the Arrange button in the Properties panel and choose Bring To Front.

Artwork that is behind other artwork was created first.

7 Choose File > Save.

8 To close all open files, choose File > Close a few times.

Review questions

1 When creating a new document, what is a document category?

2 What are the basic tools for creating shapes?

3 What is a live shape?

4 Describe what Draw Inside mode does.

5 How can you convert a raster image into editable vector shapes?

Review answers

1 You can set up a document for different kinds of output, such as print, web, video, and more, by choosing a category. For example, if you are designing a web page mock-up, you can select the Web category and select a document preset (size). The document will be set with the units in pixels, the color mode as RGB, and the raster effects to Screen (72 ppi)—all optimal settings for a web design document.

2 There are five shape tools in the Essentials workspace: Rectangle, Ellipse, Polygon, Star, and Line Segment (the Rounded Rectangle and Flare tools are not in the toolbar in the Essentials workspace). As explained in Lesson 1, "Getting to Know the Work Area," to tear off a group of tools from the toolbar, move the pointer over the tool that appears in the toolbar, and hold down the mouse button until the group of tools appears. Without releasing the mouse button, drag to the triangle on the right side of the group and then release the mouse button to tear off the group.

3 After you draw a rectangle, ellipse, or polygon (or rounded rectangle, which wasn't covered) using the shape tool, you can continue to modify its properties such as width, height, rounded corners, corner types, and radii (individually or collectively). This is what is known as a Live Shape. The shape properties, such as corner radius, are editable later in the Transform panel, in the Properties panel, or directly on the art.

4 Draw Inside mode lets you draw objects or place images inside other objects, including live text, automatically creating a clipping mask of the selected object.

5 You can convert a raster image into editable vector shapes by selecting it and then clicking the Image Trace button in the Properties panel. To convert the tracing to paths, click Expand in the Properties panel, or choose Object > Image Trace > Expand. Use this method if you want to work with the components of the traced artwork as individual objects. The resulting paths are grouped.

4 EDITING AND COMBINING SHAPES AND PATHS

Lesson overview

In this lesson, you'll learn how to do the following:

- Cut with the Scissors tool.

- Join paths.

- Work with the Knife tool.

- Outline strokes.

- Work with the Eraser tool.

- Create a compound path.

- Work with the Shape Builder tool.

- Work with Pathfinder effects to create shapes.

- Work with the Reshape tool.

- Edit strokes with the Width tool.

 This lesson will take about 45 minutes to complete. To get the lesson files used in this chapter, download them from the web page for this book at www.adobepress.com/IllustratorCIB2020. For more information, see "Accessing the lesson files and Web Edition" in the Getting Started section at the beginning of this book.

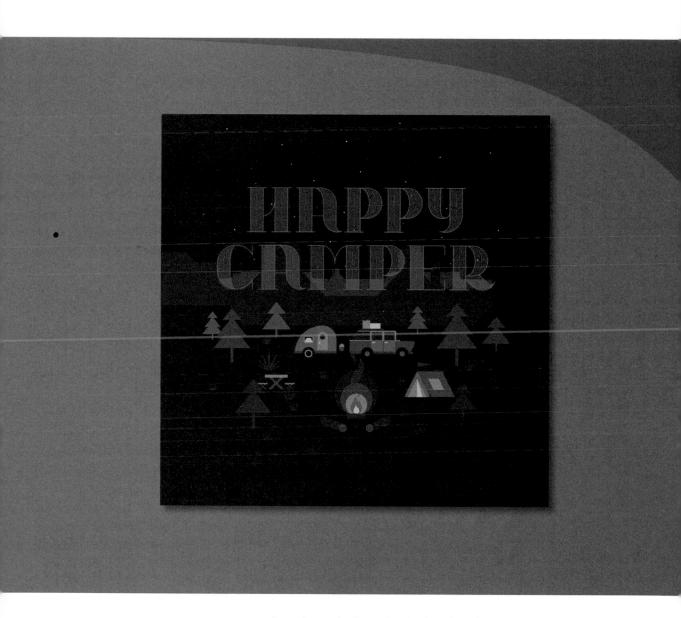

Soon after you begin creating simple paths and shapes, you will most likely want to use them to create more complex artwork. In this lesson, you'll explore how to both edit and combine shapes and paths.

Starting the lesson

In Lesson 3, "Using Shapes to Create Artwork for a Postcard," you learned about creating and making edits to basic shapes. In this lesson, you'll take basic shapes and paths and learn how to edit and combine them to create artwork to finish a poster about camping.

Note: If you have not already downloaded the project files for this lesson to your computer from your Account page, make sure to do so now. See the "Getting Started" section at the beginning of the book.

1   To ensure that the tools function and the defaults are set exactly as described in this lesson, delete or deactivate (by renaming) the Adobe Illustrator preferences file. See "Restoring default preferences" in the "Getting Started" section at the beginning of the book.

2   Start Adobe Illustrator.

3   Choose File > Open. Locate the file named L4_end.ai, which is in the Lessons > Lesson04 folder that you copied onto your hard disk, and click Open. This file contains the finished artwork.

4   Choose View > Fit All In Window; leave the file open for reference, or choose File > Close (I closed it).

5   Choose File > Open. In the Open dialog box, navigate to the Lessons > Lesson04 folder, and select the L4_start.ai file on your hard disk. Click Open.

Tip: By default, the .ai extension shows on macOS, but you can add the extension on either platform in the Save As dialog box.

6   Choose File > Save As. In the Save As dialog box, change the name to **HappyCamper.ai** (macOS) or **HappyCamper** (Windows), and choose the Lesson04 folder. Leave Adobe Illustrator (ai) chosen from the Format menu (macOS) or Adobe Illustrator (*.AI) chosen from the Save As Type menu (Windows) and then click Save.

7   In the Illustrator Options dialog box, leave the Illustrator options at their default settings, and click OK.

8   Choose Window > Workspace > Reset Essentials.

Note: If you don't see Reset Essentials in the Workspace menu, choose Window > Workspace > Essentials before choosing Window > Workspace > Reset Essentials.

Editing paths and shapes

In Illustrator, you can edit and combine paths and shapes in a variety of ways to create your own artwork. Sometimes that may mean starting with simpler paths and shapes and using different methods to produce more complex paths. This includes working with the Scissors tool (✂), the Knife tool (✐), and the Eraser tool (◆); outlining strokes; joining paths; and more.

● **Note:** You'll explore other methods for transforming artwork in Lesson 5, "Transforming Artwork."

Cutting with the Scissors tool

There are several tools that allow you to cut and divide shapes. You'll start with the Scissors tool (✂), which splits a path at an anchor point or on a line segment to create an open path. Next, you'll cut a rectangle with the Scissors tool and reshape it to make curtains in a camping trailer illustration.

1 Click the View menu, and make sure that the Smart Guides option is selected. A checkmark appears when it's selected.

2 Choose 2 Window from the Artboard Navigation menu in the lower-left corner of the Document window. Choose View > Fit Artboard In Window.

An example of what you will create is labeled "Final" on the right side of the artboard. You will work with the artwork labeled "Start" on the left.

3 Select the Selection tool (▶) in the toolbar, and click the white shape in the area labeled "Start" to select it.

4 Press Command and + (macOS) or Ctrl and + (Windows) a few times to zoom in to the selected artwork.

Note: If you don't click directly on a point or path, you will see a warning dialog box. You can simply click OK and try again.

5   With the shape selected, in the toolbar, press and hold on the Eraser tool (◆), and select the Scissors tool (✂). Move the pointer over the bottom edge of the shape (see the first part of the following figure). When you see the word "path," click to cut the path at that point and then move the pointer away.

You may have noticed the gray message "Shape Expanded" appear after cutting the shape. Rectangles are Live Shapes by default, but after cutting with the Scissors tool, they become an open path. Cuts made with the Scissors tool must be on a line or a curve rather than on an end point of an open path. When you use the Scissors tool to click the stroke of a shape, which is the rectangle in this example, the path is cut where you click so that it becomes open.

6   Select the Direct Selection tool (▷) in the toolbar. Move the pointer over the selected (blue) anchor point and drag it up.

7   From where you originally cut the shape, drag the other anchor point up and to the right (see the figure).

Notice how the stroke (the black border) doesn't go all the way around the white shape. That's because cutting a shape with the Scissors tool makes an open path. If you only want to fill the shape with a color, it doesn't have to be a closed path. It is, however, necessary for a path to be closed if you want a stroke to appear around the entire fill area.

Joining paths

Suppose you draw a "U" shape and later decide to close the shape, essentially joining the ends of the "U" with a straight path. If you select the path, you can use the Join command to create a line segment between the end points, closing the path.

Open path   Endpoints joined

When more than one open path is selected, you can join them to create a closed path. You can also join selected end points of two separate paths. Next, you'll join the ends of the white path you edited to create a single closed shape.

1 Select the Selection tool (▶) in the toolbar. Click away from the white path to deselect it and then click in the white fill to reselect it.

This step is important because only one anchor point was left selected from the previous section. If you were to choose the Join command with only one anchor point selected, an error message would appear. By selecting the whole path, when you apply the Join command, Illustrator simply finds the two ends of the path and connects them with a straight line.

▶ **Tip:** If you wanted to join specific anchor points from separate paths, select the anchor points and choose Object > Path > Join or press Command+J (macOS) or Ctrl+J (Windows).

2 Click the Join button in the Quick Actions section of the Properties panel.

When you apply the Join command to two or more open paths, by default, Illustrator first looks for and joins the paths that have end points located closest to each other. This process is repeated every time you apply the Join command until all paths are joined.

▶ **Tip:** In Lesson 6, "Using the Basic Drawing Tools," you'll learn about the Join tool (✕), which allows you to join two paths at a corner, keeping the original curve intact.

3 In the Properties panel, change the stroke to 0 by clicking the Down Arrow button until the stroke is removed.

4 Click the Fill color box (white) in the Properties panel, make sure the Swatches option (▦) is selected in the panel that appears, and click to select the color Purple3.

5 Drag across the window shapes to select them.

6 Click the Group button in the Properties panel to group them together.

7 Choose Select > Deselect and then choose File > Save.

Cutting with the Knife tool

You can also use the Knife tool () to cut vector artwork. Using the Knife tool, you drag across a shape, and instead of creating open paths, you end up with closed paths.

1 Choose 3 Tank from the Artboard Navigation menu in the lower-left corner of the Document window.

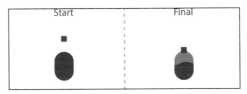

An example of what you will create is labeled "Final" on the right side of the artboard. You will work with the artwork labeled "Start" on the left.

2 Choose View > Fit Artboard In Window.

▶ **Tip:** You can select multiple vector objects and cut them at one time with the Knife tool.

3 With the Selection tool (▶) selected, click the pink oval shape under the artwork labeled "Start."

If an object is selected, the Knife tool will cut only that object. If nothing is selected, it will cut any vector objects it touches.

● **Note:** If you see a message window appear after clicking Edit Toolbar, you can close it.

4 Click Edit Toolbar (▦) at the bottom of the toolbar. Scroll in the menu that appears and toward the bottom of the menu you should see the Knife tool (✎). Drag the Knife tool onto the Scissors tool (✂) in the toolbar on the left to add it to the list of tools.

5 Press the Escape key to hide the menu.

6 With the Knife tool now selected in the toolbar, move the Knife pointer (▸✎) to the left of the selected shape. Drag across the shape to cut it into two.

▶ **Tip:** Pressing the Caps Lock key will turn the Knife tool pointer into a more precise cursor (-¦-). This can make it easier to see where the cut will happen.

Notice how dragging across a shape with the Knife tool makes a free-form cut that is not straight at all.

7 Choose Select > Deselect.

8 Select the Selection tool (▶), and click the new shape on the top (see the following figure).

9 Click the Fill color box in the Properties panel, make sure the Swatches option (▦) is selected in the panel that appears, and click to select the color Pink.

 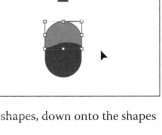

10 Drag the small, red square that is above the shapes, down onto the shapes you cut.

11 Drag across all of the tank shapes labeled "Start" to select them.

12 Click the Group button in the Quick Actions section of the Properties panel.

13 Choose Select > Deselect.

Cutting in a straight line

Next, you'll cut artwork in a straight line with the Knife tool.

1 Choose 4 Tent from the Artboard Navigation menu in the lower-left corner of the Document window.

● **Note:** The side of the tent was skewed with the Shear tool. You'll learn how to shear artwork in Lesson 5.

An example of what you will create is labeled "Final" on the right side of the artboard. You will work with the artwork labeled "Start" on the left. You'll cut the tent opening shape into several paths. This requires you to cut in straight lines.

2 Choose View > Fit Artboard In Window.

3 With the Selection tool (▶) selected, click the pink triangle shape under the artwork labeled "Start."

4 Choose View > Zoom In, twice, to zoom in to the artwork.

5 Select the Knife tool (✐). Move the pointer just above the top point of the selected triangle. Press the Caps Lock key to turn the Knife tool pointer into crosshairs (-¦-).

Start

The crosshairs pointer is more precise and can make it easier to see exactly where you begin cutting.

Note: Pressing the Option/Alt key keeps the cut straight, and pressing the Shift key in addition constrains the cutting to a multiple of 45°.

6 Press and hold Option+Shift (macOS) or Alt+Shift (Windows), and drag down, all the way across the shape to cut it into two, in a completely straight line. Release the mouse button and then the keys.

7 Press and hold Option (macOS) or Alt (Windows), and drag down from just above the top of the selected triangle, at a slight angle, all the way across the shape to cut it into two. Release the mouse button and then the key.

8 Choose Select > Deselect.

9 Select the Selection tool (▶), and click the middle, pink triangle.

10 Click the Fill color box in the Properties panel, make sure the Swatches option (▦) is selected in the panel that appears, and click to select the color Yellow.

11 Drag across all of the tent shapes labeled "Start" to select them.

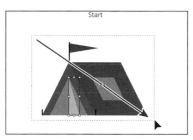

12 Click the Group button in the Quick Actions section of the Properties panel.

13 Press the Caps Lock key to turn off the pointer crosshairs.

Outlining strokes

A path, like a line, can show a stroke color but not a fill color by default. If you create a line in Illustrator and want to apply both a stroke and a fill, you can outline the stroke of a path, which converts it into a closed shape (or compound path). Next, you'll outline the stroke of a line so you can erase parts of it in the next section.

1 Choose 5 Plant from the Artboard Navigation menu in the lower-left corner of the Document window.

An example of what you will create is labeled "Final" on the right side of the artboard. You'll work with the artwork labeled "Start" on the left.

2 Choose View > Fit Artboard In Window to ensure it fits in the Document window.

3 With the Selection tool (▶), under the "Start" label, click the purple path in its center.

The rectangle is actually a path with a large stroke. In the Properties panel, you can see that the stroke weight is set to 20. To erase part of the path to make it the shape of one of the leaves, it will need to be a shape (rectangle), not a path.

Note: If you outline the stroke and it shows as "Group" in the Selection Indicator at the top of the Properties panel, then there was a fill set on the path. If the artwork is a group, choose Edit > Undo Outline Stroke, apply a fill of None to the path, and try again.

4 Choose Object > Path > Outline Stroke.

This creates a filled shape that is a closed path.

5 Drag the shape into position as you see in the following figure. Leave the shape selected.

Next, you'll erase parts of the shape.

Using the Eraser tool

Note: You cannot erase raster images, text, symbols, graphs, or gradient mesh objects.

The Eraser tool (◆) lets you erase any area of your vector artwork. You can use the Eraser tool on paths, compound paths, paths inside Live Paint groups, and clipping content. Whatever artwork you select is the only artwork you will erase. If you leave all objects deselected, you can erase any object that the tool touches across all layers. Next, you'll use the Eraser tool to erase part of the selected rectangle so it looks like a leaf.

1 Press and hold down the mouse button on the Knife tool (✐), and select the Eraser tool (◆) in the toolbar.

2 Double-click the Eraser tool () in the toolbar to edit the tool properties. In the Eraser Tool Options dialog box, change Size to **20 pt** to make the eraser larger. Click OK.

You can change the Eraser tool properties, depending on what your needs are.

▶ **Tip:** With the Eraser tool selected, and nothing selected in the document, you could also click the Tool Options button at the top of the Properties panel to see the options dialog box.

3 Move the pointer above the selected purple shape. Drag down the left side of the shape to erase it.

When you release the mouse button, part of the shape is erased, and the shape is still a closed path.

4 Move the pointer above the selected purple shape. Drag down the right side of the shape to erase it.

5 Select the Selection tool (▶), and drag across all of the plant shapes labeled "Start" to select them.

6 Click the Group button in the Quick Actions section of the Properties panel.

Erasing in a straight line

You can also erase in a straight line, which is what you'll do next.

1 Choose 6 Car from the Artboard Navigation menu in the lower-left corner of the Document window.

An example of what you will create is labeled "Final" on the right side of the artboard. You will work with the artwork labeled "Start" on the left. You'll select and erase the back of the car to make it angled like you see in the Final.

2 With the Selection tool (▶) selected, drag across the pink, purple, and dark pink shapes labeled "Start."

3 Choose View > Zoom In a few times to see more detail.

4 Double-click the Eraser tool (◆) to edit the tool properties. In the Eraser Tool Options dialog box, change Size to **40 pt** to make the eraser bigger. Click OK.

5 With the Eraser tool (◆) selected, move the pointer above the selected shapes. See the first part of the following figure. Press the Shift key, and drag at a 45-degree angle down. Release the mouse button and then the Shift key.

If nothing is erased, try again. Also, it may look like you erased other parts of the car, but since nothing else was selected, you didn't.

6 Select the Selection tool, and drag across all of the car shapes labeled "Start" to select them.

7 Click the Group button in the Quick Actions section of the Properties panel to the right of the document.

8 Choose File > Save.

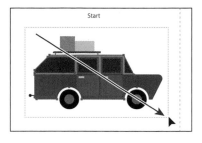

Creating a compound path

Compound paths let you use a vector object to cut a hole in another vector object. Whenever I think of a compound path, I think of a doughnut shape, which can be created from two circles. Holes appear where paths overlap. A compound path is treated like a group, and the individual objects in the compound path can still be edited or released (if you don't want them to be a compound path anymore). Next, you'll create a compound path to create some art for a wheel.

1 Choose 7 Wheel from the Artboard Navigation menu in the lower-left corner of the Document window.

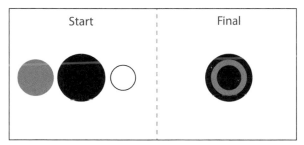

An example of what you will create is labeled "Final" on the right side of the artboard. You will work with the artwork labeled "Start" on the left. You'll create a wheel from the shapes labeled "Start."

2 Choose View > Fit Artboard In Window, if necessary.

3 With the Selection tool (▶) selected, select the gray circle on the left, and drag it so it overlaps the larger dark circle to its right.

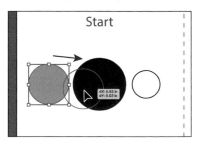

4 Drag the white shape on top of the gray circle, and make sure it's centered.

Smart Guides help you align the circles. You can also select the gray circle and the white circle and align them to each other using the Align options in the Properties panel on the right.

5 Shift-click the gray circle to select it along with the white circle.

▶ **Tip:** You can still edit the original shapes in a compound path like this one. To edit them, select each shape individually with the Direct Selection tool (▶) or double-click the compound path with the Selection tool to enter Isolation mode and select individual shapes.

6 Choose Object > Compound Path > Make, and leave the artwork selected.

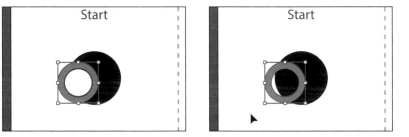

● **Note:** When creating a compound path, the appearance attributes of the object lowest in the stacking order determine the appearance of the resulting compound path.

You can now see that the white circle has seemingly disappeared, and you can see through the shape to the dark circle beneath. The white circle was used to "punch" a hole in the gray shape. With the gray shape still selected, you should see "Compound Path" at the top of the Properties panel to the right.

7 Drag the gray donut shape into the center of the darker circle behind it. The selected shape should be on top. If it isn't, choose Object > Arrange > Bring To Front.

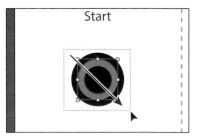

8 Drag across all of the circle shapes labeled "Start" to select them.

9 Choose Object > Group.

10 Choose File > Save.

Combining shapes

Creating more complex shapes from simpler shapes can be easier than trying to create them with drawing tools like the Pen tool. In Illustrator, you can combine vector objects in different ways. The resulting paths or shapes differ depending on the method you use to combine the paths. In this section, you'll explore a few of the more widely used methods for combining shapes.

Working with the Shape Builder tool

The first method you'll learn for combining shapes involves working with the Shape Builder tool (⊕). This tool allows you to visually and intuitively merge, delete, fill, and edit overlapping shapes and paths directly in the artwork. Using the Shape Builder tool, you'll create a more complex trailer shape from a series of simpler shapes like circles and squares.

1   Choose 8 Trailer from the Artboard Navigation menu in the lower-left corner of the Document window.

An example of what you will create is labeled "Final" on the right side of the artboard. You will work with the artwork labeled "Start" on the left.

2   Choose View > Fit Artboard In Window to ensure it fits in the Document window.

3   With the Selection tool (▶) selected, drag a marquee selection across the shapes you see in the figure, labeled "Start," to select the shapes on the artboard. *Make sure not to select the white circle.*

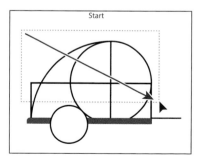

To edit shapes with the Shape Builder tool (⊕), they need to be selected. Using the Shape Builder tool, you will now combine, delete, and paint these simple shapes to create a camper.

▶ **Tip:** You can also press the Shift key and drag a marquee across a series of shapes to combine them. Pressing Shift+Option (macOS) or Shift+Alt (Windows) and dragging a marquee across selected shapes with the Shape Builder tool (⊕) selected allows you to delete a series of shapes within the marquee.

4 Select the Shape Builder tool (⊕) in the toolbar. Move the pointer off the upper-left corner of the shapes, and drag from the red X in the figure to the right into the shapes. Release the mouse button to combine the shapes.

When you select the Shape Builder tool, the overlapping shapes are temporarily divided into separate objects. As you drag from one part to another, a red outline appears, showing you the resulting shape when the shapes are merged together.

● **Note:** Your final combined shapes may have a different stroke and/or fill, and that's okay. You'll change them shortly.

5 Move the pointer off the upper-left corner of the shapes again. Press the Shift key and, from the red X in the figure, drag down and to the right. Release the mouse button and then the key to combine the shapes.

 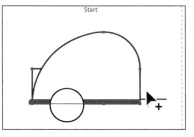

Next, you'll delete a few shapes.

● **Note:** When you position the pointer over the shapes, make sure you see the mesh within those shapes before clicking to delete.

6 With the shapes still selected, hold down the Option (macOS) or Alt (Windows) key. Notice that, with the modifier key held down, the pointer shows a minus sign (▶_). Click the shape on the far left to delete it. Refer to the figure to see which shape to remove.

7 Select the Selection tool (▶) and click in an empty area to deselect the artwork. Drag across the larger shape you combined, the purple bar, and the white circle to select all three shapes.

8 Select the Shape Builder tool (⊕), and move the pointer below the white circle. Hold down the Option (macOS) or Alt (Windows) key and drag through the white circle, stopping before the top of the circle. Release the mouse button and then the key to remove the circle from the larger shape you combined.

9 Choose Select > Deselect.

10 Select the Selection tool (▶), and click the edge of the larger shape to select it. Change the fill color in the Properties panel to the color named red 1 with the tool tip name that shows as "Red 1."

11 Change the stroke weight to **0**.

12 Drag across the red shape, purple shape, and black line to select them all.

13 Choose Object > Group.

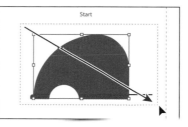

Combining objects using Pathfinders

Pathfinder effects, found in the Properties panel or the Pathfinder panel (Window > Pathfinder), are another way to combine shapes in a variety of ways. By default, when a Pathfinder effect such as Unite is applied, the original objects selected are *permanently* transformed.

1 Choose 9 Door from the Artboard Navigation menu in the lower-left corner of the Document window.

An example of what you will create is labeled "Final" on the right side of the artboard. You will work with the artwork labeled "Start" on the left. You'll combine shapes in different ways to create a single door.

2 Choose View > Fit Artboard In Window.

3 With the Selection tool (▶) selected, drag across the circle and rectangle with the black strokes to select both objects.

You need to create a shape that looks like the door to the right of the shapes you selected, labeled "Final." You will use the Properties panel and those shapes to create the final artwork.

● **Note:** The Unite button in the Properties panel produces a similar result as the Shape Builder tool by combining the shapes into one.

▶ **Tip:** Clicking More Options (•••) in the Pathfinder section of the Properties panel will reveal the Pathfinder panel, which has more options.

4 With the shapes selected, in the Properties panel on the right, click the Unite button (▣) to *permanently* combine the two shapes.

5 Choose Edit > Undo Add to undo the Unite command and bring both shapes back. Leave them selected.

Understanding shape modes

In the previous section, the pathfinders made a permanent change to the shapes. With shapes selected, Option-clicking (macOS) or Alt-clicking (Windows) any of the default set of Pathfinders showing in the Properties panel creates a compound shape rather than a path. The original underlying objects of compound shapes are preserved. As a result, you can still select each original object within a compound shape. Using a shape mode to create a compound shape can be useful if you think that you may want to retrieve the original shapes at a later time.

1 With the shapes still selected, press the Option (macOS) or Alt (Windows) key and click the Unite button (▣) in the Properties panel.

This creates a compound shape that traces the outline of what's left after the shapes are combined. You will still be able to edit both shapes separately.

2 Choose Select > Deselect to see the final shape.

3 With the Selection tool, double-click the black stroke of the newly combined shape to enter isolation mode.

4 Click the edge of the circle at the top or drag across the path to select it.

5 Drag the selected circle straight down from the blue dot in the center. As you drag, press the Shift key. Drag down until you see that a horizontal Smart Guide appears and the center of the circle is aligned with the top edge of the rectangle. When in position, release the mouse button and then the Shift key.

▶ **Tip:** To edit the original shapes in a compound shape like this one, you can also select them individually with the Direct Selection tool (▶).

● **Note:** You can also press the arrow keys to move the shape if you find it difficult to drag.

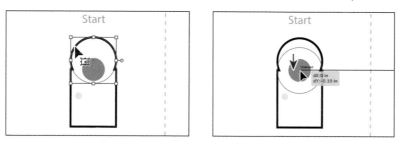

6 Press the Escape key to exit isolation mode.

You will now expand the artwork appearance. Expanding the appearance of a compound shape maintains the shape of the compound object, but you can no longer select or edit the original objects. You will typically expand an object when you want to modify the appearance attributes and other properties of specific elements within it.

7 Click away from the shape to deselect it and then click to select it again.

8 Choose Object > Expand Appearance.

The pathfinder effect is now *permanent* and the shapes are a single shape.

9 Change the Fill color in the Properties panel to the color Pink. Change the stroke weight to **0**.

10 Drag across the shapes that make up the door to select them all.

11 Click the Group button toward the bottom of the Properties panel to group the content together.

Creating the trailer

In this short section, you'll drag all of the pieces for the trailer together and group them.

1   Choose View > Zoom Out several times.

2   Press the spacebar to access the Hand tool, and drag in the Document window to see the wheel, door, window, tank, and trailer artboards.

● **Note:** You may find that with the Smart Guides on, it is difficult to position the content on the trailer. You can always turn off the Smart Guides (View > Smart Guides) and then turn them on when you are finished dragging the artwork.

3   With the Selection tool selected, drag the wheel, door, window, and tank artwork you created labeled "Start" onto the trailer artwork labeled "Start." Position them as you see in the figure.

4   Drag across the trailer artwork, and click the Group button in the Quick Actions section of the Properties panel.

Reshaping a path

In Lesson 3 you learned about creating shapes and paths (lines). You can use the Reshape tool to stretch parts of a path without distorting its overall shape. In this section, you'll change the shape of a line, giving it a bit of curve, so you can turn it into a flame.

1   Choose 10 Flame from the Artboard Navigation menu in the lower-left corner of the Document window.

An example of what you will create is labeled "Final" on the right side of the artboard. You will work with the artwork labeled "Start" on the left. You'll reshape the straight line on the left to start.

2   Make sure the Smart Guides are on by choosing View > Smart Guides.

3 Select the Selection tool (), and click the path labeled "Start."

4 Click Edit Toolbar (⬛⬛⬛) at the bottom of the toolbar. Scroll in the menu that appears, and drag the Reshape tool (✎) onto the Rotate tool (⟳) in the toolbar on the left to add it to the list of tools.

● **Note:** You may want to press the Escape key to hide the extra tools menu.

5 With the Reshape tool (✎) selected, move the pointer over the path. When the pointer changes (▷), drag away from the path to add an anchor point and reshape the path. Move the pointer farther down the path, and drag the path to the left. You can look at the flame shape labeled "Final," to the right, for guidance.

● **Note:** You can use the Reshape tool on a closed path, like a square or circle, but if the entire path is selected, the Reshape tool will add anchor points and move the path.

The Reshape tool can be used to drag an existing anchor point or path segment. If you drag from an existing path segment, an anchor point is created.

6 Move the pointer over the top anchor point of the path and drag it to the right a little. Leave the path selected.

All of the anchor points were selected in the path, which means the Reshape tool will adjust the entire path.

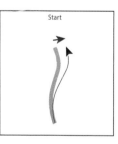

● **Note:** Only selected anchor points are adjusted when dragging with the Reshape tool.

Using the Width tool

Not only can you adjust the weight of a stroke, like you did in Lesson 3, but you can alter regular stroke widths either by using the Width tool (✎) or by applying width profiles to the stroke. This allows you to create a variable width along the stroke of a path. Next, you will use the Width tool to adjust the path you just reshaped to look like a flame.

1   Select the Width tool () in the toolbar. Move the pointer over the middle of the path you just reshaped, and notice that the pointer has a plus symbol next to it (▶₊) when it's positioned over the path. If you were to drag, you would edit the width of the stroke. Drag away from the line, to the right. Notice that, as you drag, you are stretching the stroke to the left and right equally. Release the mouse button when the measurement label shows Side 1 and Side 2 at *approximately* 0.2 in.

You just created a variable stroke on a path, not a shape with a fill. The new point on the original path is called the *width point*. The lines extending from the width point are the *handles*.

2   Click in an empty area of the artboard to deselect the point.

3   Move the pointer anywhere over the path, and the new width point you just created will appear (an arrow is pointing to it in the first part of the following figure). The width point you see on the path next to the pointer is where a new point would be created if you were to click.

4   Move the pointer over the original width point, and when you see lines extending from it and the pointer changes (▶~), drag it up and down to see the effect on the path.

5   Choose Edit > Undo Width Point Change to return the width point to its original position on the path.

In addition to dragging to reposition a width point, you can double-click and enter values in a dialog box. That's what you'll do next.

6   Move the pointer over the top anchor point of the path, and notice that the pointer has a wavy line next to it (▶~) and the word "anchor" appears (see the

first part of the following figure). Double-click the point to create a new width point and to open the Width Point Edit dialog box.

7   In the Width Point Edit dialog box, change Total Width to **0 in**, and click OK.

The Width Point Edit dialog box allows you to adjust the length of the width point handles, together or separately, with more precision. Also, if you select the Adjust Adjoining Width Points option, any changes you make to the selected width point affect neighboring width points as well.

8   Move the pointer over the bottom anchor point of the path, and double-click. In the Width Point Edit dialog box, change Total Width to **0 in**, and click OK.

9   Move the pointer over the original width point. When the width point handles appear, drag one of them away from the center of the path to make it a little wider. Leave the path selected for the next section.

▶ **Tip:** You can select a width point and Option-drag (macOS) or Alt-drag (Windows) one of the width point handles to change one side of the stroke width.

▶ **Tip:** After defining the stroke width, you can save the variable width as a *profile* that you can reuse later from the Stroke panel or the Control panel. To learn more about variable width profiles, search for "Painting with fills and strokes" in Illustrator Help (Help > Illustrator Help).

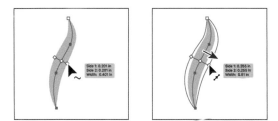

Finishing up the illustration

To finish the illustration, you'll drag the artwork you grouped on each artboard into the main illustration on the left.

1   Select the Selection tool (▶) and, with the path selected, choose Edit > Copy and then Edit > Paste to paste a copy.

2   With the copy selected, choose Object > Path > Outline Stroke so you can more easily scale the shape without having to adjust a stroke weight.

3 Shift-drag the corner of the path to make it smaller. Release the mouse button and then the key. Drag it into position as you see in the figure.

4 With the smaller copy selected, choose Edit > Copy and then Edit > Paste, scale the new copy larger, and position it as you see in the figure.

5 With the shape still selected, click the Flip Along Horizontal Axis button () in the Properties panel. Drag the shape into position as you see in the figure.

6 Drag across the three flame shapes to select them all. Click the Group button in the Properties panel.

7 Choose View > Zoom Out a few times so you can see the campfire artwork to the right of the artboard. Drag the group of flames onto the fire artwork to the right of the artboard.

8 Drag across all of the campfire shapes to select them. Click the Group button in the Properties panel.

9 Choose View > Fit All In Window.

10 Choose View > Smart Guides to turn them off.

Note: After fitting all in window, you may need to zoom out again to see the campfire artwork.

11 Drag each of the artwork groups you created into the main illustration as you see in the figure.

You may want to adjust the size of each group so it fits within the existing artwork better. With the Selection tool, you can hold down the Shift key and drag a corner point to resize artwork proportionally. When you're finished resizing, release the mouse button and then the Shift key.

12 Choose View > Smart Guides to turn them on for the next lesson.

13 Choose File > Save and then choose File > Close.

Review questions

1 Name two ways you can combine several shapes into one.

2 What is the difference between the Scissors tool (✂) and the Knife tool (🖊)?

3 How can you erase with the Eraser tool (◆) in a straight line?

4 What is the main difference between shape modes and Pathfinder effects in the Properties panel or Pathfinder panel?

5 Why would you outline strokes?

Review answers

1 Using the Shape Builder tool (�), you can visually and intuitively merge, delete, fill, and edit overlapping shapes and paths directly in the artwork. You can also use the Pathfinder effects, which can be found in the Properties panel, the Effects menu, or the Pathfinder panel, to create new shapes out of overlapping objects.

2 The Scissors tool (✂) is meant to split a path, graphics frame, or empty text frame at an anchor point or along a segment. The Knife tool (🖊) cuts objects along a path you draw with the tool, dividing objects. When you cut a shape with the Scissors tool, it becomes an open path. When you cut a shape with the Knife tool, the resulting shapes become closed paths.

3 To erase in a straight line with the Eraser tool (◆), you need to press and hold the Shift key before you begin dragging with the Eraser tool.

4 In the Properties panel, when a shape mode (such as Unite) is applied, the original objects selected are permanently transformed, but you can hold down the Option (macOS) or Alt (Windows) key and the original underlying objects are preserved. When a Pathfinder effect (such as Merge) is applied, the original objects selected are permanently transformed.

5 Paths, like a line, can show a stroke color but not a fill color by default. If you create a line in Illustrator and want to apply both a stroke and a fill, you can outline the stroke, which converts the line into a closed shape (or compound path).

5 TRANSFORMING ARTWORK

Lesson overview

In this lesson, you'll learn how to do the following:

- Add, edit, rename, and reorder artboards in an existing document.

- Navigate artboards.

- Work with rulers and guides.

- Position objects with precision.

- Move, scale, rotate, reflect, and shear objects using a variety of methods.

- Use the Free Transform tool to distort an object.

- Work with the Puppet Warp tool.

 This lesson will take about 60 minutes to complete. To get the lesson files used in this chapter, download them from the web page for this book at www.adobepress.com/IllustratorCIB2020. For more information, see "Accessing the lesson files and Web Edition" in the Getting Started section at the beginning of this book.

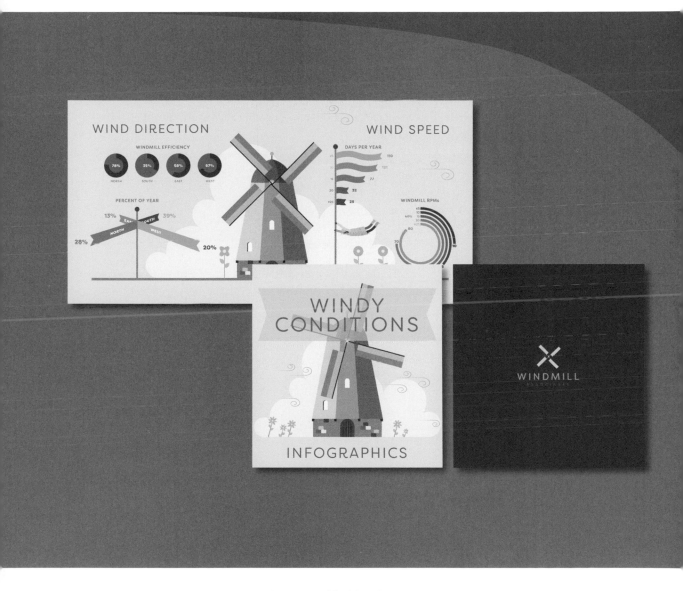

You can modify objects in many ways as you create artwork by quickly and precisely controlling their size, shape, and orientation. In this lesson, you'll explore creating and editing artboards, the various Transform commands, and specialized tools while creating several pieces of artwork.

Starting the lesson

In this lesson, you'll transform artwork and use it to complete an infographic. Before you begin, you'll restore the default preferences for Adobe Illustrator and then open a file containing the finished artwork to see what you'll create.

● **Note:** If you have not already downloaded the project files for this lesson to your computer from your Account page, make sure to do so now. See the "Getting Started" section at the beginning of the book.

1 To ensure that the tools function and the defaults are set exactly as described in this lesson, delete or deactivate (by renaming) the Adobe Illustrator preferences file. See "Restoring default preferences" in the "Getting Started" section at the beginning of the book.

2 Start Adobe Illustrator.

3 Choose File > Open, and open the L5_end.ai file in the Lessons > Lesson05 folder on your hard disk.

This file contains the three artboards that make up the front, back cover, and center for an infographic pamphlet. Any data presented is purely fictitious.

4 Choose View > Fit All In Window, and leave the artwork onscreen as you work.

5 Choose File > Open. In the Open dialog box, navigate to the Lessons > Lesson05 folder, and select the L5_start.ai file on your hard disk. Click Open.

6 Choose File > Save As. In the Save As dialog box, name the file **Infographic.ai**, and navigate to the Lesson05 folder. Leave Adobe Illustrator (ai) chosen from the Format menu (macOS) or Adobe Illustrator (*.AI) chosen from the Save As Type menu (Windows), and click Save.

● **Note:** If you don't see Reset Essentials in the Workspace menu, choose Window > Workspace > Essentials before choosing Window > Workspace > Reset Essentials.

7 In the Illustrator Options dialog box, leave the Illustrator options at their default settings and then click OK.

8 Choose Window > Workspace > Reset Essentials.

Working with artboards

Artboards represent the regions that can contain printable or exportable artwork, similar to pages in Adobe InDesign or artboards in Adobe Photoshop or Adobe XD. You can use artboards for creating a variety of project types, such as multiple-page PDF files, printed pages with different sizes or different elements, independent elements for websites or apps, or video storyboards, for instance.

Adding artboards to a document

You can add and remove artboards at any time while working in a document. Artboards can be created in different sizes. You can resize them in Artboard Editing mode, and position them anywhere in the Document window. All artboards are numbered and can be renamed. Next, you'll add a few artboards to the Infographic.ai document.

1   Choose View > Fit Artboard In Window and then press Command and – (macOS) or Ctrl and – (Windows) twice to zoom out.

2   Press the spacebar to temporarily access the Hand tool (✋). Drag the artboard to the left to see more of the darker canvas to the right of the artboard.

3   Select the Selection tool (▶) in the toolbar.

4   Click the Edit Artboards button in the Properties panel on the right to enter Artboard Editing mode and to select the Artboard tool in the toolbar.

● **Note:** You cannot have content selected in order to see the Document options in the Properties panel. If need be, choose Select > Deselect.

5   Move the pointer to the right of the existing artboard, and drag down and to the right. When the measurement label next to the pointer shows an approximate width and height of 800 pixels, release.

▶ **Tip:** You can also simply select the Artboard tool (🗗) in the toolbar to enter Artboard Editing mode.

The new artboard should be selected. You can tell it's selected because of the dashed bounding box surrounding it. In the Properties panel on the right, you'll see properties for the selected artboard like position (X, Y) and size (width and height), name, and more.

6 In the Properties panel on the right, select the width value, and type **800**. Select the height value, and type **850**. Press Return or Enter to accept the height.

7 Change the name to **Back** in the Artboards section of the Properties panel. Press Return or Enter to make the change.

Next, you'll create another artboard that's the same size.

8 Click the New Artboard button (🔲) in the Properties panel on the right to create a new artboard that is the same size as the selected artboard (named Back) and just to its right.

9 Change the name of the new artboard to **Front** in the Properties panel. Press Return or Enter to make the change.

When editing artboards in Artboard Editing mode, you can see the name of each artboard in the upper-left corner of the artboard.

Editing artboards

After creating artboards, you can edit or delete them by using the Artboard tool (⌐), menu commands, Properties panel, or Artboards panel. Next, you'll reposition and change the size of an artboard.

1   Choose View > Fit All In Window to see all of your artboards.

2   Press Command and – (macOS) or Ctrl and – (Windows) twice to zoom out.

3   While still in Artboard Editing mode and with the Artboard tool (⌐) still selected in the toolbar, drag the artboard named Front to the left of the original artboard. Don't worry about its exact position yet, but make sure it doesn't cover any artwork.

In the Properties panel on the right, in Artboard Editing mode, you'll see lots of options for editing the selected artboard. When an artboard is selected, the Preset menu lets you change the artboard to a set size. The sizes in the Preset menu include typical print, video, tablet, and web sizes. You can also switch the orientation of, rename, or delete the artboard.

▶ **Tip:** To delete an artboard, select it with the Artboard tool (⌐) and either press Delete or Backspace or click the Delete Artboard button (🗑) in the Properties panel. You can delete all but one artboard.

4   Click in the larger, original artboard in the center, and choose View > Fit Artboard In Window to fit that artboard in the Document window.

Commands such as View > Fit Artboard In Window typically apply to the selected or *active* artboard.

5   Drag the bottom-middle point of the artboard up to resize it. When the point snaps to the bottom of the blue shape, release the mouse button.

▶ **Tip:** You can also transform multiple selected artboards at one time.

Tip: To exit Artboard Editing mode, you can also select another tool in the toolbar besides the Artboard tool (⌐) or press the Escape key.

6 Click the Exit button at the top of the Properties panel to exit Artboard Editing mode.

Exiting Artboard Editing mode will deselect all artboards and also select the Selection tool (▶) in the toolbar on the left.

7 Choose View > Fit All In Window to fit all of the artboards in the Document window.

Aligning artboards

To organize the artboards in your document, maybe to keep similar artboards next to each other, you can move and align artboards to suit your working style. Next, you'll select all of the artboards and align them.

1 Select the Artboard tool (⌐) in the toolbar on the left.

This is another way to enter Artboard Editing mode and can be useful when artwork is selected since you can't see the Edit Artboards button in the Properties panel with artwork selected.

Tip: With the Artboard tool (▣) selected, you can press the Shift key and drag across a series of artboards to select them.

2 Click in the leftmost artboard, labeled "03-Front," to select it. Press the Shift key, and click in the other two artboards to the right, one at a time, to select all three.

The Shift key allows you to add artboards to the selection, rather than draw an artboard, when the Artboard tool is selected.

3 Click the Vertical Align Center button (▣) in the Properties panel on the right to align the artboards to each other. Leave the artboards selected.

Renaming artboards

By default, artboards are assigned a number and a name, as you've seen. When you navigate the artboards in a document, it can be helpful to name them. Next, you'll rename artboards so that the names are more useful.

1 While still in Artboard Editing mode, click to select the middle (largest) artboard.

2 Click the Artboard Options button in the Properties panel.

3 In the Artboard Options dialog box, change the name to **Inside**, and click OK.

The Artboard Options dialog box has a lot of extra options for artboards, as well as a few you've already seen, like width and height.

4 Choose Window > Artboards to open the Artboards panel.

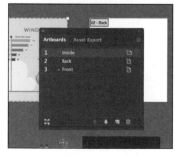

The Artboards panel allows you to see a list of all of the artboards in the document. It also allows you to reorder, rename, add, and delete artboards and to choose many other options related to artboards without being in Artboard Editing mode.

5 Choose File > Save, and keep the Artboards panel showing for the next steps.

Reordering artboards

You can navigate between artboards in your document using the Next Artboard () and Previous Artboard () buttons in the Properties panel with the Selection tool selected, with nothing selected, and while not in Artboard Editing mode, or you can do this from below the Document window. By default, artboards appear according to the order in which they are created, but you can change that order. Next, you'll reorder the artboards in the Artboards panel so that if you use the Next or Previous Artboard buttons, you navigate in an artboard order you determine.

1 With the Artboards panel open, double-click the number 2 to the left of the name "Back" and then double-click the number 1 to the left of the name "Inside" in the Artboards panel.

Double-clicking the number to the left of an artboard name that isn't selected in the Artboards panel makes that artboard the *active* artboard and fits it in the Document window.

▶ Tip: You can also reorder the artboards by selecting an artboard in the Artboards panel and clicking the Move Up () or Move Down () button at the bottom of the panel.

2 Drag the "Front" artboard name up until a line appears above the artboard named "Inside." Release the mouse button.

This makes the Front artboard the first artboard in the list.

3 Choose View > Fit Artboard In Window to fit the Front artboard in the Document window, if necessary.

▶ Tip: The Artboard Options icon () appears to the right of the name of each artboard in the Artboards panel. It not only allows access to the artboard options for each artboard but also indicates the orientation (vertical or horizontal) of the artboard.

4 Click the Exit button in the Properties panel to exit Artboard Editing mode.

5 Click the Next Artboard button () in the Properties panel.

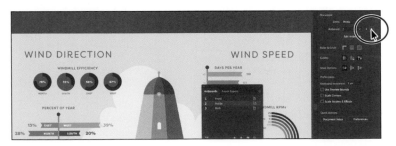

This fits the next artboard in the Artboards panel list, named "Inside," in the Document window. If you hadn't changed the order of the artboards in the Artboards panel, the Next Artboard button in the previous step would have been dimmed (you couldn't select it) because the Front artboard was the last artboard in the Artboards panel list.

6 Click the X at the top of the Artboards panel group to close it.

Now that the artboards are set up, you will concentrate on transforming artwork to create the content for your project.

Rearranging artboards

In Artboard Editing mode (with the Artboard tool selected in the toolbar), you can click the Rearrange All button in the Properties panel to open the Rearrange All Artboards dialog box.

In the Rearrange All Artboards dialog box, you can arrange your artboards in columns and set the spacing between each artboard to a set amount. For instance, if you have a document with six artboards and set the columns to 3, the artboards would be arranged in two rows (or two columns) of three artboards.

You can also click the Rearrange All Artboards button at the bottom of the Artboards panel (Window > Artboards) or choose Object > Artboards > Rearrange All Artboards.

Working with rulers and guides

With the artboards set up, next you'll learn about aligning and measuring content using rulers and guides. *Rulers* help you accurately place and measure objects and distances. They appear along the top and left sides of the Document window and can be shown and hidden. There are two types of rulers in Illustrator: *artboard rulers* and *global rulers*. The point on each ruler (horizontal and vertical) where the 0 (zero) appears is called the *ruler origin*. Artboard rulers set the ruler origin to the upper-left corner of the *active* artboard. Global rulers set the ruler origin to the upper-left corner of the *first* artboard, or the artboard that is at the top of the list in the Artboards panel, no matter which artboard is active. By default, rulers are set to artboard rulers, which means the origin is in the upper-left corner of the active artboard.

● **Note:** You could switch between the artboard and global rulers by choosing View > Rulers > and selecting Change To Global Rulers or Change To Artboard Rulers, depending on which option is currently chosen, but don't do that now.

Creating guides

Guides are nonprinting lines created from the rulers that help you align objects. Next, you'll create a guide so later you can more accurately align content on an artboard.

1 Choose View > Fit All In Window.

▶ **Tip:** You can also choose View > Rulers > Show Rulers.

2 With nothing selected and the Selection tool (▶) selected, click the Show Rulers button (▣) in the Properties panel on the right to show the rulers.

● **Note:** The toolbar you see may look different depending on whether you completed the previous lessons.

3 Click each of the artboards, and as you do, look at the horizontal and vertical rulers (along the top and left sides of the Document window).

Notice that 0 (zero) for each ruler is in the upper-left corner of the active (selected) artboard (the last artboard you clicked in). The point on each ruler (horizontal and vertical) where the 0 appears is called the *ruler origin*. By default, the ruler origin is in the upper-left corner of the *active* (selected) artboard. As you can see, the 0 point on both rulers corresponds to the edges of the active artboard.

4 With the Selection tool, click in the leftmost artboard, named "Front."

Notice the very subtle black outline around the Front artboard, with "1" showing in the Artboard Navigation menu (below the Document window) and in the Document section of the Properties panel to the right of the document, all of which indicate that the Front artboard is the currently active artboard. There can be only one active artboard at a time. Commands such as View > Fit Artboard In Window apply to the active artboard.

5 Choose View > Fit Artboard In Window.

That fits the active artboard in the window, and the ruler origin (0,0) is in the upper-left corner of that same artboard. Next you'll create a guide on the active artboard.

6 Drag from the top ruler down, into the artboard. When the guide reaches 600 pixels on the ruler, release the mouse button. Don't worry about the guide being at exactly 600 pixels. The units for this document are set to pixels.

▶ **Tip:** Dragging from a ruler while pressing the Shift key "snaps" a guide to the measurements on the ruler.

▶ **Tip:** You can double-click the horizontal or vertical ruler to add a new guide.

After creating a guide, it's selected, and when selected, its color matches the color of the layer it's on (darker blue in this case) when you move the pointer away from it.

7 With the guide still selected (in this case, it will be blue, if selected), change the Y value in the Properties panel to **600**, and press Return or Enter.

8 Click away from the guide to deselect it.

9 Click the Units menu in the Properties panel, and choose Inches to change the units for the entire document.

You can now see that the rulers show inches instead of pixels.

10 Choose File > Save.

▶ **Tip:** To change the units for a document (inches, points, etc.), you can also right-click either ruler and choose the new units.

Editing the ruler origin

On the horizontal ruler, measurements to the right of 0 (zero) are positive and to the left are negative. On the vertical ruler, measurements below 0 (zero) are positive and above are negative. You can move the ruler origin to start the horizontal and/or vertical measurements at another location, which is what you'll do next.

1 Choose View > Zoom Out.

2 Drag from the upper-left corner of the Document window, where the rulers intersect (▦), to the lower-left corner of the Front artboard.

   This sets the ruler origin (0,0) to the lower-left corner of the artboard. In other words, the measurements start in the lower-left corner of the artboard.

3 With the Selection tool (▶) selected, move the pointer over the guide, and click to select it.

4 Look in the Properties panel on the right to see the Y value. Right now, because you moved the ruler origin (0,0), the Y shows the vertical distance from the bottom of the artboard. Change the Y value to −**1.75** (inches), and press Return or Enter.

5 Move the pointer in the upper-left corner of the Document window, where the rulers intersect (▦), and *double-click* to reset the ruler origin to the upper-left corner of the artboard.

▶ **Tip:** You can also lock guides by choosing View > Guides > Lock Guides. You can hide guides by clicking the Hide Guides button in the Properties panel or pressing Command+; (macOS) or Ctrl+; (Windows).

6 Choose Select > Deselect to deselect the guide.

7 Click the Lock Guides button (▦) in the Properties panel to lock all guides and prevent them from being selected.

Transforming content

In Lesson 4, "Editing and Combining Shapes and Paths," you learned how to take simple paths and shapes and create more complex artwork by editing and combining that content. That was a form of transforming artwork. In this lesson, you'll learn how to scale, rotate, and transform content in other ways, using a variety of tools and methods.

Working with the bounding box

As you've seen in this lesson and previous lessons, a bounding box appears around selected content. You can transform content using the bounding box, but you can also turn it off. This makes it so you can't resize content by dragging anywhere on the bounding box with the Selection tool.

1   With the Front artboard showing, choose View > Zoom Out until you see the group of artwork that contains the text headline "WINDY CONDITIONS" beneath the artboards.

2   With the Selection tool (▶) selected, click to select the group. Move the pointer over the upper-left corner of the selected group. If you were to drag right now, you would resize the content.

3   Choose View > Hide Bounding Box.

    This command hides the bounding box around the group and makes it so you can't resize the group by dragging anywhere on the bounding box with the Selection tool.

4   Move the pointer over the upper-left point of the group again, and drag it onto the upper-left corner of the Front artboard. You'll find that being zoomed out can make it more difficult to be precise with placement.

5   Choose View > Show Bounding Box.

Positioning artwork using the Properties panel

At times, you may want to position objects more precisely—relative either to other objects or to the artboard. You could use the alignment options, as you saw in Lesson 2, "Techniques for Selecting Artwork," but you can also use Smart Guides and Transform options in the Properties panel to move objects to exact coordinates on the x- and y-axes and to control the positioning of objects relative to the edge of the artboard. Next you'll add content to the background of an artboard and position that content precisely.

1 Choose View > Fit All In Window to see all three artboards.

2 Click in the blank artboard that's farthest to the right to make it the active artboard. Transformation commands, as you are about to learn, apply to the active artboard.

▶ **Tip:** You could have also aligned the content to the artboard using the alignment options. You'll find there are at least a few ways to accomplish most tasks in Illustrator.

3 Click to select the blue shape with the WINDMILL logo on it, beneath the artboards. In the Transform section of the Properties panel, click the upper-left point of the reference point locator (⊞). Change the X value to **0** and the Y value to **0**, and press Return or Enter.

The group of content is moved into the upper-left corner of the active artboard. The points in the reference point locator map to the points of the bounding box for the selected content. For instance, the upper-left reference point refers to the upper-left point of the bounding box.

4 Choose Select > Deselect and then choose File > Save.

Scaling objects

So far in this book, you've scaled most content with the selection tools. In this part of the lesson, you'll use several other methods for scaling artwork.

1 Press Command and – (macOS) or Ctrl and – (Windows) (or choose View > Zoom Out), if necessary, to see the person in the raincoat off the bottom edge of the artboards.

2 With the Selection tool (▶) selected, click the artwork of the person in the yellow raincoat.

3 Press Command and + (macOS) or Ctrl and + (Windows) a few times to zoom in.

4 In the Properties panel, click the center reference point of the reference point locator (⊞), if it's not selected, to resize from the center. Ensure that Constrain Width And Height Proportions is set (🔒), type **30%** in the Width (W) field, and then press Enter or Return to decrease the size of the artwork.

▶ **Tip:** When typing values to transform content, you can type different units, such as percent (%) or pixels (px), and they will be converted to the default unit, which is inches (in) in this case.

5 Choose View > Hide Edges so you hide the inside edges.

Notice that the artwork is smaller, but the arms of the person are still the same width. That's because they are a path with a stroke applied. By default, strokes and effects, like drop shadows, are *not* scaled along with objects. For instance, if you enlarge a circle with a 1-pt stroke, the stroke remains 1 pt. By selecting Scale Strokes & Effects before you scale—and then scaling the object—that 1-pt stroke would scale (change) relative to the amount of scaling applied to the object.

6 Choose View > Show Edges so you show the inside edges again.

7 Choose Edit > Undo Scale.

8 In the Properties panel, click More Options (•••) in the Transform section. Select Scale Strokes & Effects. Type **30%** in the Width (W) field and then press Enter or Return to decrease the size of the artwork.

Now the stroke applied to the paths that make up the arms are scaled as well.

● **Note:** The figure shows selecting the Scale Strokes & Effects option only.

9 Press the spacebar to select the Hand tool, and drag to the right so you can see the flower to the left of the person, if you don't already.

10 With the Selection tool (▶) selected, click to select the flower artwork.

11 Press and hold on the Rotate tool (↻) in the toolbar, and choose the Scale tool (⬚).

● **Note:** You may see another tool instead of the Rotate tool in the toolbar. If that's the case, press and hold on the other tool to select the Scale tool.

The Scale tool is used to scale content by dragging. For a lot of the transform tools, like the Scale tool, you can also double-click the tool to edit selected content in a dialog box. This is similar to choosing Object > Transform > Scale.

▶ **Tip:** You could also choose Object > Transform > Scale to access the Scale dialog box.

12 Double-click the Scale tool (⊞) in the toolbar. In the Scale dialog box, change Uniform to **20%**, and select Scale Strokes & Effects, if it isn't already selected. Toggle Preview on and off to see the change in size. Click OK.

This method of scaling artwork may be useful if there is a lot of overlapping artwork, for instance, or when precision matters or when you need to scale content nonuniformly, and more.

13 Select the Selection tool, and drag the flower up onto the artboard so it's sitting on the gray line that the windmill and other artwork are sitting on. You may need to zoom out.

14 Choose View > Fit Artboard In Window.

15 Press the Option key (macOS) or Alt key (Windows), and drag the flower to the right. Release the mouse button and then the key to make a copy. Do this several times to place copies along the line on the artboard.

Reflecting objects

▶ **Tip:** You could also choose Object > Transform > Reflect to access the Reflect dialog box.

When you *reflect* an object, Illustrator flips the object across an invisible vertical or horizontal axis. In a similar way to scaling and rotating, when you reflect an object, you either designate the reference point or use the object's center point by default. Next, you'll copy artwork and use the Reflect tool (▷◁) to flip artwork 90° across an axis.

1 Choose View > Fit All In Window.

2 Select the Zoom tool (Q) in the toolbar, and drag from left to right across the curly green shape below the artboards to zoom in.

3 Select the Selection tool (▶), and click to select the curly green shape.

4 Choose Edit > Copy and then choose Edit > Paste In Place to create a copy on top of the selected shape.

5 Select the Reflect tool (▷◀), which is nested within the Scale tool (⊡), in the toolbar. Click the straight part of the path to set the invisible axis that the shape will reflect around, rather than the center, which is the default.

6 With the artwork still selected, move the pointer off the right edge, and drag clockwise. As you drag, press the Shift key to constrain the rotation to 45° as the artwork is reflected. When the artwork looks like the figure, release the mouse button and then release the modifier key.

7 Select the Selection tool (▶) in the toolbar, and with the shape still selected, click More Options (•••) in the Transform area of the Properties panel, making sure Scale Strokes & Effects is *not* selected.

8 Drag the lower-right point of the bounding box away from the center to make the shape larger.

9 Drag across the two curly shapes and click the Group button in the Properties panel to keep them together.

10 Choose View > Fit All In Window.

11 Drag the group onto the middle artboard.

12 Press the Option key (macOS) or Alt key (Windows), and drag the group to another area of the artboard. Release the mouse button and then the key to make a copy. You can do this several times to place copies around the artboard, if you like.

● **Note:** You may need to pan in the Document window to see the curly green shape. Press the spacebar, drag in the Document window, then release the spacebar.

▶ **Tip:** If all you want to do is flip content in place, you can also click either the Flip Along Horizontal Axis button (⋈) or the Flip Along Vertical Axis button (⧖) in the Properties panel.

▶ **Tip:** If you want to copy artwork and reflect artwork as you drag, begin dragging artwork with the Reflect tool. As you drag, hold down the Option (macOS) or Alt (Windows) key. When the artwork is where you want it, release the mouse button and then the key. Pressing Shift+Option (macOS) or Shift+Alt (Windows) will copy the reflected artwork and constrain the reflection angle to 45°.

Rotating objects

There are lots of ways to rotate artwork, including methods that range from precise to free-form rotation. In previous lessons, you learned that you can rotate selected content with the Selection tool. By default, objects are rotated around a designated reference point in the center of content. In this part of the lesson, you'll learn about the Rotate tool and the Rotate command.

1   With the Selection tool (▶) selected, click to select the artwork of the person in the yellow raincoat. Press Command and + (macOS) or Ctrl and + (Windows) a few times to zoom in.

2   Move the pointer off one of the corners of the bounding box, and when the rotate arrow (↰) appears, drag counterclockwise to rotate it. As you drag, press the Shift key to constrain the rotation to 45°. When you see 90° in the measurement label next to the pointer, release the mouse button and then the key.

The Selection tool rotates content around the center by default. Next you'll use the Rotate tool, which allows you to rotate around a different point.

3   Press the spacebar to access the Hand tool, and drag to the right to bring the group at the far left into view (see the following figure). When you see it, release the spacebar.

4   With the Selection tool selected, click to select the group.

5   Select the Rotate tool (↻) in the toolbar (it's under the Reflect tool [▷◀]). Move the pointer over the bottom edge of the selected artwork, and click to set the reference point (where it will rotate around). Look at the figure for where to click.

6 Move the pointer off the right side of the selected artwork, and begin dragging clockwise. As you drag, press Option+Shift (macOS) or Alt+Shift (Windows) to copy the artwork as you rotate it, and constrain the rotation to 45°. Release the mouse button and then the keys when you see −90° in the measurement label.

● **Note:** The measurement label you see may look different than the figure, and that's okay.

The Properties panel (or Control panel or Transform panel) is another way to rotate artwork precisely. In the Transform panel, you can always see the angle of rotation and change it later for individual objects.

7 Choose Object > Transform > Transform Again, *twice*, to repeat the previous transformations on the selected shape.

8 Select the Selection tool (▶), and drag across all four groups to select them.

9 Click the Group button in the Properties panel to group them together.

10 With the group still selected, double-click the Rotate tool in the toolbar. In the Rotate dialog box that appears, change the Angle value to **45°**. Select Preview to see the change, and then click OK.

▶ **Tip:** After transforming content using various methods, including rotation, you will notice that the bounding box may be rotated. You can choose Object > Transform > Reset Bounding Box to reset the bounding box around the artwork again.

11 Choose View > Fit All In Window.

12 With the Selection tool (▶) selected, drag the selected group up, on top of the windmill artwork.

Distorting objects with effects

● **Note:** To learn more about effects, see Lesson 13, "Exploring Creative Uses of Effects and Graphic Styles."

You can distort the original shapes of objects in different ways using various tools. Now you'll distort part of the flower and other artwork using effects. These are different types of transformations because they are applied as effects, which means you could ultimately edit the effect later or remove it in the Appearance panel.

1   With the Selection tool (▶) selected, click one of the flowers. Press Command and + (macOS) or Ctrl and + (Windows) several times to zoom in closely.

2   Double-click the flower group to enter isolation mode; then click to select the larger orange circle in the flower.

3   Click the Choose An Effect button (fx.) in the Properties panel.

4   Choose Distort & Transform > Pucker & Bloat in the menu that appears.

5   In the Pucker & Bloat dialog box, select Preview, and drag the slider to the right to change the value to roughly 35%, which distorts the shape. Click OK.

Effects you apply to shapes are live, which means they can be edited or removed at any time. You can access the effect(s) applied to selected artwork in the Appearance panel (Window > Appearance).

6   Press the Escape key to exit isolation mode.

7   Press the spacebar, and drag in the Document window to see the DAYS PER YEAR flags.

8   Click to select the top flag shape. You may need to zoom out.

9   Click the Choose An Effect button (fx.) in the Properties panel, and choose Distort & Transform > Twist.

10 In the Twist dialog box, change Angle to **20**, select Preview to see the effect, and then click OK.

11 Click the banner below the selected banner; then press the Shift key, and click the remaining three banner shapes, one at a time, to select them all.

12 Choose Effect > Apply Twist.

Choosing Apply Twist applies the last applied effect with the same options. If you were to choose Effect > Twist, the last applied effect would be applied, but the dialog box would open so you could set options.

Transforming with the Free Transform tool

The Free Transform tool (⤢) is a multipurpose tool that allows you to distort an object, combining functions such as moving, scaling, shearing, rotating, and distorting (perspective or free). The Free Transform tool is also touch-enabled, which means you can control transformation using touch controls on certain devices.

1 Press the spacebar to select the Hand tool and drag in the Document window until you see the "PERCENT OF YEAR" text to the left of the windmill.

2 With the Selection tool (▶) selected, click to select the shape labeled "EAST WEST."

3 Click Edit Toolbar (⋯) at the bottom of the toolbar. Scroll in the menu that appears, and drag the Free Transform tool (⤢) into the toolbar on the left to add it to the list of tools. Drag the Puppet Warp tool (✦) onto the Free Transform tool to group them together.

4 Press and hold on the Puppet Warp tool (✦), and select the Free Transform tool (⤢) in the toolbar.

● **Note:** To learn more about touch controls, search for "Touch Workspace" in Adobe Help (Help > Illustrator Help).

● **Note:** You may want to press the Escape key to hide the extra tools menu.

● **Note:** To learn more about the options for the Free Transform tool, search for "Free Transform" in Adobe Help (Help > Illustrator Help).

With the Free Transform tool selected, the Free Transform widget appears in the Document window. This widget, which is free-floating and can be repositioned, contains options for changing how the Free Transform tool works. By default, the Free Transform tool allows you to move, shear, rotate, and scale objects. By selecting other options, like Perspective Distort, you can change how the tool works.

Constrain
Free Transform
Selected Action (dark gray background)
Perspective Distort
Free Distort

5   With the Free Transform tool selected, click the Perspective Distort option (⬛) in the Free Transform widget (circled in the following figure).

6   Choose View > Smart Guides to temporarily turn them off.

With the Smart Guides off, you can adjust the artwork without it snapping to everything else in the document.

7   Move the pointer over the lower-right corner of the bounding box, and the pointer changes in appearance (⬚). Drag down a little, until it looks something like the figure.

8   Press the Command key (macOS) or Ctrl key (Windows) to temporarily select the Selection tool, and click to select the shape labeled "NORTH SOUTH." Release the key to return to the Free Transform tool.

9   With the Perspective Distort option (⬛) in the Free Transform widget still selected, drag the lower-left point down a little, until it looks like the figure. Leave the group selected.

10 Choose View > Smart Guides to turn them back on.

11 Choose File > Save.

Shearing objects

Shearing an object slants, or skews, the sides of the object along the axis you specify, keeping opposite sides parallel and making the object asymmetrical. Next, you'll apply shear to the selected sign artwork.

1 With the group labeled "NORTH SOUTH" still selected, select the Shear tool (⬚), nested within the Rotate tool (⟳) in the toolbar.

2 Move the pointer off the right side of the group, press the Shift key to constrain the artwork to its original width, and drag up. Release the mouse button and then the Shift key when you see a shear angle (S) of *approximately* −20.

3 Press the Command key (macOS) or Ctrl key (Windows) to temporarily select the Selection tool. Click to select the shape labeled "EAST WEST." Release the key to return to the Shear tool.

4 Press the Shift key to constrain the artwork to its original width, and drag down from off the right side of the group. Release the mouse button and then the Shift key when you see a shear angle (S) of *approximately* −160.

5 Select the Selection tool (▶), and drag the NORTH SOUTH group and then the EAST WEST group so they are each aligned with the sign pole as you see in the following figure.

6 Click the NORTH SOUTH group to select it. Click the Ungroup button in the Properties panel to the right.

7 Choose Select > Deselect.

8 Click the NORTH text to select that group.

> **Tip:** You can set a reference point, shear, and even copy in one step. With the Shear tool (⬚) selected, Option-click (macOS) or Alt-click (Windows) to set the reference point and to open the Shear dialog box, where you can set options and even copy if necessary.

9 Choose Object > Arrange > Bring To Front.

10 Drag each of the numbers with percent (%) next to the ends of the signs.
I moved the flower to the right as well.

11 Choose View > Fit All In Window and then choose File > Save.

Using Puppet Warp

In Illustrator, you can easily twist and distort artwork into different positions using the Puppet Warp tool. In this section, you'll warp the artwork of the person in the yellow raincoat using the Puppet Warp tool.

1 With the Selection tool (▶) selected, drag the artwork of the person in the yellow rain jacket onto the artboard above the artwork, to the right of the windmill, as you see in the figure.

Make sure the hands of the person are directly on the flagpole. The idea is to have the person appear to be holding on to the DAYS PER YEAR flagpole, as the wind blows him or her to the right.

2 Press Command and + (macOS) or Ctrl and + (Windows) several times to zoom in closely.

3 Press and hold the Free Transform tool (⬚) in the toolbar, and select the Puppet Warp tool (📌).

By default, Illustrator identifies the best areas to transform your artwork and automatically adds pins to the artwork. Pins are used to hold part of the selected artwork to the artboard, and you can

Note: It's difficult to see exactly where to drag the person in the figure. If you look at the following figures, you may get a better idea of what I mean by "Make sure the hands of the person are directly on the flagpole."

Note: The pins Illustrator adds to the artwork by default may not look like what you see in the figure. If that is the case, pay attention to the notes along the way.

add or delete pins to transform your object. You can rotate the artwork around a pin, reposition pins to move artwork, and more.

4   Move the pointer roughly halfway down the top arm—over where the elbow would be. When the pointer shows a plus (+) next to it, click to add a pin.

5   In the Properties panel on the right, you should see Puppet Warp options. Deselect Show Mesh.

    That will make it easier to see the pins and provide a clearer view of any transformations you make.

6   Click the pin on the hand to select it. You can tell that a pin is selected because it has a white dot in the center. Drag the selected pin up to move the hand and not the rest of the artwork.

    The pin you set, farther down the arm near the "elbow," was a point to pivot around. The other default pins on the body help to keep the body in place without moving it. Having at least three pins on your artwork usually achieves a better result.

7   With the hand pin still selected, move the pointer over the dotted circle, and drag counterclockwise a little to rotate around the pin.

● **Note:** If you don't see a pin on the hand, you can click to add one. If there is a pin between the hand pin you just added and the elbow pin you added previously, click to select it, then press Delete or Backspace to remove it.

▶ **Tip:** You can press the Shift key and click multiple pins to select them all or click the Select All Pins button in the Properties panel to select all of the pins.

8 Click the pin that was added to the leg by default. Press Backspace or Delete to remove it.

The pin is not in a good position to bend the legs, and pins currently can't be moved without affecting the artwork.

9 Click between the feet to add a pin.

10 Drag the selected pin at the feet up.

11 Move the pointer over the dotted circle of the selected pin, and drag counterclockwise a little to rotate around the pin.

12 Choose Select > Deselect and then choose View > Fit All In Window.

13 Choose File > Save and then File > Close.

Review questions

1 Name three ways to change the size of an existing active artboard.

2 What is the ruler origin?

3 What is the difference between artboard rulers and global rulers?

4 Briefly describe what the Scale Strokes & Effects option in the Properties panel or Transform panel does.

5 Briefly describe what the Puppet Warp tool does.

Review answers

1 To change the size of an existing artboard, you can do any of the following:

   • Double-click the Artboard tool (⊞), and edit the dimensions of the active artboard in the Artboard Options dialog box.

   • With nothing selected and the Selection tool selected, click the Edit Artboards button to enter Artboard Editing mode. With the Artboard tool selected, position the pointer over an edge or corner of the artboard, and drag to resize.

   • With nothing selected and the Selection tool selected, click the Edit Artboards button to enter Artboard Editing mode. With the Artboard tool selected, click in an artboard in the Document window, and change the dimensions in the Properties panel.

2 The ruler origin is the point where 0 (zero) appears on each ruler. By default, the ruler origin is set to be 0 (zero) in the upper-left corner of the active artboard.

3 Artboard rulers, which are the default rulers, set the ruler origin at the upper-left corner of the active artboard. Global rulers set the ruler origin at the upper-left corner of the first artboard, no matter which artboard is active.

4 The Scale Strokes & Effects option, which can be accessed from the Properties panel or the Transform panel, scales any strokes and effects as the object is scaled. This option can be turned on and off, depending on the current need.

5 In Illustrator, you can easily twist and distort artwork into different positions using the Puppet Warp tool.

6 USING THE BASIC DRAWING TOOLS

Lesson overview

In this lesson, you'll learn how to do the following:

- Draw curves and straight lines with the Curvature tool.

- Edit paths with the Curvature tool.

- Create dashed lines.

- Draw and edit with the Pencil tool.

- Join paths with the Join tool.

- Add arrowheads to paths.

 This lesson will take about 30 minutes to complete. To get the lesson files used in this chapter, download them from the web page for this book at www.adobepress.com/IllustratorCIB2020. For more information, see "Accessing the lesson files and Web Edition" in the Getting Started section at the beginning of this book.

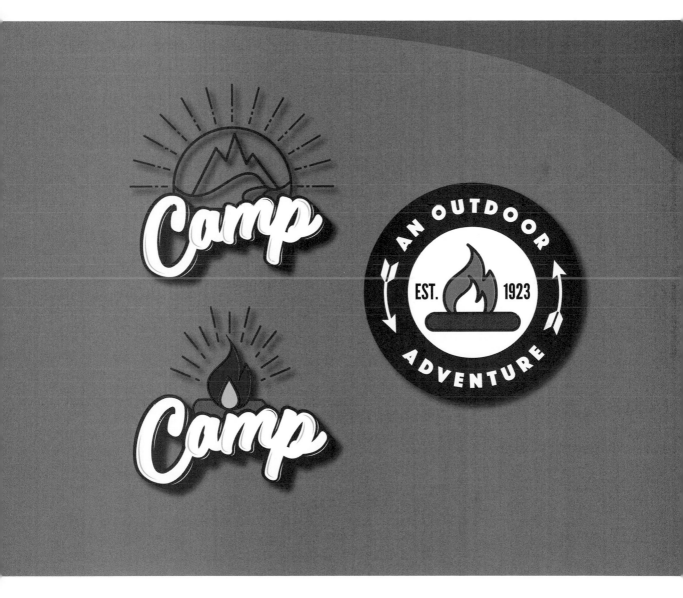

In previous lessons you created and edited shapes. Next you'll learn how to create straight lines, curves, or more complex shapes using the Pencil and Curvature tools. You'll also explore creating dashed lines, arrowheads, and more.

Starting the lesson

In the first part of this lesson, you'll start by creating and editing free-form paths with the Curvature tool and explore other methods for drawing.

● **Note:** If you have not already downloaded the project files for this lesson to your computer from your Account page, make sure to do so now. See the "Getting Started" section at the beginning of the book.

1 To ensure that the tools function and the defaults are set exactly as described in this lesson, delete or deactivate (by renaming) the Adobe Illustrator preferences file. See "Restoring default preferences" in the "Getting Started" section at the beginning of the book.

2 Start Adobe Illustrator.

3 Choose File > Open. Locate the file named L6_end.ai, which is in the Lessons > Lesson06 folder that you copied onto your hard disk, and click Open.

This file contains the finished illustrations that you'll create in this lesson.

4 Choose View > Fit All In Window; leave the file open for reference, or choose File > Close.

5 Choose File > Open, and open the L6_start.ai file in the Lessons > Lesson06 folder on your hard disk.

6 Choose File > Save As. In the Save As dialog box, navigate to the Lesson06 folder, and open it. Rename the file to **Outdoor_Logos.ai**. Choose Adobe Illustrator (ai) from the Format menu (macOS), or choose Adobe Illustrator (*.AI) from the Save As Type menu (Windows). Click Save.

7 In the Illustrator Options dialog box, leave the default settings and then click OK.

8 Choose Window > Workspace > Reset Essentials.

● **Note:** If you don't see Reset Essentials in the menu, choose Window > Workspace > Essentials before choosing Window > Workspace > Reset Essentials.

Creating with the Curvature tool

To start this lesson, you'll be introduced to the Curvature tool since it's one of the easier drawing tools to master. With the Curvature tool (✏️), you can draw and edit paths to create straight lines and smooth, refined curves. The paths the Curvature tool creates are composed of anchor points and can be edited with any of the drawing or selection tools.

Drawing paths with the Curvature tool

In this first part, you'll draw a curved path with the Curvature tool that will become the skyline for a logo.

1   Choose 1 Logo 1 from the Artboard Navigation menu below the Document window to switch artboards. To fit the artboard in the window, choose View > Fit Artboard In Window.

2   Select the Selection tool (▶) in the toolbar and click the edge of the circle. To lock it, choose Object > Lock > Selection. That way, you can draw without accidentally editing the circle.

3   Select the Curvature tool (✏️) in the toolbar on the left.

4   To set the stroke and fill of the path you will create before you draw, click the Fill box in the Properties panel, and select the None (▨) color to remove it. Click the Stroke color, and make sure the dark gray swatch with the tool tip "C=0 M=0 Y=0 K=90" is selected. Make sure the stroke weight is 4 pt.

With the Curvature tool, you start a path by clicking and releasing to create an anchor point. You then create anchor points to change the path's direction, its amount of curve, or both. For the path you are about to create, you could start drawing from either end.

5   On the left edge of the circle, click and release to start the path.

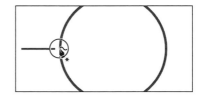

6   Move the pointer to the right, click and release to create a new point, and then move the pointer away.

Notice the rubber band preview of the curve before and after the new point. The Curvature tool works by creating anchor points where you click. The drawing curve will "flex" around the points dynamically.

7 Move the pointer to the right, as you see in the figure. Click and release to create a point. Move the pointer around to see how the path reacts.

8 Click and release to the right to create another anchor point.

9 Finally, to complete the horizon, move the pointer over the right edge of the circle, and click and release to create the last anchor point.

10 To stop drawing and lock the path so you can't accidentally edit it in the next section, choose Object > Lock > Selection.

Practice drawing a river path

In order to get more of a feel for the Curvature tool, next you'll draw a river that begins at the horizon path you just created. You'll draw one side of the river, then the other. The figure at right shows an example of how the river might look. Yours may look different and that's okay.

1 Move the pointer over the horizon path as you see in the figure. Click and release to start a new path.

For the next few steps, to draw one side of the river, you can use the figure as a guide, but try to experiment a little.

2 Move the pointer and click. Do this three more times to add points to create one side of the river. Make sure the last point you create is on the circle.

3 Press the Escape key to stop drawing the river path.

When learning the Curvature tool, it helps to click, release, and then move the pointer around to get a feel for how it affects the path. Next you'll draw the other side of the river using a similar technique.

4 Choose Select > Deselect.

5 Move the pointer over the horizon path just to the right of the start of the path you just drew. Click and release to start a new path.

It's important not to click too closely to the first river path you drew because you may edit that path instead of starting a new one. If you click and begin editing the other path, press the Escape key to stop editing the first river path.

6 Move the pointer and click to set another point. Do this two more times to add points to create the other side of the river. Make sure the last point you create is on the circle.

7 To stop drawing the river path, press the Escape key.

Editing a path with the Curvature tool

You can also edit paths with the Curvature tool by moving or deleting anchor points, or adding new ones. You can use the Curvature tool to edit a path you're drawing or any other path you've created regardless of the drawing tool used to create it. Next you'll edit the paths you've created so far.

1 With the Curvature tool selected, click the first river path you drew on the left to select it and show the anchor points.

    In order to edit a path with the Curvature tool, it needs to be selected.

▶ **Tip:** To close a path with the Curvature tool, hover the pointer over the first point you created in the path. When a circle appears next to the pointer (✎₀), click to close the path.

2 Move the pointer over the anchor point circled in the first part of the following figure. When the point changes appearance (▶₀), click to select it. Drag that point to reshape the curve a little.

3 Try clicking and dragging to move other points in the path.

    Next, you'll unlock the horizon path, select that path, and edit it.

4 Choose Object > Unlock All to be able to edit the horizon path you drew.

5 With the Curvature tool selected, click the horizon path to select just that path and see the anchor points on it.

6 Move the pointer over the path just to the right of the first anchor (on the left). When a plus sign (+) appears next to the pointer (✎₊), click to add a new point.

7 Drag the new point down a bit to reshape the path.

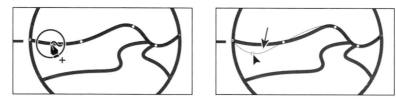

    You'll remove the point just to the right of the new point you just added so the path can have more curve.

8 Click the point to the right, and to remove it press Delete or Backspace.

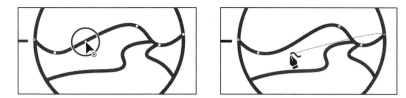

9   Press the Escape key to stop drawing.

10 To lock the path so you don't accidentally edit it in the next section, choose
    Object > Lock > Selection.

Creating corners with the Curvature tool

By default, the Curvature tool creates smooth anchor points—that is, anchor points
that cause the path to curve. Paths can have two kinds of anchor points: *corner
points* and *smooth points*. At a corner point, a path abruptly changes direction.
At a smooth point, path segments are connected as a continuous curve. With the
Curvature tool, you can also create corner points to create straight paths. Next
you'll draw a mountain for the logo.

1   With the Curvature tool ( ) selected,
    move the pointer over the left side of the
    horizon path. Click to set the first point.

2   Move the pointer up and to the right to
    create a mountain peak, and click.

3   Move the pointer down and to the right and click to create a new point.

    To make the mountain peak have a point to it and not be curved, you'll convert
    the anchor point you just created to a corner point.

4   Move the pointer over the top anchor
    point on the mountain path, and when
    the pointer changes ( ), double-click to
    convert it to a corner point.

    You can tell which points are smooth
    and which are corners by their appearance. Each point you create with the
    Curvature tool can have three appearances, indicating their current state: a
    selected point (●), a corner point that is not selected (◉), and smooth point
    that is not selected (○).

5 To continue drawing, move the pointer over and up and click to create another point and start another mountain peak.

The point you just created and the point before it also need to be converted to corner points. As a matter of fact, all of the anchor points you create for the mountain path need to be corners. You'll convert the two anchor points to corner points next.

6 Double-click the last *two* anchor points you made to make them corners.

To finish the mountain path, you'll create a few more anchor points, but you will make corner points instead of smooth points by pressing a key as you create them.

7 Press Option (macOS) or Alt (Windows) and the pointer will change (✎). Click to make another anchor.

8 While still pressing Option (macOS) or Alt (Windows), click a few more times to finish the mountain path. Make sure the last point you create is on the horizon path.

If you want to adjust any of the anchor points, feel free to move the pointer over one, click it, and either drag it to reshape the path, double-click the anchor point to convert it between a corner and smooth point, or press Delete or Backspace to remove it from the path.

9 Press the Escape key to stop drawing, and then choose Select > Deselect.

Creating dashed lines

To add some design flair to your artwork, you can add dashes to the stroke of a closed path (like a square) or an open path (like a line). Dashes are created in the Stroke panel, where you specify a sequence of dash lengths and the gaps between them. Next you'll add a dash to lines to add more artwork to the same logo.

1   Select the Selection tool (▶) and click the small path to the left of the circle.

2   In the Properties panel, click the word "Stroke" to show the Stroke panel. Change the following options in the Stroke panel:

▶ **Tip:** The Preserves Exact Dash And Gap Lengths button (▦) allows you to retain the appearance of the dashes without aligning to the corners or the dash ends.

- Weight: **3 pt**
- Dashed Line: Selected
- Preserves Exact Dash and Gap Lengths (▦): Selected
- First Dash value: **35 pt** (This creates a 35-pt dash, 35-pt gap pattern.)
- First Gap value: **4 pt** (This creates a 35-pt dash, 4-pt gap pattern.)
- Second Dash value: **5 pt** (This creates a 35-pt dash, 4-pt gap, 5-pt dash, 5 pt gap pattern.)
- Second Gap value: **4 pt** (This creates a 35-pt dash, 4-pt gap, 5-pt dash, 4-pt gap pattern.) After entering the last value, press Return or Enter to accept the value and close the Stroke panel.

Now you'll make copies of the dashed line around the circle.

3   With the dashed line selected, select the Rotate tool (↻) in the toolbar. Move the pointer into the center of the circle and when you see the word "center" Option-click (macOS) or Alt-click (Windows) to set the reference point (the point at which the artwork rotates around) and open the Rotate dialog box.

● **Note:** If the word "center" doesn't appear, make sure Smart Guides are turned on (View > Smart Guides).

4 Select Preview to see the results of the changes you make in the dialog. Change the Angle to **−15** and click Copy.

5 To copy the dashed line again using the same rotation, choose Object > Transform > Transform Again.

6 To make 10 more copies, press Command+D (macOS) or Ctrl+D (Windows) 10 times.

That keyboard command invokes the Transform Again command you chose in the previous step.

To finish the artwork, you'll cut off part of the circle and drag the text at the bottom of the artboard onto the logo.

7 Select the Rectangle tool (▢) in the toolbar and draw a rectangle that covers the lower part of the circle (see the following figure).

Notice that the dashed stroke is applied to the rectangle.

8 Select the Selection tool (▶) and drag across the rectangle and circle (only!).

9 Select the Shape Builder tool (⊕) in the toolbar. Press the Option key (macOS) or Alt key (Windows) and drag across the rectangle and bottom part of the circle to remove them. Release the mouse button and then the key.

10 Select the Selection tool and drag the text at the bottom of the artboard up, onto the logo.

11 Click the Arrange button in the Properties panel and choose Bring To Front.

12 Choose Select > Deselect, and choose File > Save.

Drawing with the Pencil tool

Another drawing tool in Illustrator is the Pencil tool. The Pencil tool (✏) lets you draw free-form open and closed paths that contain curves and straight lines, and is similar to drawing on paper. As you draw with the Pencil tool, anchor points are created on the path, where necessary, and according to the Pencil tool options you set. The path can easily be adjusted when the path is complete.

Drawing paths with the Pencil tool

Next you'll draw and edit a simple path to make fire using the Pencil tool.

1 Choose 2 Pencil from the Artboard navigation menu in the lower-left corner of the Document window.

2 Select the Pencil tool (✏) from the Paintbrush tool (🖊) group in the toolbar.

3 Double-click the Pencil tool. In the Pencil Tool Options dialog box, set the following options:

- Drag the Fidelity slider all the way to the right. This will smooth the path and reduce the number of points on a path drawn with the Pencil tool.

- Keep Selected: Selected (the default setting)

- Close Paths When Ends Are Within: Selected (the default setting)

▶ **Tip:** When it comes to the Fidelity value, dragging the slider closer to Accurate usually creates more anchor points and more accurately reflects the path you've drawn. Dragging the slider toward Smooth makes fewer anchor points and a smoother, less complex path.

4 Click OK.

5 In the Properties panel, make sure that the fill color is None (⬜) and the stroke color is the dark gray swatch with the tool tip "C=0 M=0 Y=0 K=90." Also make sure the stroke weight is 3 pt in the Properties panel.

If you move the pointer into the Document window, the asterisk (*) that appears next to the Pencil tool pointer indicates that you're about to create a new path.

● **Note:** If the pointer looks like ✕ instead of the Pencil icon (✏), the Caps Lock key is active. Caps Lock turns the Pencil tool icon into an X for increased precision.

6 Starting at the red dot of the template labeled "A," press and drag clockwise around the dashed template path. When the pointer gets close to where you started the path (the red dot), a small circle displays next to it (✏○). This means that if you release the mouse button, the path will be closed. When you see the circle, release the mouse button to close the path.

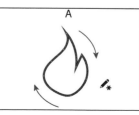

Notice that as you are drawing, the path may not look perfectly smooth. After releasing the mouse button, the path is smoothed based on the Fidelity value that you set in the Pencil Tool Options dialog box. Next you'll redraw a part of the path with the Pencil tool.

7   Move the pointer on or near the path to redraw it. When the asterisk next to the pointer disappears, press and drag to reshape the path, making the bottom different. Make sure you wind up back on the original path.

8   With the fire shape selected, change the fill color to a red in the Properties panel.

Drawing straight lines with the Pencil tool

In addition to drawing more free-form paths, you can create straight lines that can be constrained to 45° angles with the Pencil tool. Next you'll draw a log for the fire using the Pencil tool. Note that the shape you will draw could be created by drawing a rectangle and rounding the corners, but we want it to look more hand-drawn, which is why you're drawing it with the Pencil tool.

1   Move the pointer over the red dot on the left side of the path labeled "B." Press and drag up and around the top of the shape, and release the mouse button when you get to the blue dot.

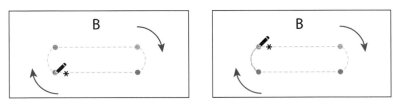

The next part of the path you draw will be straight. As you draw with the Pencil tool, you can easily continue drawing paths.

2   Move the pointer over the end of the path you just drew. When a line appears next to the Pencil tool pointer (✐), indicating that you can continue drawing the path, press Option (macOS) or Alt (Windows) and drag to the right to the orange dot. When you reach the orange dot, release the key but *not the mouse button.*

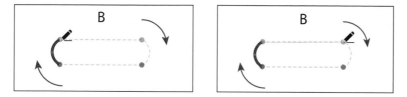

Pressing the Option (macOS) or Alt (Windows) key when you're drawing with the Pencil tool lets you create a straight path in any direction.

3 With the mouse button still held down, continue drawing around the bottom of the template path. When you reach the purple dot, keep the mouse button held down, and press the Option (macOS) or Alt (Windows) key. Continue drawing to the left until you reach the start of the path at the red dot. When a small circle displays next to the Pencil tool pointer (✐), release the mouse button and then the modifier key to close the path.

▶ **Tip:** You can also press the Shift key when drawing with the Pencil tool and drag to create a straight line that is constrained to 45 degrees.

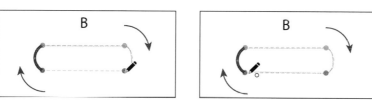

4 With the path selected, change the fill color to a brown swatch in the Properties panel.

5 Select the Selection tool (▶), and drag the fire shape down onto the log shape.

6 To bring the fire shape on top of the log shape, click the Arrange button in the Properties panel and choose Bring To Front.

7 Drag across both shapes to select them.

8 Copy the two shapes by choosing Edit > Copy.

9 To move to the next artboard, click the Next artboard button (▶) below the Document window in the Status bar.

10 To paste the shapes, choose Edit > Paste.

11 Drag the shapes onto the artwork as you see in the figure.

Joining with the Join tool

In earlier lessons you used the Join command (Object > Path > Join) to join and close paths. You can also join paths using the Join tool. With the Join tool (✕), you can use scrubbing gestures to join paths that cross, overlap, or have open ends.

1 Select the Direct Selection tool (▶) and click the yellow circle on the artboard.

2 Choose View > Zoom In a few times to zoom in.

3 Select the Scissors tool (✂) grouped with the Eraser tool (◆) in the toolbar. Move the pointer over the top anchor point. When you see the word "anchor," click to cut the path there.

A message stating that the shape has been expanded appears at the top of the Document window. This circle, by default, was a live shape. After cutting the path, it's no longer a live shape.

4 Select the Direct Selection tool and drag the top anchor point up, and slightly to the right.

5 Drag the anchor point on the other end of the path up just to the left. A purple alignment guide will appear when the anchor point is aligned with the first anchor point.

Right now the two endpoints are curved, when they need to be straight.

6 With the Direct Selection tool selected, drag across the two end points.

7 In the Properties panel on the right, click the Convert Selected Anchor Points To Corner button (⊾) to straighten the ends of the path.

You'll learn more about converting anchor points in the next lesson.

8 Click Edit Toolbar () at the bottom of the toolbar. Scroll in the menu that appears, and drag the Join tool (✄) onto the Pencil tool (✏) in the toolbar on the left to add it to the list of tools.

Next you'll join the open ends of the path with the Join tool. Know that you don't need to select paths to join them with the Join tool.

● **Note:** You may want to press the Escape key to hide the extra tools menu.

9 With the Join tool now selected, drag across the top two ends of the path (see the following figure). Make sure you drag closer to the tip.

When dragging (also called scrubbing) across paths, they will be either "extended and joined" or "trimmed and joined." In this example, the ends of the path were extended and joined. Also, the resulting joined artwork is deselected to allow you to continue working on other paths.

▶ **Tip:** Pressing the Caps Lock key will turn the Join tool pointer into a more precise cursor (-¦-). This can make it easier to see where the join will happen.

● **Note:** If you were to instead join the ends of the open path by pressing Command+J (macOS) or Ctrl+J (Windows), a straight line would connect the ends.

10 Choose View > Fit Artboard In Window.

11 Select the Selection tool (▶), and drag the yellow shape onto the fire shape, aligning it with the bottom of the shape.

12 To bring the yellow shape on top of the other artwork, click the Arrange button in the Properties panel and choose Bring To Front.

13 Drag the "Camp" text at the bottom of the artboard onto the rest of the logo.

14 To bring the text on top of the other artwork, click the Arrange button in the Properties panel and choose Bring To Front.

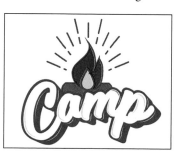

15 Choose Select > Deselect, and choose File > Save.

Adding arrowheads to paths

You can add arrowheads to both ends of a path using the Stroke panel. There are many different arrowhead styles to choose from in Illustrator, as well as arrowhead editing options. Next, you'll apply arrowheads to a few paths to finish a logo.

1 Choose 4 Logo 3 from the Artboard Navigation menu below the Document window to switch artboards.

2 Select the Selection tool (▶) and click to select the curved pink path on the left. Press the Shift key, and click the curved pink path to the right.

● **Note:** When you draw a path, the beginning is where you start drawing and the "end" is where you finish. If you need to swap the arrowheads, you can click the Swap Start And End Arrowheads button (⯳) in the Stroke panel.

3 With the paths selected, click the word "Stroke" in the Properties panel to open the Stroke panel. In the Stroke panel, change only the following options:

   • Change the Stroke Weight to **3 pt**

   • Choose Arrow 5 from the Arrowheads menu on the right. This adds an arrowhead to the end of both lines.

   • Scale (*directly beneath where you chose Arrow 5*): **70%**

   • Choose Arrow 17 from the Arrowheads menu on the left. This adds an arrowhead to the beginning of both lines.

   • Scale (*directly beneath where you chose Arrow 17*): **70%**

Experiment with some of the arrowhead settings. Maybe changing the Scale values or trying different arrowheads.

4 With the paths selected, change the stroke color to white in the Properties panel.

5 Choose Select > Deselect.

6 Choose File > Save and then choose File > Close.

Review questions

1 By default, what type of path is created by the Curvature tool, curved or straight?

2 How do you create a corner point when working with the Curvature tool?

3 How can you change the way the Pencil tool (✐) works?

4 Explain how you can redraw parts of a path with the Pencil tool.

5 How do you draw a straight path with the Pencil tool?

6 How is the Join tool different from the Join command (Object > Path > Join)?

Review answers

1 When drawing paths with the Curvature tool, curved paths are created by default.

2 When drawing with the Curvature tool, either double-click an existing point on a path to convert it to a corner or, while drawing, press Option (macOS) or Alt (Windows) and click to create a new corner point.

3 To change the way the Pencil tool (✐) works, double-click the Pencil tool in the toolbar or click the Tool Options button in the Properties panel to open the Pencil Tool Options dialog box. There you can change the fidelity and other options.

4 With a path selected, you can redraw parts of it by moving the Pencil tool pointer over the path and redrawing part of it, ending up back on the path.

5 Paths you create with the Pencil tool are free-form by default. In order to draw a straight path with the Pencil tool, press the Option (macOS) or Alt (Windows) key and drag to create a straight line.

6 Unlike the Join command, the Join tool can trim or extend overlapping paths or the ends of an open path as it joins, and it doesn't simply create a straight line between the anchor points you are joining. The angle created by the two paths to be joined are taken into account.

7 DRAWING WITH THE PEN TOOL

Lesson overview

In this lesson, you'll learn how to do the following:

- Draw straight and curved lines with the Pen tool.

- Edit curved and straight lines.

- Add and delete anchor points.

- Convert between smooth points and corner points.

 This lesson will take about 60 minutes to complete. To get the lesson files used in this chapter, download them from the web page for this book at www.adobepress.com/IllustratorCIB2020. For more information, see "Accessing the lesson files and Web Edition" in the Getting Started section at the beginning of this book.

In the previous lesson you started working with the basic drawing tools in Illustrator. In this lesson, you'll learn how to create and refine artwork using the Pen tool.

Starting the lesson

In this lesson, you'll focus on creating paths with the Pen tool. You'll start by working with a practice file to learn the fundamentals of the tool, then you'll put the Pen tool into practice by drawing a swan.

● **Note:** If you have not already downloaded the project files for this lesson to your computer from your Account page, make sure to do so now. See the "Getting Started" section at the beginning of the book.

1 To ensure that the tools function and the defaults are set exactly as described in this lesson, delete or deactivate (by renaming) the Adobe Illustrator preferences file. See "Restoring default preferences" in the "Getting Started" section at the beginning of the book.

2 Start Adobe Illustrator.

3 Choose File > Open, and open the L7_practice.ai file in the Lessons > Lesson07 folder on your hard disk.

4 Choose File > Save As. In the Save As dialog box, navigate to the Lesson07 folder, and open it. Rename the file to **Pen_practice.ai**. Choose Adobe Illustrator (ai) from the Format menu (macOS), or choose Adobe Illustrator (*.AI) from the Save As Type menu (Windows). Click Save.

● **Note:** If you don't see Reset Essentials in the menu, choose Window > Workspace > Essentials before choosing Window > Workspace > Reset Essentials.

5 In the Illustrator Options dialog box, leave the default settings and then click OK.

6 Choose View > Fit All In Window.

7 Choose Window > Workspace > Reset Essentials.

Understanding curved paths

In the previous chapter, you created curved and straight paths with the Curvature and Pencil tools. With the Pen tool (✒) you can also create curved and straight paths, but you have even more control over the shape of the paths you draw. The Pen tool is one of the main drawing tools in Illustrator and can be used for creating new vector artwork as well as for editing artwork you create both with, as well as with the other drawing tools.

The Pen tool can be found in other Adobe apps, such as Photoshop and InDesign. Understanding how to create and edit paths with it will give you more creative freedom not only in Illustrator but in those other apps as well.

Learning and mastering the Pen tool takes plenty of practice. So go through the steps in this lesson and practice, practice, practice.

With the Pen tool you can click to create corner anchor points. If you create two corner points, you've made a straight path. In order to create a curve with the Pen tool, you press and drag to create an anchor point with direction lines. Anchor point *direction lines* control the length and slope of the shape of the path before and after that anchor point.

When you create curves with the Curvature tool or Pencil tool, you are also creating direction lines, but when drawing with those tools you don't see the direction lines and you can't (and don't need to) interact with them.

Curved Path

A. Line segment
B. Anchor point
C. Direction line
D. Direction point

A direction line and direction point together are called the *direction handle*.

An introduction to drawing with the Pen tool

In this section, you'll open a practice file and get the work area set up so you can begin to explore drawing with the Pen tool.

1 Choose 1 from the Artboard Navigation menu in the lower-left corner of the Document window, if it's not already chosen. If the artboard does not fit in the document window, choose View > Fit Artboard In Window.

2 Select the Zoom tool (🔍) in the toolbar, and click once in the bottom half of the artboard to zoom in.

3 Choose View > Smart Guides to turn *off* Smart Guides.

   Smart Guides can be useful when you draw, helping you align anchor points, among other things, but you won't need them now.

Getting started with the Pen tool

Now you'll start drawing straight lines with the Pen tool to create the main path for a royal crown, like the one you see at the top of the first artboard.

1 Select the Pen tool (✒) in the toolbar.

2 In the Properties panel to the right of the document, click the Fill box, make sure the Swatches option (▣) is selected, and choose None (▱). Then, click the Stroke box, and make sure that the Black swatch is selected. Make sure the stroke weight is also **1 pt** in the Properties panel.

   When you begin drawing with the Pen tool, it's usually best to have no fill on the path you draw because the fill can cover parts of the path you are trying to create. You can add a fill later, if necessary.

Note: If you see ✕ instead of the Pen icon (✎₊), the Caps Lock key is active. Caps Lock turns the Pen tool icon into ✕ for increased precision. After you begin drawing with the Caps Lock key active, the Pen tool icon looks like this: -¦-.

3   Move the pointer into the area labeled "Work Area" on the artboard, and notice the asterisk next to the Pen icon (✎₊), indicating that you'll create a new path if you begin drawing.

4   Click and release on the orange start point "1" to set the first anchor point.

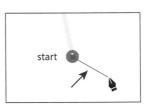

5   Move the pointer away from the point you just created, and you'll see a line connecting the first point and the pointer, no matter where you move the pointer.

That line is called the Pen tool preview (or the rubber band). Later, as you create curved paths, it will make drawing them easier because it is a preview of what the path will look like. Also notice that the asterisk has disappeared from next to the pointer, indicating that you are now drawing a path.

6   Move the pointer over the gray dot labeled "2." Click and release to create an anchor point.

You just created a straight path. A path is composed of two anchor points and a line segment connecting those anchor points.

7   Continue clicking points 3 through 7, releasing the mouse button after every click to create anchor points.

Unlike the Curvature tool, the Pen tool creates corner points and straight lines when you click to create anchor points.

Selecting paths

The type of anchor point you created in the previous section is called a corner point. *Corner points* are not smooth like a curve; instead, they create an angle at the anchor point. Now that you can create corner points, you'll learn how to create smooth points with the Pen tool, which generate curves for a path.

In Lesson 2, "Techniques for Selecting Artwork," you were introduced to selecting content with the Selection and Direct Selection tools. Next, you'll explore a few more options for selecting artwork with those same selection tools.

1 Select the Selection tool (▶) in the toolbar, and move the pointer over a straight line in the path you just created. When the pointer shows a solid black box (▶.) next to it, click.

This selects the path and all of its anchor points.

▶ **Tip:** You can also drag across a path to select it with the Selection tool.

2 Move the pointer over one of the straight lines in the path. When the pointer changes appearance (▶⊞), drag the path to a new location anywhere on the artboard and release the mouse button.

The anchor points all travel together, maintaining the shape of the path.

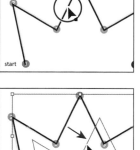

3 Choose Edit > Undo Move to move the path to its original position.

4 Click an empty area of the artboard to deselect the path.

5 Select the Direct Selection tool (▷) in the toolbar. Move the pointer anywhere over the path between anchor points. When the pointer changes (▷), click the path to reveal all of the anchor points.

You just selected a line segment (path). If you were to press Delete or Backspace (*don't*), only that part of the path between two anchor points would be removed.

Note: When you move the pointer over a line segment that isn't already selected, a black, solid square appears next to the Direct Selection tool pointer, indicating that you will select a line segment.

6 Move the pointer over the anchor point labeled 4; the anchor point will become a little larger than the others, and the pointer will show a small box with a dot in the center (▷.) next to it, as you see in the figure. Both of these indicate that if you click, you will select the anchor point. Click to select the anchor point, and the selected anchor point is filled (appears solid), whereas the other anchor points are still hollow (deselected).

▶ **Tip:** If the Pen tool (✒) were still selected, you could Command-click (macOS) or Ctrl-click (Windows) in an empty area of the artboard to deselect the path. This temporarily selects the Direct Selection tool. When you release the Ctrl or Command key, the Pen tool is selected again.

7 Drag the selected anchor point up to reposition it.

The anchor point moves, but the others remain stationary. This is one method for editing a path, as you saw in Lesson 2.

8 Click in an empty area of the artboard to deselect.

● **Note:** If the entire path disappears, choose Edit > Undo Cut, and try selecting the line segment again.

9 Move the Direct Selection pointer over the path between points 5 and 6. When the pointer changes (⬥), click to select. Choose Edit > Cut.

This removes the selected segment between anchor points 5 and 6. Next you'll learn how to connect the paths again.

10 Select the Pen tool (✐), and move the pointer onto the blue anchor point labeled 5. Notice that the Pen tool shows a forward slash (✐), indicating that if you click, you will continue drawing from that anchor point. Click the point.

11 Move the pointer over the other anchor point (point 6) that was connected to the cut line segment. The pointer now shows a merge symbol next to it (✐₀), indicating that, if you click, you are connecting to another path. Click the point to reconnect the paths.

12 Choose Select > Deselect. Leave the file open for the next section. Choose File > Save.

Drawing straight lines with the Pen tool

In previous lessons, you learned that using the Shift key as well as Smart Guides in combination with shape tools constrains the shape of objects. The Shift key and Smart Guides can also constrain paths drawn with the Pen tool, allowing you to create straight paths with 45-degree angles. Next, you'll learn how to draw straight lines and constrain angles as you draw.

1 Choose 2 from the Artboard Navigation menu in the lower-left corner of the Document window.

2 Select the Zoom tool (🔍) in the toolbar, and click in the bottom half of the artboard to zoom in.

3 Click the View menu and choose Smart Guides to turn them *on*.

4 With the Pen tool (✐) selected, in the area labeled "Work Area," click the point labeled 1, where you see "start," to set the first anchor point.

The Smart Guides most likely are attempting to "snap" the anchor point you create to other content on the artboard, possibly making it difficult to add an anchor point exactly where you want it. This is expected behavior and is why you might sometimes turn off the Smart Guides when drawing.

5 Move the pointer above the original anchor point to the point labeled 2. When you see approximately 1.5 inches in the gray measurement label that appears next to the pointer, click to set another anchor point.

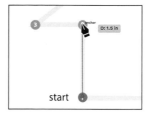

As you've learned in previous lessons, the measurement label and alignment guides are part of the Smart Guides. The measurement labels showing distance can be useful when you're drawing with the Pen tool.

6 Choose View > Smart Guides to turn *off* the Smart Guides.

With Smart Guides turned off, you'll need to press the Shift key to align points, which is what you'll do next.

7 Press the Shift key, and click the point labeled 3. Release the Shift key.

With Smart Guides turned off, there is no measurement label, and the point is only aligning with the previous point because you are pressing the Shift key.

8 Click to set point 4 and then click to set point 5.

As you've already seen, without pressing the Shift key, you can set an anchor point anywhere. The path is not constrained to angles of 45°.

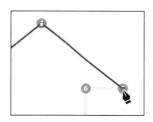

9 Press the Shift key, and click to set point 6 and then click to set point 7. Release the Shift key.

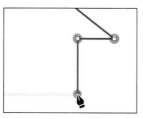

10 Move the pointer over point 1 (the first point). When the pointer shows a small circle next to it (🖊︎₀), click to close the path.

11 Choose Select > Deselect.

Starting with curved paths

In this part of the lesson, you'll learn how to draw curved paths with the Pen tool. To create a curve, you set (create) anchor points and drag out direction handles to define the shape of the curve. This type of anchor point, with direction handles, is called a *smooth point*.

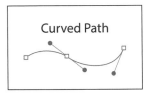

Drawing curves this way gives you some of the greatest control and flexibility in creating paths. However, mastering this technique does take some time. The goal for this exercise is not to create anything specific but to get accustomed to the feel of creating curves. First you'll just get a feel for creating a simple curved path.

1   Choose 3 from the Artboard Navigation menu in the lower-left corner of the Document window. You will draw in the area labeled "Practice."

2   Select the Zoom tool (🔍) in the toolbar, and click twice in the bottom half of the artboard to zoom in.

3   Select the Pen tool (✒) in the toolbar. In the Properties panel, make sure that the fill color is None (⬜), the stroke color is Black, and the stroke weight is still 1 pt.

4   With the Pen tool selected, click and release in an empty area of the artboard to create a starting anchor point. Move the pointer away.

5   In an empty area, press and drag to create a curved path. Release the mouse button.

As you drag away from the point, direction handles appear. *Direction handles* are *direction lines* that have a round *direction point* at the end of each. The angle and length of direction handles determine the shape and size of the curve. Direction handles do not print.

6   Move the pointer away from the anchor point you just created to see the rubber banding. Move the pointer around a bit to see how it changes.

7   Continue pressing, dragging, and releasing in different areas to create a series of points.

8   Choose Select > Deselect. Leave the file open for the next section.

Drawing a curve with the Pen tool

In this part of the lesson, you'll use what you just learned about drawing curves to trace a curved shape with the Pen tool. This will require a little more precision to follow a template path.

1   Press the spacebar to temporarily select the Hand tool (✋), and drag down until you see the curve at the top of the current artboard (on Artboard 3).

2   With the Pen tool (✒) selected, move the pointer over the point labeled 1. Press and drag up to the red dot, and then release the mouse button.

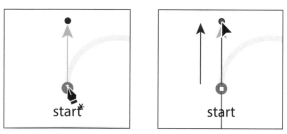

● **Note:** The artboard may scroll as you drag. If you lose visibility of the curve, choose View > Zoom Out until you see the curve and anchor point. Pressing the spacebar allows you to use the Hand tool to reposition the artwork.

So far you haven't drawn anything yet; you've simply created a direction line going in the same general direction as the path (up). Dragging out a direction line on the very first anchor point can be done to create a more "curved" path.

3   Press and drag from point 2 down toward the red dot. Drag the pointer around to see how the path reacts. When the pointer is over the red dot, release the mouse button and the path you are creating should follow the gray template path.

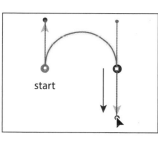

● **Note:** Pulling the direction handle longer makes a steeper curve; when the direction handle is shorter, the curve is flatter.

If the path you created is not aligned exactly with the template, select the Direct Selection tool (▷), and select the anchor points one at a time to show the direction handles. You can then drag the ends of the direction handles (called *direction points*) until your path follows the template more accurately.

4   Select the Selection tool (▶), and click the artboard in an area with no objects, or choose Select > Deselect.

Deselecting the first path allows you to create a new path. If you click somewhere on the artboard with the Pen tool while the path is still selected, the new path connects to the last point you drew.

If you want to try drawing the curve for more practice, scroll down to the Practice area in the same artboard and trace the different curves.

▶ **Tip:** While drawing with the Pen tool, to deselect objects, you can press the Command (macOS) or Ctrl (Windows) key to temporarily switch to the Direct Selection tool and then click the artboard where there are no objects. Another way to end a path is to press the Escape key when you are finished drawing.

Drawing a series of curves with the Pen tool

Now that you've experimented with drawing a curve, you will draw a shape that contains several continuous curves.

1   Choose 4 from the Artboard Navigation menu in the lower-left corner of the Document window. Select the Zoom tool (Q), and click several times in the *top* half of the artboard to zoom in.

2   Select the Pen tool (✐). In the Properties panel to the right of the document, make sure that the fill color is None (☐), the stroke color is black, and the stroke weight is still 1 pt.

3   Press and drag up from point 1, labeled "start," in the direction of the arc, stopping at the red dot. This is exactly how you started the last path.

● **Note:** Don't worry if the path you draw is not exact. You could correct the path by selecting it with the Direct Selection tool (▷) when the path is complete.

4   Move the pointer over the point labeled 2 (to the right), and drag down to the red dot, adjusting the first arc (between points 1 and 2) with the direction handle before you release the mouse button.

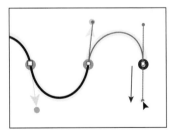

When it comes to smooth points (curved), you'll find that you spend a lot of time focusing on the path segment *behind* the current anchor point you are creating. Remember, by default there are two direction lines for an anchor point. The trailing direction line controls the shape of the segment behind the anchor point.

▶ **Tip:** As you drag out the direction handles for an anchor point, you can press and hold the spacebar to reposition the anchor point. When the anchor point is where you want it, release the spacebar and continue drawing.

5   Continue along the path, alternating between dragging up at point 3, down at point 4, and up at point 5. Put anchor points only where there are numbers, and finish with the point labeled 6.

If you make a mistake as you draw, you can undo your work by choosing Edit > Undo Pen and then draw the last point again. If your direction lines don't match the figures, that's okay.

6   When the path is complete, select the Direct Selection tool (▷), and click to select any anchor point in the path.

When an anchor point is selected, the direction handles appear, and you can readjust the curve of the path, if necessary. With a curve selected, you can also change the stroke and fill. When you do this, the next line you draw will have the same attributes. If you want to try drawing the shape again for more practice, scroll down to the bottom half of the same artboard (labeled "Practice"), and trace the shape there.

7   Choose Select > Deselect and then choose File > Save.

Converting smooth points to corner points

When you create curves, the direction handles help to determine the shape and size of the curved segments, as you've seen. If you want to create a curved path followed by a straight line, for instance, you can remove the direction lines from an anchor point to convert a smooth point into a corner point. In this next part of the lesson, you'll practice converting between smooth points and corner points.

1   Choose 5 from the Artboard Navigation menu in the lower-left corner of the Document window.

On the top of the artboard, you can see the path that you will trace. You'll use the top artboard as a template for the exercise, creating your paths directly on top of those.

2   Select the Zoom tool (Q), and click several times in the top part of the artboard to zoom in.

3   Select the Pen tool ( ). In the Properties panel, make sure that the fill color is None ( ), the stroke color is Black, and the stroke weight is still 1 pt.

4   Pressing the Shift key, press and drag up from point 1, labeled "start," in the direction of the arc, stopping at the red dot. Release the mouse button and then release the Shift key.

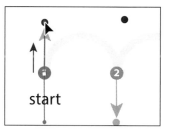

Pressing the Shift key when dragging constrains the direction handles to multiples of 45°.

5   From point 2, press and drag down to the gold dot. As you drag, press and hold the Shift key. When the curved path between 1 and 2 looks correct, and the pointer reaches the gold dot, release the mouse button and then release the Shift key. Leave the path selected.

Now you need the curve to switch directions and create another arc. You will *split* the direction lines, or move them in different directions from each other, to convert a smooth point to a corner point. When you press and drag to create a smooth anchor point with the Pen tool, you create a leading direction line and a trailing direction line. By default, they are equal and paired together.

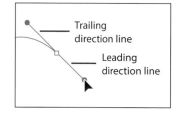

Trailing direction line

Leading direction line

Note: The Option (macOS) or Alt (Windows) key essentially allows you to split the direction lines so that they are independent of each other for that anchor point.

6   Press the Option (macOS) or Alt (Windows) key, and move the pointer over the anchor point you just created (on point 2). When a convert-point icon (^) appears next to the Pen tool pointer (♦ₖ), press and drag a direction line up to the red dot above. Release the mouse button and then release the modifier key. If you do not see the caret (^), you might end up creating an additional loop.

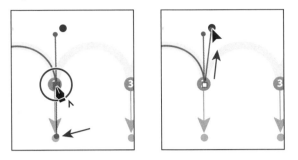

You can also Option-drag (macOS) or Alt-drag (Windows) the *end* of the direction handle (called the *direction point*). An arrow is pointing to it in the first part of the figure. Either method "splits" the direction handles so they can go in different directions.

7   Move the Pen tool pointer over point 3 to the right on the template path, and drag down to the gold dot. Release the mouse button when the path looks similar to the template path.

8   Press the Option (macOS) or Alt (Windows) key, and move the pointer over the last anchor point you created (at 3). When a convert-point icon (^) appears next to the Pen tool pointer (♦ₖ), press and drag a direction line up to the red dot above. Release the mouse button and then release the modifier key.

For the next point, you will not release the mouse button to split the direction handles, so pay close attention.

▶ **Tip:** You can watch these steps in a video! Check out the videos that are a part of the Web Edition. For more information, see the "Web Edition" section of "Getting Started" at the beginning of the book.

9   For anchor point 4, press and drag down to the gold dot until the path looks correct. This time, *do not release the mouse button*. Press the Option (macOS) or Alt (Windows) key, and drag up to the red dot for the next curve. Release the mouse button and then release the modifier key.

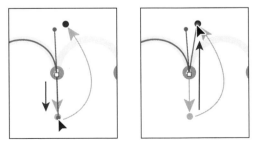

10 Continue this process using the Option (macOS) or Alt (Windows) key to create corner points. Keep doing this until the path is completed.

11 Use the Direct Selection tool to fine-tune the path and then deselect the path.

If you want to try drawing the same shape again for more practice, scroll down to the Practice area in the same artboard, and trace the shape down there.

Combining curves and straight lines

When you're drawing your own artwork with the Pen tool, you'll need to transition easily between curves and straight lines. In this next section, you'll learn how to go from curves to straight lines and from straight lines to curves.

1 Choose 6 from the Artboard Navigation menu in the lower-left corner of the Document window. Select the Zoom tool (Q), and click several times in the top half of the artboard to zoom in.

2 Select the Pen tool ( ). Move the pointer over point 1, labeled "start," and press and drag up, stopping at the red dot. Release the mouse button.

Up to this point, you've been dragging to a gold or red dot in the templates. In the real world those obviously won't be there, so for the next point you will drag to create a point without much guidance. Don't worry, you can always choose Edit > Undo Pen and try again!

3 Press and drag down from point 2, and release the mouse button when the path between 1 and 2 roughly matches the gray template path.

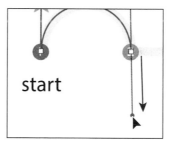

This method of creating a curve should be familiar to you by now.

If you were to continue drawing by clicking point 3, even pressing the Shift key (to produce a straight line), the path would be curved (don't do either). The last point you created is a smooth anchor point and has a leading direction handle (the one you pulled out). The figure to the right shows what the path would look like if you clicked with the Pen tool on the next point.

You will now continue the path as a straight line by removing the leading direction handle.

4 Move the pointer over the last point created (point 2). When the convert-point icon appears (⬧ₖ), click. This deletes the *leading* direction handle from the anchor point (not the trailing direction handle), as shown in the second part of the following figure.

5 Move the pointer over point 3. Pressing the Shift key, click and release to create the next point. Release the Shift key after clicking, and you've created a straight line.

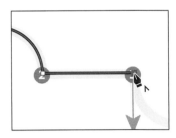

6 For the next arc, move the pointer over the last point created. When the convert-point icon appears (⬧ₖ), press and drag down from that point to the red dot. This creates a new, independent direction line.

For the rest of this section, I'm going to ask you to complete the path, following the remaining part of the template. I don't include any figures, so go through the figures in the previous steps if you need guidance.

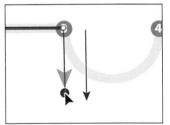

7 For the next point (point 4), press and drag up to complete the arc.

8 Click the last anchor point you just created to remove the direction line.

9 Shift-click the next point to create the second straight segment.

10 Press and drag up from the last point you created to create a direction line.

11 Press and drag down on the end point (point 6) to create the final arc.

If you want to try drawing the same shape for more practice, scroll down to the Practice area in the same artboard, and trace the shape down there. Make sure you deselect the previous artwork first.

12 Choose File > Save and then choose File > Close.

Remember, you can always go back and work on those Pen tool templates in the L7_practice.ai file as many times as you need. Take it as slowly as you need and *practice, practice, practice.*

Creating artwork with the Pen tool

Next, you'll take what you've learned and create some artwork to be used in your project. To start you'll draw a swan, which combines curves and corners. Take your time as you practice with this shape, and use the template guides provided.

▶ **Tip:** Don't forget, you can always undo a point you've drawn (Edit > Undo Pen) and then try again.

1. Choose File > Open, and open the L7_end.ai file in the Lessons > Lesson07 folder to see the final artwork.

2. Choose View > Fit Artboard In Window to see the finished artwork. If you don't want to leave the artwork open, choose File > Close.

3. Choose File > Open, and open the L7_start.ai file in the Lessons > Lesson07 folder to open the file you'll be working in.

4. Choose File > Save As, name the file **Swan.ai**, and select the Lessons > Lesson07 folder in the Save As dialog box. Leave Adobe Illustrator (ai) chosen from the Format menu (macOS) or Adobe Illustrator (*.AI) chosen from the Save As Type menu (Windows), and click Save.

5. In the Illustrator Options dialog box, leave the options set at the defaults and then click OK.

6. Choose View > Fit Artboard In Window to ensure that you see the entire artboard.

7. Open the Layers panel (Window > Layers), and click to select the layer named "Artwork."

8. Select the Pen tool (✒) in the toolbar.

9. In the Properties panel (Window > Properties), make sure that the fill color is None (◻), the stroke color is Black, and the stroke weight is 1 pt.

Drawing the swan

Now that you have the file open and ready, you're going to put the Pen tool practice you did in previous sections to use by drawing a beautiful swan. This next section has more than the average number of steps, so *take your time*.

● **Note:** You do not have to start at the blue square (point A) to draw this shape. You can set anchor points for a path with the Pen tool in a clockwise or counterclockwise direction.

1 With the Pen tool (✐) selected, press and drag from the blue square labeled "A" on the swan body template, to the red dot to set the starting anchor point and direction of the first curve.

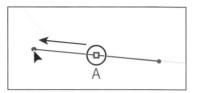

2 Move the pointer over point B. Press and drag, stopping at the gold dot. Release the mouse button.

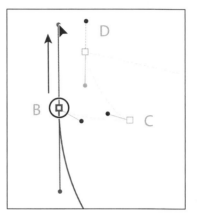

Remember to pay attention to how the path looks as you drag the direction line. It's easier when dragging to color dots on a template, but when you're creating your own content, you'll need to be aware of the path you are creating! Next, you'll split the direction handles so the path can go in a different direction.

3 Move the pointer over point B again and when the pointer changes (▸ₙ), press Option (macOS) or Alt (Windows) and drag away from the point to the red dot to create a new direction line. Release the mouse button and then the key.

4 Move the pointer over point C. Click and release to add a point.

5 To make the next path a curve, move the pointer over the anchor point you just created at point C—press and drag to the red dot to add a direction handle.

6 Move the pointer over point D. Press and drag to the red dot.

The next part of the path needs to be straight, so the direction line on point D needs to be removed.

7 Move the Pen tool pointer over point D again. When the convert-point icon appears (✎ₙ) next to the pointer, click point D to remove the leading direction handle (the handle pointing up).

8 Click and release on point E to make a straight line.

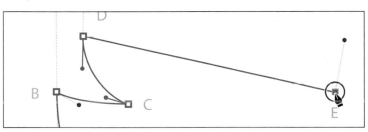

As you draw with the Pen tool, you may want to edit part of a path you previously drew. Pressing a modifier key with the Pen tool selected, you can move the pointer over a previous path segment and drag to modify it, which is what you'll do next.

9 Move the pointer over the path between points D and E. Press the Option (macOS) or Alt (Windows) key. The pointer changes appearance (▶.). Drag the path up to make it curved, as you see in the figure. Release the mouse button and then the key. This adds direction handles to the anchor points at both ends of the line segment.

After releasing the mouse button, notice that as you move the pointer, you can see the Pen tool rubber banding, which means you are still drawing the path.

▶ **Tip:** You can also press the Option+Shift (macOS) or Alt+Shift (Windows) keys to constrain the handles to a perpendicular direction, which ensures that the handles are the same length.

The path that continues from point E needs to be curved, so you'll need to add a leading direction handle to the point.

● **Note:** After releasing the mouse button in the previous step, if you move the pointer away and then bring it back to point E, the convert-point icon [^] will appear next to the pointer.

10 With the Pen tool pointer over point E, press and drag up to the red dot to create a new direction handle.

This creates a new leading direction handle and sets up the next path to be a curve.

11 Continue drawing by dragging from the anchor point at F to the red dot.

12 Drag from point G to the red dot.

The next part of the path needs to be straight, so you'll remove the leading direction handle from the point at G.

13 Move the pointer back over point G. When the convert-point icon appears (✎ₙ) next to the pointer, click to remove the direction handle.

14 Click point H to create a new anchor point.

The next part of the path needs to be curved, so you will need to add a leading direction handle to point H.

15 Move the Pen tool pointer over point H again. When the convert-point icon appears (✎ₙ) next to the pointer, press and drag from point H up to the red dot to add a leading direction handle.

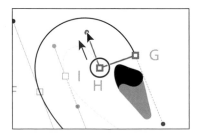

16 Continue drawing the point at I by dragging from the anchor point to the gold dot. Release the mouse button.

17 Press Option (macOS) or Alt (Windows), and when the pointer changes (⊼), drag the end of the direction handle down to the red dot from the gold dot.

18 Drag from point J to the red dot.

Next, you'll complete the drawing of the swan by closing the path.

19 Move the Pen tool pointer over point A *without clicking*.

Notice that an open circle appears next to the Pen tool pointer (🖋₀), indicating that the path would close if you were to click the anchor point (*don't click yet*). If you were to drag, the direction handles on either side of the point would move as a single straight line. You need to extend one of the direction handles to match the template.

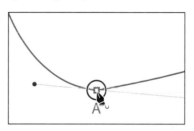

20 Drag left and a little up. Notice that a direction handle shows but is going in the opposite direction (it's going down and to the right). Drag until the curve looks right.

Normally, as you drag away from a point, direction lines appear before and after the point. Without the modifier key, as you drag away from a closing point, you are reshaping the path before *and* after the anchor point. Pressing the Option (macOS) or Alt (Windows) modifier key on the closing point allows you to edit the previous direction handle independently.

21 Click the Properties panel tab. Click the Fill color and select white.

22 Command-click (macOS) or Ctrl-click (Windows) away from the path to deselect it, and then choose File > Save.

▶ **Tip:** When creating an anchor point, you can press the spacebar to move the point as you create it.

● **Note:** This is a shortcut method for deselecting a path while keeping the Pen tool selected. You could also choose Select > Deselect, among other methods.

Editing paths and points

Next you'll edit a few of the paths and points for the swan you just created.

1 Select the Direct Selection tool (▶), and click the anchor point labeled J to select it. Drag the anchor point to the left so it roughly matches the figure.

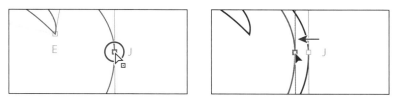

> **Tip:** As you are dragging a path with the Direct Selection tool, you can also press the Shift key to constrain the handles to a perpendicular direction, which ensures that the handles are the same length.

2 Move the pointer over the part of the path between points F and G (at the top of the swan). When the pointer looks like this: ▶., drag the path up and to the left a little to change the curve of the path. This is an easy way to make edits to a curved path without having to edit the direction handles for each anchor point.

Notice that the pointer changes appearance (▶.) with the pointer over the path. This indicates that you can drag the path, which will adjust the anchor points and direction handles as you drag.

3 Choose Select > Deselect and then choose File > Save.

Deleting and adding anchor points

Most of the time, the goal of drawing paths with a tool like the Pen tool or Curvature tool is to avoid adding more anchor points than necessary. You can reduce a path's complexity or change its overall shape by deleting unnecessary points (and therefore gain more control over the shape), or you can extend a path by adding points to it. Next you'll delete anchor points from, and add anchor points to, different parts of the swan path.

1 Open the Layers panel (Window > Layers). In the Layers panel, click the eye icon (👁) for the layer named "Bird template" to hide the layer contents.

2 With the Direct Selection tool (▶) selected, click the swan path to select it.

To start you'll delete a few points in the tail to simplify the swan path.

3 Select the Pen tool (✐) in the toolbar, and move the pointer over the anchor point you see in the first part of the following figure. When a minus sign (−) appears to the right of the Pen tool pointer (♦_), click to remove the anchor point.

▶ **Tip:** With an anchor point selected, you can also click Remove Selected Anchor Points (⬛) in the Properties panel to delete the anchor point.

4 Move the pointer over the anchor point in the second part of the following figure. When a minus sign (−) appears to the right of the Pen tool pointer (♦_), click to remove the anchor point.

Next you'll reshape the remaining path. With the Pen tool selected, you can press Command (macOS) or Ctrl (Windows) to temporarily select the Direct Selection tool so you can edit a path and then release the key and continue drawing.

5 Press Command (macOS) or Ctrl (Windows) to temporarily select the Direct Selection tool. With the key held down, move the pointer over the anchor point shown in the figure. When the pointer shows a box next to it (▷), click to select the anchor point if it isn't already.

6 With the key still held down, drag the direction line pointing down from the selected anchor point to reshape the path, and release the key.

With that part of the path reshaped, now you'll add a new anchor point to the path so you can reshape it further.

● **Note:** It can be tricky to drag the end of a direction line. If you wind up missing and deselecting the path, with the modifier key still held down, click the path and then click the anchor point to see the direction handles and try again.

7 Move the pointer over the left side of the swan path, below the selected anchor point. When a plus sign (+) appears to the right of the Pen tool pointer (♦+), click to add an anchor point.

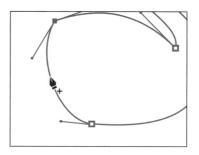

8 Press Command (macOS) or Ctrl (Windows) to temporarily select the Direct Selection tool and drag the new anchor to the left to reshape the path. Release the key.

Lastly, you'll add a new anchor point to the bottom of the swan path so that in the next section you can reshape the bottom.

9 Move the pointer over the bottom part of the path. When a plus sign (+) appears to the right of the Pen tool pointer (🖋₊), click to add an anchor point.

Converting between smooth points and corner points

To more precisely control the path you create, you can convert points from smooth points to corner points and from corner points to smooth points, using several methods.

1 Select the Direct Selection tool (▷). With the last point you added still selected, Shift-click the anchor point to the left (formerly labeled "A") to select both.

▶ **Tip:** You could also convert between corner and smooth points by double-clicking an anchor point (or Option-clicking [macOS] or Alt-clicking [Windows]) with the Curvature tool, as you'll see later.

2 In the Properties panel to the right, click the Convert Selected Anchor Points To Corner button (⬎) to convert the anchor points to corners.

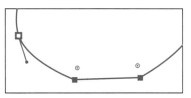

● **Note:** If the points align to the artboard after clicking the align button, try again. Make sure that Align To Key Anchor is selected in the Properties panel first.

3 Click the Vertical Align Bottom button (⬛) in the Properties panel to align the point you first selected to the second point you selected.

As you saw in Lesson 2, selected anchor points align to the last selected anchor point, which is known as the *key anchor*.

4 Choose Select > Deselect and then File > Save.

Working with the Anchor Point tool

Another way to convert anchor points between smooth and corner points is using the Anchor Point tool (�ᐱ). You'll do that next to finish the head of the swan.

1 Select the Selection tool and click the swan path to select it.

2 Press and hold on the Pen tool (✒) in the toolbar to reveal more tools. Select the Anchor Point tool (ᐱ).

   If you click an anchor point with the Anchor point tool, the direction lines are removed and it becomes a corner point. The Anchor point tool is also used either to remove both or one of the direction handles from an anchor point, converting it to a corner point, or to drag out direction handles from an anchor point. Dragging handles out with the Anchor point tool can be a great way to restore handles that have been split.

3 Move the pointer over the point in the swan's head in the figure. When the pointer looks like this: ᐱ, press and drag *up* from the corner point to drag the direction handles out. Drag until the neck looks similar to how it did before you started dragging.

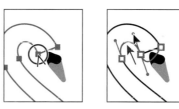

● **Note:** Don't drag if the pointer looks like this: ▸₋. This means that the pointer is not over the anchor point, and if you drag, you will reshape the curve.

   Depending on which direction you drew the path in, dragging in one direction may reverse the direction handles.

4 Move the pointer over the anchor point to the right of the anchor point you just edited. Press and drag *down* when the pointer looks like this: ᐱ. Make sure the top of the swan's head looks similar to the way it did.

▶ **Tip:** If you move the Anchor Point tool pointer over the end of a direction handle that is split, you can press the Option (macOS) or Alt (Windows) key and, when the pointer changes (▸), click to make the direction handles a single straight line again (not split).

5 Select the Direct Selection tool, and drag the end of the bottom direction handle up to shorten it and make the line less curvy.

   The direction handles for an anchor point are split when you create them with the Anchor Point tool, which means you can move them independently. Next you'll convert an anchor point from a smooth point (with direction handles) to a corner point.

6 Open the Layers panel (Window > Layers). In the Layers panel, click the visibility column for the layer named "Wing" and the layer named "Background" to show the content for both.

You should now see the wing of the swan on top of the swan shape you drew. It's made up of a series of simple paths that are overlapping each other. You need to make the right edge of the wing a corner point, not a smooth point.

7 Select the Direct Selection tool in the toolbar. Click the larger wing shape to select it and see the anchor points.

● **Note:** Another way to convert a smooth anchor point to a corner anchor point is to click the Convert Selected Anchor Points To Corner button (◥) in the Properties panel.

8 Select the Anchor Point tool (◣) in the toolbar. Move the pointer over the point circled in the first part of the following figure. Click to convert the point from a smooth point (with direction handles) to a corner point.

9 Select the Direct Selection tool, and drag the anchor point you converted. Snap it to the anchor point at the base of the swan's neck.

10 Move the pointer over the end of the direction handle coming from the top anchor point, and drag to change the shape of the path.

11 Choose Select > Deselect.

12 Choose View > Fit Artboard In Window.

13 Save and close the file by choosing File > Save and then File > Close.

Review questions

1 Describe how to draw straight vertical, horizontal, or diagonal lines using the Pen tool (✐).

2 How do you draw a curved line using the Pen tool?

3 What are the two types of anchor points you can create with the Pen tool?

4 Name two ways to convert a smooth point on a curve to a corner point.

5 Which tool would you use to edit a segment on a curved line?

Review answers

1 To draw a straight line, click with the Pen tool (✐) and then move the pointer and click again. The first click sets the starting anchor point, and the second click sets the ending anchor point of the line. To constrain the straight line vertically, horizontally, or along a 45° diagonal, press the Shift key as you click to create the second anchor point with the Pen tool.

2 To draw a curved line with the Pen tool, click to create the starting anchor point, drag to set the direction of the curve, and then click to end the curve.

3 With the Pen tool, you can create corner points or smooth points. Corner points allow the path to change direction and have either no direction lines or split direction lines. Smooth points have direction lines that are paired together.

4 To convert a smooth point on a curve to a corner point, use the Direct Selection tool (▷) to select the anchor point and then use the Anchor Point tool (⌐) to drag a direction handle to change the direction. Another method is to choose a point or points with the Direct Selection tool and then click the Convert Selected Anchor Points To Corner button (⬢) in the Properties panel.

5 To edit a segment on a curved line, select the Direct Selection tool and drag the segment to move it; or drag a direction handle on an anchor point to adjust the length and shape of the segment. Pressing the Option (macOS) or Alt (Windows) key and dragging a path segment with the Pen tool is another way to reshape a path.

8 USING COLOR TO ENHANCE SIGNAGE

Lesson overview

In this lesson, you'll learn how to do the following:

- Understand color modes and the main color controls.

- Create, edit, and paint with colors using a variety of methods.

- Name and save colors.

- Copy and paint appearance attributes from one object to another.

- Work with color groups.

- Be inspired creatively with the Color Guide panel.

- Explore the Recolor Artwork command.

- Work with Live Paint groups.

 This lesson will take about 75 minutes to complete. To get the lesson files used in this chapter, download them from the web page for this book at www.adobepress.com/IllustratorCIB2020. For more information, see "Accessing the lesson files and Web Edition" in the Getting Started section at the beginning of this book.

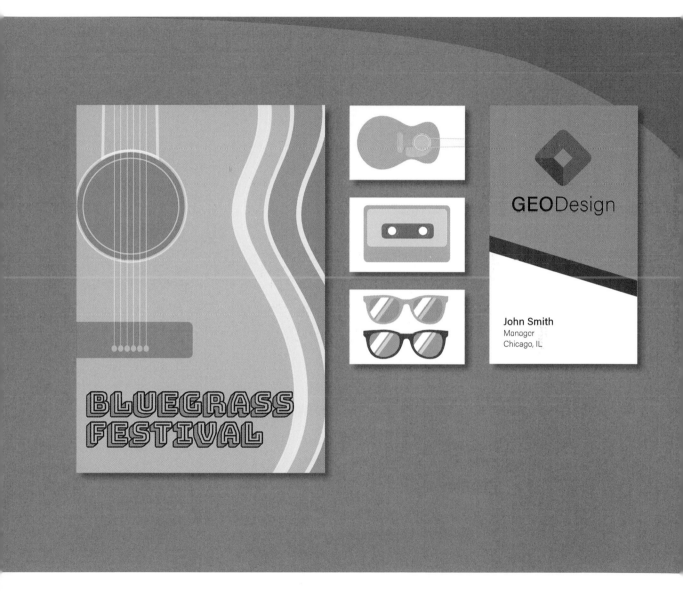

Spice up your illustrations with color by taking advantage of color controls in Adobe Illustrator. In this information-packed lesson, you'll discover how to create and paint fills and strokes, use the Color Guide panel for inspiration, work with color groups, recolor artwork, and more.

Starting the lesson

In this lesson, you'll learn about the fundamentals of color by creating and editing colors for a festival sign and artwork, using the Swatches panel and more.

● **Note:** If you have not already downloaded the project files for this lesson to your computer from your Account page, make sure to do so now. See the "Getting Started" section at the beginning of the book.

1   To ensure that the tools function and the defaults are set exactly as described in this lesson, delete or deactivate (by renaming) the Adobe Illustrator preferences file. See "Restoring default preferences" in the "Getting Started" section at the beginning of the book.

2   Start Adobe Illustrator.

3   Choose File > Open, and open the L8_end1.ai file in the Lessons > Lesson08 folder to view a final version of the artwork.

4   Choose View > Fit All In Window. You can leave the file open for reference or choose File > Close to close it.

5   Choose File > Open. In the Open dialog box, navigate to the Lessons > Lesson08 folder, and select the L8_start1.ai file on your hard disk. Click Open to open the file. This file has all the pieces already in it; they just need to be painted.

6   Choose View > Fit All In Window.

7   Choose File > Save As. In the Save As dialog box, navigate to the Lesson08 folder, and name the file **Festival.ai**. Leave Adobe Illustrator (ai) chosen from the Format menu (macOS) or Adobe Illustrator (*.AI) chosen from the Save As Type menu (Windows), and click Save.

8   In the Illustrator Options dialog box, leave the options at their default settings and then click OK.

● **Note:** If you don't see Reset Essentials in the menu, choose Window > Workspace > Essentials before choosing Window > Workspace > Reset Essentials.

9   Choose Window > Workspace > Reset Essentials.

Exploring color modes

There are many ways to experiment with and apply color to your artwork in Adobe Illustrator. As you work with color, it's important to consider the medium in which the artwork will be published, such as print or the web. The colors you create need to be suitable for the medium. This usually requires that you use the correct color mode and color definitions for your colors. Color modes will be described next.

Before starting a new document, you should decide which color mode the artwork should use, *CMYK* or *RGB*.

- **CMYK**—Cyan, magenta, yellow, and black are the colors of ink used in four-color process printing. These four colors are combined and overlapped in a pattern of dots to create a multitude of other colors.

- **RGB**—Red, green, and blue light are added together in various ways to create an array of colors. Select this mode if you are using images for onscreen presentations, the internet, or mobile apps.

When you create a new document by choosing File > New, each new document preset, like Print or Web, has a specific color mode. For instance, the Print category uses the CMYK color mode. You can easily change the color mode by choosing a different option from the Color Mode menu after clicking Advanced Options in the New Document dialog box.

▶ **Tip:** To learn more about color and graphics, search for "About color" in Illustrator Help (Help > Illustrator Help).

● **Note:** You may see a series of templates in the New Document dialog box, unlike in the figure.

Once a color mode is chosen, solid colors in the document are displayed in and created from that color mode. Once a document is created, you can change the color mode of a document by choosing File > Document Color Mode and then switching to either CMYK Color or RGB Color from the menu.

Working with color

In this lesson, you'll learn about the traditional methods of coloring (also called *painting*) objects in Illustrator using a combination of panels and tools, such as the Properties panel, Swatches panel, Color Guide panel, Color Picker, and paint options in the toolbar.

● **Note:** The toolbar you see may be a double column, depending on the resolution of your screen.

In previous lessons, you learned that objects in Illustrator can have a fill, a stroke, or both. At the bottom of the toolbar, notice the Fill and Stroke boxes. The Fill box is white (in this case), and the Stroke box is black. If you click those boxes one at a time, you'll see that whichever is clicked is brought in front of the other (it's selected). When a color is chosen, it is applied to the fill or stroke, whichever is selected. As you explore more of Illustrator, you'll see these fill and stroke boxes in lots of other places, like the Properties panel, Swatches panel, and more.

As you will see in this section, Illustrator provides a lot of ways to arrive at the color you need. You'll start by applying an existing color to a shape and then work your way through the most widely used methods for creating and applying color.

Applying an existing color

● **Note:** Throughout this lesson, you'll be working on a document with a color mode that was set to CMYK when the document was created. That means that colors you create will, by default, be composed of cyan, magenta, yellow, and black.

Every new document in Illustrator has a series of default colors available for you to use in your artwork in the form of swatches in the Swatches panel. The first color method you'll explore is applying an existing color to a shape.

1   With the Festival.ai document showing, choose 1 Festival Sign from the Artboard Navigation menu in the lower-left corner of the Document window (if it's not chosen already) and then choose View > Fit Artboard In Window.

2   With the Selection tool (▶), click in the red guitar shape to select it.

3   Click the Fill box (■) in the Properties panel on the right to reveal a panel. Click the Swatches button (▦) toward the top of the panel, if it isn't already selected, to show the default swatches (colors). As you move the pointer over the swatches, tool tips appear revealing each swatch's name. Click to apply the orange swatch named "Orange" to change the color of the fill for the selected guitar shape.

4 Press the Escape key to hide the panel of colors.

Creating a custom color

There are lots of ways to create your own custom colors in Illustrator. Using the Color panel (Window > Color) or Color Mixer, which you'll learn more about in this section, you can apply custom colors you create to an object's fill and stroke and also edit and mix colors using different color models (CMYK, for example). The Color panel and Color Mixer display the current fill and stroke of the selected content, and you can either visually select a color from the color spectrum bar at the bottom of the panel or mix your own colors in various ways. Next, you'll create a custom color using the Color Mixer.

1 With the Selection tool (▶), click in the gray guitar shape to select it (see the figure).

2 Click the Fill box (■) in the Properties panel on the right to reveal a panel. Click the Color Mixer button (🎨) in the top of the panel that appears.

3 At the bottom of the panel, click in the yellow-orange part of the color spectrum to sample a yellow-orange color, and apply it to the fill (see the following figure).

Since the spectrum bar is so small, you most likely won't achieve the same color as you see in the book. That's okay, because you'll edit it shortly to match.

▶ **Tip:** To see a larger color spectrum, you can open the Color panel (Window > Color) and drag the bottom of the panel down.

4 In the Color Mixer panel, which should still be showing, type the following values in the CMYK fields: C=**3**, M=**2**, Y=**98**, K=**0**. Press Return or Enter after the last value entered. This ensures that we are all using the same yellow.

Colors created in the Color Mixer panel are not saved anywhere except in the fill or stroke of the selected artwork. If you want to easily reuse the color you just created elsewhere in this document, you can save it as a swatch in the Swatches panel, which is what you'll do next.

Saving a color as a swatch

You can name and save different types of colors, gradients, and patterns in the document as swatches so that you can apply and edit them later. Swatches are initially listed in the Swatches panel in the order in which they were created, but you can reorder or organize the swatches into groups to suit your needs. All documents start with a default number of swatches, as mentioned earlier. Any colors you save or edit in the Swatches panel are available to the current document only, by default, since each document has its own defined swatches.

Next, you'll save a color you create as a swatch so you can easily reuse it later.

1 With the Selection tool selected, click to select the black circle.

2 Click the Fill box (■) in the Properties panel to show the panel. With the Color Mixer option (🎨) selected, change the CMYK values to C=**0**, M=**84**, Y=**100**, K=**0**. Press Return or Enter after the last value entered. The following figure shows just before pressing Return or Enter for the K value.

Now you'll save the color as a swatch.

3 Click the Fill box again, if the colors panel isn't showing.

4 Click the Swatches button () at the top of the panel to see the swatches. Click the New Swatch button (🔲) at the bottom of the panel to create a swatch from the fill color of the selected artwork.

5 In the New Swatch dialog box that appears, change the following options:

- Swatch Name: **Dark Orange**

- Add To My Library: Deselected (In Lesson 14, you'll learn all about Libraries.)

Notice the Global option that is selected by default. New swatches you create are global by default. That means that if you later edit this swatch, everywhere it is applied is updated, regardless of whether or not the artwork is selected.

▶ **Tip:** Naming colors can be an art form. You can name them according to their values (C=45, …), appearance (light orange), or description (like "text header"), among other attributes.

6 Click OK to save the swatch.

Notice that the new Dark Orange swatch is highlighted in the Swatches panel (it has a white border around it). That's because it's applied to the selected shape automatically. Also notice the little white triangle in the lower-right corner of the swatch. This indicates that it's a global swatch.

Leave the orange circle selected and the panel showing for the next section.

Creating a copy of a swatch

One of the easiest ways to create and save a color as a swatch is to make a copy of an existing swatch and edit the color of the copy. Next, you'll create another swatch by copying and editing the swatch named "Dark Orange."

1   With the circle still selected and the Swatches panel still showing, choose Duplicate Swatch from the panel menu (▤).

This creates a copy of the selected Dark Orange swatch. The new swatch is now applied to the selected circle shape in place of the original color.

2   Click to apply the *original* Dark Orange swatch to the selected circle.

3   With the Selection tool (▶), click the light blue guitar shape to select it. An arrow is pointing to it in the following figure.

4   Click the Fill box (▣) in the Properties panel, and double-click the Dark Orange *copy* swatch to both apply it to the selected artwork and edit the color settings.

▶ **Tip:** In the Swatch Options dialog box, the Color Mode menu lets you change the color mode of a specific color to RGB, CMYK, Grayscale, or another mode.

5   In the Swatch Options dialog box, change the name to **Mustard**; change the values to C=**11**, M=**23**, Y=**100**, K=**0**; and make sure that Add To My Library is deselected. Select Preview to see the change, and then click OK.

Make sure the new Mustard swatch is applied to the selected shape.

Editing a global swatch

Next you'll learn about *global color*. When you edit a global color, all artwork with that swatch applied is updated, regardless of which artwork is and isn't selected.

1   With the Selection tool (▶), click to select the gray shape above the "BLUEGRASS FESTIVAL" text. Press the Shift key, and click in the green guitar shape to select it as well.

You'll apply the Dark Orange swatch to both shapes and then change the color.

2   Click the Fill box (?) in the Properties panel, and click the Swatches button (▦) at the top of the panel to see the swatches, if necessary. Click to apply the swatch named "Dark Orange."

The question mark (?) in the Fill box indicates that there are different fills in the selected artwork.

3   Double-click the Dark Orange swatch. In the Swatch Options dialog box, change the M value (Magenta) to **64**, select Preview to see the change (you may need to click in another field in the dialog box to see the change happen), and then click OK.

All of the shapes with the global swatch applied are updated—even the circle that wasn't selected.

Editing a nonglobal swatch

The default color swatches that come with each Illustrator document are not global swatches by default. As a result, when you edit one of those color swatches, the artwork that uses the color will update only if that artwork is selected. Next, you'll apply and edit a swatch that was not saved as a global swatch.

1 With the Selection tool (▶) selected, click to select the first guitar shape you changed the color for. An arrow is pointing to it in the figure.

2 Click the Fill box (■) in the Properties panel and you will see that the swatch named "Orange" is applied to the fill. This was the first color you applied to content at the beginning of this lesson.

You can tell that the orange color swatch you applied is *not* a global swatch because it doesn't have the small white triangle in the lower-right corner of the swatch in the Swatches panel.

3 Press the Escape key to hide the Swatches panel.

4 Choose Select > Deselect.

5 Choose Window > Swatches to open the Swatches panel as a separate panel. Double-click the swatch named "Orange" to edit it.

Most of the formatting options you find in the Properties panel can also be found in separate panels. Opening the Swatches panel, for instance, can be a useful way to work with color without having to select artwork.

6 In the Swatch Options dialog box, change the name to **Guitar Orange** and the values to C=**0**, M=**29**, Y=**100**, K=**0**, select Global to ensure that it's a global swatch, and select Preview.

● **Note:** You can change an existing swatch into a global swatch, but it requires a bit more effort. Either you need to select all of the shapes that swatch was applied to before you edit the swatch and make it global, or you edit the swatch to make it global and then reapply the swatch to the content.

Notice that the color of the guitar doesn't change. That's because global wasn't selected in the Swatch Options dialog box when the color was applied to the guitar shape. After changing a nonglobal swatch, you need to reapply it to artwork that wasn't selected when you made the edit.

7 Click OK.

8 Click the X at the top of the Swatches panel group to close it.

9 Click to select the guitar shape again. Click the Fill box (■) in the Properties panel, and notice that what was the orange color swatch is no longer applied.

10 Click the Guitar Orange swatch you just edited to apply it.

11 Choose Select > Deselect and then choose File > Save.

Using the Color Picker to create color

Another method for creating color is to use the Color Picker. The Color Picker lets you select a color in a color field or in a spectrum, either by defining colors numerically or by clicking a swatch. The Color Picker is also found in Adobe applications like InDesign and Photoshop. Next you'll create a color using the Color Picker and then save that color as a swatch in the Swatches panel.

1 With the Selection tool (▶), click in the blue guitar shape.

2 Double-click the blue Fill box at the bottom of the toolbar, to the left of the document, to open the Color Picker.

In the Color Picker dialog box, the larger color field shows saturation (horizontally) and brightness (vertically). The color spectrum bar to the right of the color field shows the hue.

3 In the Color Picker dialog box, drag up and down in the color spectrum bar to change the color range. Make sure that you wind up with the triangles in an orange color—it doesn't have to match the figure exactly.

4 Drag in the color field (where you see the circle in the following figure). As you drag right and left, you adjust the saturation, and as you drag up and down, you adjust the brightness. The color you create when you click OK (don't click yet)

appears in the New Color rectangle (an arrow is pointing to it in the figure). Don't worry about matching the color in the figure yet.

5 In the CMYK fields, change the values to C=**8**, M=**50**, Y=**100**, and K=**0**.

Note: The Color Swatches button in the Color Picker shows you the swatches in the Swatches panel and the default color books (the sets of swatches that come with Illustrator). It also lets you select a color from one. You can return to the color spectrum by clicking the Color Models button and then editing the swatch color values, if necessary.

6 Click OK, and you should see that the orange color is applied to the fill of the shape.

7 Click the Fill box (■) in the Properties panel to show the swatches. Click the New Swatch button (▣) at the bottom of the panel, and change the following options in the New Swatch dialog box:

   • Swatch Name: **Burnt Orange**
   • Global: Selected (the default setting)
   • Add To My Library: Deselected

8 Click OK to see the color appear as a swatch in the Swatches panel.

9 Choose Select > Deselect.

10 Choose File > Save.

Using Illustrator swatch libraries

● **Note:** Sometimes it's practical to use process (typically CMYK) and spot (PANTONE, for instance) inks in the same job. For example, you might use one spot ink to print the exact color of a company logo on the same pages of an annual report where photographs are reproduced using process color. You can also use a spot-color printing plate to apply a varnish over areas of a process color job. In both cases, your print job would use a total of five inks—four process inks and one spot ink or varnish.

Swatch libraries are collections of preset colors, such as Pantone and TOYO, and thematic libraries, such as Earthtone and Ice Cream. Illustrator has default swatch libraries that appear as separate panels when you open them, and they cannot be edited. When you apply color from a library to artwork, the color in the library becomes a swatch that is saved only in that document and appears in the Swatches panel. Libraries are a great starting point for creating colors.

Next you'll create a spot color using a Pantone Plus library, which prints using a spot ink. After creating it, you'll apply it to artwork. When color is defined in Illustrator and later printed, the appearance of the color may vary. This is why most printers and designers rely on a color-matching system, like the PANTONE system, to help maintain color consistency and, in some cases, to access a wider range of colors.

Adding a spot color

In this section, you'll see how to open a color library, such as the PANTONE color system, and how to add a Pantone Matching System (PMS) color to the Swatches panel.

1 Choose Window > Swatch Libraries > Color Books > PANTONE+ Solid Coated.

   The PANTONE+ Solid Coated library appears in its own panel.

2 Type **137** in the Find field.

   As you type, the list is filtered, showing a smaller and smaller range of swatches.

3 Click the swatch PANTONE 137 C beneath the search field to add it to the Swatches panel for this document. Click the X to the right of the search field to stop the filtering.

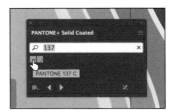

4 Close the PANTONE+ Solid Coated panel.

● **Note:** If you exit Illustrator with the PANTONE library panel still open and then relaunch Illustrator, the panel does not reopen. To automatically open the panel whenever Illustrator opens, choose Persistent from the PANTONE+ Solid Coated panel menu (▤).

5 Choose 2 Pantone from the Artboard Navigation menu in the lower-left corner of the Document window.

   The artboard should be fit in the Document window. If it is not, you can choose View > Fit Artboard In Window.

6 With the Selection tool (▶), click the larger light gray guitar shape.

7 Click the Fill box (▢) in the Properties panel to show the swatches, and select the PANTONE 137 C swatch to fill the shape.

8 Choose Select > Deselect and then choose File > Save.

● **Note:** After saving, you may see a warning dialog box about spot colors and transparency. To learn more about this message, visit: helpx. adobe.com/illustrator/ kb/spot-colors-transparency-illustrator. html.

PANTONE swatches vs. other swatches in the Swatches panel

In the Swatches panel, you can identify spot-color swatches by the spot-color icon (⬚) when the panel is in List view or by the dot in the lower corner (⬚) when the panel is in Thumbnail view. Process colors do not have a spot-color icon or a dot.

Creating and saving a tint of a color

A *tint* is a mixture of a color with white to make the color lighter. You can create a tint from a *global* process color, like CMYK, or from a spot color. Next, you'll create a tint of the Pantone swatch you added to the document.

1 With the Selection tool (▶), press the Shift key and click the two darker gray shapes on the guitar to select them both.

2 Click the Fill box in the Properties panel (■) on the right. Select the PANTONE 137 C swatch to fill both shapes.

3 Click the Color Mixer button (🎨) at the top of the panel.

In the section "Creating a custom color," you created a custom color using the Color Mixer sliders. In that section, you were creating a custom color from scratch—that's why there were CMYK sliders. Now you will see a single slider labeled "T" for tint. When using the color mixer for a global swatch, you will create a tint instead of mixing CMYK values.

4 Drag the tint slider to the left to change the tint value to 70%.

5 Click the Swatches button (▦) at the top of the panel to show the swatches. Click the New Swatch button (⬜) at the bottom of the panel to save the tint.

6 Move the pointer over the swatch icon to see its name, which is PANTONE 137 C 70%.

7 Choose Select > Deselect and then choose File > Save.

Converting colors

Illustrator offers Edit Colors commands (Edit > Edit Colors) that allow you to convert colors between color modes, blend colors, invert colors, and much more, for selected artwork. Next, you'll change the guitar with the PANTONE 137 C color applied to use CMYK colors instead of Pantone.

1 Choose Select > All On Active Artboard to select all artwork on the artboard, including the shapes with the Pantone color and tint applied.

2 Choose Edit > Edit Colors > Convert To CMYK.

Any colors in the selected shapes that had Pantone applied as a spot color are now composed of CMYK. Using this method for converting to CMYK does *not* affect Pantone color swatches (PANTONE 137 C and the tint, in this case) in the Swatches panel. It simply converts the selected *artwork* colors to CMYK. The swatches in the Swatches panel are no longer applied to the artwork.

3 Choose Select > Deselect.

● **Note:** Currently, Convert To RGB in the Edit Color menu is dimmed (you cannot select it). That's because the document color mode is CMYK. To convert the selected content color to RGB using this method, first choose File > Document Color Mode > RGB Color.

Copying appearance attributes

At times you may want to simply copy appearance attributes, such as text formatting, fill, and stroke, from one object to another. This can be done with the Eyedropper tool (🖊) and can really speed up your creative process.

1 Using the Selection tool (▶), select the pink shape.

2 Select the Eyedropper tool (🖊) in the toolbar on the left. Click in the circle shape that you applied the tint to. See the figure.

The once pink shape now has the attributes from the circle shape applied, including a 2-pt white stroke.

▶ **Tip:** You can double-click the Eyedropper tool in the toolbar before sampling to change the attributes that the Eyedropper picks up and applies.

3 Click the Stroke color (■) in the Properties panel, and change the color to None (◻).

4 Select the Selection tool (▶) in the toolbar.

5 Choose Select > Deselect and then choose File > Save.

Creating a color group

In Illustrator, you can save colors in color groups, which consist of related color swatches in the Swatches panel. Organizing colors by use, such as grouping all colors for a logo, can be helpful for organization and more, as you'll soon see. Color groups cannot contain patterns, gradients, the None color, or the Registration color. Next, you'll create a color group of some of the swatches you've created to keep them organized.

1 Choose Window > Swatches to open the Swatches panel. In the Swatches panel, drag the bottom of the panel down to see more of the content.

2 Click the swatch named "Guitar Orange" to select it. Pressing the Shift key, click the swatch named "PANTONE 137 C" to select five color swatches.

3 Click the New Color Group button () at the bottom of the Swatches panel. Change Name to **Guitar colors** in the New Color Group dialog box, and click OK to save the group.

4 With the Selection tool (▶) selected, click a blank area of the Swatches panel to deselect all in the panel.

Each swatch in a color group can still be edited independently by double-clicking a swatch in the group and editing the values in the Swatch Options dialog box. You could also edit the colors in the group together by double-clicking the group folder icon.

5 Drag the swatch named "PANTONE 137 C" in the color group to the right of the PANTONE 137 C 70% swatch. Leave the Swatches panel open.

You can drag colors into or out of a color group. When dragging into a color group, make sure that you see a line appear on the right edge of a swatch within the group. Otherwise, you may drag the swatch to the wrong place. You can always choose Edit > Undo Move Swatches and try again.

Using the Color Guide panel for creative inspiration

The Color Guide panel can provide you with color inspiration as you create your artwork. You can use it to pick color tints, analogous colors, and much more, and then apply them directly to artwork, edit them using several methods, or save them as a group in the Swatches panel.

Next, you'll select a color from artwork and then use the Color Guide panel to create new colors based on that original color.

1   Choose 3 Cassette artwork from the Artboard Navigation menu in the lower-left corner of the Document window.

2   With the Selection tool (▶), click the green rounded rectangle. Make sure that the Fill box is selected toward the bottom of the toolbar.

3   Choose Window > Color Guide to open the panel.

4   In the Color Guide panel, click the Set Base Color To The Current Color button (▣) (circled in the figure).

The Color Guide panel suggests colors based on the color showing in the Set Base Color To The Current Color button. The colors you see in the Color Guide panel may differ from what you see in the figure. That's okay.

Next, you'll experiment with colors using harmony rules.

5   Choose Analogous from the Harmony Rules menu (circled in the first part of the following figure) in the Color Guide panel.

A base group of colors is created to the right of the base color (green), and a series of tints and shades of those colors appears in the body of the panel. There are lots of harmony rules to choose from, each instantly generating a color scheme based on any color you want. The base color you set (green) is the basis for generating the colors in the color scheme.

▶ **Tip:** You can also choose a different color variation (different from the default Tints/Shades), such as Show Warm/Cool, by clicking the Color Guide panel menu icon (▤) and choosing one.

6 Click the Save Color Group To Swatch Panel button () at the bottom of the Color Guide panel to save the base colors (the five colors at the top) in the Swatches panel as a group.

7 Click the X at the top of the Color Guide panel group to close it.

8 Choose Select > Deselect.

In the Swatches panel you should see the new group added. You may need to scroll down in the panel. Next you'll use colors in the group to change the appearance of the cassette artwork.

9 Close the Swatches panel group.

● **Note:** For more information about working with the Color Themes panel, search for "Color themes" in Illustrator Help (Help > Illustrator Help).

Working with Adobe Color Themes

The Adobe Color Themes panel (Window > Color Themes) displays color themes you have created and synced with your account on the Adobe Color website (color.adobe.com/create). The Adobe ID used in Illustrator is automatically used to sign in to the Adobe Color website, and the Adobe Color Themes panel is refreshed with your Adobe color themes.

Applying colors from the Color Guide panel

After creating colors with the Color Guide panel, you can either click a color in the Color Guide panel to apply it to selected artwork, or apply colors you saved in the Swatches panel as a color group. Next you'll apply a color from the color group to the cassette artwork and edit that color.

1 Click the yellow shape in the cassette artwork to select it.

2 Click the Fill box (□) in the Properties panel and click to apply the lighter blue swatch from the group you just saved.

3. To edit the lighter blue color, double-click the swatch in the panel. In the Swatch Options dialog box, select Global so any artwork will update if you change the color. Also, change the C (Cyan) value to **0**.

4. Click OK to make the change.

● **Note:** The color values you see may be a bit different and that's okay.

Using Recolor Artwork to edit colors in artwork

You can edit colors in selected artwork using the Recolor Artwork command. It's especially useful when global swatches weren't used in the artwork. Without using global colors in your artwork, updating a series of colors may take a lot of time. Using Recolor Artwork, you can edit colors, change the number of colors, map an existing color to a new color, and much more.

Next you'll edit the colors for cassette artwork that was created with colors that weren't global swatches.

1. Choose Select > All On Active Artboard to select all of the artwork.

2. Click the Recolor button in the Properties panel to open the Recolor Artwork dialog box.

▶ **Tip:** You can also choose Edit > Edit Colors > Recolor Artwork.

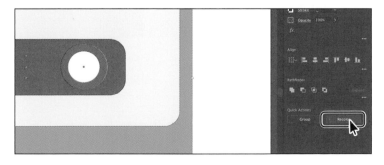

The options in the Recolor Artwork dialog box allow you to edit, reassign, or reduce the colors in your *selected* artwork and to create and edit color groups like those you created previously.

All of the color groups in the Swatches panel appear on the right side of the Recolor Artwork dialog box (in the Color Groups storage area). In the Recolor Artwork dialog box you can apply colors from these color groups to the selected artwork. In this part of the lesson, you'll simply edit the colors found in the selected cassette artwork.

3   In the Recolor Artwork dialog box, click the Hide Color Group Storage icon (◀) on the right side of the dialog box (an arrow is pointing to it in the following figure) to hide the color groups.

4   Click the Edit tab to edit the colors in the artwork using the color wheel.

You'll see the color wheel in the middle of the dialog, with the colors found in the selected cassette artwork represented on the color wheel as circles, called *markers*. You can edit the colors individually or together, and edit them visually or precisely using specific color values (found at the bottom of the dialog).

5   Make sure that the Link Harmony Colors icon is disabled so you can edit colors independently. The Link Harmony Colors icon should look like this: 🔗, not like this: 🔗. The lines between the color markers (circles) and the center of the color wheel should be dotted.

If the Link Harmony Colors option were on and if you were to edit one of the colors, the rest would change relative to the color you edited.

▶ **Tip:** You can save edited colors as a color group by clicking the Show Color Group Storage icon (▶) on the right side of the dialog box and then clicking the New Color Group button (🗔).

6   Click the yellow marker (circle) to select the color. Drag it away from the center of the color wheel into the light orange area to change the color.

Know that if you make a mistake when editing the colors and want to start over, you can click the Get Colors From Selected Art button (⬚) in the upper-right corner of the Recolor Artwork dialog box to reset the colors to their original values.

7 Click the green marker (circle) on the left side of the color wheel (circled in the following figure). This time, in order to change the color, you'll edit the actual color values.

8 Click the Color Mode icon (▤) to the right of the H, S, B values below the color wheel, and choose CMYK from the menu, if the CMYK sliders are not already visible.

9 Change the Y value to 15.

Notice that the marker has moved in the color wheel, and it's the only one that moved. That's because the Unlink Harmony Colors option is set.

10 Click OK in the Recolor Artwork dialog box.

11 Choose Select > Deselect and then choose File > Save.

Changing the number of colors in artwork

In the previous section, you learned that you can edit colors in existing selected artwork in the Recolor Artwork dialog box. You can also reduce the number of colors in artwork like a logo, maybe to use a single CMYK color with tints or to apply a Pantone color to artwork instead of CMYK. You can also "assign" colors from an existing color group to your artwork in the Recolor Artwork dialog box. Next, you'll recolor a pair of sunglasses.

1 Choose 4 Sunglasses artwork from the Artboard Navigation menu in the lower-left corner of the Document window.

2 With the Selection tool (▶) selected, click the green sunglasses to select them.

3 Click the Recolor button in the Properties panel to open the Recolor Artwork dialog box. Make sure that the Assign option is selected toward the top of the Recolor Artwork dialog box.

● **Note:** White, black, and grays are typically preserved, or unchanged.

The colors from the selected sunglasses artwork are listed in the Current Colors (4) column, in what is called *hue-forward* sorting. That means they are arranged, from top to bottom, in the ordering of the color wheel: red, orange, yellow, green, blue, indigo, and violet. The Current Colors column shows what the color originally was in the sunglasses artwork, and an arrow to the right of each of those colors points to the New column, which contains what the color has become (or has been *reassigned to*). In this example the colors in the sunglasses will be changed to a single color and tints of that color.

4 Choose 1 from the Colors menu to force the colors to "map" to the main green color.

In this case the green color is the color that the other colors are made from. Depending on how light the color is, a tint of the green is made for each. The darkest color (the red in this case), becomes the green, and the other colors are lighter versions or tints of the green.

To change the color from green to another color, you could edit the color using the CMYK sliders at the bottom of the dialog. In this case, you'll choose one of the swatches you've already created.

5   Double-click the green color in the New column to open the Color Picker (circled in the following figure).

6   In the Color Picker dialog box, click the Color Swatches button to see the color swatches found in the Swatches panel. Scroll in the list to find the Burnt Orange color and select it. Click OK to apply the color.

7   Click OK to close the Recolor Artwork dialog box.

8   Choose Select > Deselect and then choose File > Save.

There are a lot of color edits that can be made to selected artwork in the Recolor Artwork dialog box, including applying other colors (like Pantone colors), and much more. If you want a bit of practice, try selecting the purple sunglasses and editing the color!

9   Choose File > Close.

Assign colors to your artwork

To learn how to assign colors from a group to your artwork, check out the video *Convert colors to tints* that is part of the Web Edition. For more information, see the "Web Edition" section of "Getting Started" at the beginning of the book.

Working with Live Paint

Note: To learn more about Live Paint and all that it can do, search for "Live Paint groups" in Illustrator Help (Help > Illustrator Help).

Live Paint lets you paint vector graphics intuitively by automatically detecting and correcting gaps that might otherwise affect the application of fills and strokes. Paths divide the drawing surface into areas that can be colored, whether the area is bounded by a single path or by segments of multiple paths. Painting objects with Live Paint is like coloring in a coloring book or using watercolors to paint a sketch. The underlying shapes are not edited.

In this first part, you'll draw some artwork and then apply color using the Live Paint Bucket tool.

1   Choose File > Open, and open the L8_start2.ai file in the Lessons > Lesson08 folder.

2   Choose File > Save As. In the Save As dialog box, navigate to the Lesson08 folder, and name the file **GeoDesign.ai**. Leave Adobe Illustrator (ai) chosen from the Format menu (macOS) or Adobe Illustrator (*.AI) chosen from the Save As Type menu (Windows), and click Save.

3   In the Illustrator Options dialog box, leave the options at their default settings and then click OK.

4   Choose View > Fit All In Window.

5   Click to select the white rounded corner square on the top of the left artboard.

6   Press Command and + (macOS) or Ctrl and + (Windows) a few times to zoom in.

7   Choose Select > Deselect.

You'll draw a few lines so you can color parts of the logo with different colors using Live Paint.

8   Select the Line Segment tool (/) from the Rectangle tool (▢) group in the toolbar.

9   Press the D key to set the default fill of white and stroke of black for the lines you are about to draw.

10 Move the pointer over the top corner of the smaller black square. Drag up to make a line to the top corner of the larger white square.

11 Repeat this for the three other corners of the smaller black square (see the figure).

Creating a Live Paint group

Next you'll turn the logo artwork you just created into a Live Paint group.

1 Choose View > Outline to see the artwork in Outline mode.

2 Select the Selection tool (▶), and drag across the logo artwork to select it.

3 Choose View > Preview (or GPU Preview) to see the selected artwork.

4 Click Edit Toolbar (•••) at the bottom of the toolbar. Scroll in the menu that appears, and drag the Live Paint Bucket tool (🐾) into the toolbar on the left to add it to the list of tools. Make sure it's selected in the toolbar.

● **Note:** You may want to press the Escape key to hide the extra tools menu.

5 Click the Fill box in the Properties panel on the right to reveal a panel. Click the Swatches button (▣) at the top of the panel to see the swatches. Click to select the purple swatch named "Purple 1." Press the Escape key to hide the panel.

6 With the Live Paint Bucket tool selected, move the pointer over the smaller black square in the center of the selected artwork (see the first part of the following figure). Click to convert the selected shapes to a Live Paint group, and fill the shape with the purple color.

▶ **Tip:** You can convert selected artwork to a Live Paint group by choosing Object > Live Paint > Make.

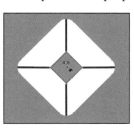

You can click any of the shapes to convert them to a Live Paint group. The shape you click is filled with the currently selected fill color of purple. Clicking selected shapes with the Live Paint Bucket tool creates a Live Paint group that you can paint with that same tool. Once a Live Paint group is created, the paths are fully editable, but they are treated like a group. Colors are automatically reapplied to new regions created when you move or adjust a path's shape.

Painting with the Live Paint Bucket tool

After objects are converted to a Live Paint group, you can paint them using several methods, which is what you'll do next.

1   Move the pointer over the area you see in the first part of the following figure.

    A red highlight appears around the area that will be painted, and three color swatches appear above the pointer. The selected color (Purple 1) is in the middle, and the two adjacent colors in the Swatches panel are on either side.

● **Note:** As you press the arrow key to change colors, the color is highlighted in the Swatches panel. You can press the Up Arrow or Down Arrow key, along with the Right Arrow or Left Arrow key to select a new swatch to paint with.

2   Open the Swatches panel by choosing Window > Swatches.

    In the next step, you'll switch colors by pressing an arrow key. As you press the key, look in the Swatches panel to see the selected color swatch change.

3   Press the Right Arrow key once to select the Purple 2 swatch (shown in the three swatches above the pointer). You can see that the Purple 2 swatch is now selected in the Swatches panel. Click to apply the color to the area.

4   Press the Right Arrow key once to select the Purple 3 swatch (shown in the three swatches above the pointer). Click to apply the color to the right of the center square. See the following figure.

5   Click the Fill box in the Properties panel on the right, and click to select the swatch named "Purple 2" again. Press the Escape key to hide the panel. Click in the area below and to the right of the center shape.

6   Click the Fill box in the Properties panel on the right, and click to select the swatch named "Purple 4." Press the Escape key to hide the panel. Click in the area below and to the left of the center shape. See the last part of the following figure.

By default, you can paint only fills with the Live Paint Bucket tool. Next, you'll see how to paint strokes with the Live Paint Bucket tool.

7 Double-click the Live Paint Bucket tool (🔲) in the toolbar. This opens the Live Paint Bucket Options dialog box. Select the Paint Strokes option and then click OK.

▶ **Tip:** With the live Paint Bucket tool selected in the toolbar, and nothing else selected in the Document window, you can also click the Tool Options button at the top of the Properties panel to open the Live Paint Bucket Options dialog box.

8 Click the Stroke color box in the Properties panel (🔲) on the right, and select None (⬜) for the stroke color, if it isn't already selected. Press the Escape key to hide the panel.

9 Move the pointer over any black stroke in the middle of the logo artwork, as shown in the figure. When the pointer changes to a paintbrush (🖊), click the stroke to remove the stroke color (by applying the None swatch). Do the same for the three other strokes (see the last part of the following figure).

10 Close the Swatches panel group.

11 Choose Select > Deselect and then choose File > Save.

Modifying a Live Paint group

When you make a Live Paint group, each path remains editable. When you move or adjust a path, the colors that were previously applied don't just stay where they were, as they do in natural media paintings or with image-editing software. Instead, the colors are automatically reapplied to the new regions that are formed by the intersecting paths. Next you'll edit a path in another Live Paint group you create.

1 Choose View > Fit Artboard In Window.

2 Select the Selection tool (▶). Click the light purple rectangle shape in the background of the artboard on the left.

3 Choose Object > Live Paint > Make.

● **Note:** The purple path is a line with a large stroke. To select it, you'll need to click in the middle of the path, not just anywhere in the purple.

4 With the Selection tool, Shift-click the purple path going across the background to select both objects.

5 Choose Object > Live Paint > Merge to add the new purple path to the Live Paint group.

6 Select the Live Paint Bucket tool (🖥) in the toolbar. Click the Fill color box in the Properties panel and select a white color. Move the pointer over the purple background below the purple line. When you see a red outline, click to paint it white.

7 Select the Selection tool, and with the Live Paint object selected, double-click the Live Paint object to enter isolation mode.

8 Select the Direct Selection tool. Move the pointer over the left anchor point on the purple line and click to select it. Drag the point up to reshape it.

Notice that the color fill and stroke changes every time you release the mouse button.

9 Choose Select > Deselect and then press the Escape key to exit isolation mode.

10 Choose File > Save and then choose File > Close.

Review questions

1 Describe what a *global color* is.

2 How can you save a color?

3 Describe what a *tint* is.

4 How can you choose color harmonies for color inspiration?

5 Name two things that the Recolor Artwork dialog box allows you to do.

6 Explain what Live Paint allows you to do.

Review answers

1 A global color is a color swatch that, when you edit it, automatically updates all artwork to which it is applied. All spot colors are global; however, process colors you save as swatches are global by default, but they can be either global or nonglobal.

2 You can save a color for painting other objects in your artwork by adding it to the Swatches panel by doing one of the following:

   • Drag the color from a Fill box, and drop it over the Swatches panel.

   • Click the New Swatch button (▤) at the bottom of the Swatches panel.

   • Choose New Swatch from the Swatches panel menu (▤).

   • Choose Create New Swatch from the Color panel menu (▤).

3 A *tint* is a mixture of a color with white to make the color lighter. You can create a tint from a global process color, like CMYK, or from a spot color.

4 You can choose color harmonies from the Color Guide panel. Color harmonies are used to generate a color scheme based on a single color.

5 You use the Recolor Artwork dialog box to change the colors used in selected artwork, create and edit color groups, or reassign or reduce the colors in your artwork, among other functions.

6 Live Paint lets you paint vector graphics intuitively by automatically detecting and correcting gaps that might otherwise affect the application of fills and strokes. Paths divide the drawing surface into areas, any of which can be colored, regardless of whether the area is bounded by a single path or by segments of multiple paths.

9 ADDING TYPE TO A POSTER

Lesson overview

In this lesson, you'll learn how to do the following:

- Create and edit area and point type.
- Import text.
- Change text formatting.
- Fix missing fonts. ◼
- Modify text with the Touch Type tool.
- Work with glyphs. ◼
- Create columns of text.
- Create and edit paragraph and character styles.
- Wrap type around an object.
- Reshape text with a warp.
- Create type on a path.
- Create text outlines.

This lesson will take about 75 minutes to complete. To get the lesson files used in this chapter, download them from the web page for this book at www.adobepress.com/IllustratorCIB2020. For more information, see "Accessing the lesson files and Web Edition" in the Getting Started section at the beginning of this book.

STRAWBERRY LEMONADE

SERVES: 6-8   TIME: 15 min   ● ● ●

INGREDIENTS:

1 cup freshly squeezed lemons (6-7 lemons)
lemon slices (1 lemon)

4 cups fresh strawberries
1/2 cup honey
5 cups water
1 cup ice

DIRECTIONS:

Lorem ipsum dolor sit amet, consectetuer adipiscing elit, sed diam nonummy nibh euismod tincidunt ut laoreet dolore magna aliquam erat vo. Lorem ipsum dolor sit amet, tincidunt ut laoreet dolore magna aliquam erat volutpat.

Ut wisi enim ad minim veniam, quis nostrud exerci tation ullamcorper suscipit lobortis nisl ut aliquip ex ea commodo consequat.

Duis autem vel eum iriure dolor in hendrerit in vulputate velit esse molestie consequat, vel illum dolore eu blandit praesent luptatum zzril delenit augue duis dolore te feugait nulla

---

SERVES: 6-8   ● ●   TIME: 15 min

GRILLED RAINBOW TROUT

GOOD FOR YOU
OMEGA

INGREDIENTS:

4 2 lb. rainbow trout
2 tbs. roughly chopped rosemary
12 sprigs fresh rosemary
2 tbs. roughly chopped thyme
12 sprigs fresh thyme
3 garlic cloves
2 lemons sliced in rounds
1/2 cup olive oil
salt & pepper

DIRECTIONS:

Lorem ipsum dolor sit amet, consectetuer adipiscing elit, sed diam nonummy nibh euismod tincidunt ut laoreet dolore magna aliquam erat vo. Lorem ipsum dolor sit amet, tincidunt ut laoreet dolore magna aliquam erat volutpat.

Ut wisi enim ad minim veniam, quis nostrud exerci tation ullamcorper suscipit lobortis nisl ut aliquip ex ea commodo consequat.

Duis autem vel eum iriure dolor in hendrerit in vulputate velit esse molestie consequat, vel illum dolore eu blandit praesent luptatum zzril delenit augue duis dolore te feugait nulla facilisi.

Text is an important design element in your illustrations. Like other objects, type can be painted, scaled, rotated, and more. In this lesson, you'll create basic text and add interesting text effects.

Starting the lesson

You'll be adding type to recipe cards during this lesson, but before you begin, restore the default preferences for Adobe Illustrator. Then open the finished art file for this lesson to see the illustration.

● **Note:** If you have not already downloaded the project files for this lesson to your computer from your Account page, make sure to do so now. See the "Getting Started" section at the beginning of the book.

1 To ensure that the tools function and the defaults are set exactly as described in this lesson, delete or deactivate (by renaming) the Adobe Illustrator preferences file. See "Restoring default preferences" in the "Getting Started" section at the beginning of the book.

2 Start Adobe Illustrator.

3 Choose File > Open. Locate the file named L9_end.ai in the Lessons > Lesson09 folder. Click Open.

You will most likely see a Missing Fonts dialog box since the file is using specific Adobe fonts. Simply click Close in the Missing Fonts dialog box. You will learn all about Adobe fonts later in this lesson.

Leave the file open for reference later in the lesson, if you like. I closed it.

4 Choose File > Open. In the Open dialog box, navigate to the Lessons > Lesson09 folder, and select the L9_start.ai file on your hard disk. Click Open to open the file.

This file already has non-text components in it. You will add all of the text elements to complete the cards.

5 Choose File > Save As. In the Save As dialog box, navigate to the Lesson09 folder, and name the file **Recipes.ai**. Leave Adobe Illustrator (ai) chosen from the Format menu (macOS) or Adobe Illustrator (*.AI) chosen from the Save As Type menu (Windows), and click Save.

● **Note:** If you don't see Reset Essentials in the Workspace menu, choose Window > Workspace > Essentials before choosing Window > Workspace > Reset Essentials.

6 In the Illustrator Options dialog box, leave the Illustrator options at their default settings and then click OK.

7 Choose Window > Workspace > Reset Essentials.

Adding type to the recipe card

Type features are some of the most powerful tools in Illustrator. As in Adobe InDesign, you can create columns and rows of text, place text, flow text into a shape or along a path, work with letterforms as graphic objects, and more. In Illustrator, you can create text in three main ways: as point type, area type, and type on a path.

Adding text at a point

Point type is a horizontal or vertical line of text that begins where you click and expands as you enter characters. Each line of text is independent—the line expands or shrinks as you edit it but doesn't wrap to the next line unless you add a paragraph return or a soft return. Entering text this way is useful for adding a headline or a few words to your artwork. Next, you'll add some text to one of the recipe cards as point type.

1 Ensure that Artboard 1 is chosen in the Artboard Navigation menu in the lower-left corner of the Document window. Choose View > Fit Artboard In Window.

2 Press Command and + (macOS) or Ctrl and + (Windows) to zoom in.

3 Select the Type tool (**T**) in the toolbar on the left. Click (*don't drag*) in between the dashed lines as you see in the figure. Some placeholder text, "Lorem ipsum," is now on the artboard and is automatically selected. Type **SERVES: 6-8**.

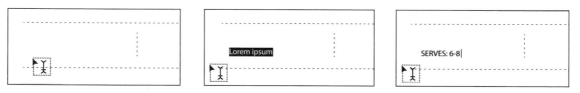

4 Select the Selection tool (▶) in the toolbar, and drag the lower-right bounding point of the text down and to the left.

Scaling point type this way will stretch the text if you drag any bounding point. This may result in a font size that is not a round number (12.93 pt, for instance).

5 Choose Edit > Undo Scale and drag the text into the position you see in the figure.

6 In order to practice adding text, select the Type tool (**T**) and click in the area just to the right to add more text. Type **TIME: 15 min**.

Adding area type

Area type uses the boundaries of an object (like a rectangle) to control the flow of characters, either horizontally or vertically. When the text reaches a boundary, it automatically wraps to fit inside the defined area. Entering text in this way is useful when you want to create one or more paragraphs, such as for a poster or a brochure.

To create area type, you click with the Type tool (**T**) where you want the text and drag to create an area type object (also called a *type object, text area*, or *text object*). You can also convert an existing shape or object to a type object by clicking the edge of an object with the Type tool. When the insertion point appears, you can type. Next, you'll create a type object and enter more text.

1 Select the Type tool (**T**) and move the pointer into the empty area at the top of the artboard. Press and drag down and to the right to create a type object that is about an inch in width; the height should roughly match the following figure.

By default, type objects are filled with selected placeholder text that you can replace with your own.

2 With the placeholder text selected, type **STRAWBERRY LEMONADE**.

Notice how the text wraps horizontally to fit within the type object.

3 Select the Selection tool (▶), and drag the lower-right bounding point to the left and then back to the right to see how the text wraps within.

You can drag any of the eight bounding points on the type object to resize it, not just the lower right.

4 Drag the same point to make the type object shorter, so you still see all of the text and it wraps as you see in the figure.

Working with Auto Sizing

By default, when you create area type by dragging with the Type tool, the type object will not resize to fit the text within (similar to how InDesign treats text frames). If there is too much text, any text that doesn't fit will be considered overset text and will not be visible. For each type area object, you can enable a feature called *Auto Sizing* so that the area type object will resize to fit the text within, which is what you'll do next.

1   Look at the bottom-middle bounding point of the text object and you'll see a widget (⬙), which means the type object is not set to auto size.

2   Move the pointer over the box at the end of the widget (the pointer will change [⬙]), and double-click.

    By double-clicking the widget, you turned Auto Sizing on. The text bounding box should now fit snugly around the text within.

● **Note:** The figure shows the type object prior to double-clicking.

▶ **Tip:** If Auto Sizing is enabled for a selected type area object, dragging down one of the bottom bounding points on the type object disables Auto Sizing for the type object.

3   Select the Type tool (T), and move the pointer *immediately after* the word "LEMONADE." Make sure you see this pointer (Ɪ), not this pointer (⬚Ɪ⬚). Click to insert the cursor. Press Return or Enter, and type **WITH MINT**.

    As the text is edited and re-edited, the frame shrinks and grows vertically (only) to accommodate the changing amount of copy. It also eliminates overset text (text that won't fit) without manually sizing and resizing frames.

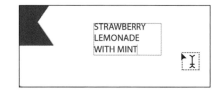

● **Note:** In this instance, if you click when you see this pointer (⬚Ɪ⬚) you'll create a new point type object.

4   Click within the text to insert the cursor, then click three times to select the line "WITH MINT." Press Delete or Backspace to remove it.

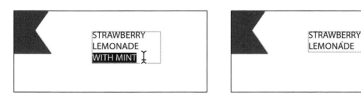

The type object will expand or shrink vertically to fit the text. If you were to double-click the Auto Sizing widget, Auto Sizing would be turned off for the area type. The type object would then remain the current size no matter how much text was added.

5   Choose Select > Deselect and then File > Save.

Converting between area type and point type

You can easily convert between area type objects and point type objects. This can be useful if you type a headline by clicking, which creates point type, but later want to resize and add more text without stretching the text inside. This method is also useful if you paste text from InDesign into Illustrator because text pasted from InDesign into Illustrator (with nothing selected) is pasted as point type. Most of the time, it would work better as an area type object so that the text could flow within. Next, you will convert a type object from area type to point type.

1   Choose View > Fit Artboard In Window.

2   With the Type tool selected in the toolbar, above the red banner on the left, press and drag to create a type area object. Type **fresh**.

This text will be placed on the red banner and would work better if it were point type. You'll adjust the size of the text to fit in the banner, and that will be easier if you can simply drag a corner to resize the text.

3   Press the Escape key to select the Selection tool (▶).

4   Move the pointer over the annotator (─●) off the right edge of the type object. A filled end on the annotator indicates that it's area type. When the pointer changes (▶ᴛ), double-click the annotator to convert the area type to point type.

The annotator end should now be hollow (─○), indicating that it is a point type object. If you were to resize the bounding box, the text would scale as well. With a type object selected, you can also choose Type > Convert To Point Type or Convert To Area Type, depending on what the selected type object is.

5   Drag the text onto the red banner.

6   Press the Shift key, and drag the lower-right bounding point down and to the right until the text just fits between the line above and the line below. Release the mouse button and then the key.

Because the text is point type, it stretches when the type object is resized. Pressing the Shift key is very important because otherwise the text would likely be distorted.

Importing a plain-text file

You can import text into artwork from a file that was created in another application. As of the writing of this book, Illustrator supports DOC, DOCX, RTF, Plain text (ASCII) with ANSI, Unicode, Shift JIS, GB2312, Chinese Big 5, Cyrillic, GB18030, Greek, Turkish, Baltic, and Central European encoding. One of the advantages of importing text from a file, rather than copying and pasting it, is that imported text retains its character and paragraph formatting (by default). For example, text from an RTF file retains its font and style specifications in Illustrator, unless you choose to remove formatting when you import the text. In this section, you'll place text from a plain-text file into your design.

1 Choose Artboard 2 in the Artboard Navigation menu in the lower-left corner of the Document window to switch to another recipe.

2 Choose Select > Deselect.

3 Choose File > Place. In the Lessons > Lesson09 folder, select the L9_text.txt file. In the Place dialog box on macOS, click the Options button to see the import options, if necessary. Select Show Import Options, and click Place.

In the Text Import Options dialog box that appears, you can set some options prior to importing text.

4 Leave the default settings and then click OK.

5 Move the loaded text icon into the lower-left part of the artboard, below the dotted line. Press and drag down and to the right and then release the mouse button. Use the figure as a guide.

 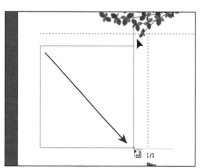

If you were to simply click with the loaded text pointer, a type object would be created that is smaller than the size of the artboard.

6 Choose File > Save.

▶ **Tip:** When you place (File > Place) RTF (Rich Text Format) or Word documents (DOC or DOCX) in Illustrator, the Microsoft Word Options dialog box appears. In the Microsoft Word Options dialog box, you can select to keep the generated table of contents, footnotes and endnotes, and index text, and you can even choose to remove the formatting of the text before you place it (the styles and formatting are brought in from Word by default).

▶ **Tip:** You can place text into an existing type object as well.

Threading text

When working with area type (*not* point type), each area type object contains an *in port* and an *out port*. The ports enable you to link type objects and flow text between them.

In port → Some Street Hometown ← Out port

An empty out port indicates that all the text is visible and that the type object isn't linked. An arrow in a port indicates that the type object is linked to another type object. A red plus sign (⊞) in an out port indicates that the object contains additional text, which is called *overflow text*. To show all of the overflow text, you can adjust the text, resize the type object, or thread the text to another type object. To *thread*, or continue, text from one object to the next, you have to link the objects. Linked type objects can be of any shape; however, the text must be entered in an object or along a path, not as point type (by simply clicking to create text).

Next, you'll thread text between two type objects.

● **Note:** If you double-click an out port, a new type object appears. If this happens, you can either drag the new object where you would like it to be positioned or choose Edit > Undo Link Threaded Text, and the loaded text icon will reappear.

1 With the Selection tool (▶), click the out port (⊞) in the lower-right corner of the type object you just created. After releasing the mouse button, move the pointer away.

The pointer changes to a loaded text icon (⌷) when you move it away from the original type object.

2 Move the pointer to the right, aligned with the top edge of the text object you just created. A horizontal Smart Guide will show when the pointer is aligned with the top edge of the text object. Click to create an area type object that is the same size as the original.

▶ **Tip:** Another way to thread text between objects is to select an area type object, select the object (or objects) you want to link to, and then choose Type > Threaded Text > Create.

With the second type object still selected, notice the line connecting the two type objects. This (non-printing) line is the *thread* that tells you that the two objects are connected. If you don't see this thread (line), choose View > Show Text Threads.

The out port (▶) of the top type object on the artboard and the in port (▶) of the bottom type object on the artboard have small arrows in them indicating how the text is flowing from one to the other.

3 With the second type object still selected, drag the right-middle point to the right to make it as wide as you see in the figure. Leave the text object selected.

The text will flow between the type objects. If you delete the second type object, the text is pulled back into the original object as overflow text. Although not visible, the overflow text isn't deleted.

Formatting type

You can format text using character and paragraph formatting, apply fill and stroke attributes to it, and change its transparency. You can apply these changes to one character, a range of characters, or all characters in a type object that you select. As you'll soon see, selecting the type object, rather than selecting the text inside, lets you apply formatting options to all of the text in the object, including options from the Character and Paragraph panels, fill and stroke attributes, and transparency settings.

In this section, you'll discover how to change text attributes, such as size and font, and later learn how to save that formatting as text styles.

Changing font family and font style

In this section, you'll apply a font to text. Aside from applying local fonts to text from your machine, Creative Cloud members have access to a library of fonts for use in desktop applications such as InDesign or Microsoft Word and on websites. Trial Creative Cloud members have access to a selection of fonts from Adobe for web and desktop use. Fonts you choose are activated and appear alongside other locally installed fonts in the fonts list in Illustrator. By default, Adobe fonts are turned on in the Creative Cloud desktop application so that it can activate fonts and make them available in your desktop applications.

▶ **Tip:** For general help with fonts, you can visit: fonts.adobe.com/help.

● **Note:** The Creative Cloud desktop application must be installed on your computer, and you must have an internet connection to initially activate fonts. The Creative Cloud desktop application is installed when you install your first Creative Cloud application, like Illustrator.

Activating Adobe Fonts

Note: For questions about Adobe Fonts licensing, visit helpx. adobe.com/fonts/using/ font-licensing.html. For more information on working with Adobe fonts, visit helpx.adobe. com/creative-cloud/ help/add-fonts.html.

Note: To learn about the Creative Cloud desktop application, visit www.adobe.com/ creativecloud/desktop-app.html.

Next, you'll select and activate Adobe fonts so that you can use them in your project.

1 Ensure that the Creative Cloud desktop application has been launched and you are signed in with your Adobe ID (*this requires an internet connection*).

2 Select the Type tool (**T**) in the toolbar, move the pointer over the text in either threaded type object, and click to insert the cursor.

3 Choose Select > All or press Command+A (macOS) or Ctrl+A (Windows) to select all of the text in both threaded type objects.

4 In the Properties panel, click the arrow to the right of the Font Family menu, and notice the fonts that appear in the menu.

The fonts you see by default are those that are installed locally. In the font menu, an icon appears to the right of the font names in the list indicating what type of font it is ($\bigcirc$ is an activated Adobe font, O is OpenType, $\overset{\tiny{VAR}}{\mathbf{G}}$ is a variable font, $\overset{\tiny{SVG}}{\mathbf{G}}$ is an SVG font, **T** is TrueType, and $\boldsymbol{a}$ is Adobe Postscript).

5 Click Find More to see a list of Adobe fonts you can choose from.

The menu content may take a few seconds to initialize. My list will look different from yours since Adobe is constantly updating the fonts available.

6 Click the Filter Fonts icon (▼) to open a menu. You can filter the font list by selecting classification and properties criteria. Click the Sans Serif option under Classification to filter the fonts.

7   Scroll down in the font list to find Montserrat Light. Click the arrow to the left of "Montserrat," if necessary, to see the font styles.

Tip: Instead of scrolling in the font list, you can also begin typing "Mont..." in the Font Family field to see all of the styles.

8   Click the Activate icon (△) to the far right of the name "Montserrat Light."

If you see this icon: (◇), or when the pointer is over the font name in the list, this icon: (◒), the font is already activated, so you don't need to do anything in this step.

Tip: The fonts are activated on all computers where you've installed the Creative Cloud application and logged in. To view fonts you've activated, open the Creative Cloud desktop application and click the Fonts icon (f) in the upper-right.

9   Click OK in the dialog box that appears.

10 Click the Activate button (△) to the far right of the name "Montserrat Medium." Click OK in the dialog box that appears.

11 Next, find the Oswald Regular font in the font list and then click Activate (△) to the far right of the font name to activate it. Click OK in the warning dialog box that appears.

12 Click the Activate button (△) to the far right of the name "Oswald Light." Click OK in the warning dialog box that appears.

Once the fonts are activated (be patient; it may take some time), you may begin to use them.

13 After activating the fonts, click the words "Clear All" toward the top of the menu to remove the Sans Serif filtering and see all of the fonts again.

Applying fonts to text in Illustrator

Now that the Adobe fonts are activated, you can use them in any application. That's what you'll do next.

1 With the threaded text still selected, and the Font Family menu still showing, click the Show Activated Fonts button (⬤) to filter the font list and show only activated Adobe fonts.

The list in the figure may be different than yours and that's okay as long as you see the Montserrat and Oswald fonts.

▶ **Tip:** When viewing any fonts in the Font Family menu (not just Adobe fonts), you can also use the Up Arrow and Down Arrow keys to navigate the list of fonts. When the font you want is chosen, you can press Enter or Return to apply it if it's not an Adobe font.

2 Move the pointer over the fonts in the menu. You should see a preview of the font the pointer is over, which is applied to the selected text. Click the arrow to the left of Montserrat in the menu, and choose Light (or Montserrat Light).

3 Choose 1 Artboard 1 from the Artboard Navigation menu in the lower-left corner of the Document window.

4 With the Selection tool (▶) selected, click the "STRAWBERRY LEMONADE" text toward the top of the artboard to select the type object.

If you want to apply the same font to all of the text in a point type or area type object, you can simply select the object, not the text, and then apply the font.

▶ **Tip:** With the cursor in the Font Name field, you can also click the X on the right side of the Font Family field to clear the search field.

5 With the type object selected, click the font name in the Properties panel (I see Myriad Pro). Begin typing the letters **monts**.

A menu appears beneath where you are typing. Illustrator filters through the list of fonts and displays the font names that contain "monts," regardless of where "monts" is in the font name and regardless of whether it's capitalized. The Show Activated Fonts () filter is still turned on from before, so you'll turn it off next.

6   Click Clear Filter (◉) in the menu that is showing to see all of the available Adobe fonts. In the menu that appears beneath where you are typing, move the pointer over the fonts in the list (my list will be different from yours because of the other fonts I already had activated). Illustrator shows a live font preview of the text.

▶ **Tip:** You can click the Eyeglass icon (Q) to the left of the Font Name field and choose to search the first word only. You can also open the Character panel (Window > Type > Character) and search for a font on your system by typing the font name.

7   Click to select Montserrat Medium to apply the font. You may need to resize the text area to see each word on its own line.

8   Click the "fresh" text. To select other text objects, press the Shift key and click the "SERVES: 6-8" text and then click the "TIME: 15 min" text.

9   With the type objects selected, click the font name in the Properties panel and type the letters **osw** (for Oswald). Select the Oswald Light font to apply it.

Fixing missing fonts ▰◀

To learn how to fix missing fonts, check out the video *Fixing Missing Fonts* that is part of the Web Edition. For more information, see the "Web Edition" section of "Getting Started" at the beginning of the book.

Changing font size

By default, typeface size is measured in points (a point equals 1/72 of an inch). In this section, you will change the font size of text and also see what happens to point type that is scaled.

1   Click to select the type object that contains the "STRAWBERRY LEMONADE" text.

Note: After resizing, your text may look different than what you see in the figure. You may need to drag the lower-right bounding point to resize the text frame to see all of the text.

2   Choose 48 pt from the Font Size menu in the Properties panel.

3   Drag the middle bounding point on the right edge of the text frame to the right to fit the text better.

Tip: You can dynamically change the font size of selected text using keyboard shortcuts. To increase the font size in increments of 2 points, press Command+Shift+> (macOS) or Ctrl+Shift+> (Windows). To reduce the font size, press Command+Shift+< (macOS) or Ctrl+Shift+< (Windows).

4   Click the up arrow to the left of the font size field in the Properties panel several times to make the font size 52.

Drag the right edge of the text frame again to make it larger if the text doesn't fit. Make sure you see STRAWBERRY on one line and LEMONADE on the next line.

5   Click in the "fresh" text to select the text object.

Looking in the Character section of the Properties panel, you'll see that the font size is not a whole number (see the first part of the following figure). That's because you scaled the point type earlier by dragging.

6   Choose 48 pt from the Font Size menu. Leave the "fresh" text selected.

Changing font color

You can change the appearance of text by applying fills, strokes, and more. In this section, you'll simply change the fill of selected text by selecting type objects. Know that you can also select text with the Type tool to apply different color fills and strokes to text.

1 With the text object still selected, click the Fill box in the Properties panel. With the Swatches option (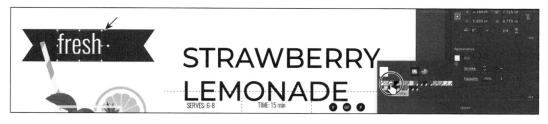) selected in the panel, select the white swatch.

2 Click the STRAWBERRY LEMONADE type object.

3 Click the Fill color box in the Properties panel. With the Swatches option (▦) selected in the panel that appears, select the red swatch named "Strawberry."

4 Choose Select > Deselect and then choose File > Save.

Changing additional character formatting

In Illustrator you can change a lot of text attributes besides font, font size, and color. As in InDesign, text attributes are split between character and paragraph formatting and can be found in the Properties panel, Control panel, and two main panels: the Character panel and the Paragraph panel. The Character panel, which you can access by clicking More Options (•••) in the Character section of the Properties panel or by choosing Window > Type > Character, contains formatting for selected text such as font, font size, kerning, and more. In this section, you will apply some of the many possible attributes to experiment with the different ways you can format text.

1 With the Selection tool (▶) selected, click the STRAWBERRY LEMONADE type object.

2 In the Properties panel, change Leading (▦) to 52 pt by selecting the value and typing **52**. Press Return or Enter to accept the value.

> ▶ **Tip:** By default, text is set to a value called Auto for leading. When looking at the Leading value in the Properties panel, you can tell it's set to Auto if the value has parentheses around it (). To return the leading to the default auto value, choose Auto from the Leading menu.

Leading is the vertical space between lines of text. Adjusting the leading can be useful for fitting text into a type object.

Note: If the text wraps differently in the type object, select the Selection tool and drag the middle-right point of the type object left or right to match the figure.

3   Click the "fresh" text to select the text object.

4   With the text selected, click More Options ( ) (circled in the following figure) in the Character section of the Properties panel to show the Character panel. Click the ALL CAPS button ( ) to capitalize the word.

Next, you'll align the "FRESH" text to the red banner and then rotate them both.

5   To align the text to the banner, drag the text object approximately into the center of the banner.

6   Shift-click the red banner to select it as well.

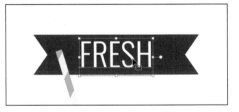

7   To rotate the banner, move the pointer off of a corner and drag when you see the rotate arrows (↻). Rotate it so it looks something like the figure.

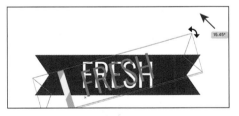

Changing paragraph formatting

As with character formatting, you can set paragraph formatting, such as alignment or indenting, before you enter new type or change the appearance of existing type. Paragraph formatting applies to entire paragraphs rather than just selected content. Most of this type of formatting can be done in the Properties panel, Control panel, or Paragraph panel. You can access the Paragraph panel options by clicking More Options (●●●) in the Paragraph section of the Properties panel or by choosing Window > Type > Paragraph.

1 Choose 2 Artboard 2 from the Artboard Navigation menu in the lower-left corner of the Document window.

2 With the Type tool (T) selected, click in the threaded text toward the bottom of the artboard. Press Command+A (macOS) or Ctrl+A (Windows) to select all of the text between the two type objects.

3 With the text selected, click More Options (●●●) in the Paragraph section of the Properties panel to show the Paragraph panel options.

4 Change Space After Paragraph (▣) to **6 pt** in the Paragraph panel.

Setting a spacing value after paragraphs, rather than pressing the Enter or Return key, helps you maintain consistency and makes editing easier.

5 Press the Escape key to hide the Paragraph panel.

6 Choose 10 pt from the Font Size menu in the Properties panel.

7 Choose Select > Deselect and then choose File > Save.

If you see the overset text icon (⊞) in the bottom type object, don't worry about it for now. We'll address that later.

Modifying text with the Touch Type tool

Using the Touch Type tool (🔲), you can modify the properties of a character, such as size, scale, and rotation, using a mouse pointer or touch controls. This is a very visual (and in my opinion, more enjoyable) way to apply character formatting properties: baseline shift, horizontal and vertical scale, rotation, and kerning. Next you'll modify letters in the "LEMONADE" heading.

1   Click the Previous artboard button (◀) at the bottom of the Document window to return to the first artboard with the lemonade.

2   With the Selection tool (▶), click to select the "STRAWBERRY LEMONADE" type object you created earlier. Drag it into position, as in the following figure.

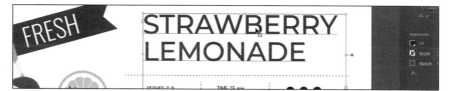

3   Choose View > Zoom In a few times.

● **Note:** Your list of tools in the toolbar may be different and that's okay.

4   Click Edit Toolbar (•••) at the bottom of the toolbar. Scroll in the menu that appears in the section labeled "Type." Drag the Touch Type tool (🔲) onto the Type tool (T) in the toolbar on the left to add it to the list of tools.

After selecting the Touch Type tool, a message briefly appears at the top of the Document window telling you to click a character to select it.

5   Click the letter "M" in "LEMONADE" to select it.

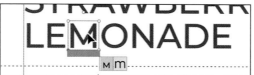

A box appears around the letter after you select it. The different points around the box allow you to adjust the character in different ways.

▶ **Tip:** You can also nudge a selected letter with the arrow keys or press Shift+arrow key to move the letter in bigger increments.

6   Drag the letter "M" down a little to reposition it.

There are limits to how far you can drag in any direction. Those limits are based on the kerning and baseline shift value limits.

7 Click the "N" in "LEMONADE" to select it. Move the pointer over the rotate handle (the rotate circle above the letter "N"). When the pointer changes (↶), drag clockwise until you see approximately –10° in the measurement label.

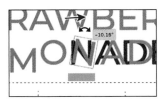

8 Drag the letter N down a little to reposition it.

If you want, you can experiment with the rest of the letters. Just know that your text may not match the figures going forward.

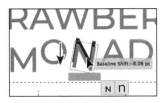

9 Choose Select > Deselect.

Working with glyphs ▮◀

To learn about working with the Glyphs panel, check out the video *Working with the Glyphs Panel*, which you'll find in the Web Edition. For more information, see the "Web Edition" section of "Getting Started" at the beginning of the book.

Resizing and reshaping type objects

You can create unique type object shapes by reshaping them using a variety of methods, including adding columns to area type objects or reshaping type objects using the Direct Selection tool. To start this section, you'll place some more text on artboard 1 so you have more text to work with.

1 Choose View > Fit Artboard In Window.

2 Select the Selection tool (▶) (or press the letter V to select it).

3 Choose File > Place. In the Lessons > Lesson09 folder, select the L9_column_text.txt file. In the Place dialog box on macOS, ensure that Show Import Options is *not* selected, and click Place.

● **Note:** If the Text Import Options dialog opens, click OK.

4 Move the loaded text icon to where you see it in the figure. Press and drag down and to the right and then release the mouse button. Use the figure as a guide. Leave the text object selected.

5 Choose File > Save.

Creating columns of text

You can easily create columns and rows of text by using the Type > Area Type Options command. This can be useful for creating a single type object with multiple columns or for organizing text, such as a table or simple chart, for instance. Next, you'll add a few columns to a type object.

▶ **Tip:** To learn more about the large number of options in the Area Type Options dialog box, search for "Creating Text" in Illustrator Help (Help > Illustrator Help).

1 With the Selection tool (▶) selected, and the text you just placed selected, choose Type > Area Type Options. In the Area Type Options dialog box, change Number to **2** in the Columns section, and select Preview. Click OK.

The text is now flowing between two columns.

2 Drag the bottom-middle bounding point up and down to see the text flow between the columns and the threaded text below it. Drag so the text is split between the columns evenly.

Reshaping type objects

In this next section, you'll reshape and resize a type object to better fit text.

1 With the Selection tool (▶), click the text object with the "Directions…" text.

2 Press Command and + (macOS) or Ctrl and + (Windows) a few times to zoom in to the selected type object.

3 Select the Direct Selection tool (▷). Click the lower-left corner of the type object to select the anchor point.

4 Begin dragging that point to the right to adjust the shape of the path so the text goes around the lemon artwork. As you drag, press the Shift key. Release the mouse button and then the Shift key when finished.

Sampling text formatting

Using the Eyedropper tool (🖊), you can quickly sample type attributes and copy them to text without having to create a type style.

1. To see everything, choose View > Fit All In Window.

2. Select the Type tool (**T**) by pressing and holding down on the Touch Type tool (🗇) in the toolbar and selecting the Type tool. Click in an empty area just above the fish on the artboard on the right. Type **GRILLED**.

3. Press the Escape key to select the text object and Selection tool.

4. To sample and apply formatting from other text, select the Eyedropper tool (🖊) in the toolbar, and click one of the letters in the "STRAWBERRY" text on the artboard on the left to apply the same formatting to the selected text.

   Be careful not to click the letters in the word "LEMONADE" you adjusted with the Touch Type tool; otherwise, those adjustments would also be sampled.

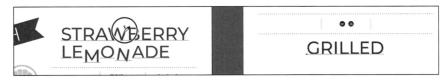

5. In the Properties panel, click the Fill box and select the color swatch named "Brown" to apply it.

6. Choose Select > Deselect and then File > Save.

Creating and applying text styles

Note: If you place a Microsoft Word document and choose to keep the formatting, the styles used in the Word document may be brought into the Illustrator document and may appear in the Paragraph Styles panel.

Styles allow you to format text consistently and are helpful when text attributes need to be updated globally. Once a style is created, you only need to edit the saved style, and then all text formatted with that style is updated. Illustrator has two types of text styles.

- **Paragraph**—Retains character and paragraph attributes and applies them to an entire paragraph.

- **Character**—Retains character attributes and applies them to selected text.

Creating and applying a paragraph style

You'll start by creating a paragraph style for the body copy.

1 Select the Selection tool (▶). On the artboard on the right, below the fish artwork, double-click in the text that begins with "Lorem ipsum dolor..." to switch to the Type tool and insert the cursor.

2 Choose Window > Type > Paragraph Styles, and click the Create New Style button (⬚) at the bottom of the Paragraph Styles panel.

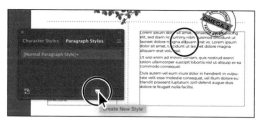

This creates a new paragraph style in the panel, called "Paragraph Style 1." The character and paragraph formatting from the paragraph with the cursor in it has been captured and saved in this new style. To create a paragraph style from text, you don't have to select the text first. You can also simply insert the cursor in text when you create a paragraph style. This saves the formatting attributes from the paragraph that the cursor is in.

3 Double-click directly on the style name "Paragraph Style 1" in the list of styles. Change the name of the style to **Body**, and press Return or Enter to edit the name inline.

By double-clicking the style to edit the name, you are also applying the new style to the paragraph (where the cursor is). This means that if you edit the Body paragraph style, this paragraph will update as well.

4 Select the Selection tool (▶) and with the text object selected, press the Shift key and if it's not already selected, click the other column of text under the fish, as well as the text on the left-hand artboard that begins with "Ingredients…" and "DIRECTIONS."

5 Click the Body style in the Paragraph Styles panel to apply the formatting.

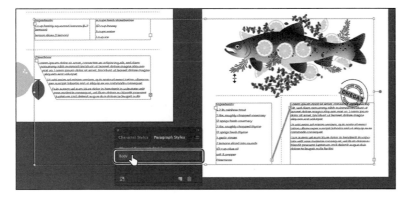

Paragraph style practice

With one paragraph style made, you'll practice by creating another for the headings in the same selected text.

1 Choose Select > Deselect.

2 Click the text in the middle of the left-hand artboard that begins with "Ingredients." Choose View > Fit Artboard In Window.

3 Select the Type tool and triple-click the "Ingredients:" heading text to select the entire paragraph.

4 Change the Font Style in the Properties panel to Medium so it's bolder.

● **Note:** If you see the overset text icon (⊞) in the out port of the type object, with the Selection tool selected, drag the corner to make it larger so you can see all of the text.

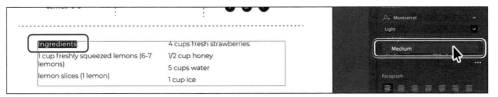

5 To make a new paragraph style, click the Create New Style button (▣) at the bottom of the Paragraph Styles panel. Double-click directly on the new style name "Paragraph Style 2" (or other) in the list of styles. Change the name of the style to **Heading**, and press Return or Enter to edit the name inline.

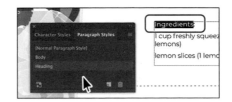

6 Insert the cursor in the Directions text, and click the Heading style in the Paragraph Styles panel to apply the Heading style to the text.

7 Click the Next artboard button (▶) at the bottom of the Document window to see the next artboard.

8 Insert the cursor in the "Ingredients" text, and click the Heading style in the Paragraph Styles panel to apply the Heading style to the text.

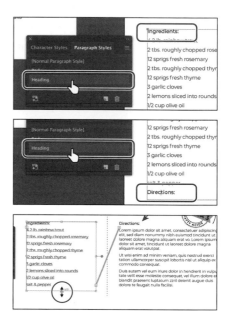

9 Insert the cursor in the "Directions" text, and click the Heading style in the Paragraph Styles panel to apply the Heading style.

10 If the "Directions" text is not at the top of the second column, select the Selection tool and drag the bottom-middle point of the selected text frame up or down so the text flows between the frames.

You may see a red plus in the "Directions" type object now. Usually, you would "copyfit" the text by changing appearance properties such as font size and leading or by editing the text. But you'll leave it in this case.

Editing a paragraph style

▶ **Tip:** There are many more options for working with paragraph styles, most of which are found in the Paragraph Styles panel menu, including duplicating, deleting, and editing paragraph styles. To learn more about these options, search for "paragraph styles" in Illustrator Help (Help > Illustrator Help).

After creating a paragraph style, you can easily edit the style formatting. Then anywhere the style has been applied, the formatting will be updated automatically. Next, you'll edit the Body style to see firsthand why paragraph styles can save you time and maintain consistency.

1 Double-click the column of text that you just resized to insert the cursor and switch to the Type tool.

2 Click in the "Ingredients" text.

3 To edit the Heading style, double-click to the *right* of the style name "Heading" in the Paragraph Styles panel list to open the Paragraph Style Options dialog box. Select the Basic Character Formats category on the left side of the dialog box and change the following:

- Font Family: Oswald
- Font Style: Regular
- Font Size: 12 pt
- Case: All Caps
- Tracking: **25**

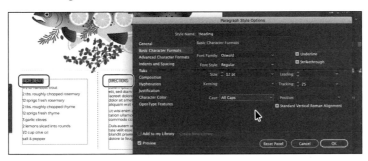

Since Preview is selected by default, you can move the dialog box out of the way to see the text change everywhere the Heading style is applied.

4 Click OK.

5 Choose View > Fit All In Window to see the headings on the left-hand artboard.

Creating and applying a character style

Character styles, unlike paragraph styles, can be applied only to selected text and can contain only character formatting. Next, you will create a character style from text styling.

1 Select the Selection tool (▶), and click the "SERVES: 6-8" text on the left-hand artboard. Choose View > Zoom In, a few times, to zoom in to the selected type.

2 Double-click the text object to select the Type tool (**T**) and then drag across the "SERVES:" text to select it.

3 In the Properties panel, choose Regular from the Font Style menu to change the font to Oswald Regular.

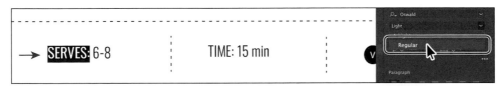

4 Click the Fill box in the Properties panel and choose the red Strawberry swatch.

5 In the Paragraph Styles panel group, click the Character Styles panel tab.

6 In the Character Styles panel, Option-click (macOS) or Alt-click (Windows) the Create New Style button () at the bottom of the Character Styles panel.

Option-clicking (macOS) or Alt-clicking (Windows) the Create New Style button in a Styles panel lets you edit the style options before the style is added to the panel.

7 In the dialog box that opens, change the following options:

- Style Name: BoldText
- Add To My Library: Deselected

8 Click OK. The style records the attributes applied to your selected text.

Note: If you apply the character style and a plus appears next to the style name, which indicates formatting applied to the text that is different from the style formatting, you can Option-click (macOS) or Alt-click (Windows) the style name to apply it.

9 With the text still selected, click the style named "BoldText" in the Character Styles panel to assign the style to that text and the text will change if the style formatting changes.

10 In the "TIME: 15 min" text to the right, select the "TIME:" text and click to apply the BoldText style in the Character Styles panel.

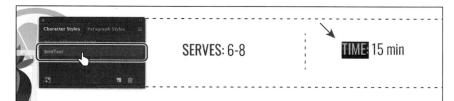

11 Choose Select > Deselect.

Editing a character style

After creating a character style, you can easily edit the style formatting, and anywhere that style is applied, the formatting will be updated automatically.

1 Double-click *to the right of* the BoldText style name in the Character Styles panel (not the name). In the Character Style Options dialog box, click the Character Color category on the left side of the dialog box, and change the following:

- Character Color: Black (it shows in the color list as "R=0 G=0 B=0")
- Add To My Library: Deselected
- Preview: Selected

2 Click OK.

3 Close the Character Styles panel group.

Wrapping text

In Illustrator, you can easily wrap text around objects, such as type objects, imported images, and vector artwork, to avoid text running over those objects or to create interesting design effects. Next, you'll wrap text around part of the artwork. In Illustrator, as in InDesign, you apply text wrap to the content that the text will wrap around.

1 Choose 2 Artboard 2 from the Artboard Navigation menu in the lower-left corner of the Document window.

2 Select the Selection tool (▶), and click the OMEGA 3 badge.

3 Choose Object > Text Wrap > Make. Click OK if a dialog box appears.

To wrap text around an object, that object must be in the same layer as the text that will wrap around it, and the object must also be located above the text in the layer hierarchy.

4 With the badge selected, click the Arrange button in the Properties panel and choose Bring To Front.

The badge should now be on top of the text in the stacking order and the text should be wrapping around the badge artwork.

5 Choose Object > Text Wrap > Text Wrap Options. In the Text Wrap Options dialog box, change Offset to **20 pt**, and select Preview to see the change. Click OK.

6 Drag the OMEGA 3 badge to the right so the text flows like it does in the figure. Click in an empty area to deselect the badge.

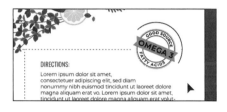

You may see a red plus in the bottom text object now. The text is flowing around the badge artwork, so some of it was pushed into the bottom type object. Usually, you would need to "copyfit" the text by changing appearance properties such as font size and leading or by editing the text.

Warping text

You can create some great design effects by warping text into different shapes using envelopes. You can make an envelope out of an object on your artboard, or you can use a preset warp shape or a mesh grid as an envelope. As you explore warping with envelopes, you'll also discover that you can use envelopes on any object except graphs, guides, or linked objects.

Reshaping text with a preset envelope warp

● **Note:** For more information about envelopes, see "Reshape using envelopes" in Illustrator Help (Help > Illustrator Help).

Illustrator comes with a series of preset warp shapes that you can warp text with. Next, you'll make a creative heading by applying a preset warp shape that Illustrator provides.

1 Click the "GRILLED" type object with the Selection tool to select it. To make a copy of it, press the Option (macOS) or Alt (Windows) key and drag the text down just below the original. Release the mouse button and then the key.

2 Select the Type tool and double-click the new "GRILLED" text to select it. Change the font family to Oswald Light and the font size to **84** in the Properties panel.

3 With the text selected, type **RAINBOW TROUTS** to replace it.

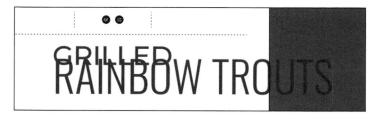

4   Press the Escape key to select the text object. Choose Object > Envelope Distort > Make With Warp.

5   In the Warp Options dialog box that appears, select Preview. The text appears as an arc by default. Make sure Arc Upper is chosen from the Style menu. Drag the Bend, Horizontal, and Vertical Distortion sliders to see the effect on the text.

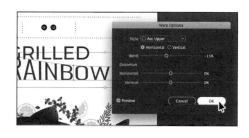

When you are finished experimenting, drag both Distortion sliders to 0%, make sure that Bend is −15%, and then click OK.

Editing the envelope warp

If you want to make any changes, you can edit the text and shape that make up the envelope warp object separately. Next, you will edit the text and then the warp shape.

1   With the envelope object still selected, click the Edit Contents button (⊞) at the top of the Properties panel.

2   Select the Type tool (T), and move the pointer over the warped text. Notice that the unwarped text appears in blue. Select and delete the "S" so it shows as "RAINBOW TROUT."

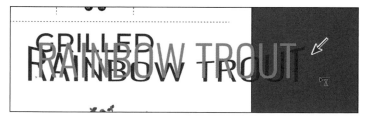

You can also edit the preset shape, which is what you'll do next.

3 Select the Selection tool (▶), and make sure the envelope object is still selected. Click the Edit Envelope button (▦) at the top of the Properties panel.

▶ **Tip:** If you double-click with the Selection tool instead of with the Type tool, you enter isolation mode. This is another way to edit the text within the envelope warp object. Press the Escape key to exit isolation mode.

4 Click the Warp Options button in the Properties panel to show the same Warp Options dialog box you saw when you first applied the warp. Change the Style to Arc Lower and the Bend to **−12%**, and click OK.

▶ **Tip:** To take the text out of the warped shape, select the text with the Selection tool and choose Object > Envelope Distort > Release. This gives you two objects: the type object and an arc lower shape.

5 With the Selection tool, drag it into the approximate center of the artboard, making sure to closely match the position you see in the figure.

6 Choose Select > Deselect and then choose File > Save.

Working with type on a path

In addition to having text in point and type objects, you can have type along a path. Text can flow along the edge of an open or closed path and can lead to some uniquely creative ways to display text. In this section, you'll add some text to an open path.

1 With the Selection tool (▶), select the OMEGA 3 badge.

2 Press Command and + (macOS) or Ctrl and + (Windows) a few times to zoom in.

3 Select the Type tool (T), and move the cursor over the left end of the black path above the badge to see an insertion point with an intersecting wavy path ( ) (see the figure). Click when this cursor appears.

Placeholder text is added to the path, and it starts where you clicked. Your text may have different formatting than you see in the previous figure, and that's okay.

4 Choose Window > Type > Paragraph Styles to open the Paragraph Styles panel. Click [Normal Paragraph Style] to apply the style. Close the panel group.

5 Type **good for you!** The new text follows the path.

6 Press Command+A (macOS) or Ctrl+A (Windows) to select all of the text.

7 In the Properties panel to the right of the document, change the following formatting options:

- Fill color: Strawberry

- Font Family: Oswald

- Font Style: Regular

- Font Size: **16 pt**

8 Choose Type > Change Case > UPPERCASE.

9 Press Command and + (macOS) or Ctrl and + (Windows) to zoom in further.

10 Select the Selection tool, and move the pointer over the line on the left edge of the text (just to the left of the "G" in "GOOD"). When you see this cursor (⊦), press and drag to the right, trying to center the text as best you can on the path. Use the following figure as a guide.

▶ **Tip:** With the path or the text on the path selected, you can choose Type > Type On A Path > Type On A Path Options to set more options.

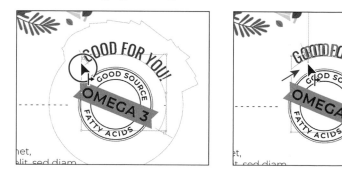

From the point where you click a path to the end of the path is where the text can flow. If you align the text left, center, or right, it's aligned within that area on the path.

Creating text outlines

Note: Bitmap fonts and outline-protected fonts cannot be converted to outlines, and outlining text that is less than 10 points in size is not recommended.

Converting text to outlines means converting text into vector shapes that you can edit and manipulate as you would any other vector graphic. When you create outlines from text, that text is no longer editable as text. Text outlines are useful for changing the look of large display type or sending a file to someone when you can't or don't want to send the font. They are rarely useful for body text or other type formatted at small sizes. The file recipient doesn't need to have your fonts installed to open and view the file correctly if you convert all text to outlines.

When type is converted to outlines, the type loses its *hints*—instructions built into outline fonts to adjust their shape to display or print optimally at many sizes. You must also convert all type in a selection to outlines; you cannot convert a single letter within a type object. Next, you will convert the main heading to outlines.

1   Choose View > Fit All In Window.

2   With the Selection tool (▶) selected, drag across the text GRILLED and RAINBOW TROUT to select both text objects.

3   Choose Edit > Copy and then choose Object > Hide > Selection.

> The original text is still there; it's just hidden. This way, you can always choose Object > Show All to see the original text if you need to make changes.

4   Choose Edit > Paste In Front.

5   Choose Type > Create Outlines.

> The text is no longer linked to a particular font. Instead, it is now editable artwork.

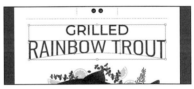

6   Click to select the "SERVES: 6-8" text on the left-hand artboard. To make a copy of the text, press the Option (macOS) or Alt (Windows) key and drag the text to the artboard on the right. Release the mouse button and then the key. See the following figure for where to drag.

7   Make a copy of the "TIME: 15 min" text from the left artboard to the right artboard using the same method.

8   Choose Select > Deselect.

9   Choose File > Save and then choose File > Close.

Review questions

1 Name a few methods for creating text in Adobe Illustrator.

2 What is overflow text?

3 What is text threading?

4 What does the Touch Type tool (⬚) let you do?

5 What is the difference between a character style and a paragraph style?

6 What is the advantage of converting text to outlines?

Review answers

1 The following methods can be used for creating text:

- With the Type tool (T), click the artboard, and start typing when the cursor appears. A point type object is created to accommodate the text.

- With the Type tool, drag to create a type area object. Type when a cursor appears.

- With the Type tool, click a path or closed shape to convert it to text on a path, or click in a type object. Option-clicking (macOS) or Alt-clicking (Windows) when crossing over the stroke of a closed path creates text around the shape.

2 Overflow text is text that does not fit within an area type object or path. A red plus sign (⊞) in an out port indicates that the object contains additional text.

3 Text threading allows you to flow text from one object to another by linking type objects. Linked type objects can be of any shape; however, the text must be entered in an area or along a path (not at a point).

4 The Touch Type tool (⬚) allows you to edit certain character formatting options for individual characters directly on the text. You can edit the character rotation, kerning, baseline shift, and horizontal and vertical scale of text, and the text remains editable.

5 A character style can be applied to selected text only. A paragraph style is applied to an entire paragraph. Paragraph styles are best for indents, margins, and line spacing.

6 Converting text to outlines eliminates the need to send the fonts along with the Illustrator file when sharing with others and makes it possible to add effects to type that aren't possible when the type is still editable (live).

10 ORGANIZING YOUR ARTWORK WITH LAYERS

Lesson overview

In this lesson, you'll learn how to do the following:

- Work with the Layers panel.

- Create, rearrange, and lock layers and sublayers.

- Move objects between layers.

- Merge layers into a single layer.

- Locate objects in the Layers panel.

- Isolate content in a layer.

- Copy and paste objects and their layers from one file to another.

- Apply an appearance attribute to objects and layers.

- Make a layer clipping mask.

 This lesson will take about 45 minutes to complete. To get the lesson files used in this chapter, download them from the web page for this book at www.adobepress.com/IllustratorCIB2020. For more information, see "Accessing the lesson files and Web Edition" in the Getting Started section at the beginning of this book.

Layers let you organize your work into distinct
levels that can be edited and viewed individually
or together. Every Adobe Illustrator document has
at least one layer. Creating multiple layers in your
artwork lets you easily control how artwork is printed,
displayed, selected, and edited.

Starting the lesson

In this lesson, you'll organize the artwork for an app design as you explore various ways to work with layers in the Layers panel.

Note: If you have not already downloaded the project files for this lesson to your computer from your Account page, make sure to do so now. See the "Getting Started" section at the beginning of the book.

1   To ensure that the tools function and the defaults are set exactly as described in this lesson, delete or deactivate (by renaming) the Adobe Illustrator preferences file. See "Restoring default preferences" in the "Getting Started" section at the beginning of the book.

2   Start Adobe Illustrator.

3   Choose File > Open, and open the L10_end.ai file in the Lessons > Lesson10 folder, located on your hard disk.

4   Choose View > Fit All In Window.

5   Choose Window > Workspace > Reset Essentials.

Note: If you don't see Reset Essentials in the Workspace menu, choose Window > Workspace > Essentials before choosing Window > Workspace > Reset Essentials.

6   Choose File > Open. In the Open dialog box, navigate to the Lessons > Lesson10 folder, and select the L10_start.ai file on your hard disk. Click Open.

The Missing Fonts dialog box may appear, indicating that fonts were used in the file that Illustrator can't find on your machine. The file uses Adobe fonts that you most likely don't have activated, so you will fix the missing font(s) before moving on.

Note: For more information on activating fonts, visit helpx.adobe.com/creative-cloud/help/add-fonts.html.

7   In the Missing Fonts dialog box, ensure that Activate is selected for each font in the Activate column, and click Activate Fonts. After some time, the font(s) should be activated, and you should see a success message in the Missing Fonts dialog box. Click Close.

Note: If you see a warning message in the Missing Fonts dialog box or cannot select Activate Fonts, you can click Find Fonts to replace the font with a local font. In the Find Font dialog box, make sure that a missing font is selected in the Fonts In Document section, and choose System from the Replace With Font From menu. This shows all the local fonts that are available to Illustrator. Select a font from the Fonts In System section, and click Change All to replace the font. Do the same for all missing fonts. Click Done.

8 Choose File > Save As, name the file **TravelApp.ai**, and select the Lesson10 folder. Leave Adobe Illustrator (ai) chosen from the Format menu (macOS) or Adobe Illustrator (*.AI) chosen from the Save As Type menu (Windows) and then click Save. In the Illustrator Options dialog box, leave the Illustrator options at their default settings and then click OK.

9 Choose Select > Deselect (if available).

10 Choose View > Fit All In Window.

Understanding layers

Layers are like invisible folders that help you hold and manage all of the items (some of which can be difficult to select or track) that make up your artwork. If you shuffle those folders, you change the stacking order of the items in your artwork. (You learned about stacking order in Lesson 2, "Techniques for Selecting Artwork.")

The structure of layers in your document can be as simple or as complex as you want. When you create a new Illustrator document, all of the content you create is organized in a single layer. However, you can create new layers and sublayers (like subfolders) to organize your artwork, as you'll learn about in this lesson.

1 Click the L10_end.ai tab at the top of the document window to show that document.

2 Click the Layers panel tab in the upper-right corner of the workspace, or choose Window > Layers.

In addition to organizing content, the Layers panel gives you an easy way to select, hide, lock, and change your artwork's appearance attributes. In the following figure, the Layers panel is showing the content for the L10_end.ai file. It won't match what you see in the file. You can refer to this figure as you progress through the lesson.

A. Layer color
B. Visibility column (eye icon)
C. Template Layer icon
D. Edit column (lock/unlock)
E. Disclosure triangle (expand/collapse)
F. Collect For Export
G. Locate Object
H. Make/Release Clipping Mask
I. Create New Sublayer
J. Create New Layer
K. Delete Selection
L. Current layer indicator (the triangle)
M. Target column
N. Selection column

● **Note:** The figure shows the top and bottom of the Layers panel. The Layers panel in the Essentials workspace is very tall, which is why the figure shows a split (dashed line) in the panel.

3 Choose File > Close to close the L10_end.ai file.

Creating layers and sublayers

By default, every document begins with a single layer, named "Layer 1." As you create artwork, you can rename and add layers and sublayers at any time. Placing objects on separate layers lets you more easily select and organize them because you can temporarily hide the content for a layer, lock the content on a layer, and more. For example, by placing type on a separate layer, you could lock the rest of the artwork in the document so you can focus on the type without affecting the rest of the artwork, or you could have several versions of an icon—one is showing while the rest are hidden.

Creating new layers

▶ Tip: Know that there is no "wrong" layer structure, but as you gain more experience with layers, you'll see what makes sense for you.

Next you'll change the default layer name and then create new layers using different methods. The idea for this project is to organize the artwork so you can more easily work with it later. Ideally, when you're working in Illustrator, you'll set up layers before you begin creating or editing the artwork. In this lesson, you'll organize artwork with layers *after* the artwork is created, which can be a bit more challenging. Instead of keeping all the content on a single layer, you'll create several layers as well as sublayers to better organize the content and to make it easier to select later.

1 With the TravelApp.ai document showing, if the Layers panel isn't visible, click the Layers panel tab on the right side of the workspace, or choose Window > Layers.

In the Layers panel, Layer 1 is highlighted, indicating that it is active. Anything you create or add to the document will go on the active layer.

2 Click the disclosure triangle (▶) to the left of the Layer 1 name to show the content on the layer.

Each object you create is listed under that layer. Illustrator shows groups as <Groups>, paths as <Paths>, images as <Images>, and so on. That makes it easier to glance at the content and see what is there.

3 Click the disclosure triangle (⌄) to the left of the Layer 1 name to hide the content on that layer.

4 In the Layers panel, double-click directly on the layer name "Layer 1" to edit it inline. Type **Phone Body** and then press Enter or Return.

5 Click the Create New Layer button () at the bottom of the Layers panel.

Layers and sublayers that aren't named are numbered in sequence. For example, the new layer is named Layer 2. When a layer or sublayer in the Layers panel contains other items, a disclosure triangle (▶) appears to the left of the layer or sublayer name. You can click the disclosure triangle to show or hide the contents. If no triangle appears, the layer has no content on it.

6 Double-click the white layer thumbnail to the left of the layer name "Layer 2" or to the right of the name in the Layers panel to open the Layer Options dialog box. Change the name to **Navigation**, and notice all the other options available. Click OK.

● **Note:** The Layer Options dialog box has a lot of the options you've already worked with, including naming layers, setting Preview or Outline mode, locking layers, and showing and hiding layers. You can also deselect the Print option in the Layer Options dialog box, and any content on that layer will not print.

By default, the new layer is added above the currently selected layer in the Layers panel (Phone Body, in this case) and becomes active. Notice that the new layer has a different layer color (a light red) to the left of the layer name. This will become more important later, as you select content.

Next you'll create a new layer and name it in one step, using a modifier key.

7 Option-click (macOS) or Alt-click (Windows) the Create New Layer button () at the bottom of the Layers panel (circled in the following figure). In the Layer Options dialog box, change the name to **Phone Content** and then click OK.

Creating a sublayer

Think of sublayers as subfolders within a layer—essentially they are a layer nested within a layer. Sublayers can be useful for organizing content within a layer without grouping or ungrouping content. Next you'll create a sublayer to put the footer content in so you can keep it together.

▶ **Tip:** To create a new sublayer and name it in one step, Option-click (macOS) or Alt-click (Windows) the Create New Sublayer button or choose New Sublayer from the Layers panel menu to open the Layer Options dialog box.

1   Click the layer named "Phone Content" to select it, if it isn't already, and then click the Create New Sublayer button () at the bottom of the Layers panel.

A new sublayer is created on the Phone Content layer and is selected. You can think of this new sublayer as a "child" of the "parent" layer named Phone Content.

2   Double-click the new sublayer name (Layer 4, in my case), change the name to **Footer**, and then press Enter or Return.

Creating a new sublayer opens the selected layer to show existing sublayers and content.

3   Click the disclosure triangle (▾) to the left of the Phone Content layer to hide the content of the layer.

In a few sections, you'll add content to the Footer sublayer.

Editing layers and objects

By rearranging the layers in the Layers panel, you can change the stacking order of objects in your artwork. On an artboard, objects in layers that are higher in the Layers panel list are in front of objects located on layers lower in the list. Within each layer there is also a stacking order applied to the objects on that layer. Layers are useful for a variety of reasons, including the ability to move objects between layers and sublayers to organize and more easily select your artwork.

Finding content in the Layers panel

When working in artwork, there may be times when you select content on the artboard and then want to locate that content in the Layers panel. This can help you determine how content is organized.

1 Drag the left edge of the Layers panel to the left to make it wider.

When the names of layers and objects are long enough or objects become further nested one in another, the names can become truncated—in other words, you can't see all of them.

2 With the Selection tool (▶), click the "Terraform Hikers" text on the artboard.

3 Click the Locate Object button (🔍) at the bottom of the Layers panel to reveal the selected content (a text group) within the Layers panel.

Clicking the Locate Object button will reveal the content for the layer that the selected text is on in the Layers panel. You'll see a selection indicator (■) to the far right of the layer that the selected content is on (Phone Body), as well as a <Group> object and the individual text objects. You can see that the selected text is in a group on a layer.

4 On the artboard, Shift-click the "$145.00" text to select it as well.

In the Layers panel, you should also see a selection indicator (■) to the far right of the $145.00 text object.

5 To group the selected text, press Command+G (macOS) or Ctrl+G (Windows).

When content is grouped, a group object (<Group>) is created that contains the grouped content.

6 Click the disclosure triangle (⌄) to the left of the selected <Group> to show the original group and the $145.00 text object that is now grouped with it.

You can rename a <Group> by double-clicking the name in the Layers panel. Renaming a group doesn't ungroup it, but it can make it easier to recognize what is in the group in the Layers panel.

7 Double-click the main <Group> name and type **Description**. Press Return or Enter to accept the name.

8 To collapse the group again so you hide the content, click the disclosure triangle (⌄) to the left of Description.

9 Click the disclosure triangle (⌄) to the left of the Phone Body layer name to collapse the layer and hide the contents of the entire layer.

Keeping layers, sublayers, and groups collapsed is a great way to make the Layers panel less visually cluttered. The Phone Content layer and Phone Body layer are the only layers with a disclosure triangle because they're the only layers with content on them.

10 Choose Select > Deselect.

Moving content between layers

Next you'll move the artwork to the different layers to take advantage of the layers and sublayers you've created.

1 In the artwork, using the Selection tool (▶), click the text "Terraform Hikers" to select that group of content.

In the Layers panel, notice that the Phone Body layer name has the selected-art indicator (the color square); it's circled in the figure.

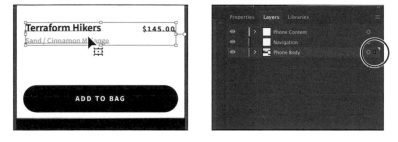

Also notice that the color of the bounding box, paths, and anchor points of the selected artwork matches the color of the layer (the small color strip [❙] you see to the left of the layer name in the Layers panel).

If you want to move selected artwork from one layer to another, you can either drag the selected-art indicator to the right of each sublayer or drag the selected-art indicator to the right of the layer name. That's what you'll do next.

2 Drag the selected-art indicator (the little blue box) from the far right of the Phone Body layer name straight up to the right of the target icon (◉) on the Phone Content layer.

This action moves all of the selected artwork to the Phone Content layer. The color of the bounding box, paths, and anchor points in the artwork changes to the color of the Phone Content layer, which is green (in my case).

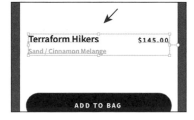

3 Choose Select > Deselect.

4 Click the disclosure triangle (▶) to the left of the Phone Body layer and the Phone Content layer to show the content for each layer.

▶ **Tip:** You can also press Option (macOS) or Alt (Windows) and drag the selected-art indicator to another layer to duplicate the content. Remember to release the mouse button first and then the key.

5 With the Selection tool (▶) selected, move the pointer above the ADD TO BAG button. Drag across the "ADD TO BAG" text and black rectangle at the bottom of the artboard to select a series of objects, making sure not to select the rectangle on the edge of the artboard.

You should see the blue selection indicator to the right of that content in the Layers panel. Also, notice the icons that are selected but can't be seen on the artboard because they are behind the black rectangle at the bottom. In the next section you'll arrange those icons so they are in front. Next you'll select those objects in the Layers panel and move them to another layer.

● **Note:** You didn't need to select the artwork on the artboard to drag content from one layer to another, but it was easier to find it that way in the layers.

6 In the Layers panel, click one of the <Group> objects that has the selection indicator to the right of the name. To select the other two groups, Command-click (macOS) or Ctrl-click (Windows) the other two <Group> objects where you see the selected indicator to the right of the name. Drag any of the selected objects to the Footer sublayer in the Phone Content layer above it. When the Footer sublayer shows a highlight, release the mouse button.

This is another way to move artwork between layers. Any content that is dragged to another layer or sublayer is automatically at the top of the layer or sublayer ordering. Notice that the color of the bounding box, paths, and anchor points of the selected artwork now matches the color of the Footer sublayer.

7 Click the disclosure triangle (▼) to the left of the Phone Body and Phone Content layers to hide the layer contents.

8 Choose Select > Deselect, and then choose File > Save.

Viewing layer content differently

In the Layers panel, you can display layers or objects individually in either Preview or Outline mode. In this section, you'll learn how to view layers in Outline mode, which can make artwork easier to select.

1   Choose View > Outline. This displays the artwork so that only its outlines (or paths) are visible.

You should be able to see the menu icons that are hidden beneath the black shape. They are circled in the figure.

Notice the eye icons (👁) in the Layers panel now. They indicate that the content on that layer is in outline mode.

2   Choose View > Preview (or GPU Preview) to see the painted artwork.

Sometimes you may want to view part of the artwork in outline mode while retaining the strokes and fills for the rest of the artwork. This can be useful if you need to see all artwork in a given layer, sublayer, or group.

3   In the Layers panel, click the disclosure triangle (▶) for the Phone Content layer to reveal the layer content. Command-click (macOS) or Ctrl-click (Windows) the eye icon (👁) to the left of the Phone Content layer name to show the content for *only that layer* in Outline mode.

You should be able to see the icons near the bottom of the artboard again. Displaying a layer in Outline mode is also useful for selecting the anchor points or center points of objects.

4   Select the Selection tool (▶), and click one of the mobile icons to select the group of icons.

5 Click the disclosure triangle (▶) to the left of the Footer sublayer to show the content on the sublayer.

You should be able to find the group of icons in the Footer sublayer.

6 Choose Object > Arrange > Bring To Front.

The Arrange commands simply move the content up or down in the layer stack on an individual layer. The Bring To Front command only brought the icons group to the top of the Footer sublayer. If you decide to create layers and organize your content, and later need to move content in front of other content, for instance, it can be a bit more challenging to use the Arrange commands if that content is not on the same layer. Sometimes you wind up moving content from one layer to another or reordering layers altogether so some content can be in front of other content.

7 Click the disclosure triangle (⌄) to the left of the Phone Content layer to hide the layer content.

8 Command-click (macOS) or Ctrl-click (Windows) the eye icon (👁) to the left of the Phone Content layer name to show the content for that layer in Preview mode again. You should now see the icons.

9 Choose Select > Deselect, and then File > Save.

Reordering layers and content

In earlier lessons you learned that objects have a stacking order, depending on when and how they were created. That stacking order applies to each of the layers in the Layers panel. By creating multiple layers in your artwork, you can control how overlapping objects are displayed. Next you'll reorder content to change the stacking order.

1   With the Selection tool (▶) selected, on the artboard, drag across the content at the top of the artboard to select the header content.

After attempting to select just the header content, you'll see that the selection appears to capture other content. You can tell because the bounding box surrounding the selection covers the artboard.

2   Click the disclosure triangle (▶) to the left of the Phone Body layer name to show the content.

You should see the content that is selected. You need to remove a few items from the selection. There is a gradient-filled rectangle and something else.

3   To remove the rectangle with the gradient fill from the selection, Shift-click the rectangle on the artboard. See the figure.

There is still a shape that is the size of the artboard that is selected and needs to be deselected.

4   In the Layers panel, Shift-click the selection indicator to the right of the bottom <Rectangle> object to remove it from the selection.

That happened to be the right thing to deselect, in this case. If it weren't, you could have Shift-clicked the selection indicator column again and tried another object. Just as in the document, you can use the Shift key to add or remove items from a selection in the Layers panel. As I'm sure you've figured out by now, selecting the name of a layer or object in the Layers panel does not select it in the document. That's why you Shift-clicked the selection indicator and not the name of the rectangle.

5 Click the disclosure triangle (⌄) to the left of the Phone Body layer to hide the content.

6 To move the selected content to the Navigation layer where it belongs, drag the selection indicator to the right of the Phone Body layer up to the Navigation layer and release.

The selection indicator to the right of a layer means that there is selected content on that layer. It doesn't tell you what or how much is selected, but dragging it to another layer moves only the currently selected content.

7 With the Selection tool (▶) selected, click in a blank area, away from artwork, to deselect, if necessary. Shift-drag the image from off the left edge of the artboard into the approximate center of the artboard. Release the mouse button and then the Shift key.

8 The image needs to be on the Phone Content layer, so with it selected, drag the selection indicator in the Layers panel up to the Phone Content layer.

Unfortunately, the image now covers the content on the Navigation layer. Next you'll reorder the layers so you can once again see the navigation content.

9 Drag the Phone Content layer down below the Navigation layer. When you see a blue line below the Navigation layer, release the mouse button to move the Phone Content layer below the Navigation layer. You should now see the navigation content since it's above the Phone Content layer content.

10 Choose Select > Deselect.

11 Choose File > Save.

Locking and hiding layers

In Lesson 2, you learned about locking and hiding content. When you lock and hide content using menu commands or keyboard shortcuts, you are actually setting lock, unlock, hide, and show in the Layers panel. The Layers panel lets you hide layers, sublayers, or individual objects from view. When a layer is hidden, the content on the layer is also locked and cannot be selected or printed. In this section, you'll lock some content and hide other content to make it easier to select things.

1 Click the image on the artboard. Click the Locate Object button (🔍) at the bottom of the Layers panel to find it in the layers. Notice the eye icon (👁) to the far left of the <Image> name.

2 Choose Object > Hide > Selection.

The image is hidden, and the eye for the <Image> object is gone in the Layers panel.

3 Click where the eye icon (👁) was, to the far left of the <Image> name in the Layers panel, to show the image again.

That is the same as choosing Object > Show > All. But in the Layers panel, you don't have to show everything that you hide, like the command does. You can show or hide layers, sublayers, individual objects, or a combination.

4 Option-click (macOS) or Alt-click (Windows) the eye icon () to the left of the Phone Body layer to hide the *other* layers.

Hiding all layers except those that you want to work with can make it easier to focus on the content at hand.

5 Click the gradient-filled rectangle in the center of the artboard. In the Layers panel, drag the selection indicator up to the Phone Content layer and release.

The rectangle will disappear since it is now on a layer that is hidden.

6 To view the artwork in Outline mode, press Command+Y (macOS) or Ctrl+Y (Windows). You should see four small circles near the center of the artboard that are meant to show navigation for an image slideshow in the app. Click to select them.

7 Drag the selection indicator in the Layers panel up to the Phone Content layer and release. The circles disappear since they are now on a layer that is hidden.

8 Press Command+Y (macOS) or Ctrl+Y (Windows) to exit Outline mode.

9 Choose Show All Layers from the Layers panel menu ( ), or Option-click (macOS) or Alt-click (Windows) the eye icon ( ) to the left of the Phone Body layer, to show all layers again.

10 Click the empty Lock column to the left of the Navigation layer to lock *all* of the content on that layer.

11 Try clicking the "KICKSAPP" text at the top of the artboard and you'll wind up selecting the gradient-filled rectangle on the layer beneath.

Locking a layer makes it so you can't even select the content on that layer. This can be useful if you don't want to accidentally move content, for instance. You can also click in the Lock column for an object on a layer to lock or unlock objects on a layer.

12 Choose Select > Deselect and then choose File > Save.

Duplicating layer content

You can also use the Layers panel as another method for duplicating layers and content. Next you'll duplicate content on a layer and duplicate a layer.

1 With the Phone Content layer content showing in the Layers panel, click to select the group you renamed "Description." Pressing Option (macOS) or Alt (Windows), drag it down until you see a line appear just below the original. Release the mouse button and then the key to duplicate it.

Dragging with the modifier key copies the selected content. This is the same as selecting the content on the artboard, choosing Edit > Copy and then choosing Edit > Paste In Place.

2 Option-click the *original* group name "Description" to select the text on the artboard.

3 Drag the selected text, off the artboard to the right.

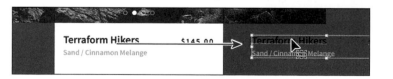

You'll keep a copy of the original text in case you convert the text on the artboard to outlines. Next you'll make a copy of the Navigation layer and drag the content for the copy off the artboard. This can be a way to make a design version of the navigation off to the side.

> **Tip:** You can also Option-drag (macOS) or Alt-drag (Windows) the selected-art indicator to duplicate content. You can also select the <Description> row in the Layers panel and choose Duplicate "<Description>" from the Layers panel menu to create a copy of the same content.

> **Note:** The original Description group was selected because if you had selected the copy and then attempted to drag it on the artboard, you would have instead dragged the original Description group that was above it in the layer stack. It really didn't matter which you dragged off the artboard, since they are the same.

4 Click the Navigation layer name and drag it down to the Create New Layer button () at the bottom of the Layers panel.

This duplicates the layer, and the content is pasted in place, on top of the original Navigation layer content. Notice that the copied layer, named "Navigation copy" is also locked.

5 Click the lock icon (🔒) to the left of the Navigation *copy* layer name in the panel to unlock it.

6 To select the copied content so you can move it off the artboard, click the selection indicator column to the far right of the "Navigation copy" name, to select all of the layer content.

7 On the artboard, drag the selected navigation content off the artboard to the right.

Pasting layers

To complete the app design, you'll copy and paste the remaining pieces of artwork from another file. You can paste a layered file into another file and even keep the layers intact. In this section, you'll also learn a few new things, including how to apply appearance attributes to layers and how to reorder layers.

1 Choose Window > Workspace > Reset Essentials.

2 Choose File > Open. Open the Sizes.ai file in the Lessons > Lesson10 folder on your hard disk.

3 Choose View > Fit Artboard In Window.

4 Click the Layers panel tab to show the panel and see the layer named "Sizes" that the content is on.

5 Choose Select > All and then choose Edit > Copy to select and copy the content to the clipboard.

6 Choose File > Close to close the Sizes.ai file without saving any changes. If a warning dialog box appears, click Don't Save (macOS) or No (Windows).

7 In the TravelApp.ai file, choose Paste Remembers Layers from the Layers panel menu (▤). A checkmark next to the option indicates that it's selected.

When Paste Remembers Layers is selected, artwork is pasted into the layer(s) from which it was copied, regardless of which layer is active in the Layers panel. If the option is not selected, all objects are pasted into the active layer, and the layers from the original file are not pasted in.

8 Choose Edit > Paste to paste the content into the center of the Document window.

The Paste Remembers Layers option causes the Sizes.ai layer to be pasted as a layer at the top of the Layers panel. Now you'll move the newly pasted layer into the Phone Content layer.

9 Drag the Sizes layer down on top of the Phone Content layer to move the content to the new layer. The pasted layer becomes a sublayer of the Phone Content layer.

10 Drag the selected artwork on the artboard down into position.

11 Choose Select > Deselect.

Applying appearance attributes to a layer

● **Note:** To learn more about working with appearance attributes, see Lesson 13, "Exploring Creative Uses of Effects and Graphic Styles."

You can use the Layers panel to apply appearance attributes, such as styles, effects, and transparency to layers, groups, and objects. When an appearance attribute is applied to a layer, any object on that layer takes on that attribute. If an appearance attribute is applied only to a specific object on a layer, it affects only that object, not the entire layer. Next you'll apply an effect to all of the artwork on one layer.

● **Note:** Clicking the target icon also selects the object(s) on the artboard. You could simply select the content on the artboard to apply an effect.

1 Click the target icon (⊙) to the right of the "Navigation copy" layer in the target column.

Clicking the target icon indicates that you want to apply an effect, style, or transparency change to that layer, sublayer, group, or object. In other words, the layer, sublayer, group, or object is *targeted*. The content is also selected in the Document window. When the target button appears as a double-ring icon (either ⊙ or ⊙), the item is targeted; a single-ring icon indicates that the item is not targeted.

2 To apply an effect, choose Effect > (Illustrator Effects) Stylize > Drop Shadow.

3 In the Drop Shadow dialog box, select Preview and change the following options:

- Mode: Multiply (default)
- Opacity: **50%**
- X Offset: **0 px**
- Y Offset: **10 px**
- Blur: **3 px**
- Color: Selected

4 Click OK.

If you look in the Layers panel, the target icon (⊙) for the Navigation copy layer is now shaded, indicating that the layer has at least one appearance attribute (the drop shadow added) applied to it. All content on the layer has the drop shadow applied.

5 Choose Select > Deselect.

Creating a clipping mask

The Layers panel lets you create clipping masks to control whether artwork on a layer (or in a group) is hidden or revealed. A *clipping mask* is an object or group of objects (with its shape) that masks artwork below it in the same layer or sublayer so that only artwork within the shape is visible. In Lesson 15, "Using Illustrator with Other Adobe Applications," you will learn about creating clipping masks that are independent of the Layers panel. Now you'll create a clipping mask from the layer content.

1 Click the disclosure triangle (▶) to the left of the Phone Body layer to show its contents, and click the disclosure triangle (▼) to the left of the Phone Content layer to hide its contents.

    The <Rectangle> object on the Phone Body layer will be used as the mask. In the Layers panel, a masking object must be above the objects it masks. In the case of a layer mask, the masking object must be the topmost object on a *single* layer. You can create a clipping mask for an entire layer, a sublayer, or a group of objects. You want to mask all of the content in the Phone Content *and* Navigation layers, so the clipping object needs to be at the top of a single merged layer that contains the Phone Content and Navigation layer content.

2 Click the lock icon (🔒) to the left of the Navigation layer name in the Layers panel to unlock it.

3 Click the Phone Content layer and Shift-click the Navigation layer name in the Layers panel. See the first part of the following figure.

4 Choose Collect In New Layer from the Layers panel menu to create a new layer and put the Phone Content and Navigation layers in it as sublayers.

You probably noticed these other options in the Layers panel menu: Merge Selected and Flatten Artwork. Merge Selected would have merged the content of the two layers into the top layer (Navigation). Flatten Artwork would have collected all of the artwork into a single layer that it chooses.

5 Double-click the new layer name directly (I see "Layer 7") and name it **Phone**. Press Return or Enter to accept the change.

6 Drag the object named <Rectangle> from the Phone Body layer onto the new Phone layer to move it to that layer.

This path will be used as the clipping mask for all of the content on the layer.

7 Click the disclosure triangle (▶) to the left of the Phone layer to show the layer content.

▶ **Tip:** To release the clipping mask, you can select the Phone layer again and click the Make/Release Clipping Mask button (▣).

8 Select the Phone layer to highlight it in the Layers panel. Click the Make/Release Clipping Mask button (▣) at the bottom of the Layers panel.

The name of the <Rectangle> content is underlined to indicate that it is the masking shape. On the artboard, the <Rectangle> content has hidden the parts of the phone content that extended outside of the shape.

● **Note:** For a complete list of shortcuts that you can use with the Layers panel, see "Keyboard shortcuts" in Illustrator Help (Help > Illustrator Help).

Now that the artwork is complete, you may want to combine all the layers into a single layer and then delete the empty layers. This is called *flattening* artwork. Delivering finished artwork in a single-layer file can prevent accidents, such as hiding layers or omitting parts of the artwork during printing. To flatten specific layers without deleting hidden layers, you can select the layers you want to flatten and then choose Merge Selected from the Layers panel menu (≡).

9 Choose File > Save and then choose File > Close.

Review questions

1 Name at least two benefits of using layers when creating artwork.

2 Describe how to reorder layers in a file.

3 What is the purpose of changing the color for a layer?

4 What happens if you paste a layered file into another file? Why is the Paste Remembers Layers option useful?

5 How do you create a layer clipping mask?

Review answers

1 The benefits of using layers when creating artwork include organizing content, selecting content more easily, protecting artwork that you don't want to change, hiding artwork that you aren't working with so that it's not distracting, and controlling what prints.

2 You reorder layers by selecting a layer name in the Layers panel and dragging the layer to its new location. The order of layers in the Layers panel controls the document's layer order—topmost in the panel is frontmost in the artwork.

3 The color for a layer controls how selected anchor points and direction lines are displayed on a layer and helps you identify which layer an object resides on in your document.

4 The paste commands paste layered files or objects copied from different layers into the active layer by default. The Paste Remembers Layers option keeps the original layers intact when the objects are pasted.

5 Create a clipping mask on a layer by selecting the layer and clicking the Make/Release Clipping Mask button (▣) in the Layers panel. The topmost object in the layer becomes the clipping mask.

11 GRADIENTS, BLENDS, AND PATTERNS

Lesson overview

In this lesson, you'll learn how to do the following:

- Create and save a gradient fill.

- Apply and edit a gradient on a stroke.

- Apply and edit a radial gradient.

- Adjust the direction of a gradient.

- Adjust the opacity of color in a gradient.

- Create and edit freeform gradients.

- Blend the shapes of objects in intermediate steps.

- Create smooth color blends between objects.

- Modify a blend and its path, shape, and color.

- Create and paint with patterns.

 This lesson will take about 60 minutes to complete. To get the lesson files used in this chapter, download them from the web page for this book at www.adobepress.com/IllustratorCIB2020. For more information, see "Accessing the lesson files and Web Edition" in the Getting Started section at the beginning of this book.

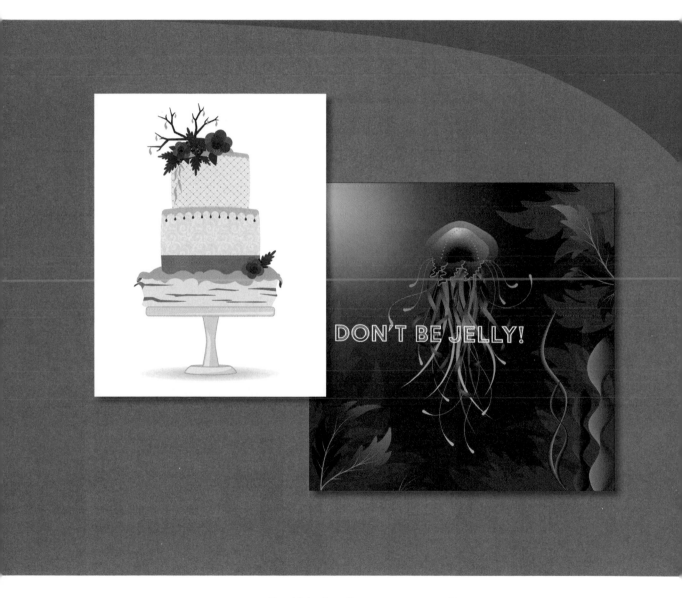

DON'T BE JELLY!

To add depth and interest to your artwork in Illustrator, you can apply gradient fills, which are graduated blends of two or more colors, patterns, shapes, and colors. In this lesson, you'll explore how to work with each of these to complete several projects.

Starting the lesson

In this lesson, you'll explore various ways to work with gradients, blend shapes and colors, and create and apply patterns. Before you begin, you'll restore the default preferences for Adobe Illustrator. Then you'll open a finished art file for the first part of the lesson to see what you'll create.

● **Note:** If you have not already downloaded the project files for this lesson to your computer from your Account page, make sure to do so now. See the "Getting Started" section at the beginning of the book.

1   To ensure that the tools function and the defaults are set exactly as described in this lesson, delete or deactivate (by renaming) the Adobe Illustrator preferences file. See "Restoring default preferences" in the "Getting Started" section at the beginning of the book.

2   Start Adobe Illustrator.

3   Choose File > Open, and open the L11_end1.ai file in the Lessons > Lesson11 folder on your hard disk.

4   Choose View > Fit All In Window. If you don't want to leave the document open as you work, choose File > Close.

To begin working, you'll open an art file that you need to finish.

5   Choose File > Open. In the Open dialog box, navigate to the Lessons > Lesson11 folder, and select the L11_start1.ai file on your hard disk. Click Open to open the file.

Don't worry, you'll make it look a lot better by the end of this lesson!

6   Choose View > Fit All In Window.

7   Choose File > Save As, name the file **Jellyfish_poster.ai**, and select the Lessons > Lesson11 folder in the Save As menu. Leave Adobe Illustrator (ai) chosen from the Format menu (macOS) or Adobe Illustrator (*.AI) chosen from the Save As Type menu (Windows) and then click Save.

8   In the Illustrator Options dialog box, leave the Illustrator options at their default settings and then click OK.

● **Note:** If you don't see Reset Essentials in the workspace switcher menu, choose Window > Workspace > Essentials before choosing Window > Workspace > Reset Essentials.

9   Choose Reset Essentials from the workspace switcher in the Application bar.

Working with gradients

A *gradient fill* is a graduated blend of two or more colors, and it always includes a starting color and an ending color. You can create different types of gradient fills in Illustrator, including *linear*, in which the beginning color blends into the ending color along a line; *radial*, in which the beginning color radiates outward, from the center point to the ending color; and *freeform*, which is a graduated blend of color stops within a shape in an ordered or random sequence that gives the blending a smooth appearance, like natural color. You can use the gradients provided with Adobe Illustrator or create your own gradients and save them as swatches for later use (all except for freeform gradient).

Linear gradient   Radial gradient   Freeform gradient

Using gradients, you can create blends between colors, add volume or a light and shadow effect to your artwork. As you go through this lesson, you'll see examples of each type of gradient and understand why you are using each.

You can apply, create, and modify gradients with the Gradient panel (Window > Gradient) or the Gradient tool (▇) in the toolbar. In the Gradient panel, the Gradient Fill box or Stroke box displays the current gradient colors and gradient type applied to the fill or stroke of an object.

A. Gradient
B. Fill box/ Stroke box
C. Reverse Gradient
D. Gradient midpoint
E. Gradient slider
F. Color stop
G. Color Picker

H. Gradient type
I. Edit Gradient
J. Stroke gradient type
K. Angle
L. Aspect ratio
M. Delete Stop
N. Opacity
O. Location

● **Note:** If you opened the Gradient panel, what you see won't match the figure, and that's okay.

In the Gradient panel under the gradient slider (labeled "E" in the previous figure), the leftmost gradient stop (labeled "F") is called a *color stop*. This marks the starting color; the right gradient stop (the dark purple circle to the far right) marks the ending color. A *color stop* is the point at which a gradient has completely changed from one color to the next. Between the color stops, the color is blending or transitioning from one color to another. You can add more color stops by clicking below the gradient slider. Double-clicking a color stop opens a panel where you can choose a color from swatches or color sliders.

Applying a linear gradient to a fill

With the simplest two-color linear gradient, the starting color blends into an ending color along a straight line. To begin the lesson, you'll apply a gradient fill that comes with Illustrator to the tentacles of a jellyfish to add depth and shadowing to the shape.

1 With the Selection tool (▶) selected, click the small yellow jellyfish shape.

2 Click the Fill box (☐) in the Properties panel, click the Swatches button (▦), and select the gradient swatch named "White, Black." Leave the swatches showing.

The default black-and-white gradient is applied to the fill of the selected shape.

Editing a gradient

Next, you'll edit the colors in the default black and white gradient you applied.

1 Click the Fill box (▦) in the Properties panel again to show the swatches, if they're not still showing. Click the Gradient Options button at the bottom of the panel to open the Gradient panel (Window > Gradient), and perform the following:

   • Double-click the black color stop on the right side of the gradient slider (circled in the figure) to edit the color in the Gradient panel. In the panel that appears, click the Color button (▨) to open the color panel.

   • Click the menu icon (▤), and choose CMYK from the menu, if CMYK values aren't showing.

   • Change the CMYK values to C=**1**, M=**97**, Y=**21**, and K=**0**.

▶ **Tip:** To move between text fields, press the Tab key. Press Enter or Return to apply the last value typed.

2 Click in a blank area of the Gradient panel to hide the color panel.

3 In the Gradient panel, perform the following:

- Make sure that the Fill box is still selected (circled in the figure) so that you edit the fill color and not the stroke color.

- Double-click the white, leftmost gradient stop to select the starting color of the gradient (an arrow is pointing to it in the figure).

- Click the Swatches button ( ) in the panel that appears.

- Click to select the dark purple swatch named "Dark purple."

● **Note:** You can press the Escape key to hide panels, but be careful. If you press the Escape key in this case, the K value *may* revert to the previous value.

Saving a gradient

Next, you'll save the gradient as a swatch in the Swatches panel. Saving a gradient is a great way to be able to apply it to other artwork easily and maintain consistency in the gradient appearance.

1 In the Gradient panel, click the Gradient menu arrow ( ) to the left of the word "Type," and click the Add To Swatches button ( ) at the bottom of the panel that appears.

The Gradient menu you saw lists all the default and saved gradients that you can apply.

2 Click the X at the top of the Gradient panel to close it.

3 With the jellyfish shape still selected, click the Fill box in the Properties panel. With the Swatches option ( ) selected, double-click the "New Gradient Swatch 1" thumbnail to open the Swatch Options dialog box.

4 In the Swatch Options dialog box, type **Jelly1** in the Swatch Name field and then click OK.

▶ **Tip:** Like most things in Illustrator, there is more than one method for saving a gradient swatch. You can also save a gradient by selecting an object with a gradient fill or stroke, clicking the Fill box or Stroke box in the Swatches panel (whichever the gradient is applied to), and then clicking the New Swatch button ( ) at the bottom of the Swatches panel.

5 Click the Show Swatch Kinds Menu button ( ) at the bottom of the Swatches panel, and choose Show Gradient Swatches from the menu to display only gradient swatches in the Swatches panel.

The Swatches panel lets you sort colors based on type, like gradient swatches.

6 With the shape still selected on the artboard, apply some of the different gradients to the shape fill by selecting them in the Swatches panel.

7 Click the gradient named "Jelly1" (the one you just saved) in the Swatches panel to make sure it's applied before continuing to the next step.

8 Click the Show Swatch Kinds Menu button ( ) at the bottom of the Swatches panel, and choose Show All Swatches from the menu.

9 Save the file by choosing File > Save, and leave the shape selected.

Adjusting a linear gradient fill

Once you have applied a gradient to the fill of artwork, you can adjust the direction, the origin, and the beginning and end points of the gradient using the Gradient tool. Now you'll adjust the gradient fill in the selected shape so the colors follow the direction of the shape, and the colors follow the direction of a light source.

1 With the Selection tool (▶) selected, double-click the shape to isolate it.

This is a great way to enter Isolation mode for a single shape so you can focus on it without the other content (in this case) on top of it.

2 Choose View > Zoom In several times.

3 Click the Edit Gradient button in the Properties panel.

▶ **Tip:** You can hide the gradient annotator (bar) by choosing View > Hide Gradient Annotator. To show it again, choose View > Show Gradient Annotator.

Clicking the Edit Gradient button selects the Gradient tool ( ) in the toolbar and enters gradient editing mode. With the Gradient tool, you can apply a gradient to the fill of an object or edit an existing gradient fill.

Notice the horizontal gradient slider that appears in the middle of the artwork, much like the one found in the Gradient panel. The slider indicates the direction and length of the gradient. You can use the gradient slider on the art to edit the gradient without opening the Gradient panel. The two color circles on either end represent the color stops. The very small circle on the left shows the starting point of the gradient, and the very small square on the right is the ending point. The diamond you see in the middle of the slider is the midpoint of the gradient.

4   With the Gradient tool selected, drag from the bottom of the shape up, to the top of the shape to change the position and direction of the starting and ending colors of the gradient.

Where you begin dragging is where the first color starts, and where you end is where the last color stops. As you drag, you see a live preview of the gradient as it's adjusted in the object.

5   With the Gradient tool, move the pointer just off the small black square at the *top* of the gradient annotator. A rotation icon (⟳) appears. Drag to the right to rotate the gradient in the rectangle, and then release the mouse button.

6   Double-click the Gradient tool in the toolbar to open the Gradient panel (if it isn't already open). Ensure that the Fill box is selected in the panel (circled in the figure) and then change the Angle value to **80** by typing in the value. Press Return or Enter.

● **Note:** Entering the gradient rotation in the Gradient panel, rather than adjusting it directly on the artboard, is useful when you want to achieve consistency and precision.

7   Choose Object > Lock > Selection to lock the shape so you don't accidentally move it later and to make selecting other artwork easier.

8   Select the Selection tool, and press the Escape key to exit Isolation mode. You should be able to select other artwork again.

Applying a linear gradient to a stroke

You can also apply a gradient blend to the stroke of an object. Unlike with a gradient applied to the fill of an object, you cannot use the Gradient tool to edit a gradient on the stroke of an object. A gradient on a stroke, however, has more options available in the Gradient panel than does a gradient fill. Next, you'll add colors to a stroke to give seaweed a three-dimensional appearance.

1   Choose View > Fit Artboard In Window.

▶ **Tip:** Curious how the light orange path is tapered on the ends? I drew a path with the Pencil tool and then applied a variable-width profile in the Control panel (Window > Control)!

2   With the Selection tool (▶) selected, click the light orange squiggly path in the lower-right corner to select that path.

You'll make this simple path into seaweed that looks something like the purple squiggly path in front of it.

● **Note:** After clicking the Stroke box in the toolbar, the Color panel group may open. If it does, you can close it.

3   Click the Stroke box at the bottom of the toolbar, and click the Gradient box below the Stroke box in the toolbar to apply the last used gradient for the current session.

4   To zoom in, press Command and + (macOS) or Ctrl and + (Windows) a few times.

Editing a gradient on a stroke

For a gradient applied to a stroke, you can choose how to align the gradient to the stroke: within, along, or across. In this section, you'll explore how to align a gradient to the stroke and also edit the colors of the gradient.

● **Note:** You can apply a gradient to a stroke in three ways: within a stroke (default) (▣), along a stroke (▣), and across a stroke (▣).

1   In the Gradient panel (Window > Gradient), click the Stroke box (if not already selected; an arrow if pointing to it in the figure) to edit the gradient applied to the stroke. Leave Type as Linear Gradient (circled in the figure), and click the Apply Gradient Across Stroke button (▣) to change the gradient type.

With this type of shape, aligning the gradient across the stroke is useful for achieving a three-dimensional appearance.

2 Move the pointer below the gradient slider, between the two color stops, in the Gradient panel. When the pointer with a plus sign (▷₊) appears, click to add another color stop, as you see in the first part of the following figure.

3 Double-click that new color stop and, with the swatches selected (▨), click the swatch named "Pink." Press the Escape key to hide the swatches and return to the Gradient panel.

4 With the color stop still selected (you can tell it's selected because it has a highlight around it), change Location to 50%.

You could have also dragged the color stop along the gradient slider to change the Location value.

Next you'll add a new color to the gradient by dragging to create a copy of a color stop in the Gradient panel.

5 Pressing the Option (macOS) or Alt (Windows) key, drag the darker color stop on the far left end to the right; release the mouse button when you see *roughly* 90% in the Location value, and then release the modifier key.

There are now four color stops. Next you'll see how to remove a color stop.

▶ **Tip:** When copying a color stop by pressing Option or Alt, if you release the mouse button on top of another color stop, you'll swap the two color stops instead of creating a duplicate.

● **Note:** The second part of the figure shows dragging the color stop, before releasing the mouse button and then the key.

6 Drag the lighter color stop on the far right down, away from the gradient slider. When you see that it's gone from the slider, release the mouse to remove it.

7 Double-click the new color stop, and with the Swatches option selected, select the Light pink color to apply it.

8 Click the X at the top of the Gradient panel to close it.

9 Choose File > Save.

Applying a radial gradient to artwork

As previously noted, with a radial gradient, the starting color (leftmost color stop) of the gradient defines the center point of the fill, which radiates outward to the ending color (rightmost color stop). Radial gradients are really useful for giving elliptical shapes a circular type of gradient. Next you'll create and apply a radial gradient fill to the large rectangle in the background.

1 Choose View > Fit Artboard In Window.

2 With the Selection tool (▶) selected, click the pink shape in the background.

3 Make sure the Fill box near the bottom of the toolbar is selected .

4 Click the Fill box in the Properties panel and change the fill color to the White, Black gradient. Press the Escape key to hide the Swatches panel.

5 Click the Radial Gradient button in the Properties panel to convert the linear gradient to a radial gradient.

● **Note:** The Fill box needs to be selected in the toolbar to see the Gradient options in the Properties panel. You can also click the Gradient Options button in the Swatches panel to open the Gradient panel and change the gradient type.

Editing the colors in the radial gradient

Previously in this lesson, you edited gradient colors in the Gradient panel. You can also edit the colors in a gradient using the Gradient tool right on the artwork, which is what you'll do next.

1 Double-click the Gradient tool (▓) in the toolbar to select the tool and also open the Gradient panel.

2 In the Gradient panel, with the rectangle still selected, click the Reverse Gradient button (▓) to swap the white and black colors in the gradient.

3 Move the pointer over the gradient slider in the ellipse, and perform the following:

● **Note:** You may need to move the Gradient panel out of the way.

- Double-click the black color stop in the center of the ellipse to edit the color (it's circled in the following figure).
- In the panel that appears, click the Swatches button (▓), if it's not already selected.
- Select the swatch named "Light blue."

Notice that the gradient slider starts from the center of the shape and points to the right. The dashed circle around the gradient slider indicates that it's a radial gradient. You can set additional options for radial gradients, as you'll soon see.

4 Press Escape to hide the swatches panel.

5 Move the pointer beneath the gradient slider, in the middle. When the pointer with a plus sign (▷₊) appears, click to add another color to the gradient (see the first part of the following figure).

▶ **Tip:** When you edit a color stop that has a swatch applied, you can easily see which swatch is applied because it is highlighted in the panel.

6 Double-click the new color stop. In the panel that appears, make sure that the Swatches option is selected, and select the swatch named "Blue," *not* "CMYK Blue."

7 Change Location to **45%** by typing in the value. Press Enter or Return to change the value and hide the panel.

8 Double-click the white color stop on the far right. In the panel that appears, make sure that the Swatches option is selected, and select the swatch named "Dark blue."

9 Press the Escape key to hide the panel.

10 Choose File > Save.

Adjusting the radial gradient

Next you'll change the aspect ratio of the radial gradient and change the radius and the origin of the radial gradient.

1 With the Gradient tool (▦) selected in the toolbar and the rectangle still selected, move the pointer near the upper-left corner of the artboard. Drag toward the lower-right corner of the artboard to change the gradient in the rectangle.

2   Move the pointer over the gradient slider on the artwork so you can see the dashed circle around the gradient. Press Command and – (macOS) or Ctrl and – (Windows) a few times to zoom out enough to see the entire dashed circle.

● **Note:** After zooming out, you may need to move the pointer back over the gradient slider to see the dashed circle.

3   Move the pointer over the double-circle on the dashed circle (see the first part of the following figure). When the pointer changes (▶), drag toward the center of the artboard a little. Release the mouse button to shorten the gradient.

4   In the Gradient panel, ensure that the Fill box is selected and then change the Aspect Ratio (◫) to 80% by choosing it from the menu. Move the pointer over the gradient slider to see the dashed circle again. Leave the Gradient panel open.

The aspect ratio changes a radial gradient into an elliptical gradient and makes the gradient better match the shape of the artwork. Another way to edit the aspect ratio is to do so visually. If you move the pointer over the gradient on the selected artwork with the Gradient tool selected and then move the pointer over the black circle that appears on the dotted path, the pointer changes to ▷. You can then drag to change the aspect ratio of the gradient.

▶ **Tip:** You can also drag the gradient slider to reposition the gradient in the ellipse.

● **Note:** The aspect ratio is a value between 0.5% and 32,767%. As the aspect ratio gets smaller, the ellipse flattens and widens.

5   Choose View > Fit Artboard In Window.

6   Choose Select > Deselect and then choose File > Save.

Applying gradients to multiple objects

You can apply a gradient to multiple objects by selecting all the objects, applying a gradient color, and then dragging across the objects with the Gradient tool.

Now you'll apply a linear gradient fill to the seaweed shapes.

1   With the Selection tool (▶) selected, click the purple seaweed artwork in the lower-left corner (an arrow is pointing to it in the following figure).

2   To select all objects with that same purple color fill, choose Select > Same > Fill Color.

3   Click the Fill box in the Properties panel. In the panel that appears, make sure the Swatches button (▦) is selected, and select the Plant gradient swatch.

● **Note:** You may not see the gradient annotators in each shape and that's okay. Before the book went to press, they were not showing in the software.

4   Select the Gradient tool (▮) in the toolbar.

You can see that every object now has the gradient fill applied separately. With the Gradient tool selected, you can see that each object has its own annotator bar.

5   Drag from the upper-right corner of the artboard to the lower-left corner.

Dragging across multiple shapes with the Gradient tool allows you to apply a gradient across those shapes.

6   With the shapes still selected, change the Opacity value in the Properties panel to **30%**.

Adding transparency to gradients

By specifying varying opacity values for the different color stops in your gradient, you can create gradients that fade in or out and that show or hide underlying artwork. Next you'll apply a gradient that fades to transparent on the jellyfish shape.

1   Select the Selection tool (▶), and click to select the green shape in the design.

2   In the Gradient panel, ensure that the Fill box is selected. Click the Gradient menu arrow (▼) and then select White, Black to apply the generic gradient to the fill.

3   Select the Gradient tool (▦) in the toolbar, and drag from the top edge of the shape down to just past the bottom edge at a slight angle.

4   With the pointer over the shape, double-click the black color stop at the bottom. Make sure the Swatches button (▦) is selected, and then select the color named "Light blue" from the swatches. Choose 0% from the Opacity menu. Press Return or Enter to hide the swatches.

5   Double-click the white color stop on the other end of the gradient slider. Select the color named "Light blue" from the swatches. Choose 70% from the Opacity menu. Press Return or Enter to hide the swatches.

6   Drag the bottom blue color stop up to shorten the gradient a little.

7   Drag the gradient midpoint (the diamond shape) up a little. More of the shape will become transparent.

8   Choose File > Save.

Applying a freeform gradient

Aside from creating linear and radial gradients, you can also create freeform gradients. Freeform gradients are made of a series of color stops that you can place anywhere within a shape randomly or as a path. The colors blend together between the color stops to create a freeform gradient. Freeform gradients are useful for adding color blends that follow the contour of a shape, adding more realistic shading to artwork, and more. Next you'll apply a freeform gradient to the top of the jellyfish and edit it.

1   Select the Selection tool (▶), and click the white shape at the top of the jellyfish artwork to select it.

2   Press Command and + (macOS) or Ctrl and + (Windows) a few times to zoom in.

3   Select the Gradient tool (▤) in the toolbar.

4   Click the Freeform Gradient option (▦) in the Properties panel on the right.

5   Ensure that the Points option is selected in the Gradient section of the Properties panel (an arrow is pointing to it in the figure).

● **Note:** The colors you see in your shape may be different, and that's okay.

● **Note:** By default, Illustrator chooses color from surrounding artwork. This is because the preference Illustrator > Preferences > General > Enable Content Aware Defaults (macOS) or Edit > Preferences > General > Enable Content Aware Defaults (Windows) is on. You can deselect this option to create your own color stops.

By default, a freeform gradient is applied in points mode. Illustrator automatically adds individual solid color stops to the object whose colors blend into each other. The number of color stops Illustrator automatically adds depends on the shape and surrounding artwork.

Editing a freeform gradient in points mode

With points mode selected, you can add, move, edit, or delete the color stops independently to change the overall gradient. In this section, you'll edit the default individual color stops in the freeform gradient.

1   Double-click the color stop you see in the figure to show the color options. With the swatches showing, select the Dark purple swatch to apply it.

    With each color stop, you can drag it, double-click to edit its color, and more.

2 Drag the dark purple color stop to the bottom center of the shape.

Next you'll add color stops, as well as edit and move color stops.

3 Click in the shape near the top to add another color stop (see the first part of the following figure).

4 Double-click the new color stop and change the color to the Yellow swatch.

The dark purple area of the gradient needs to be bigger or more spread out. To do that, you can adjust the spread of the color.

5 Move the pointer over the dark purple color stop at the bottom of the shape. When you see the dotted circle appear, drag the widget at the bottom of the circle away from the color stop. The dark purple color will "spread" farther away from the color stop.

6 Click in the shape to add a new color stop (see the figure for the position). Double-click the new color stop you just added, and change the color to the Pink swatch.

7 Click the color stop circled in the figure. In the Gradient panel, click the Color Picker (🖉) to sample some color. Click in the pink area below the selected shape to sample the color and apply it to the point.

Applying color stops in lines mode

You can also add multiple solid colors that blend along a line in lines mode. In this section, you'll add more color to the jellyfish using lines mode.

1   With the Gradient tool still selected, drag the color stop you see below to the left side of the shape.

2   Double-click the color stop to show the color options. With the swatches option selected, click to apply the swatch named "Purple."

3   Select Lines in the Gradient panel to be able to draw a gradient along a path.

4   Click the purple color stop you just changed the color of, so you can start drawing from that point.

● **Note:** The first part of the following figure shows the gradient before clicking to add the next color stop.

5   Move the pointer into the center of the shape, and you'll see the path preview. Click to create a new color stop. Double-click the new color stop, and ensure that the Purple swatch is applied.

6   Click to make a final color stop to the right and toward the bottom of the shape. It should already be purple.

7   Drag the middle color stop up and to the left a little to see the effect on the gradient.

8   Close the Gradient panel.

9   Choose Select > Deselect, and then choose File > Save.

Working with blended objects

You can blend two distinct objects to create and distribute shapes evenly between two objects. The two shapes you blend can be the same or different. You can also blend between two open paths to create a smooth transition of color between objects, or you can combine blends of colors and objects to create color transitions in the shape of a particular object.

The following are examples of different types of blended objects you can create:

Blend between two of
the same shape.

Blend between two
of the same shapes,
each with a different
color fill.

Blend between two
different shapes with
different fill colors.

Blend between two of
the same shape along
a path.

Smooth color blend
between two stroked
lines (original lines on
left, blend on right).

When you create a blend, the blended objects are treated as one object, called a *blend object*. If you move one of the original objects or edit the anchor points of the original object, the blend changes accordingly. You can also expand the blend to divide it into distinct objects.

Creating a blend with specified steps

Next you'll use the Blend tool ( ) to blend two shapes that you will use to create a pattern for the jellyfish.

1   In the Layers panel (Window > Layers), click the visibility column for the layer named Blends to show the layer content.

    You should now see three small circles on top of the freeform gradient object.

2   Select the Blend tool ( ) in the toolbar. Move the little box part of the pointer ( ) over the center of the leftmost circle, and click.

    By clicking, you are telling Illustrator that this will be the starting point of the blend. Nothing will appear to happen.

▶ **Tip:** You can add more than two objects to a blend.

● **Note:** If you wanted to end the current path and blend other objects, you would first click the Blend tool in the toolbar and then click the other objects, one at a time, to blend them.

3   Move the pointer over the center of the small circle at the top of the freeform gradient shape. When the pointer looks like this: □₊, click to create a blend between these two objects.

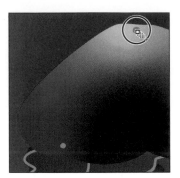

▶ **Tip:** To edit the blend options for an object, you can also select the blend object and then double-click the Blend tool. You can also double-click the Blend tool (🖮) in the toolbar to set tool options *before* you create the blend object.

4   With the blended object still selected, choose Object > Blend > Blend Options. In the Blend Options dialog box, select Preview to see any changes and choose Specified Steps from the Spacing menu. Change Specified Steps to **10**, and then click OK.

Modifying a blend

Now you'll edit one of the shapes in the blend as well as the spine of the blend you just created so the shapes blend along a curve.

1   Select the Selection tool (▶) in the toolbar, and double-click anywhere right on the blend object to enter isolation mode.

This temporarily ungroups the blended objects and lets you edit each original shape, as well as the spine. The *spine* is a path along which the steps in a blended object are aligned. By default, the spine is a straight line.

2   Choose View > Outline.

In outline mode, you can see the outlines of the two original shapes and a straight path (spine) between them. These three objects are what a blend object is composed of, by default. It can be easier to edit the path between the original objects in outline mode.

● **Note:** It's a small circle to begin with, so you may want to zoom in for this step and then zoom back out.

3   Click the edge of the top circle to select it. Pressing the Shift key, drag a corner of the bounding box to make it about half the size. Release the mouse button and then the key.

4   Choose Select > Deselect, and remain in isolation mode.

320   LESSON 11   Gradients, Blends, and Patterns

5 Select the Pen tool () in the toolbar. Press the Option key (macOS) or Alt key (Windows), and position the pointer over the path between the shapes. When the pointer changes (▸), drag the path up and to the left a little, as in the figure.

6 Choose View > Preview (or GPU Preview).

7 Press the Escape key to exit isolation mode.

Now you'll continue the blend to include the last circle.

8 Select the Blend tool (🖋) and click the top circle.

9 Click in the circle on the lower right to continue the blend path.

● **Note:** The circles are pretty small. You may want to zoom in to complete this step, and then zoom out when finished.

10 Select the Pen tool (🖋) in the toolbar. Press the Option key (macOS) or Alt key (Windows), and move the pointer over the path between the shapes. When the pointer changes (▸), drag the path up and to the right a little, as in the figure.

11 Choose Select > Deselect.

Creating and editing a smooth color blend

You can choose several options for blending the shapes and colors of objects to create a new object. When you choose the Smooth Color blend option in the Blend Options dialog box, Illustrator combines the shapes and colors of the objects into many intermediate steps, creating a smooth, graduated blend between the original objects, as you see in the figure above.

If objects are filled or stroked with different colors, the steps are calculated to provide the optimal number of steps for a smooth color transition. If the objects contain identical colors or if they contain gradients or patterns, the number of steps is based on the longest distance between the bounding box edges of the two objects. Now you'll combine two shapes into a smooth color blend to make seaweed.

1   Choose View > Fit Artboard In Window.

> If you look off the right edge of the artboard, you'll see a wavy pink path and a wavy purple path. You will blend them together so they look like the shape just to the left of them. The pink and purple paths have a stroke color and no fill. Objects that have strokes blend differently than those that have no stroke.

2   Select the Selection tool (▶), and click the pink path off the right edge of the artboard. Press the Shift key and click the purple path on the right to select both.

● **Note:** Your blend object may look different to start, and that's okay. You'll adjust it next.

3   Choose Object > Blend > Make.

> This is another way to create a blend and can be useful if creating a blend using the Blend tool proves challenging. The blend you created is using the last settings from the Blend Options dialog box (Smooth Color).

▶ **Tip:** You can also click the Blend Options button in the Properties panel to edit the options for a selected blend object.

● **Note:** Creating smooth color blends between paths can be difficult in certain situations. For instance, if the lines intersect or the lines are too curved, unexpected results may occur.

4   With the blend object still selected, double-click the Blend tool (🖫) in the toolbar. In the Blend Options dialog box, make sure that Smooth Color is chosen from the Spacing menu. Select Preview and then click OK.

5   Choose Select > Deselect.

> Next you'll edit the paths that make up the blend.

6 Select the Selection tool (➤), and double-click within the color blend to enter isolation mode. Click the path on the right to select it. Drag it to the left until it looks like the figure. Notice how the colors are now blended.

7 Double-click away from the blend object to exit isolation mode. Drag across both seaweed objects to select them, then drag them onto the artboard.

8 Drag the transparent gradient shape onto the jellyfish.

9 Click the Arrange button in the Properties panel, and choose Bring To Front to bring the selected shape on top of the freeform gradient artwork.

10 In the Layers panel, make all of the layers visible by clicking the visibility column for each layer that is currently hidden.

11 Choose File > Save and then choose File > Close.

Creating patterns

In addition to process colors, spot colors, and gradients, the Swatches panel can also contain pattern swatches. A *pattern* is artwork saved in the Swatches panel that can be applied to the stroke or fill of an object. Illustrator provides sample swatches of each type in the default Swatches panel as separate libraries and lets you create your own patterns as well. In this section, you will focus on creating, applying, and editing patterns.

Applying an existing pattern

You can design patterns from scratch and customize existing patterns with any of the Illustrator tools. Patterns can start with artwork (a tile) that is repeated (tiled) within a fill or stroke, starting at the ruler origin and continuing to the right. Next you'll apply a pattern that comes with Illustrator to a cake shape.

1 Choose File > Open. In the Open dialog box, navigate to the Lessons > Lesson11 folder, and select the L11_start2.ai file on your hard disk. Click Open to open the file.

2 Choose File > Save As, name the file **Cake_poster.ai**, and select the Lessons > Lesson11 folder in the Save As menu. Leave Adobe Illustrator (ai) chosen from the Format menu (macOS) or Adobe Illustrator (*.AI) chosen from the Save As Type menu (Windows) and then click Save. In the Illustrator Options dialog box, leave the Illustrator options at their default settings and then click OK.

3 Choose View > Fit All In Window.

4 With the Selection tool (▶) selected, click to select the lower tan cake layer.

● **Note:** You'll learn all about the Appearance panel in Lesson 13, "Exploring Creative Uses of Effects and Graphic Styles."

5 Click More Options (•••) in the Appearance section of the Properties panel to open the Appearance panel (or choose Window > Appearance).

6 Click the Add New Fill button at the bottom of the Appearance panel. This adds a copy of the existing fill to the shape and layers the new fill on top of the existing stroke and fill.

▶ **Tip:** You can find more pattern swatches in Illustrator by choosing Window > Swatch Libraries > Patterns and choosing a pattern library.

7 Click the new fill box to the right of the word "Fill" to show a panel of swatches. An arrow is pointing to it in the second part of the following figure. Select the Pompadour swatch.

The pattern swatch fills the shape as a second fill on top of the first. The swatch named "Pompadour" is a default swatch for a Print document.

8   In the Appearance panel, just below the *top* word "Fill," click the word "Opacity" to open the transparency panel (or choose Window > Transparency). Change the Opacity value to **10**.

● **Note:** If you don't see the word "Opacity" below the top Fill row, click the disclosure triangle (▶) to the left of the top word "Fill" to show it.

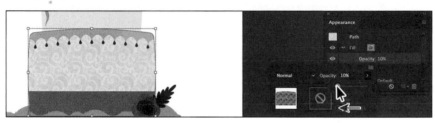

9   Close the Appearance panel.

Creating your own pattern

In this section, you'll create your own custom pattern. Patterns you create are saved as a swatch in the Swatches panel for the document you're working in.

1   Choose 2 Artboard 2 from the Artboard menu in the lower-left corner of the Document window to show the smaller artboard on the right.

2   With the Selection tool (▶) selected, choose Select > All On Active Artboard to select the artwork you'll use to create a pattern.

3   Choose Object > Pattern > Make. Click OK in the dialog box that appears.

When you create a pattern, Illustrator enters pattern editing mode, which is similar to the isolation mode you've worked with in previous lessons. Pattern editing mode allows you to create and edit patterns interactively, while previewing the changes to the pattern on the artboard. All other artwork is dimmed and cannot be edited while in this mode. The Pattern Options panel (Window > Pattern Options) also opens, giving you all the necessary options to create your pattern.

● **Note:** You don't need to have anything selected when you create a pattern. You can add content to the pattern when you edit it in pattern editing mode, as you'll see.

● **Note:** A pattern can be composed of shapes, symbols, or embedded raster images, among other objects that you can add in pattern editing mode. For instance, to create a flannel pattern for a shirt, you can create three overlapping rectangles or lines, each with varying appearance options.

4   Choose Select > All On Active Artboard to select the artwork.

5   Press Command and + (macOS) or Ctrl and + (Windows) to zoom in.

The series of lighter-colored objects around the artwork in the center are the repetition of the pattern. They are there for a preview and are a little dimmed so you can focus on the original. The blue box around the original group of objects is the *pattern tile* (the area that repeats).

6 In the Pattern Options panel, change Name to **Cake Top**.

7 Try choosing different options from the Tile Type menu to see the effect on the pattern. Before continuing, make sure Grid is selected.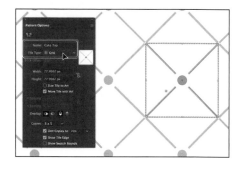

The name in the Pattern Options panel becomes the name of the swatch saved in the Swatches panel and can be useful to distinguish multiple versions of a pattern swatch, for instance. Tile Type determines how the pattern is tiled. You have three main Tile Type choices: the default grid pattern, a brick-style pattern, and the hex pattern.

8 Choose 1 x 1 from the Copies menu at the bottom of the Pattern Options panel. This will remove the repeat and let you temporarily focus on the main pattern artwork.

9 Click in a blank area to deselect the artwork.

● **Note:** Don't forget to release the mouse button first and then the keys.

10 Option+Shift-drag (macOS) or Alt+Shift-drag (Windows) the blue circle in the center to a little outside the upper-right corner of the blue pattern tile box.

  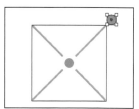

11 Click in a blank area to deselect the artwork.

12 In the Pattern Options panel, change the following options:

• Choose 5 x 5 from the Copies menu to see the repeat again.

Notice that the new circle is not repeated. That's because it's not within the pattern tile. Only artwork within the pattern tile is repeated.

- Select the Size Tile To Art option in the Pattern Options panel.

The Size Tile To Art selection fits the tile area (the blue square) to the bounds of the artwork, changing the spacing between the repeated objects. With Size Tile To Art deselected, you could manually change the width and the height of the pattern definition area in the Width and Height fields to include more content or to edit the spacing between. You can also edit the tile area manually with the Pattern Tile Tool button (⬛) in the upper-left corner of the Pattern Options panel.

▶ **Tip:** The H Spacing and V Spacing values can be either positive or negative, and they move the tiles apart or bring them closer together either horizontally (H) or vertically (V).

If you set the spacing values (H Spacing or V Spacing) to negative values, the artwork in the pattern tile will overlap. By default, when objects overlap horizontally, the left object is on top; when objects overlap vertically, the top object is on top. You can set the overlap values: Left In Front, Right In Front to change overlap horizontally, or Top In Front, Bottom In Front to change the overlap vertically (they are the small buttons in the Overlap section of the panel).

13 Click Done in the bar along the top of the Document window. If a dialog box appears, click OK.

14 Choose File > Save.

Applying your pattern

You can assign a pattern using a number of different methods. In this section, you'll apply your pattern using the fill color in the Properties panel.

1 With nothing selected, click the Previous Artboard button (◀) in the Properties panel to show the larger artboard on the left.

2 With the Selection tool (▶), click the top cake shape (see the following figure). Choose Edit > Copy and then Edit > Paste In Front.

3 Select the swatch named "Cake Top" from the Fill box in the Properties panel.

▶ **Tip:** If you want to create pattern variations, you can click Save A Copy in the bar along the top of the Document window when in pattern editing mode. This saves the current pattern in the Swatches panel as a copy and allows you to continue creating.

▶ **Tip:** Instead of making a copy of the shape, you could have applied a second fill to the shape like you did previously.

Editing your pattern

Next you'll edit the Cake Top pattern swatch in pattern editing mode.

1 With the shape still selected, click the Fill box in the Properties panel. Double-click the Cake Top pattern swatch to edit it in pattern editing mode.

2 Press Command and + (macOS) or Ctrl and + (Windows) several times to zoom in.

3 In pattern editing mode, with the Selection tool (▶) selected, click one of the blue circles; then, while pressing the Shift key, click to select the other.

4 In the Properties panel, change the fill color to the brown swatch named "BG."

5 Click Done in the gray bar along the top of the Document window to exit pattern editing mode.

6 Choose View > Fit Artboard In Window.

7 Click the top cake shape with the pattern fill to select it, if necessary.

▶ Tip: In the Scale dialog box, if you want to scale the pattern *and* the shape, you can select Transform Objects and select Transform Patterns. You can also transform patterns in the Transform panel (Window > Transform) by choosing Transform Pattern Only, Transform Object Only, or Transform Both from the panel menu (▤) before applying a transformation.

8 With the shape selected, choose Object > Transform > Scale to scale the pattern but not the shape. In the Scale dialog box, change the following options (if not already set):

- Uniform Scale: **50%**
- Scale Corners: Deselected (default setting)
- Scale Strokes & Effects: Deselected (default setting)
- Transform Objects: Deselected
- Transform Patterns: Selected

9 Select Preview to see the change. Click OK.

10 Choose Select > Deselect and then choose File > Save.

11 Choose File > Close.

Review questions

1 What is a *gradient*?

2 How do you adjust the blend between colors in a linear or radial gradient?

3 Name two ways you can add colors to a linear or radial gradient.

4 How can you adjust the direction of a linear or radial gradient?

5 What is the difference between a gradient and a blend?

6 When you save a pattern in Illustrator, where is it saved?

Review answers

1 A gradient is a graduated blend of two or more colors or tints of the same color. Gradients can be applied to the stroke or fill of an object.

2 To adjust the blend between colors in a linear or radial gradient, with the Gradient tool (▧) selected and with the pointer over the gradient annotator or in the Gradient panel, drag the diamond icons or the color stops of the gradient slider.

3 To add colors to a linear or radial gradient, in the Gradient panel, click beneath the gradient slider to add a gradient stop to the gradient. Then double-click the color stop to edit the color, using the panel that appears to mix a new color or to apply an existing color swatch. You can select the Gradient tool in the toolbar, move the pointer over the gradient-filled object, and then click beneath the gradient slider that appears in the artwork to add or edit a color stop.

4 Drag with the Gradient tool to adjust the direction of a linear or radial gradient. Dragging a long distance changes colors gradually; dragging a short distance makes the color change more abruptly. You can also rotate the gradient using the Gradient tool and change the radius, aspect ratio, starting point, and more.

5 The difference between a gradient and a blend is the way that colors combine—colors blend together within a gradient and between objects in a blend.

6 When you save a pattern in Illustrator, it is saved as a swatch in the Swatches panel. By default, swatches are saved with the currently active document.

12 USING BRUSHES TO CREATE A POSTER

Lesson overview

In this lesson, you'll learn how to do the following:

- Use four brush types: Calligraphic, Art, Bristle, and Pattern.

- Apply brushes to paths.

- Paint and edit paths with the Paintbrush tool.

- Change brush color and adjust brush settings.

- Create new brushes from Adobe Illustrator artwork.

- Work with the Blob Brush tool and the Eraser tool.

 This lesson will take about 60 minutes to complete. To get the lesson files used in this chapter, download them from the web page for this book at www.adobepress.com/IllustratorCIB2020. For more information, see "Accessing the lesson files and Web Edition" in the Getting Started section at the beginning of this book.

The variety of brush types in Adobe Illustrator lets you create a myriad of effects by painting with the Paintbrush tool or drawing with the drawing tools. You can work with the Blob Brush tool; choose from the Art, Calligraphic, Pattern, Bristle, and Scatter brushes; and create new brushes based on your artwork.

Starting the lesson

In this lesson, you will learn how to work with the different brush types in the Brushes panel, how to change brush options and create your own brushes. Before you begin, you'll restore the default preferences for Adobe Illustrator. Then you'll open the finished art file for the lesson to see the finished artwork.

● **Note:** If you have not already downloaded the project files for this lesson to your computer from your Account page, make sure to do so now. See the "Getting Started" section at the beginning of the book.

1   To ensure that the tools function and the defaults are set exactly as described in this lesson, delete or deactivate (by renaming) the Adobe Illustrator preferences file. See "Restoring default preferences" in the "Getting Started" section at the beginning of the book.

2   Start Adobe Illustrator.

3   Choose File > Open. In the Open dialog box, navigate to the Lessons > Lesson12 folder, and select the L12_end.ai file on your hard disk. Click Open to open the file.

4   If you want, choose View > Zoom Out to make the finished artwork smaller, and then adjust the window size and leave the artwork on your screen as you work. (Use the Hand tool [🖐] to move the artwork to where you want it in the Document window.) If you don't want to leave the artwork open, choose File > Close.

To begin working, you'll open an existing art file.

5   Choose File > Open. In the Open dialog box, navigate to the Lessons > Lesson12 folder and select the L12_start.ai file on your hard disk. Click Open to open the file.

6   Choose View > Fit All In Window.

7   Choose File > Save As. In the Save As dialog box, name the file **VacationPoster.ai**, and select the Lesson12 folder. Leave Adobe Illustrator (ai) chosen from the Format menu (macOS) or Adobe Illustrator (*.AI) chosen from the Save As Type menu (Windows) and then click Save.

8   In the Illustrator Options dialog box, leave the Illustrator options at their default settings and then click OK.

● **Note:** If you don't see Reset Essentials in the workspace switcher menu, choose Window > Workspace > Essentials before choosing Window > Workspace > Reset Essentials.

9   Choose Reset Essentials from the workspace switcher in the Application bar to reset the workspace.

Working with brushes

Using brushes, you can decorate paths with patterns, figures, brush strokes, textures, or angled strokes. You can also modify the brushes provided with Illustrator and create your own brushes.

You can apply brush strokes to existing paths, or you can use the Paintbrush tool to draw a path and apply a brush stroke simultaneously. You can change the color, size, and other features of a brush, and you can edit paths after brushes are applied (including adding a fill).

Types of brushes

A. Calligraphic brush

B. Art brush

C. Bristle brush

D. Pattern brush

E. Scatter brush

There are five types of brushes that appear in the Brushes panel (Window > Brushes): Calligraphic, Art, Bristle, Pattern, and Scatter. In this lesson, you will discover how to work with all of these except the Scatter brush.

A. Brushes

B. Brush Libraries Menu

C. Libraries panel

D. Remove Brush Stroke

E. Options of selected object

F. New Brush

G. Delete Brush

Note: The Brushes panel you see will most likely look different than the figure. The figure shows the default Brushes panel for a new document.

▶ **Tip:** To learn more about Scatter brushes, search for "Scatter brushes" in Illustrator Help (Help > Illustrator Help).

Using Calligraphic brushes

The first type of brush you'll learn about is the Calligraphic brush. Calligraphic brushes resemble strokes drawn with the angled point of a calligraphic pen. Calligraphic brushes are defined by an elliptical shape whose center follows the path, and you can use these brushes to create the appearance of hand-drawn strokes made with a flat, angled pen tip.

Calligraphic brush examples

Applying a Calligraphic brush to artwork

To get started, you'll filter the types of brushes shown in the Brushes panel so that it shows only Calligraphic brushes.

1 Choose Window > Brushes to show the Brushes panel. Click the Brushes panel menu icon (☰), and choose List View.

Note: A checkmark next to the brush type in the Brushes panel menu indicates that the brush type is visible in the panel.

2 Click the Brushes panel menu icon (☰) again, and deselect Show Art Brushes, Show Bristle Brushes, and Show Pattern Brushes, leaving only the Calligraphic brushes visible in the Brushes panel. You can't deselect them all at once, so you'll have to keep clicking the menu icon (☰) to access the menu.

3 Select the Selection tool (▶) in the toolbar, and click one of the curved pink paths to select it. To select the rest, choose Select > Same > Stroke Color.

4 Select the 40 pt. Flat brush in the Brushes panel to apply it to the pink paths.

Note: Similarly to drawing with an actual calligraphic pen, when you apply a Calligraphic brush, such as the 40 pt. Flat brush, the more vertically the path is drawn, the thinner the path's stroke appears.

5 Change the Stroke weight to **3 pt** in the Properties panel.

6 Click the Stroke box in the Properties panel, make sure the Swatches option (▦) is selected, and select White. Press the Escape key to hide the Swatches panel, if necessary.

7   Change Opacity to 20% in the Properties panel by clicking the arrow to the right
    of the value and dragging the Opacity slider.

8   Choose Select > Deselect and then choose File > Save.

Drawing with the Paintbrush tool

The Paintbrush tool allows you to apply a brush as you paint. Painting with the
Paintbrush tool creates vector paths that you can edit with the Paintbrush tool or
other drawing tools. Next you'll use the Paintbrush tool to paint waves in the water
with a Calligraphic brush from a brush library. Your waves won't look identical to
what you see in the lesson, and that's okay—just have some fun!

1   Select the Paintbrush tool (✏) in the toolbar.

2   Click the Brush Libraries Menu
    button (▦) at the bottom of
    the Brushes panel, and choose
    Artistic > Artistic_Calligraphic.
    A brush library panel with
    various brushes appears.

    Illustrator comes with a host
    of brush libraries that you can
    use in your artwork. Each brush
    type, including those discussed
    previously, has a series of
    libraries to choose from.

3 Click the Artistic_Calligraphic panel menu icon (▤), and choose List View. Click the brush named "15 pt. Flat" to add it to the Brushes panel.

4 Close the Artistic_Calligraphic brush library panel.

Selecting a brush from a brush library, such as the Artistic_Calligraphic library, adds that brush to the Brushes panel for the active document only.

5 Make sure the fill color is None (▨), change the stroke color to the Water swatch, and change the stroke weight to **1 pt** in the Properties panel.

6 Change the Opacity to **100%** in the Properties panel.

With the pointer in the Document window, notice that the Paintbrush pointer has an asterisk next to it (✐*), indicating that you are about to paint a new path.

● **Note:** This Calligraphic brush creates random angles on the paths, so yours may not look like what you see in the figures, and that's okay.

7 Move the pointer over the water in the lake. Paint a short curving path from left to right. You can consult the figure for how I painted it.

8 Try creating a few more paths, painting from left to right.

9 Choose Select > Deselect (if necessary) and then choose File > Save.

Editing paths with the Paintbrush tool

Now you'll use the Paintbrush tool to edit one of the paths you painted.

1 Select the Selection tool (▶) in the toolbar, and click to select one of the paths you drew on the water.

2 Select the Paintbrush tool (✎) in the toolbar. Move the pointer over the selected path. An asterisk will *not* appear next to the pointer when it's positioned over a selected path. Drag to redraw the path. The selected path is edited from the point where you began drawing.

3 Press and hold the Command (macOS) or Ctrl (Windows) key to toggle to the Selection tool, and click to select another one of the curved paths you drew with the Paintbrush tool. After clicking, release the key to return to the Paintbrush tool.

4 With the Paintbrush tool, move the pointer over some part of the selected path. When the asterisk disappears next to the pointer, drag to the right to redraw the path.

5 Choose Select > Deselect (if necessary) and then choose File > Save.

Next you'll edit the Paintbrush tool options to change how it paints.

6 Double-click the Paintbrush tool (✎) in the toolbar to display the Paintbrush Tool Options dialog box, and make the following changes:

   • Fidelity: Drag the slider all the way to Smooth (to the right).

   • Keep Selected: Selected.

7 Click OK.

The Paintbrush Tool Options dialog box changes the way the Paintbrush tool functions. For the Fidelity option, the closer to Smooth you drag the slider, the smoother the path will be, and with fewer points. Also, because you selected Keep Selected, the paths remain selected after you finish drawing them.

8   Change the stroke weight to **2 pt** in the Properties panel.

9   With the Paintbrush tool selected, paint several more paths from either left to right or right to left across the water.

Notice that after painting each path, the path is still selected, so you could edit it if you need to.

● **Note:** When the Keep Selected option is deselected, you can edit a path by selecting it with the Selection tool (▶) or by selecting a segment or point on the path with the Direct Selection tool (▷) and then redrawing part of the path with the Paintbrush tool, as you saw previously.

10 Double-click the Paintbrush tool in the toolbar. In the Paintbrush Tool Options dialog box, deselect the Keep Selected option and then click OK.

Now the paths will *not* remain selected after you finish drawing them, and you can draw overlapping paths without altering previously drawn paths.

11 Choose Select > Deselect, if necessary, and then choose File > Save.

Editing a brush

To change the options for a brush, you can double-click the brush in the Brushes panel. When you edit a brush, you can also choose whether to change artwork that the brush has been applied to. Next you'll change the appearance of the 15 pt. Flat brush you've been painting with.

1   In the Brushes panel, double-click the brush thumbnail to the left of the text "15 pt. Flat" (or to the right of the name in the Brushes panel) to open the Calligraphic Brush Options dialog box.

● **Note:** The edits you make will change the brush for this document only.

2 In the dialog box make the following changes:

- Name: **20 pt. Angled**
- Angle: **20°**
- Choose Fixed from the menu to the right of Angle. (When Random is chosen, a random variation of brush angles is created every time you draw.)
- Roundness: **0%** (the default setting)
- Size: **20 pt**

▶ **Tip:** The Preview window in the dialog box (below the Name field) shows the changes that you make to the brush.

3 Click OK.

4 In the dialog box that appears, click Leave Strokes so as not to apply the brush change to the existing waves that have the brush applied.

5 Choose Select > Deselect, if necessary, and then choose File > Save.

● **Note:** The artwork should be deselected already, and if it is, the Select > Deselect command will be dimmed (you can't select it).

Removing a brush stroke

You can easily remove a brush stroke applied to artwork where you don't want it. Now you'll remove the brush stroke from the stroke of a path.

1 Select the Selection tool (▶), and click the purple path with the purple stroke applied (see the following figure).

    When creating the artwork, I was trying out different brushes on the artwork. The brush applied to the stroke of the selected path needs to be removed.

▶ **Tip:** You can also select the [Basic] Brush in the Brushes panel to remove a brush applied to a path.

2 Click the Remove Brush Stroke button (✖) at the bottom of the Brushes panel.

    Removing a brush stroke doesn't remove the stroke color and weight; it just removes the brush applied.

3 Change the stroke weight to **10 pt** in the Properties panel.

4 Choose Select > Deselect and then choose File > Save.

Using Art brushes

Art brushes stretch artwork or an embedded raster image evenly along the length of a path. As with other brushes, you can edit the brush options to affect how the brush is applied to artwork.

Art brush examples

Applying an existing Art brush

Next you'll apply an existing Art brush to create a fern plant on the lake shore.

1   In the Brushes panel, click the Brushes panel menu icon (▤), and deselect Show Calligraphic Brushes. Then choose Show Art Brushes from the same panel menu to make the Art brushes visible in the Brushes panel.

2   Click the Brush Libraries Menu button (▥.) at the bottom of the Brushes panel, and choose Artistic > Artistic_ChalkCharcoalPencil.

3   Click the Artistic_ChalkCharcoalPencil panel menu icon (▤), and choose List View. Click the brush named "Charcoal" in the list to add the brush to the Brushes panel for this document. Close the Artistic_ChalkCharcoalPencil panel group.

4   Select the Paintbrush tool (✐) in the toolbar.

5   Ensure that the fill color is None (⬚), change the stroke color to the Fern green swatch, and change the stroke weight to **10 pt** in the Properties panel.

6   Move the Paintbrush pointer (✐.) on the left side of the lake (marked with an X in the figure). Drag to create the plant path.

    Refer to the figure to see how it was painted, and don't worry about being exact. You can always choose Edit > Undo Art Stroke and repaint the path.

▶ **Tip:** With the Paintbrush pointer selected, press the Caps Lock key to see a precise cursor (X). In certain situations, this can help you paint with more precision.

7 Try adding a few more painted paths, always starting from the same point as the original path you painted, to add more fronds (leaves).

8 Select the Selection tool, and click to select one of the paths. To select the rest of the paths that make up the fern, choose Select > Same > Stroke Color.

9 Click the Group button in the Properties panel to keep them together.

10 Choose Select > Deselect and then choose File > Save.

If you followed the tip on the previous page and pressed the Caps Lock key to see a precise cursor, press the Caps Lock key again to return to a normal cursor.

Creating an Art brush

● **Note:** To learn about guidelines for creating brushes, see "Create or modify brushes" in Illustrator Help (Help > Illustrator Help).

In this section, you'll create a new Art brush from existing artwork.

1 Choose 2 from the Artboard menu in the Properties panel to navigate to the second artboard with the tree artwork on it.

2 With the Selection tool (▶) selected, click the tree artwork to select it.

▶ **Tip:** You can create an Art brush from a raster image. The image you use to create the brush must be embedded in the Illustrator document.

Next you'll make an Art brush from the selected artwork. You can make Art brushes from embedded raster images or from vector artwork, but that artwork must not contain gradients, blends, other brush strokes, mesh objects, graphs, linked files, masks, or text that has not been converted to outlines.

3 Choose Window > Brushes to open the Brushes panel, if it isn't open already. With the tree artwork still selected, click the New Brush button (▣) at the bottom of the Brushes panel.

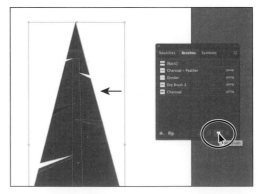

This begins the process of creating a new brush from the selected artwork.

4 In the New Brush dialog box, select Art Brush and then click OK.

▶ **Tip:** You can also create an Art brush by dragging artwork into the Brushes panel and choosing Art brush in the New Brush dialog box that appears.

5 In the Art Brush Options dialog box that appears, change the name to **Tree**. Click OK.

6 Choose Select > Deselect.

7 Choose 1 from the Active Artboard menu in the Properties panel to navigate to the first artboard with the main scene.

8 With the Selection tool selected, click to select the purple line to the right of the cabin artwork.

9 Click the brush named "Tree" in the Brushes panel to apply it.

Notice that the original tree artwork is stretched along the path. This is the default behavior of an Art brush.

Editing an Art brush

Next you'll edit the tree Art brush you applied to the path and update the appearance of the tree on the artboard.

1   With the path still selected on the artboard, in the Brushes panel, double-click the brush thumbnail to the left of the text "Tree" (or to the right of the name in the Brushes panel) to open the Art Brush Options dialog box.

2   In the Art Brush Options dialog box, select Preview to see the changes as you make them, and move the dialog box so you can see the line with the brush applied. Make the following changes:

*   Stretch Between Guides: Selected. The guides referred to in the settings are not physical guides on the artboard. They are used to indicate a portion of the art that stretches or contracts to make the Art brush fit the path length. Any part of the art that is not within the guides will be able to stretch or contract. The Start and End settings are how you indicate where the guides are positioned on the original art.

*   Start: **5.875 in**

*   End: **7.5414 in** (the default setting)

3   Click OK.

4   In the dialog box that appears, click Apply To Strokes to apply the change to the path that has the Tree brush applied.

5   Choose Select > Deselect and then choose File > Save.

Using Bristle brushes

Bristle brushes allow you to create strokes with the appearance of a natural brush with bristles. Painting with a Bristle brush using the Paintbrush tool creates vector paths with the Bristle brush applied.

In this section, you'll start by adjusting options for a brush to change how it appears in the artwork and then paint with the Paintbrush tool and a Bristle brush to create smoke

Bristle brush examples

Changing Bristle brush options

As you've seen, you can change the appearance of a brush by adjusting its settings in the Brush Options dialog box, either before or after brushes have been applied to artwork. In the case of Bristle brushes, it's usually best to adjust the brush settings prior to painting since it can take some time to update the brush strokes.

1   In the Brushes panel, click the panel menu icon (▦), choose Show Bristle Brushes, and then deselect Show Art Brushes.

2   Double-click the thumbnail for the default Mop brush, or double-click directly to the right of the brush name in the Brushes panel, to change the options for that brush. In the Bristle Brush Options dialog box, make the following changes:

● **Note:** To learn more about the Bristle Brush Options dialog box and its settings, see "Using the Bristle brush" in Illustrator Help (Help > Illustrator Help).

▶ **Tip:** Illustrator comes with a series of default Bristle brushes. Click the Brush Libraries Menu button (▥) at the bottom of the Brushes panel, and choose Bristle Brush > Bristle Brush Library.

- Shape: **Flat Fan**

- Size: **3 mm** (The brush size is the diameter of the brush.)

- Bristle Length: **150%** (This is the default setting. The bristle length starts from the point where the bristles meet the handle of the bristle tip.)

- Bristle Density: **33%** (This is the default setting. The bristle density is the number of bristles in a specified area of the brush neck.)

- Bristle Thickness: **50%** (The bristle thickness can vary from fine to coarse [from 1% to 100%].)

- Paint Opacity: **75%** (This is the default setting. This option lets you set the opacity of the paint being used.)

- Stiffness: **50%** (This is the default setting. Stiffness refers to the rigidness of the bristles.)

3   Click OK.

Painting with a Bristle brush

Now you'll use the Mop brush to draw some smoke above the chimney of the cabin. Painting with a Bristle brush can create an organic, fluid path.

1 Select the Zoom tool (Q) in the toolbar, and click a few times, slowly, on the chimney at the top of the cabin to zoom in on it.

2 Select the Selection tool (▶) in the toolbar, and click to select the chimney.

This selects the layer that the shape is on so that any artwork you paint will be on the same layer.

3 Choose Select > Deselect.

4 Select the Paintbrush tool (🖌) in the toolbar. Choose the Mop brush from the Brush menu in the Properties panel, if it's not already chosen.

▶ **Tip:** If you want to edit paths as you draw, you can select the Keep Selected option in the Paintbrush Tool Options for the Paintbrush tool, or you can select paths with the Selection tool.

5 Make sure that the fill color is None (⊘) and the stroke color is White in the Properties panel. Press the Escape key to hide the Swatches panel. Change the stroke weight to **4 pt** in the Properties panel.

6 Move the pointer over the top of the chimney. Drag up in an S shape. Release the mouse button when you reach the end of the path you want to draw.

7 With the Paintbrush tool, use the Mop brush to paint more paths. Try drawing from where you started the first path, at the top of the chimney. The idea is to create smoke coming from the fireplace in the cabin.

Cleaning up the shapes

Next you'll change the stroke color of a few of the paths you drew.

1 Choose View > Outline to see all of the paths you just created when painting.

2 Select the Selection tool (▶) in the toolbar, and click to select one of the paths.

3 Change the stroke color in the Properties panel to the swatch named "Light gray."

4 Choose View > Preview (or GPU Preview).

Next you'll select all of the Bristle brush paths you painted and group them together.

5 Choose Select > Object > Bristle Brush Strokes to select all of the paths created with the Paintbrush tool using the Mop brush.

6 Click the Group button in the Properties panel to group them together.

7 Change Opacity to **50%** in the Properties panel.

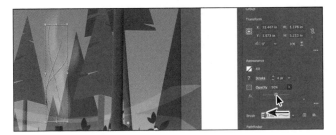

8 Choose Select > Deselect and then choose File > Save.

Using Pattern brushes

Pattern brushes paint a pattern made up of separate sections, or *tiles*. When you apply a Pattern brush to artwork, different tiles of the pattern are applied to different sections of the path, depending on where the section falls on the path—the end, middle, or corner. There are hundreds of interesting Pattern brushes that you can choose from when creating your own projects, from grass to cityscapes. Next you'll apply an existing Pattern brush to paths to give the side of the cabin the appearance of wood.

Pattern brush examples

1 Choose View > Fit Artboard In Window.

2 In the Brushes panel, click the panel menu icon (▤), choose Show Pattern Brushes, and then deselect Show Bristle Brushes.

▶ Tip: Just as with other brush types, there is a series of default Pattern brush libraries that come with Illustrator. To access them, click the Brush Libraries Menu button (▦), and choose a library from one of the menus (the Borders menu, for example).

3 With the Selection tool (▶) selected, double-click one of the yellow paths on the cabin group to enter isolation mode; then click to select one of the yellow paths to select the group.

4 Click the Brush Libraries Menu button (▦) at the bottom of the Brushes panel, and choose Borders > Borders_Frames.

5 Click the brush named "Mahogany" in the list to apply it to the paths and add the brush to the Brushes panel for this document. Close the Borders_Frames panel group.

6 Click the Options Of Selected Object button (▤) in the Properties panel to edit the brush options for only the selected paths on the artboard.

7 Select Preview in the Stroke Options (Pattern Brush) dialog box. Change the Scale to **70%** either by dragging the Scale slider or by typing in the value. Click OK.

▶ **Tip:** You'll also see the Options Of Selected Object button (▤) at the bottom of the Brushes panel or in the Properties panel.

When you edit the brush options of the selected object, you see only some of the brush options. The Stroke Options (Pattern Brush) dialog box is used to edit the properties of the brushed path without updating the corresponding brush.

8 Press the Escape key to exit isolation mode.

9 Choose Select > Deselect and then choose File > Save.

Creating a Pattern brush

You can create a Pattern brush in several ways. For a simple pattern applied to a straight line, for instance, you can select the content that you're using for the pattern and click the New Brush button (▤) at the bottom of the Brushes panel.

To create a more complex pattern to apply to objects with curves and corners, you can select artwork in the Document window to be used in a pattern brush, create swatches in the Swatches panel from the artwork that you are using in the Pattern brush, and even have Illustrator autogenerate the Pattern brush corners. In Illustrator, only a side tile needs to be defined. Illustrator automatically generates four different types of corners based on the art used for the side tile. These four autogenerated options fit the corners perfectly. Next you'll create a Pattern brush for some lights on the cabin.

1 Choose 3 from the Artboard menu in the Properties panel to navigate to the third artboard with the light bulb artwork on it.

2 With the Selection tool (▶) selected, click to select the yellow light bulb group.

3 Click the panel menu icon (▤) in the Brushes panel, and choose Thumbnail View.

Notice that Pattern brushes in the Brushes panel are segmented in Thumbnail view. Each segment corresponds to a pattern tile.

4 In the Brushes panel, click the New Brush button () to create a pattern out of the light bulb.

5 In the New Brush dialog box, select Pattern Brush. Click OK.

A new Pattern brush can be made regardless of whether artwork is selected. If you create a Pattern brush without artwork selected, it is assumed that you will add artwork by dragging it into the Brushes panel later or by selecting the artwork from a pattern swatch you create as you edit the brush. You will see the latter method later in this section.

Note: Some brushes don't require corner tiles because they're designed for straight lines or curved paths.

6 In the Pattern Brush Options dialog box, name the brush **Lights**.

Pattern brushes can have up to five tiles—the side, start, and end tiles, plus an outer-corner tile and an inner-corner tile to paint sharp corners on a path.

You can see all five tiles as buttons below the Spacing option in the dialog box. The tile buttons let you apply different artwork to different parts of the path. You can click a tile button for the tile you want to define, and then you select an autogenerated selection (if available) or a pattern swatch from the menu that appears.

Tip: Move the pointer over the tile squares in the Pattern Brush Options dialog box to see a tool tip indicating which tile it is.

Tip: Selected artwork becomes the side tile, by default, when creating a Pattern brush.

7 Under the Spacing option, click the Side Tile box (the second tile from the left). The artwork that was originally selected is in the menu that appears, along with None and any pattern swatches found in the Swatches panel.

Tip: To save a brush and reuse it in another file, you can create a brush library with the brushes you want to use. For more information, see "Work with Brush libraries" in Illustrator Help.

8 Click the Outer Corner Tile box to reveal the menu. You may need to click twice, once to close the previous menu and another click to open this new one.

The outer-corner tile has been generated automatically by Illustrator, based on the original light bulb artwork. In the menu, you can choose from four types of corners that are generated automatically:

- **Auto-Centered**: The side tile is stretched around the corner and centered on it.

- **Auto-Between**: Copies of the side tile extend all the way into the corner, with one copy on each side. Folding elimination is used to stretch them into shape.

- **Auto-Sliced**: The side tile is sliced diagonally, and the pieces come together, similar to a miter joint in a wooden picture frame.

- **Auto-Overlap**: Copies of the tiles overlap at the corner.

9 Choose Auto-Between from the menu. This generates the outer corner of any path that the Pattern brush will be applied to from the light bulb artwork.

10 Click OK. The Lights brush appears in the Brushes panel.

11 Choose Select > Deselect.

Applying a Pattern brush

In this section, you'll apply the Border Pattern brush to a path on the cabin. As you've seen, when you use drawing tools to apply brushes to artwork, you first draw the path with the drawing tool and then select the brush in the Brushes panel to apply the brush to the path.

1 Choose 1 from the Active Artboard menu in the Properties panel to navigate to the first artboard with the main scene artwork on it.

2 Choose View > Zoom In a few times to zoom in.

3 With the Selection tool (▶) selected, click the horizontal green path on the cabin.

4 Toward the bottom of the toolbar, click the Fill box, and make sure that None (⧄) is selected, and then click the Stroke box and select None (⧄).

5 With the path selected, click the Lights brush in the Brushes panel to apply it.

6 Choose Select > Deselect.

The path is painted with the Lights brush. Because the path does not include sharp corners, outer-corner and inner-corner tiles are not applied to the path.

Editing the Pattern brush

▶ **Tip:** For more information on creating pattern swatches, see "About patterns" in Illustrator Help.

Now you'll edit the Lights Pattern brush using a pattern swatch that you create.

1 Choose 3 from the Active Artboard menu in the Properties panel to navigate to the third artboard with the light bulb artwork on it. There is a white light bulb in the group that you won't be able to see since it's on a white artboard.

2 Click the Swatches panel tab to show the Swatches panel.

3 With the Selection tool (▶), drag the artwork with the white light bulb into the Swatches panel.

The artwork is saved as a new pattern swatch in the Swatches panel. After you create a pattern brush, you can delete the pattern swatches from the Swatches panel, if you don't plan to use them for additional artwork.

4 Choose Select > Deselect.

5 Choose 1 from the Active Artboard menu in the Properties panel to navigate to the first artboard with the main scene artwork on it.

6 Click the Brushes panel tab to show the panel and double-click the Lights pattern brush to open the Pattern Brush Options dialog box.

7 Change Scale to **20%**. Click the Outer Corner Tile box, and choose the pattern swatch named New Pattern Swatch 1, which you just created, from the menu that appears (you'll need to scroll). Click OK.

▶ **Tip:** You can also change the pattern tiles in a Pattern brush by pressing the Option (macOS) or Alt (Windows) key and dragging artwork from the artboard onto the tile of the Pattern brush you want to change in the Brushes panel.

8 In the dialog box that appears, click Apply To Strokes to update the lights on the cabin.

The lights on the horizontal path won't change since there are no corners.

9 With the Selection tool selected, click to select the green rectangle path on the door of the cabin. You may want to zoom in.

10 Click the Lights brush in the Brushes panel to apply it.

Notice that the white light bulbs are added to the path. The path is painted with the side tile from the Lights brush and the outer-corner tile.

11 Choose Select > Deselect and then choose File > Save.

Working with the Blob Brush tool

You can use the Blob Brush tool () to paint filled shapes that intersect and merge with other shapes of the same color. With the Blob Brush tool, you can draw with Paintbrush tool artistry. Unlike the Paintbrush tool, which lets you create open paths, the Blob Brush tool lets you create a closed shape with only a fill (no stroke) that you can then easily edit with the Eraser or Blob Brush tool. Shapes that have a stroke cannot be edited with the Blob Brush tool.

Path created with the Paintbrush tool.

Shape created with the Blob Brush tool.

Drawing with the Blob Brush tool

Next you'll use the Blob Brush tool to create a flower.

1   Choose 4 from the Active Artboard menu in the Properties panel to navigate to the fourth artboard, which is empty.

2   In the Swatches panel, select the Fill box and then select the swatch named "Flower." Select the Stroke color box, and select None (⊘) to remove the stroke.

When drawing with the Blob Brush tool, if a fill and stroke are set before drawing, the stroke color becomes the fill color of the shape made by the Blob Brush tool. If only a fill is set before drawing, it ultimately becomes the fill of the shape created.

3   Press and hold down on the Paintbrush tool (✏) in the toolbar, and select the Blob Brush tool ().

4   Double-click the Blob Brush tool in the toolbar. In the Blob Brush Tool Options dialog box, change the following:

   •   Keep Selected: Selected

   •   Size: **70 pt**

5 Click OK.

6 Press and drag to create a flower shape.

When you draw with the Blob Brush tool, you create filled, closed shapes. Those shapes can contain several types of fill, including gradients, solid colors, patterns, and more. Notice that the Blob Brush pointer has a circle around it before you begin painting. That circle indicates the size of the brush (70 pt, which you set in the previous step).

● **Note:** You can release the mouse and then continue painting with the Blob Brush. As long as the new artwork is overlapping the existing flower artwork, it will merge.

▶ **Tip:** You can also change the Blob Brush size by pressing the right bracket key ( ]) or left bracket key ([ ) several times to increase or decrease the size of the brush.

Merging paths with the Blob Brush tool

In addition to drawing new shapes with the Blob Brush tool, you can use it to intersect and merge shapes of the same color. Objects merged with the Blob Brush tool need to have the same appearance attributes, have no stroke, be on the same layer or in the same group, and be adjacent to each other in the stacking order.

If you find that the shapes are not merging, it may be that they have different strokes and fills. You can select both shapes with the Selection tool (▶) and ensure that the fill color is the same and the stroke is None in the Properties panel. Then you can select the Blob Brush tool and try dragging from one shape to the other.

Editing with the Eraser tool

As you draw and merge shapes with the Blob Brush tool, you may draw too much and want to edit what you've done. You can use the Eraser tool (◆) in combination with the Blob Brush tool to mold the shape and to correct any changes you don't like.

1 With the Selection tool (▶), click to select the flower shape.

Selecting the shape(s) before erasing limits the Eraser tool to erasing only the selected shape(s).

2 Double-click the Eraser tool (◆) in the toolbar. In the Eraser Tool Options dialog box, change Size to **40 pt**, and click OK.

▶ **Tip:** As you draw with the Blob Brush and Eraser tools, it is recommended that you use shorter strokes and release the mouse button often. You can undo the edits that you make, but if you draw in one long stroke without releasing the mouse button, undoing removes the entire stroke.

3 Move the pointer over the center of the flower shape and, with the Eraser tool selected, press and drag to remove some of the center. Try switching between the Blob Brush tool and the Eraser tool to edit the flower.

The Blob Brush and Eraser tools both have pointers that include a circle that indicates the diameter of the brush.

4 Choose Select > Deselect.

5 Select the flower shape with the Selection tool.

6 Choose Edit > Copy.

7 Choose 1 Lake scene from the Active Navigation menu in the Status bar to navigate to the first artboard with the scene artwork on it.

8 Click the bush with flowers on the right side of the artboard, and press Command and + (macOS) or Ctrl and + (Windows) a few times to zoom in.

9 Click the Arrange button in the Properties panel, and choose Bring To Front.

10 Choose Edit > Paste to paste the flower. Pressing the Shift key, drag a corner to make the flower smaller. Release the mouse button and then the key.

11 Option-drag (macOS) or Alt-drag (Windows) the flower shape onto another part of the bush. Release the mouse button and then the key to place a new copy.

12 Repeat this several times to create flowers on the bush.

13 Choose Select > Deselect and then choose View > Fit Artboard In Window.

14 Choose File > Save, and close all open files.

Review questions

1 What is the difference between applying a brush to artwork using the Paintbrush tool (✐) and applying a brush to artwork using one of the drawing tools?

2 Describe how artwork in an Art brush is applied to content.

3 Describe how to edit paths with the Paintbrush tool as you draw. How does the Keep Selected option affect the Paintbrush tool?

4 For which brush types must you have artwork selected on the artboard before you can create a brush?

5 What does the Blob Brush tool (✐) allow you to create?

Review answers

1 When painting with the Paintbrush tool (✐), if a brush is chosen in the Brushes panel and you draw on the artboard, the brush is applied directly to the paths as you draw. To apply brushes using a drawing tool, you select the tool and draw in the artwork. Then you select the path in the artwork and choose a brush in the Brushes panel. The brush is applied to the selected path.

2 An Art brush is made from artwork (vector or embedded raster). When you apply an Art brush to the stroke of an object, the artwork in the Art brush, by default, is stretched along the selected object stroke.

3 To edit a path with the Paintbrush tool, drag over a selected path to redraw it. The Keep Selected option keeps the last path selected as you draw with the Paintbrush tool. Leave the Keep Selected option selected when you want to easily edit the previous path as you draw. Deselect the Keep Selected option when you want to draw layered paths with the paintbrush without altering previous paths. When Keep Selected is deselected, you can use the Selection tool (▶) to select a path and then edit it.

4 For Art (and Scatter) brushes, you need to have artwork selected in order to create a brush using the New Brush button (▣) in the Brushes panel.

5 Use the Blob Brush tool (✐) to edit filled shapes that you can intersect and merge with other shapes of the same color or to create artwork from scratch.

13 EXPLORING CREATIVE USES OF EFFECTS AND GRAPHIC STYLES

Lesson overview

In this lesson, you'll learn how to do the following:

- Work with the Appearance panel.

- Edit and apply appearance attributes.

- Copy, enable, disable, and remove appearance attributes.

- Reorder appearance attributes.

- Apply and edit a variety of effects.

- Save and apply an appearance as a graphic style.

- Apply a graphic style to a layer.

- Scale strokes and effects.

This lesson will take about 60 minutes to complete. To get the lesson files used in this chapter, download them from the web page for this book at www.adobepress.com/IllustratorCIB2020. For more information, see "Accessing the lesson files and Web Edition" in the Getting Started section at the beginning of this book.

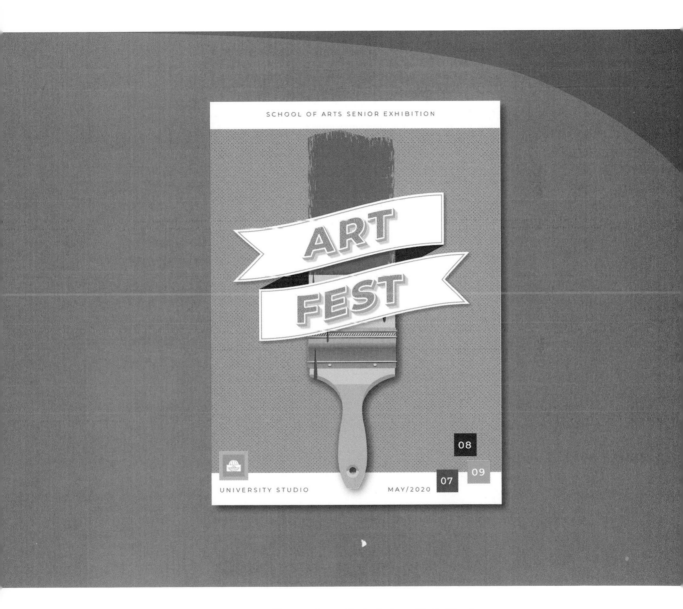

You can change the look of an object without changing its structure simply by applying attributes, such as fills, strokes, and effects, from the Appearance panel. Since the effects themselves are live, they can be modified or removed at any time. This allows you to save the appearance attributes as graphic styles and apply them to another object.

Starting the lesson

In this lesson, you'll change the appearance of artwork for a poster using the Appearance panel, various effects, and graphic styles. Before you begin, you'll need to restore the default preferences for Adobe Illustrator. Then you'll open a file containing the final artwork to see what you'll create.

● **Note:** If you have not already downloaded the project files for this lesson to your computer from your Account page, make sure to do so now. See the "Getting Started" section at the beginning of the book.

1 To ensure that the tools function and the defaults are set exactly as described in this lesson, delete or deactivate (by renaming) the Adobe Illustrator preferences file. See "Restoring default preferences" in the "Getting Started" section at the beginning of the book.

2 Start Adobe Illustrator.

3 Choose File > Open, and open the L13_end.ai file in the Lessons > Lesson13 folder on your hard disk.

This file displays a completed illustration of a poster for a student art festival.

● **Note:** You will need an internet connection to activate fonts.

4 In the Missing Fonts dialog box that most likely will appear, click Activate Fonts to activate all of the missing fonts. After they are activated and you see the message stating that there are no more missing fonts, click Close.

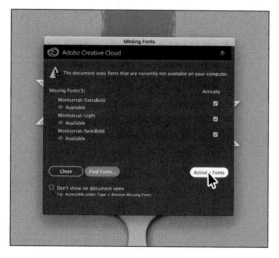

If you can't get the fonts to activate, you can go to the Creative Cloud desktop application and click the Fonts icon (f) in the upper-right to see what the issue may be (refer to the section "Changing font family and font style" in Lesson 9, "Adding Type to a Poster," for more information on how to resolve it).

You can also just click Close in the Missing Fonts dialog box and ignore the missing fonts as you proceed. A third method is to click the Find Fonts button in the Missing Fonts dialog box and replace the fonts with a local font on your machine. You can also go to Help (Help > Illustrator Help) and search for "Find missing fonts."

5   Choose View > Fit Artboard In Window. Leave the file open as a reference or choose File > Close to close it.

To begin working, you'll open an existing art file.

6   Choose File > Open. In the Open dialog box, navigate to the Lessons > Lesson13 folder, and select the L13_start.ai file on your hard disk. Click Open to open the file.

● **Note:** For help on resolving any missing fonts, refer to step 4.

The L13_start.ai file uses the same fonts as the L13_end.ai file. If you've activated the fonts already, you don't need to do it again. If you didn't open the L13_end.ai file, then the Missing Fonts dialog box will most likely appear for this step. Click Activate Fonts to activate all of the missing fonts. After they are activated and you see the message stating that there are no more missing fonts, click Close.

7   Choose File > Save As, name the file **ArtShow.ai**, and select the Lesson13 folder. Leave Adobe Illustrator (ai) chosen from the Format menu (macOS) or Adobe Illustrator (*.AI) chosen from the Save As Type menu (Windows), and then click Save.

8   In the Illustrator Options dialog box, leave the Illustrator options at their default settings and then click OK.

9   Choose Reset Essentials from the workspace switcher in the Application bar to reset the workspace.

● **Note:** If you don't see Reset Essentials in the workspace switcher menu, choose Window > Workspace > Essentials before choosing Window > Workspace > Reset Essentials.

10 Choose View > Fit Artboard In Window.

Using the Appearance panel

An *appearance attribute* is an aesthetic property—such as a fill, stroke, transparency, or effect—that affects the look of an object but usually does not affect its basic structure. Up to this point, you've been changing appearance attributes in the Properties panel, Swatches panel, and more. Appearance attributes like these can also be found in the Appearance panel for selected artwork. In this lesson, you'll focus on using the Appearance panel to apply and edit appearance attributes.

1 Select the Selection tool (▶), and click to select the large dark gray shape in the background.

▶ **Tip:** You can also choose Window > Appearance to open the Appearance panel.

2 Click More Options (•••) in the Appearance section of the Properties panel on the right (an arrow is pointing to it in the following figure) to open the Appearance panel.

The Appearance panel shows what the selected content is (a path, in this case) and the appearance attributes applied to it (Stroke, Fill, etc.).

▶ **Tip:** You may want to drag the bottom of the Appearance panel down to make it taller, as you see in the figure.

The different options available in the Appearance panel are shown here:

A. Selected artwork and thumbnail

B. Attribute row

C. Visibility column

D. Link to edit the effect options

E. Add New Stroke

F. Add New Fill

G. Add New Effect

H. Clear Appearance

I. Duplicate Selected Item

J. Delete Selected Item

K. Indicates that an effect is applied

The Appearance panel (Window > Appearance) can be used to view and adjust the appearance attributes for a selected object, group, or layer. Fills and strokes are listed in stacking order; top to bottom in the panel correlates to front to back in the artwork. Effects applied to artwork are listed from top to bottom in the order in which they are applied to the artwork. An advantage of using appearance attributes is that they can be changed or removed at any time without affecting the underlying artwork or any other attributes applied to the object in the Appearance panel.

Editing appearance attributes

You'll start by changing the appearance of artwork using the Appearance panel.

1   With the dark gray shape selected, in the Appearance panel, click the gray Fill box in the fill attribute row as many times as needed until the Swatches panel appears. Select the swatch named "Background" to apply it to the fill. Press the Escape key to hide the Swatches panel.

Note: You may need to click the Fill box more than once to open the Swatches panel. The first click of the Fill box selects the Fill row in the panel, and the next click shows the Swatches panel.

2   Click the words "1 pt" in the Stroke row to show the Stroke Weight option. Change the stroke weight to 0 to remove it (the Stroke Weight field will be blank or show "0 pt" when it's 0).

Tip: In the
Appearance panel, you
can drag an attribute
row, such as Drop
Shadow, to the
Delete Selected Item
button (🗑) to delete
it, or you can select the
attribute row and click
the Delete Selected
Item button.

Tip: You can view
all hidden attributes
(attributes you have
turned off) by choosing
Show All Hidden
Attributes from the
Appearance panel
menu (▤).

3 Click the visibility column (👁) to the left of the Drop Shadow attribute name
in the Appearance panel.

Appearance attributes can be temporarily hidden or deleted so that they are no
longer applied to the selected artwork.

4 With the Drop Shadow row selected (click to the right of the link "Drop
Shadow" if it isn't selected), click the Delete Selected Item button (🗑) at the
bottom of the panel to completely remove the shadow, rather than just turning
off the visibility. Leave the shape selected.

Adding another fill to content

Artwork and text in Illustrator can have more than one stroke and fill applied. This
can be a great way to add interest to design elements like shapes and paths, while
adding multiple strokes and fills to text can be a great way to add pop to your text.
Next you'll add another fill to the shape.

1 With the background shape still selected,
in the Appearance panel, click the Add
New Fill button (▣) at the bottom of the
Appearance panel.

The figure shows what the panel looks like after clicking the Add New Fill button. A second Fill row is added to the Appearance panel. By default, new fill or stroke attribute rows are added directly above a selected attribute row or, if no attribute rows are selected, at the top of the Appearance panel list.

2 Click the *bottom* (original) Fill box in the fill attribute row a few times until the Swatches panel appears. Click the pattern swatch named "Crosses" to apply it to the original fill. Press the Escape key to hide the Swatches panel.

The pattern won't show in the selected artwork because the second fill you added in the first step is covering the "Crosses" fill. The two fills are stacked on top of each other.

▶ **Tip:** You can also close panels that appear when you click an underlined word, like "Stroke," by pressing the Escape key, clicking the Stroke attribute row, or pressing Enter or Return.

3 Click the eye icon (👁) to the left of the *top* fill attribute row to hide it.

You should now see the pattern fill in the shape. In the next section, you'll reorder the attribute rows in the Appearance panel so the pattern is on top of the color fill.

4 Click where the eye icon was to the left of the *top* fill attribute row to make it visible again.

5 Choose Select > Deselect and then choose File > Save.

Adding multiple strokes and fills to text

Aside from adding multiple strokes and fills to artwork, you can also do the same for text. The text remains editable and you can use a number of effects to achieve the look that you want.

1 Select the Type tool (T), and select the text "ART SHOW."

Notice that "Type: No Appearance" appears at the top of the Appearance panel. This is referring to the type object, not the text within. You will also see the word "Characters." Formatting for the text (not the type object) is listed below the word "Characters." You should see the stroke (none) and the fill (gold). Also notice that you cannot add another stroke or fill to the text since the Add New Stroke and Add New Fill buttons are dimmed at the bottom of the panel. To add a new stroke or fill to text, you need to select the type object, not the text within.

▶ **Tip:** You could also click Type: No Appearance at the top of the Appearance panel to select the type object (not the text within).

2 Select the Selection tool (▶). The type object will now be selected (not the text).

3 Click the Add New Fill button (▣) at the bottom of the Appearance panel to add a fill above the word "Characters."

● **Note:** If you are wondering why I would name a swatch "USGS 22 Gravel Beach," know that I didn't. That pattern swatch can be found in Illustrator by default (Window > Swatch Libraries > Patterns > Basic Graphics > Basic Graphics_Textures).

The new black fill is covering the original fill of the text. If you were to double-click the word "Characters" in the Appearance panel, you would select the text and see the formatting options for it (fill, stroke, etc.).

4 Click the fill attribute row to select it, if it's not already selected. Click the black Fill box, and select the pattern swatch named "USGS 22 Gravel Beach." Press the Escape key to hide the swatches.

When you apply a fill to a text object, an extra stroke with no color is also applied. You don't have to use it.

5   Click the disclosure triangle (▶) to the left of the same fill row to show other properties, if necessary. Click the word "Opacity" to show the Transparency panel and change Opacity to **50%**. Press the Escape key to hide the Transparency panel.

Each appearance row (stroke, fill) has its own opacity that you can adjust. The bottom Opacity appearance row affects the transparency for the entire selected object. Next you'll add two strokes to the text using the Appearance panel. This is another great way to achieve unique design effects with a single object.

6   Click the Stroke box a few times in the Appearance panel to show the swatches. Select the light green swatch named "Text stroke." Press the Escape key to hide the swatches.

7   Change the Stroke Weight to 5 pt.

8 Click the Add New Stroke button (■) at the bottom of the Appearance panel.

A second stroke, which is a copy of the original, is now added to the text. This is a great way to add interest to your designs without having to make copies of shapes and put them on top of each other to add multiple strokes and fills.

9 With the new (top) stroke attribute row selected, change the color to white.

10 Click the word "Stroke" in the same attribute row to open the Stroke panel. Click the Round Join option (⬜) in the Corner section of the panel to *slightly* round the corners of the stroke. Press the Return or Enter to accept the value and hide the Stroke panel.

Clicking underlined words in the Appearance panel, as in the Properties panel, shows more formatting options—usually a panel such as the Swatches or Stroke panel. Appearance attributes, such as Fill or Stroke, can have other options, such as Opacity or an effect applied to only that attribute. These additional options are listed as a subset under the attribute row and can be shown or hidden by clicking the disclosure triangle (▶) on the left end of the attribute row.

11 Leave the type object selected.

Reordering appearance attributes

The ordering of the appearance attribute rows can greatly change how your artwork looks. In the Appearance panel, fills and strokes are listed in stacking order—top to bottom in the panel correlates to front to back in the artwork. You can reorder attribute rows in a way similar to dragging layers in the Layers panel to rearrange the stacking order. Next you'll change the appearance of artwork by reordering attributes in the Appearance panel.

1 With the text still selected, press Command and + (macOS) or Ctrl and + (Windows) a few times to zoom in.

● **Note:** You can drag the bottom of the Appearance panel to make it taller.

2 In the Appearance panel, click the eye icon to the left of the white Stroke row to hide it temporarily.

3 Then drag the light green stroke row in the Appearance panel down below the word "Characters." When a line appears below the word "Characters," release the mouse button to see the result.

The light green stroke is now behind both fills. The word Character represents where the stroke and fill (the mustard color) of the text (not the text object) sits in the stacking order.

4 Click where the eye icon ( ) was for the white stroke row to show it again.

5 Select the Selection tool (▶), and click to select the large rectangle in the background. In the Appearance panel, drag the pink Fill row down, below the Fill row with the Cross pattern, and release.

Moving the pink Fill attribute below the pattern Fill attribute changes the look of the artwork. The pattern fill is now on top of the solid color fill.

6 Choose Select > Deselect and then choose File > Save.

Using live effects

Note: When you apply a raster effect, the original vector data is rasterized using the document's raster effects settings, which determine the resolution of the resulting image. To learn about document raster effects settings, search for "Document raster effects settings" in Illustrator Help.

In most instances effects alter the appearance of an object without changing the underlying artwork. They're added to the object's appearance attribute, which you can edit, move, hide, delete, or duplicate, at any time, in the Appearance panel.

There are two types of effects in Illustrator: *vector effects* and *raster effects*. In Illustrator, click the Effect menu item to see the different types of effects available.

Artwork with a drop shadow effect applied.

- **Illustrator Effects (vector):** The top half of the Effect menu contains vector effects. You can apply these effects only to vector objects or to the fill or stroke of a vector object in the Appearance panel. The following vector effects can be applied to both vector and bitmap objects: 3D effects, SVG filters, Warp effects, Transform effects, Drop Shadow, Feather, Inner Glow, and Outer Glow.

- **Photoshop Effects (raster):** The bottom half of the Effect menu contains raster effects. You can apply them to either vector or bitmap objects.

In this section, you will first explore how to apply and edit effects. You will then explore a few of the more widely used effects in Illustrator to get an idea of the range of effects available.

Applying an effect

Effects are applied using the Properties panel, the Effect menu, and the Appearance panel, and they can be applied to objects, groups, or layers. You are first going to learn how to apply an effect using the Effect menu, and then you will apply an effect using the Properties panel.

1 Choose View > Fit Artboard In Window.

2 With the Selection tool (▶) selected, click the handle of the paintbrush artwork.

3 Click the Add New Effect button (fx) at the bottom of the Appearance panel, or click the Choose An Effect button (fx) in the Appearance section of the Properties panel. Choose Stylize > Drop Shadow from the Illustrator Effects section of the menu that appears.

4   In the Drop Shadow dialog box, select Preview and change the
    following options:

    •   Mode: Multiply (the default setting)

    •   Opacity: **50%**

    •   X Offset: **0.14 in**

    •   Y Offset: **0.14 in**

    •   Blur: **0.21 in**

    •   Color: Selected

5   Click OK.

Since the drop shadow is applied to the group,
it appears around the perimeter of the group,
not on each object independently. If you look in
the Appearance panel right now, you'll see the
word "Group" at the top and the Drop Shadow
effect applied. The word "Contents" refers to the
content within the group. Each object in a group
can have its own appearance properties.

6   Choose File > Save.

Editing an effect

● **Note:** If you attempt to apply an effect to artwork that already has the same effect applied, Illustrator will warn you that you are about to apply the same effect.

Effects are live, so they can be edited after they are applied to an object. You can edit the effect in the Properties panel or Appearance panel by selecting the object with the effect applied and then clicking the name of the effect or, in the Appearance panel, double-clicking the attribute row. This displays the dialog box for that effect. Changes you make to the effect update in the artwork. In this section, you will edit the Drop Shadow effect applied to the group of background shapes.

▶ **Tip:** If you were to choose Effect > Drop Shadow, the Drop Shadow dialog box would appear, allowing you to make changes before applying the effect.

1 Click the ART SHOW text. With the text object selected, choose Effect > Apply Drop Shadow.

The Apply Drop Shadow menu item applies the last used effect with the same options set.

2 With the text still selected, click the text "Drop Shadow" in the Appearance panel.

3 In the Drop Shadow dialog box, select Preview to see the changes. Change the Opacity to **10%** and the Blur to **0.03 in**. Click OK. Leave the text object selected.

Styling text with a Warp effect

Text can have all sorts of effects applied, including warp, as you saw in Lesson 9. Next, you will use the Warp effect to warp text. The difference between the warp you applied in Lesson 9 and this Warp effect is that this one is an effect and can be turned on and off, edited, or removed easily.

1 With the text still selected, click the Choose An Effect button (fx) in the Appearance section of the Properties panel. Choose Warp > Rise from the menu.

   This is just another way to apply an effect to content and will be handy if you don't have the Appearance panel open, for instance.

2 In the Warp Options dialog box select Preview to see the changes you make. To create an arcing effect, set Bend to 15%. Try choosing other styles from the Style menu and then return to Rise. Try adjusting the Horizontal and Vertical Distortion sliders to see the effect. Make sure that the Distortion values are returned to 0 and then click OK. Leave the text selected.

Tip: You can also click the Choose An Effect button (fx) at the bottom of the Appearance panel.

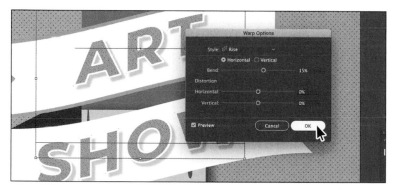

Temporarily disabling effects to make edits

You can edit text with a Warp effect applied, but sometimes it's easier to turn off the effect, make the change to the text, and then turn the effect back on.

1 With the text selected, click the visibility icon (👁) to the left of the "Warp: Rise" row in the Appearance panel to temporarily turn off the effect.

   Notice that the text is no longer warped on the artboard (see the following figure).

Tip: You can drag the bottom edge of the Appearance panel down to make it taller if you want to more easily see the content in the panel.

Tip: You can press the Escape key to select the Selection tool and select the type object, not the text.

2   Select the Type tool (**T**) in the toolbar, and change the text to **ART FEST**.

3   Select the Selection tool (▶) in the toolbar. This selects the type object, not the text.

4   Click the visibility column to the left of the "Warp: Rise" row in the Appearance panel to turn on visibility for the effect.

The text is once again warped, but since the text changed, the amount of warp may need to be different due to the overall size of the text.

5   In the Appearance panel, click the "Warp: Rise" text to edit the effect. In the Warp Options dialog box, change Bend to 11%. Click OK.

You may want to drag the text down to center it in the ribbon artwork.

6   Choose Select > Deselect and then choose File > Save.

Applying other effects

Next you'll apply a few other effects to finish parts of the artwork. Know that you can apply multiple effects to the same objects to get the appearance you are after.

1   With the Selection tool (▶) selected, click the top banner shape to select it.

2   Click the Stroke row in the Appearance panel to select it.

3   With the stroke attribute row selected, in the Appearance panel, click the Add New Effect button (*fx*) at the bottom of the panel, and choose Path > Offset Path to apply it to the stroke only.

4   In the Offset Path dialog box, change Offset to **−0.13 in**, select Preview, and then click OK.

Now you'll move one of the strokes on the text so you can see it.

5   With the Selection tool selected, click the
    ART FEST text. In the Appearance panel,
    click the light green stroke row to select it.
    The effect you apply will now affect only
    the selected stroke.

6   In the Appearance panel, click the
    Add New Effect button (fx) at the bottom of
    the panel, and choose Distort & Transform >
    Transform.

7   In the Transform dialog box, select Preview
    and change the following:

    •   Horizontal *Move*: **0.013 in**

    •   Vertical *Move*: **0.013 in**

    •   Copies: **10**

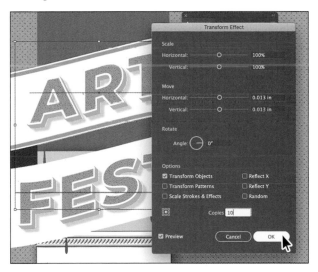

8   Click OK.

    The Transform effect, in this case, will copy the stroke 10 times and move those
    copies to the right and down.

9   In the Appearance panel, click the disclosure triangle (▶) to the left of the
    words "Stroke: 5 pt" for the light green stroke to toggle it open (if it's not
    already open).

    Notice that the Transform effect is a subset of Stroke. This indicates that the
    Transform effect is applied to only that stroke.

10 Choose Select > Deselect and then choose File > Save.

Applying a Photoshop effect

As described earlier in the lesson, raster effects generate pixels rather than vector data. Raster effects include SVG filters, all of the effects in the bottom portion of the Effect menu, and the Drop Shadow, Inner Glow, Outer Glow, and Feather commands in the Effect > Stylize submenu. You can apply them to either vector or bitmap objects. Next, you'll apply a Photoshop effect (raster) to some of the artwork.

1 Click the paintbrush bristle artwork to select it.

2 Click the Choose An Effect button ($fx.$) in the Appearance section of the Properties panel. Choose Brush Strokes > Sprayed Strokes.

When you choose the raster (Photoshop) effects, the Filter Gallery dialog box opens for most, but not all, effects. Similarly to working with filters in Adobe Photoshop, where you can also access a Filter Gallery, in the Illustrator Filter Gallery, you can try different raster effects to see how they affect your artwork.

3 With the Filter Gallery dialog box open, you can see the type of filter (Sprayed Strokes) displayed at the top. Choose Fit In View from the view menu in the lower-left corner of the dialog box so you can see how the effect alters one of the shapes.

The Filter Gallery dialog box, which is resizable, contains a preview area (labeled A), effect thumbnails that you can click to apply (labeled B), settings for the currently selected effect (labeled C), and the list of effects applied (labeled D). If you want to apply a different effect, expand a category in the middle panel of the dialog box (labeled B), and click an effect thumbnail.

4 Change the Sprayed Strokes settings in the upper-right corner of the dialog box as follows (if necessary):

- Brush Stroke: Sprayed Strokes
- Stroke Length: **20**
- Spray Radius: **25**
- Stroke Direction: Vertical

5 Click OK to apply the raster effect to the shape.

6 Choose Select > Deselect.

Tip: You can click the eye icon (⬤) to the left of the name "Sprayed Strokes" in the section labeled "D" to see the artwork without the effect applied.

Note: The Filter Gallery lets you apply only one effect at a time. If you want to apply multiple Photoshop effects, you can click OK to apply the current effect and then choose another from the Effect menu.

Working with 3D effects ▬◀

To learn about other working with 3D effects, check out the video *Working with 3D Effects,* which is part of the Web Edition. For more information, see the "Web Edition" section of "Getting Started" at the beginning of the book.

Using graphic styles

A *graphic style* is a saved set of appearance attributes that you can reuse. By applying graphic styles, you can quickly and globally change the appearance of objects and text.

The Graphic Styles panel (Window > Graphic Styles) lets you create, name, save, apply, and remove effects and attributes for objects, layers, and groups. You can also break the link between an object and an applied graphic style to edit that object's attributes without affecting other objects that use the same graphic style.

The different options available in the Graphic Styles panel are shown here:

A. Graphic style thumbnail

B. Graphic Styles Libraries menu

C. Break Link To Graphic Style

D. New Graphic Style

E. Delete Graphic Style

For example, if you have a map that uses a shape to represent a city, you can create a graphic style that paints the shape green and adds a drop shadow. You can then use that graphic style to paint all the city shapes on the map. If you decide to use a different color, you can change the fill color of the graphic style to blue. All the objects that use that graphic style are then updated to blue.

Applying an existing graphic style

You can apply graphic styles to your artwork from graphic style libraries that come with Illustrator. Next, you'll explore a built-in graphic style and apply it to artwork.

▶ **Tip:** Use the arrows at the bottom of the library panel to load the previous or next Graphic Styles library in the panel.

1   Choose Window > Graphic Styles. Click the Graphic Styles Libraries Menu button (▣) at the bottom of the panel (circled in the following figure), and choose Illuminate Styles.

2   With the Selection tool (▶), click to select the artwork that will become the metal band on the paintbrush (see the following figure).

3   Click the Aluminium Highlight style and then click the Steel Highlight graphic style in the Illuminate Styles panel. Close the Illuminate Styles panel.

Clicking the first style applies the appearance attributes from that style to the selected artwork. Clicking the second style replaces the appearance attributes of the first style with the new attributes. Both graphic styles are added to the Graphic Styles panel for the active document.

▶ **Tip:** You can right-click a graphic style thumbnail in the Graphic Styles panel to show a preview of the graphic style on the selected artwork. Previewing a graphic style is a great way to see how it will affect the selected object, without actually applying it.

4   With the artwork still selected, click the Appearance panel tab to see the fills applied to the selected artwork. You may need to scroll in the panel, but notice "Path: Steel Highlight" at the top of the panel list. This indicates that the graphic style named "Steel Highlight" is applied.

5   Click the Graphic Styles panel tab to show the panel again.

You should now see the two graphic styles, Aluminium Highlight and Steel Highlight, listed in the panel.

Creating and applying a graphic style

Now you'll create a new graphic style and apply that graphic style to artwork.

1 With the Selection tool (▶) selected, click the banner shape beneath the "ART" text.

2 Click the New Graphic Style button () at the bottom of the Graphic Styles panel.

▶ **Tip:** When you make a graphic style by selecting an object, you can then either drag the object directly into the Graphic Styles panel or, in the Appearance panel, drag the appearance thumbnail at the top of the listing into the Graphic Styles panel. The panels can't be in the same panel group.

The appearance attributes from the selected shape are saved as a graphic style.

3 In the Graphic Styles panel, double-click the new graphic style thumbnail. In the Graphic Style Options dialog box, name the new style **Banner**. Click OK.

4 Click the Appearance panel tab, and at the top of the Appearance panel you'll see "Path: Banner."

This indicates that a graphic style named "Banner" is applied to the selected artwork.

5 With the Selection tool, click the banner artwork beneath the "FEST" text. In the Graphic Styles panel, click the graphic style named Banner to apply the styling.

▶ **Tip:** You can also apply a graphic style by dragging the graphic style thumbnail found in the Graphic Styles panel onto artwork in the document.

6 Leave the shape selected and then choose File > Save.

Applying a graphic style to text

When you apply a graphic style to a type area, the fill color of the graphic style overrides the fill color of the text by default. If you deselect Override Character Color from the Graphic Styles panel menu (▤), the fill color in the text (if there is one) will be preserved.

You can right-click and hold down the mouse button on a graphic style to preview the graphic style on the text.

If you choose Use Text For Preview from the Graphic Styles panel menu (▤), you can view the style on a letter "T" in the panel.

Updating a graphic style

Once you create a graphic style, you can update the graphic style, and all artwork with that style applied will update its appearance as well. If you edit the appearance of artwork that a graphic style is applied to, the graphic style is overridden, and the artwork will not update when the graphic style is updated.

1 With the banner shape beneath the "FEST" text still selected, look in the Graphic Styles panel; you will see that the Banner graphic style thumbnail is highlighted (it has a border around it), indicating that it's applied.

2 Click the Appearance panel tab. Notice the text "Path: Banner" at the top of the panel, indicating that the Banner graphic style is applied. As you learned earlier, this is another way to tell whether a graphic style is applied to selected artwork.

3 With the shape selected, in the Stroke row in the Appearance panel, click the stroke color box a few times to open the Swatches panel. Select the light green swatch named "Text stroke." Press the Escape key to hide the swatches. Change the stroke weight to **3 pt**.

Notice that the "Path: Banner" text at the top of the Appearance panel is now just "Path," telling you that the graphic style is no longer applied to the selected artwork.

4   Click the Graphic Styles panel tab to see that the Banner graphic style no longer has a highlight (border) around it, which means that the graphic style is no longer applied.

5   Press the Option (macOS) or Alt (Windows) key, and drag the selected shape on top of the Banner graphic style thumbnail in the Graphic Styles panel. Release the mouse button and then release the modifier key when the thumbnail is highlighted.

▶ **Tip:** You can also update a graphic style by selecting the graphic style you want to replace. Then you select artwork (or target an item in the Layers panel) that has the attributes you want to use, and choose Redefine Graphic Style "Style name" from the Appearance panel menu.

Both banner shapes now look the same since the Banner graphic style was applied to both objects.

6   Choose Select > Deselect and then choose File > Save.

7   Click the Appearance panel tab. You should see "No Selection: Banner" at the top of the panel (you may need to scroll up).

When you apply appearance settings, graphic styles, and more to artwork, the next shape you draw will have the same appearance settings listed in the Appearance panel as the previous one.

Applying a graphic style to a layer

Note: If you apply a graphic style to artwork and then apply a graphic style to the layer (or sublayer) that it's on, the graphic style formatting is added to the appearance of the artwork—it's cumulative. This can change the artwork in ways you didn't expect, since applying a graphic style to the layer will be added to the formatting of the artwork.

When a graphic style is applied to a layer, everything added to that layer has that same style applied to it. Now you'll apply a drop shadow graphic style to the layer named "Text banner," which will apply the style to every object on that layer at once.

1 Click the Layers panel tab on the right to show the Layers panel. Click the target icon (◉) for the Text Banner layer.

This selects the layer content and targets the layer for any appearance attributes.

2 Click the Graphic Styles panel tab and then click the graphic style named Drop Shadow to apply the style to the layer and all its contents.

The target icon in the Layers panel for the Text Banner layer is now shaded.

Tip: In the Layers panel, you can drag a target icon to the Delete Selection icon (🗑) at the bottom of the Layers panel to remove the appearance attributes.

Tip: In the Graphic Styles panel, graphic style thumbnails that show a small box with a red slash (⌀) indicate that the graphic style does not contain a stroke or fill. It may just be a drop shadow or outer glow, for instance.

3 Click the Appearance panel tab, and you should see, with all of the artwork on the Text Banner layer still selected, the words "Layer: Drop Shadow." You can close the Appearance panel group.

This is telling you that the layer target icon is selected in the Layers panel and that the Drop Shadow graphic style is applied to that layer.

Scaling strokes and effects

In Illustrator, by default, when scaling (resizing) content, any strokes and effects that are applied do not change. For instance, suppose you scale a circle with a 2 pt stroke from small to the size of the artboard. The shape may change size, but the stroke will remain 2 point by default. That can change the appearance of scaled artwork in a way that you didn't intend, so you'll need to watch out for that when transforming artwork. Next, you'll make an icon group smaller.

1 Choose Select > Deselect, if necessary.

2 Choose View > Fit Artboard In Window, if necessary.

3 Click the small building icon in the lower-left corner of the artboard to select the group.

4 Double-click the group to enter isolation mode so you can edit the parts of the group. Click the mustard-colored rectangle to select it. Notice the stroke weight of 36 pt in the Properties panel.

5 To get out of isolation mode, press the Escape key. Click away from the artwork to deselect, then click the building icon again to select the group.

6 Click More Options () in the Transform section of the Properties panel, and select Scale Strokes & Effects at the bottom of the panel that appears. Press the Escape key to hide the options.

Without this option selected, scaling the spokes would not affect the stroke weights or effects when it is scaled. You are selecting this option so the spokes will scale smaller and not remain the same stroke weight.

7 Pressing the Shift key, drag the upper-right corner of the building icon to make it smaller. Drag until you see a width and height of approximately 1.3 inches.

After scaling the spokes, if you were to select the stroked box again in isolation move, you would see that the stroke weight in the Properties panel has changed (scaled).

8 Choose Select > Deselect.

9 Choose File > Save and then choose File > Close.

Review questions

1 How do you add a second fill or stroke to artwork?

2 Name two ways to apply an effect to an object.

3 When you apply a Photoshop (raster) effect to vector artwork, what happens to the artwork?

4 Where can you access the options for effects applied to an object?

5 What's the difference between applying a graphic style to a *layer* versus applying it to *selected artwork*?

Review answers

1 To add a second fill or stroke to artwork, click the Add New Stroke button (▣) or Add New Fill button (▢) at the bottom of the Appearance panel, or choose Add New Stroke/Add New Fill from the Appearance panel menu. A stroke is added to the top of the appearance list. It has the same color and stroke weight as the original.

2 You can apply an effect to an object by selecting the object and then choosing the effect from the Effect menu. You can also apply an effect by selecting the object, clicking the Choose An Effect button (▣) in the Properties panel or the Add New Effect button (▣) at the bottom of the Appearance panel, and then choosing the effect from the menu that appears.

3 Applying a Photoshop effect to artwork generates pixels rather than vector data. Photoshop effects include all of the effects in the bottom portion of the Effect menu and the Drop Shadow, Inner Glow, Outer Glow, and Feather commands in the Effect > Stylize submenu. You can apply them to either vector or bitmap objects.

4 You can edit effects applied to selected artwork by clicking the effect link in the Properties panel or Appearance panel to access the effect options.

5 When a graphic style is applied to a single object, other objects on that layer are not affected. For example, if a triangle object has a Roughen effect applied to its path and you move it to another layer, it retains the Roughen effect.

   After a graphic style is applied to a layer, everything you add to the layer has that style applied to it. For example, if you create a circle on Layer 1 and then move that circle to Layer 2, which has a Drop Shadow effect applied, the circle adopts that effect.

14 CREATING ARTWORK FOR A T-SHIRT

Lesson overview

In this lesson, you'll learn how to do the following:

- Work with existing symbols.

- Create, modify, and redefine a symbol.

- Store and retrieve artwork in the Symbols panel.

- Understand Creative Cloud libraries.

- Work with Creative Cloud libraries.

- Work with Global Edit.

 This lesson will take about 45 minutes to complete. To get the lesson files used in this chapter, download them from the web page for this book at www.adobepress.com/IllustratorCIB2020. For more information, see "Accessing the lesson files and Web Edition" in the Getting Started section at the beginning of this book.

In this lesson, you'll explore a variety of useful concepts for working smarter and faster in Illustrator by using symbols, working with Creative Cloud libraries to make your design assets available anywhere, and editing content using Global Edit.

Starting the lesson

In this lesson, you'll explore concepts such as symbols and the Libraries panel to create artwork for a T-shirt. Before you begin, you'll restore the default preferences for Adobe Illustrator. Then, you'll open the finished art file for this lesson to see what you'll create.

Note: If you have not already downloaded the project files for this lesson to your computer from your Account page, make sure to do so now. See the "Getting Started" section at the beginning of the book.

1 To ensure that the tools function and the defaults are set exactly as described in this lesson, delete or deactivate (by renaming) the Adobe Illustrator preferences file. See "Restoring default preferences" in the "Getting Started" section at the beginning of the book.

2 Start Adobe Illustrator.

3 Choose File > Open, and open the L14_end1.ai file in the Lessons > Lesson14 folder on your hard disk.

You're going to create artwork for a T-shirt design.

4 Choose View > Fit All In Window and leave the file open for reference, or choose File > Close.

5 Choose File > Open. In the Open dialog box, navigate to the Lessons > Lesson14 folder, and select the L14_start1.ai file on your hard disk. Click Open to open the file.

6 Choose View > Fit All In Window.

7 Choose File > Save As. In the Save As dialog box, navigate to the Lesson14 folder, and name the file **TShirt.ai**. Leave Adobe Illustrator (ai) chosen from the Format menu (macOS) or Adobe Illustrator (*.AI) chosen from the Save As Type menu (Windows), and click Save.

8 In the Illustrator Options dialog box, leave the Illustrator options at their default settings and then click OK.

9 Choose Reset Essentials from the workspace switcher in the Application bar.

Note: If you don't see Reset Essentials in the menu, choose Window > Workspace > Essentials before choosing Window > Workspace > Reset Essentials.

Working with symbols

A *symbol* is a reusable art object that is stored in the Symbols panel (Window > Symbols). For example, if you create a symbol from a flower you drew, you can then quickly add multiple *instances* of that flower symbol to your artwork, which saves you from having to draw each flower. All instances in the document are linked to the original symbol in the Symbols panel. When you edit the original symbol, all instances of that symbol (a flower in this example) that are linked to the original are updated. You can turn all those flowers from white to red instantly! Not only do symbols save time, but they also greatly reduce file size.

● **Note:** Illustrator comes with a series of symbol libraries, which range from tiki icons to hair to web icons. You can access those symbol libraries in the Symbols panel or by choosing Window > Symbol Libraries and easily incorporate them into your own artwork.

• Choose Window > Symbols to open the Symbols panel. The symbols you see in the Symbols panel are the symbols you can use with this document. Each document has its own set of saved symbols. The different options available in the Symbols panel are shown here:

A. Symbol thumbnail
B. Symbol Libraries Menu
C. Place Symbol Instance
D. Break Link To Symbol
E. Symbol Options
F. New Symbol
G. Delete Symbol

Using default Illustrator symbol libraries

You'll start by adding to your project a symbol from one of the many symbol libraries that come with Illustrator.

1 Select the Selection tool (▶) in the toolbar and click in the larger artboard.

2 Choose View > Fit Artboard In Window to fit the active artboard in the Document window.

3 Click the Hide Smart Guides option in the Properties panel to turn the Smart Guides off temporarily.

▶ **Tip:** You can also choose View > Smart Guides to turn them off.

4 In the Symbols panel (Window > Symbols), click the Symbol Libraries Menu button () at the bottom of the panel, and choose Tiki from the menu.

The Tiki library opens as a free-floating panel. The symbols in this library are not part of the file that you are working on, but you can import any of the symbols into the document and use them in the artwork.

▶ **Tip:** If you want to see the symbol names along with the symbol pictures, click the Symbols panel menu icon (▤) and then choose Small List View or Large List View.

5 Move the pointer over the symbols in the Tiki panel to see their names as tool tips. Click the symbol named "Fish" to add it to the Symbols panel. Close the Tiki panel.

▶ **Tip:** You can also copy a symbol instance on the artboard and paste as many as you need. This is the same as dragging a symbol instance out of the Symbols panel onto the artboard.

When you add symbols to the Symbols panel, they are saved with the active document only.

6 With the Selection tool (▶) selected, drag the Fish symbol from the Symbols panel onto the artboard into the approximate center of the artboard. Do this a total of *two times* to create two instances of the fish next to each other.

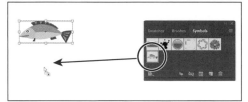

Each time you drag a symbol like the fish onto the artboard, an instance of the original symbol is created. Next you'll resize one of the symbol instances.

7   With one of the Fish symbol instances selected, Shift-drag the upper-right bounding point toward the center to make it a little smaller while also constraining its proportions. Release the mouse button and then the key.

● **Note:** Although you can transform symbol instances in many ways, specific properties of instances from static symbols like the fish cannot be edited. For example, the fill color is locked because it is controlled by the original symbol in the Symbols panel.

A symbol instance is treated like a group of objects and can have only certain transformation and appearance properties changed (scale, rotate, move, transparency, and more). You cannot edit the individual artwork that makes up an instance without breaking the link to the original symbol. With the symbol instance still selected on the artboard, notice that, in the Properties panel, you see "Symbol (Static)" and symbol-related options.

8   With the same fish instance still selected, make a copy of it by pressing Option (macOS) or Alt (Windows) and dragging a copy. Release the mouse button and then the key.

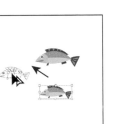

Creating a copy of an instance is the same thing as dragging an instance of a symbol from the Symbols panel.

9   To resize the new fish instance, Shift-drag a corner to make it smaller. Release the mouse button and then the key.

10 Drag all three fish instances into position, as in the figure. Choose Select > Deselect.

Editing a symbol

In this next section, you'll edit the original Fish symbol, and all instances in the document will be updated. There are several ways to edit a symbol, and in this section you will focus on one method.

▶ **Tip:** There are a lot of ways to edit a symbol. You can select the symbol instance on the artboard and then click the Edit Symbol button in the Properties panel, or double-click a symbol thumbnail in the Symbols panel to edit the symbol.

1   With the Selection tool (▶) selected, double-click any of the Fish symbol instances on the artboard. A warning dialog box appears, stating that you are about to edit the original symbol and that all instances will update. Click OK.

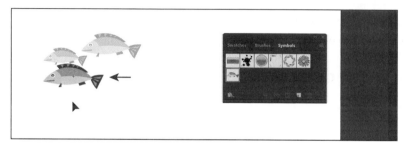

This takes you into symbol editing mode, so you can't edit any other objects on the page. The Fish symbol instance you double-clicked will show as the size of the original symbol artwork. That's because in symbol editing mode, you are looking at the *original* symbol artwork rather than the transformed instance (if you double-clicked one that was resized). You can now edit the artwork that makes up the symbol.

2   Select the Zoom tool (Q), and drag across the symbol content to zoom in closely.

3   Select the Direct Selection tool (▷), and click to select the light green head of the fish. An arrow is pointing to it in the following figure.

4   Click the Fill color box in the Swatches panel, and select the Color Mixer (⊞). Press the Shift key and drag the Cyan (C) slider to the right a little, to change the color.

Pressing the Shift key when dragging a slider changes all of the colors (CMYK, for instance) proportionally.

5 Double-click away from the symbol content, or click the Exit Symbol Editing Mode button (⬅) in the upper-left corner of the Document window until you exit symbol editing mode so that you can edit the rest of the content.

Notice that all of the Fish symbol instances on the artboard have been changed.

Working with dynamic symbols

As you just saw, editing a symbol updates all of the instances in your document. Symbols can also be set to be *dynamic*, which means you can change certain appearance properties of individual instances using the Direct Selection tool (▶) without editing the original symbol. In this section, you'll edit the properties of the Fish symbol so that it is dynamic, and then you'll edit each instance separately.

1 In the Symbols panel, click the Fish symbol thumbnail to select it, if it's not already selected. Click the Symbol Options button (▤) at the bottom of the Symbols panel.

2 In the Symbol Options dialog box, select Dynamic Symbol, and click OK. The symbol and its instances are now dynamic.

You can tell if a symbol is dynamic by looking at the thumbnail in the Symbols panel. If there is a small plus sign (+) in the lower-right corner of the thumbnail, it is a dynamic symbol.

3 Select the Direct Selection tool (▷) in the toolbar. Click within the fish head of the smallest fish instance. See the following figure.

With part of the symbol instance selected, notice the words "Symbol (Dynamic)" at the top of the Properties panel, telling you it's a dynamic symbol.

4 Click the Fill box in the Properties panel. With the Swatches option selected, change the fill color to a blue green swatch in the Swatches panel.

One fish now looks a little different from the others. Know that if you were to edit the original symbol, like you did previously, all symbol instances would still update, but that blue-green part of the smallest fish instance would remain different.

Creating a symbol

Illustrator also lets you create and save your own symbols. You can make symbols from objects, including paths, compound paths, text, embedded (not linked) raster images, mesh objects, and groups of objects. Symbols can even include active objects, such as brush strokes, blends, effects, or other symbol instances. Next you'll create your own symbol from existing artwork.

1 Choose 2 Symbol Artwork from the Artboard Navigation menu in the Status bar below the Document window.

2 With the Selection tool (▶) selected, click the flower on the artboard to select it.

3 Click the New Symbol button (▣) at the bottom of the Symbols panel to make a symbol from the selected artwork.

4 In the Symbol Options dialog box that opens, change the name to **Flower**. Ensure that Dynamic Symbol is selected, just in case you want to edit the appearance of one of the instances later. Click OK to create the symbol.

In the Symbol Options dialog box, you'll see a note that explains that there is no difference between a movie clip and a graphic type in Illustrator. If you don't plan on exporting this content to Adobe Animate, you don't need to worry about choosing an export type. After creating the symbol, the flower artwork on the artboard is converted to an *instance* of the Flower symbol. The symbol also appears in the Symbols panel.

Now you'll create another symbol by dragging artwork into the Symbols panel.

Tip: You can drag the symbol thumbnails in the Symbols panel to change their ordering. Reordering symbols in the Symbols panel has no effect on the artwork. It can simply be a way to organize your symbols.

5 Drag the surfboard artwork into a blank area of the Symbols panel. In the Symbol Options dialog box, change the name to **Surfboard** and click OK.

6 Choose 1 T-Shirt from the Artboard menu in the Status bar below the Document window.

7 Drag the Flower symbol from the Symbols panel onto the artboard four times, and position the instances around the fish, as you see in the following figure.

8 Resize and rotate each of the flower instances on the artboard using the Selection tool, making them different sizes. Make sure to press the Shift key to constrain the proportions as you scale.

9 Choose Select > Deselect and then choose File > Save.

Breaking a link to a symbol

At times you will need to edit a specific instance on the artboard in ways that require you to break the link between the original symbol artwork and an instance. As you've learned, you can make certain changes, such as scaling, opacity, and flipping, to a symbol instance, and saving the symbol as dynamic only lets you edit certain appearance attributes using the Direct Selection tool. When you break the link between a symbol and an instance, that instance will no longer update if the symbol is edited.

Next you'll see how to break the link to a symbol instance so you can make a change to just that one.

1 Turn on the Smart Guides by choosing View > Smart Guides.

▶ **Tip:** You can also break the link to a symbol instance by selecting the symbol instance on the artboard and then clicking the Break Link To Symbol button (⊠) at the bottom of the Symbols panel.

2 With the Selection tool (▶) selected, drag *three* copies of the Surfboard symbol on top of the other artwork already on the artboard. Arrange them like you see in the following figure.

3 Select each symbol instance and resize it, making the center artboard taller than the other two. I wound up making all three larger. Don't forget to Shift-drag a corner in order to resize proportionally.

4 Select the center surfboard, and in the Properties panel, click the Break Link button.

This surfboard is now a series of paths; if you click to select the artwork, you'll see "Group" at the top of the Properties panel. You should be able to edit the artwork directly now. This content will no longer update if the Surfboard symbol is edited.

5 Select the Zoom tool (🔍), and drag across the top of the selected surfboard artwork on the artboard to zoom in.

6 Choose Select > Deselect.

7 Select the Direct Selection tool, and drag across the top of the middle surfboard. Move the pointer over the anchor points at the top of the surfboard and when you see the word "anchor," drag one of them down a little to reshape the top.

8 Choose Select > Deselect.

Now you'll arrange the surfboards behind the flowers and fish.

9 Select the Selection tool (▶) and Shift-click all three of the surfboards to select them all. Choose Object > Arrange > Send To Back.

10 Click the Group button in the Properties panel to group them together.

11 Choose File > Save.

The Symbolism tools

The Symbol Sprayer tool (⬚⬚) in the toolbar allows you to spray symbols on the artboard, creating symbol sets.

A *symbol set* is a group of symbol instances that you create with the Symbol Sprayer tool. This can be really useful if, for instance, you were to create grass from individual blades of grass. Spraying the blades of grass speeds up this process greatly and makes it much easier to edit individual instances of grass or the sprayed grass as a group. You can create mixed sets of symbol instances by using the Symbol Sprayer tool with one symbol and then using it again with another symbol.

You use the symbolism tools to modify multiple symbol instances in a set. For example, you can disperse instances over a larger area using the Symbol Scruncher tool or gradually tint the color of instances to make them look more realistic.

—From Illustrator Help

● **Note:** The Symbolism tools are not in the default toolbar. To access them, click the Edit Toolbar option (▪▪▪) at the bottom of the toolbar and drag any of the Symbolism tools into the toolbar.

Replacing symbols

You can easily replace a symbol instance in the document with another symbol. You can also replace a symbol like a fish if you made changes to the dynamic symbol instance. That way, the symbol instance matches the original symbol artwork again. Next you'll replace one of the Fish symbol instances.

1   With the Selection tool (▶), select the smallest Fish symbol instance, the one whose head you recolored.

When you select a symbol instance, you can tell which symbol it came from because the symbol for the selected instance is highlighted in the Symbols panel.

2   In the Properties panel, click the arrow to the right of the Replace Symbol field to open a panel showing the symbols in the Symbols panel. Click the Flower symbol in the panel.

If the original symbol instance you are replacing had a transformation applied, such as a rotation, the symbol instance replacing it would have the same transformations applied.

● **Note:** After making edits to a dynamic symbol instance with the Direct Selection tool, you can reselect the entire instance with the Selection tool and click the Reset button in the Properties panel to reset the appearance to the same as the original symbol.

3   With the Flower symbol instance still selected on the artboard, in the Properties panel click the arrow to the right of the Replace Symbol field and click the Fish symbol in the panel.

The change you made to the Fish symbol instance earlier (changing the color of the head) is gone and the original Fish symbol artwork replaces the flower.

4   Choose Select > Same > Symbol Instance.

This is a great way to select all instances of a symbol in the document.

5   Click the Group button in the Properties panel to keep them together as a group.

6   Choose Select > Deselect and close the Symbols panel group.

Working with Creative Cloud libraries

Creative Cloud libraries are an easy way to create and share stored content such as images, colors, text styles, Adobe Stock assets, and more between Adobe applications like Photoshop, Illustrator, InDesign, and most Adobe mobile apps.

Creative Cloud libraries connect to your Creative Profile, putting the creative assets you have saved at your fingertips. When you create content in Illustrator and save it to a Creative Cloud library, that asset is available to use in all of your Illustrator files. Those assets are automatically synced and can be shared with anyone with a Creative Cloud account. As your creative team works across Adobe desktop and mobile apps, your shared library assets are always up to date and ready to use anywhere. In this section, you'll explore libraries and use assets you save there, in your project.

Adding assets to a Creative Cloud library

The first thing you'll learn about is how to work with the Libraries panel (Window > Libraries) in Illustrator and add assets to a Creative Cloud library. You'll open an existing document in Illustrator and capture assets from it.

1 Choose File > Open. In the Open dialog box, navigate to the Lessons > Lesson14 folder, and select the Sample.ai file on your hard disk. Click Open.

2 Choose View > Fit All In Window.

   Using this document, you will capture artwork, text, and colors to be used in the TShirt.ai document.

Note: To use Creative Cloud libraries, you will need to be signed in with your Adobe ID and have an internet connection.

Note: The Missing Fonts dialog box may appear. You need an internet connection to activate the fonts. The activation process may take a few minutes. Click Activate Fonts to activate all of the missing fonts. After they are activated and you see the message stating that there are no more missing fonts, click Close. If you have an issue with activation, you can go to Help (Help > Illustrator Help) and search for "Find missing fonts."

3 Choose Window > Libraries, or click the Libraries panel tab to open the Libraries panel.

To start you have one library to work with, called "My Library." You can add your design assets to this default library and you can create more libraries—maybe to save assets for specific clients or projects.

4 Choose Select > Deselect, if anything is selected.

5 Select the Selection tool (▶), and click the text object that contains the text "PLAY ZONE." Drag the text into the Libraries panel. When a plus sign (+) appears in the panel, release to save the text object in the default library. If you see a missing profile warning dialog box, click OK.

The text object is now saved in the currently selected library and is still editable as text—retaining the text formatting as well. As you save assets and formatting in the Libraries panel, the content is organized by asset type.

6 Make sure that View By Type is chosen from the View By menu.

▶ **Tip:** You can change the appearance of the items in the library (icons or list) by clicking the buttons to the right of the View By Type option.

7 To change the name of the saved text object, double-click the name "Text 1" in the Libraries panel, and change it to **SURF ZONE**. Press Enter or Return to accept the name change. That name will make more sense when you update the text to "SURF ZONE" later in the lesson.

You can change the names of other assets like graphics, colors, character styles, and paragraph styles saved in the Libraries panel as well. In the case of character and paragraph styles you save, you can also move the pointer over the asset and see a tool tip that shows the saved formatting.

8   With the PLAY ZONE text still selected on the artboard, click the plus sign (+) at the bottom of the Libraries panel and choose Text Fill Color to save the blue color.

9   Click the T-shirt artwork to select it. Drag the selected artwork into the Libraries panel. When a plus sign (+) and a name (such as "Artwork 1") appear, release the mouse button to add the artwork as a graphic.

The assets you store as graphics in a Creative Cloud library remain editable vectors wherever you use the graphic.

10 Click the shape on the artboard above the PLAY ZONE text. You'll simply copy this artwork since you will use it to mask or hide parts of the surfboards. Choose Edit > Copy.

11 Choose File > Close to close the Sample.ai file and return to the TShirt.ai file. Don't save the file if asked.

Notice that even with a different document open, the Libraries panel still shows those assets in the library. The libraries and their assets are available no matter which document is open in Illustrator.

12 Choose Edit > Paste to paste the shape. Drag it to the right of the surfboards.

▶ **Tip:** You can share a copy of your library with others by choosing the library you want to share in the Libraries panel and then choosing Share Link from the panel menu.

Using library assets

Now that you have some assets in the Libraries panel, once synced with your Creative Cloud account, those assets will be available to other applications and apps that support libraries, as long as you are signed in with the same Creative Cloud account. Next you'll use some of those assets in the TShirt.ai file.

1 While still on the 1 T-Shirt artboard, choose View > Fit Artboard In Window.

▶ **Tip:** To apply the color or styles saved in the Libraries panel, select artwork or text and click to apply. When it comes to text styles in the Libraries panel, if you apply them to text in a document, a style of the same name and formatting will appear in the Paragraph Styles panel or Character Styles panel (depending on which you selected in the Libraries panel).

2 Drag the SURF ZONE asset from the Libraries panel onto the artboard.

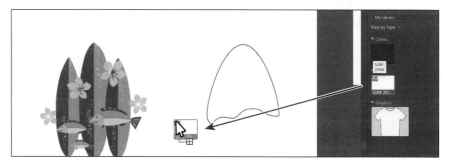

3 Click to place the text.

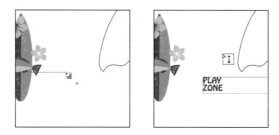

4 With the Type tool selected, click in the PLAY ZONE text, select the word "PLAY," and type **SURF**.

5 Select the Selection tool (▶), and drag the T-shirt graphic asset from the Libraries panel onto the artboard. You will need to click the artboard after dragging to place it. Don't worry about position for now.

6 Choose Select > Deselect.

Updating a library asset

When you drag a graphic from your Creative Cloud library to an Illustrator project, it is automatically placed as a linked asset. You can tell that an asset you dragged from a library is linked by the X that appears on the object bounding box when it's selected in the document. If you make a change to a library asset, the linked instances will update in your projects. Next you'll see how to update the asset.

1 In the Libraries panel, double-click the T-shirt asset thumbnail. The artwork will appear in a new, temporary document.

▶ **Tip:** You can also edit a linked library asset like the T-shirt by clicking Edit Original (▨) at the bottom of the Links panel.

2 With the Selection tool (▶) selected, click to select the T-shirt shape. Change the stroke color to a lighter gray with the tool tip "C=0, M=0, Y=0, K=40" in the Properties panel.

3 Choose File > Save and then choose File > Close.

In the Libraries panel, the graphic thumbnail should update to reflect the appearance change you made. Back in the TShirt.ai document, the T-shirt graphic on the artboard should have updated. If it hasn't, with the T-shirt artwork still selected on the artboard, click the text "Linked File" at the top of the Properties panel. In the Links panel that shows, with the T-shirt asset row selected, click the Update Link button (▨) at the bottom of the panel.

4 Click the T-shirt artwork. To embed the graphic, click the Properties panel tab to see the panel again. Click the Embed button in the Quick Actions section of the panel.

The asset is no longer linked to the library item and will not update if the library item is updated.

That also means the artwork is now editable in the TShirt.ai document. Libraries panel artwork that is embedded after it has been placed will typically have a clipping mask applied. Next you'll move and scale the artwork.

5   With the Selection tool (▶) selected and the T-shirt artwork also selected, click the Arrange button in the Properties panel and choose Send To Back. The artwork is now behind all other content. Drag it into the approximate center of the artboard.

6   To lock the T-shirt artwork, press Command+2 (macOS) or Ctrl+2 (Windows).

7   Click the shape you pasted into the document and drag it on top of the surfboards. Shift-drag a corner to make it bigger; then release the mouse button and key when finished. See the figure for approximate position and size.

The shape will be used as a mask to hide parts of the surfboards. You'll learn more about creating and editing masks in Lesson 15.

8   With the shape selected, Shift-click the artwork in the surfboard group.

9   Choose Object > Clipping Mask > Make.

The surfboard artwork that's outside of the shape is now hidden.

10 To arrange the surfboard group behind the fish and flowers, click the Arrange button in the Properties panel and choose Send To Back. This will put the artwork behind the T-shirt. Then click the Arrange button and choose Bring Forward.

11 Drag across the flowers, fish, and surfboards to select it all. Click the Group button in the Properties panel to group it.

▶ **Tip:** You may also want to adjust text formatting like leading, font size, and more in the Properties panel.

12 Drag that new group into position, along with the text. You may want to enlarge the text in the Properties panel. If you do make it larger, you will need to resize the text area so all of the text shows.

13 Choose Select > Deselect.

14 Choose File > Save and then choose File > Close.

Working with Global Edit

There will be times where you create multiple copies of artwork and use it across multiple artboards within a single document. If you need to make changes to an object everywhere it's used, you can use Global Edit to edit all similar objects. In this section, you'll open a new file with icons and make a global edit to its content.

Note: The final version of the file, L14_end2.ai, is in the Lessons > Lesson14 folder.

1 Choose File > Open, and open the L14_start2.ai file in the Lessons > Lesson14 folder on your hard disk.

2 Choose File > Save As. In the Save As dialog box, navigate to the Lesson14 folder, and name the file **Icons.ai**. Leave Adobe Illustrator (ai) chosen from the Format menu (macOS) or Adobe Illustrator (*.AI) chosen from the Save As Type menu (Windows), and click Save.

3 In the Illustrator Options dialog box, leave the Illustrator options at their default settings and then click OK.

4 Choose View > Fit All In Window.

5 With the Selection tool selected, click the black circle behind the larger microphone icon.

If you need to edit all of the circles found behind each of the icons, you can select them using several methods, including the Select > Similar commands, assuming they all share similar appearance attributes. To make use of Global Edit, you can select objects that share attributes, such as stroke, fill, or size, on the same artboard or all artboards.

Tip: You can also start global editing by choosing Select > Start Global Edit.

6 Click Start Global Edit in the Quick Actions section of the Properties panel.

All circles (in this case) are now selected, and you can edit them. The object you originally selected has a red highlight, and the similar objects have a blue highlight. You can also use the Global Edit options to further narrow down the objects that will be selected, which is what you'll do next.

● **Note:** The Appearance option is enabled by default when the selection includes a plug-in art or a mesh art.

7 Click the arrow to the right of the Stop Global Edit button to reveal a menu of options. Select Appearance to select all of the content that has the same appearance attributes as the selected circle. Leave the menu showing.

8 Select Size from the Global Edit options menu to further refine the search to include objects that have the same shape, appearance properties, and size. There should now only be two circles selected.

You can further refine your selection by choosing to search for similar objects on certain artboards.

9 Click the Stroke color in the Properties panel, make sure the Swatches option is selected, and apply a color to the stroke. If you see a warning dialog, click OK.

10 Click away from the panel to hide it, and both of the selected objects should change appearance.

11 Choose Select > Deselect and then choose File > Save.

12 Choose File > Close.

Review questions

1 What are three benefits of using symbols?

2 How do you update an existing symbol?

3 What is a dynamic symbol?

4 In Illustrator, what type of content can you save in a library?

5 Explain how to embed a linked library graphic asset.

Review answers

1 Three benefits of using symbols are as follows:

- You can edit one symbol, and all instances are updated.

- You can map artwork to 3D objects (not discussed in the lesson).

- Using symbols reduces file size.

2 To update an existing symbol, double-click the symbol icon in the Symbols panel, double-click an instance of the symbol on the artboard, or select the instance on the artboard and then click the Edit Symbol button in the Properties panel. Then you can make edits in Isolation mode.

3 When a symbol is saved as dynamic, you can change certain appearance properties of instances using the Direct Selection tool (▶) without editing the original symbol.

4 In Illustrator, currently you can save colors (fill and stroke), type objects, graphic assets, and type formatting.

5 By default, when a graphic asset is dragged from the Libraries panel into a document, a link is created to the original library asset. To embed a graphic asset, select the asset in the document and click Embed in the Properties panel. Once embedded, the graphic will no longer update if the original library asset is edited.

15 USING ILLUSTRATOR WITH OTHER ADOBE APPLICATIONS

Lesson overview

In this lesson, you'll learn how to do the following:

- Place linked and embedded graphics in an Illustrator file.

- Transform and crop images.

- Create and edit clipping masks.

- Use text to mask an image.

- Make and edit an opacity mask.

- Work with the Links panel.

- Embed and unembed images.

This lesson will take about 60 minutes to complete. To get the lesson files used in this chapter, download them from the web page for this book at www.adobepress.com/IllustratorCIB2020. For more information, see "Accessing the lesson files and Web Edition" in the Getting Started section at the beginning of this book.

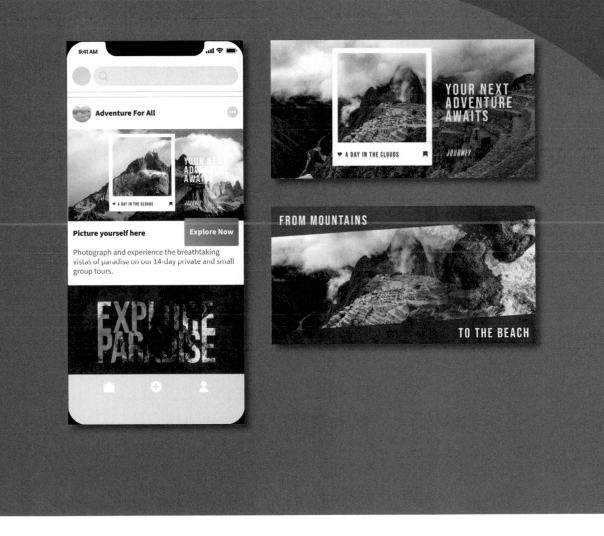

You can easily add images to an Adobe Illustrator file. This is a great way to incorporate raster images into your vector artwork to combine the two.

Starting the lesson

Before you begin, you'll need to restore the default preferences for Adobe Illustrator. Then you'll open the finished art file for this lesson to see what you'll create.

Note: If you have not already downloaded the project files for this lesson to your computer from your Account page, make sure to do so now. See the "Getting Started" section at the beginning of the book.

1 To ensure that the tools function and the defaults are set exactly as described in this lesson, delete or deactivate (by renaming) the Adobe Illustrator preferences file. See "Restoring default preferences" in the "Getting Started" section at the beginning of the book.

2 Start Adobe Illustrator.

3 Choose File > Open, and open the L15_end.ai file in the Lessons > Lesson15 folder that you copied onto your hard disk.

This is a series of social images for a travel company. The fonts in the L15_end.ai file have been converted to outlines (Type > Create Outlines) to avoid having missing fonts, and the images are embedded.

4 Choose View > Fit All In Window and leave it open for reference, or choose File > Close.

5 Choose File > Open. In the Open dialog box, navigate to the Lessons > Lesson15 folder, and select the L15_start.ai file on your hard disk. Click Open to open the file.

This is an unfinished version of the social content for a travel company. You will add and edit graphics to it in this lesson.

Note: You need an internet connection to activate fonts. The process may take a few minutes.

6 The Missing Fonts dialog box will most likely appear. Click Activate Fonts to activate all the missing fonts. After they are activated and you see the message stating that there are no more missing fonts, click Close.

If you can't get the fonts to activate, you can go to the Creative Cloud desktop application and click the Fonts icon (f) in the upper-right to see what the issue may be (refer to the section "Changing font family and font style" in Lesson 9, "Adding Type to a Poster," for more information on how to resolve it).

You can also just click Close in the Missing Fonts dialog box and ignore the missing fonts as you proceed. A third method is to click the Find Fonts button in the Missing Fonts dialog box and replace the fonts with a local font on your machine.

● **Note:** You can also go to Help (Help > Illustrator Help) and search for "Find missing fonts."

7   Choose File > Save As. In the Save As dialog box, navigate to the Lesson15 folder, and open it. Name the file **SocialTravel.ai**. Leave Adobe Illustrator (ai) chosen from the Format menu (macOS) or Adobe Illustrator (*.AI) chosen from the Save As Type menu (Windows), and then click Save.

8   In the Illustrator Options dialog box, leave the Illustrator options at their default settings. Click OK.

9   Choose Window > Workspace > Reset Essentials to reset the Essentials workspace.

10 Choose View > Fit All In Window.

Working with Adobe Bridge

Adobe Bridge is an application available with your Adobe Creative Cloud membership. Bridge provides you with centralized access to all the media assets you need for your creative projects.

Bridge simplifies your workflow and keeps you organized. You can batch edit with ease, add watermarks, and even set centralized color preferences. You can access Adobe Bridge from within Illustrator by choosing File > Browse In Bridge (if it's installed on your machine).

Combining artwork

You can combine Illustrator artwork with images from other graphics applications in a variety of ways for a wide range of creative results. Sharing artwork among applications lets you combine continuous-tone paintings and photographs with vector art. Illustrator lets you create certain types of raster images, and Adobe Photoshop excels at many additional image-editing tasks. The images edited or created in Photoshop can then be inserted into Illustrator.

This lesson steps you through the process of creating a composite image, including combining bitmap images with vector art and working between applications. You will add photographic images created in Photoshop to social content created in Illustrator. Then you'll mask an image and replace a placed image.

Placing image files

You can bring raster artwork from Photoshop or other applications into Illustrator using the Open command, the Place command, the Paste command, drag-and-drop operations, and the Libraries panel. Illustrator supports most Adobe Photoshop data, including layer comps, layers, editable text, and paths. This means that you can transfer files between Photoshop and Illustrator and still be able to edit the artwork.

Note: Illustrator includes support for DeviceN rasters. For instance, if you create a Duotone image in Photoshop and place it in Illustrator, it separates properly and the spot colors are printed.

When placing a file using the File > Place command, no matter what type of image file it is (JPEG, GIF, PSD, AI, etc.), it can be either embedded or linked. *Embedding* files stores a copy of the image in the Illustrator file, which often increases the Illustrator file size to reflect the addition of the placed file. *Linking* files creates a link to external files, and that link is placed in the Illustrator file. A linked file does not significantly add to the size of the Illustrator file. Linking to files can be a great way to ensure that image updates are reflected in the Illustrator file. The linked file must always accompany the Illustrator file, or the link will break and the placed file will not appear in the Illustrator artwork.

Placing an image

First, you'll place a JPEG (.jpg) image in your document.

1   Choose File > Place.

Note: On macOS, you may need to click the Options button in the Place dialog box to reveal the Link option.

2   Navigate to the Lessons > Lesson15 > images folder, and select the Mountains2.jpg file. Make sure that Link is selected in the Place dialog box.

3   Click Place.

The pointer should now show the loaded graphics cursor. You can see "1/1" next to the pointer, indicating how many images are being placed (1 of 1), and a thumbnail so you can see what image you are placing.

4   Move the loaded graphics cursor off the left side of the mobile design on the artboard on the left (see the figure), and click to place the image. Leave the image selected.

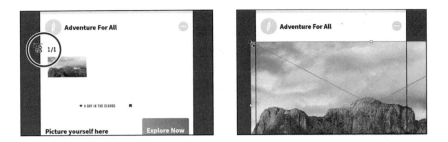

Tip: The X on a selected image indicates that the image is linked (with edges showing, View > Show Edges).

The image appears on the artboard at 100% of its original size, with the upper-left corner of the image placed where you clicked. You could also have dragged with the loaded graphics cursor to size the image as you placed it.

Notice in the Properties panel (Window > Properties) that, with the image selected, you see the words "Linked File" at the top, indicating that the image is linked to its source file. By default a placed image is linked to the source file, so if the source file is edited (outside of Illustrator), the placed image in Illustrator is also updated. Deselecting the Link option while placing embeds the image file in the Illustrator file.

Transforming a placed image

You can duplicate and transform placed raster images just as you do other objects in an Illustrator file. Unlike with vector artwork, with raster images you need to consider the image resolution since raster images with lower resolution may look pixelated when printed. Working in Illustrator, if you make an image smaller, the resolution of the image increases. If you make an image larger, the resolution decreases. Transformations performed on a linked image in Illustrator, and any resulting resolution changes, do not change the original image. The changes affect only how the image is rendered in Illustrator. Next you'll transform the Mountains2.jpg image.

Tip: To transform a placed image, you can also open the Properties panel or Transform panel (Window > Transform) and change settings in either.

1 With the Selection tool (▶) selected, press and hold the Shift key and drag the lower-right bounding point toward the center of the image until it is just wider than the artboard. Release the mouse button and then release the key.

Tip: Much as with other artwork, you can also Option+Shift-drag (macOS) or Alt+Shift-drag (Windows) the image's bounding box to resize from the center while maintaining the image proportions.

2 In the Properties panel, click the text "Linked File" at the top of the Properties panel to see the Links panel. With the Mountains2.jpg file selected in the Links panel, click the Show Link Info arrow in the lower-left corner of the panel to see information about the image.

You can see the scale percentage as well as rotation information, size, and much more. Specifically, notice the PPI (pixels per inch) value is approximately 100. PPI refers to the current resolution of the image. If you scale a placed raster image like you just did, the image resolution in Illustrator will change (the original placed image isn't affected). Generally, if you scale the image to be larger, the resolution becomes lower. Conversely, if you scale an image to be smaller, the resolution becomes higher. Other transformations, like rotation, can also be applied to images using the various methods you learned in Lesson 5, "Transforming Artwork."

3 Press the Escape key to hide the panel.

4 Click the Flip Along Horizontal Axis option (⬚) in the Properties panel to flip the image horizontally, across the center.

5 Leave the image selected, and choose File > Save.

Cropping an image

In Illustrator, you can mask or hide part of an image, as you'll learn about in this lesson, but you can also crop images to *permanently* remove part of an image. While cropping an image, you can define the resolution, which can be a useful way to reduce file size and improve performance. When cropping an image, on Windows 64-bit and macOS, Illustrator automatically identifies the visually significant portions of the selected image. This is powered by Adobe Sensei and is called Content-Aware cropping. Next you'll crop part of the image of the mountains.

1 With the image still selected, click the Crop Image button in the Properties panel. Click OK in the warning dialog box that appears.

A linked image, like the mountain image, becomes embedded after you crop it. Illustrator automatically identifies the visually significant portions of the selected image, and a default cropping box is displayed on the image. You can adjust the dimensions of this cropping box, if needed. The rest of the artwork is dimmed, and you cannot select it until you are finished cropping.

▶ **Tip:** To crop a selected image, you can also choose Object > Crop Image or right-click the image and choose Crop Image from the context menu.

▶ **Tip:** You can turn off the Content Aware feature by choosing Illustrator > Preferences > General (macOS) or Edit > Preferences > General (Windows) and deselecting Enable Content Aware Defaults.

2 Drag the crop handles so the bottom and top of the image are cut off and the image stops at the edge of the artboard on the right and left. The crop you see initially may be different from the figure and that's okay. Use the second part of the following figure as a guide for the final crop.

You can drag the handles that appear around the image to crop different parts of the image. You can also define a size in the Properties panel (width and height) to crop to.

3 Click the PPI (resolution) menu in the Properties panel.

The PPI is the resolution of the image. Any options in the PPI menu that are higher than the original resolution of the image are disabled. The maximum value that you can enter equals the resolution of the original image or 300 PPI for linked artwork. Choosing a lower resolution than the original can be useful if you want to save file size.

● **Note:** A lower PPI may result in an image that is not suitable for printing.

● **Note:** Depending on the size of your image, the "Medium (150 ppi)" option may not be dimmed, and that's okay.

4 Move the pointer over the center of the image, and drag the crop area down a little to crop more of the top of the image.

5 Click Apply in the Properties panel to *permanently* crop the image.

Since the image is embedded when cropping, the crop does not affect the original image file you placed.

6 If you need to, drag the image into place, as in the following figure.

7 To send the image behind the other content on the artboard, click the Arrange button in the Properties panel and choose Send Backward. Do this a few times so the image is behind the artwork and text, like you see in the figure.

8 Choose Select > Deselect and then choose File > Save.

Placing a Photoshop image with Show Import Options

When you place a Photoshop file with multiple layers in Illustrator, you can change image options when the file is imported. For instance, if you place a Photoshop file (.psd), you can choose to flatten the image or even to preserve the original Photoshop layers in the file. Next you'll place a Photoshop file, set import options, and embed it in the Illustrator file.

1 Choose File > Place.

2 In the Place dialog box, navigate to the Lessons > Lesson15 > images folder, and select the PhotoFrame.psd file. In the Place dialog box, set the following options (on macOS, if you don't see the options, click the Options button):

- Link: Deselected (Deselecting the Link option embeds an image file in the Illustrator file. Embedding the Photoshop file allows for more options when it is placed, as you'll see.)

- Show Import Options: Selected (Selecting this option will open an Import Options dialog box where you can set import options before placing.)

3   Click Place.

    The Photoshop Import Options dialog box appears because you selected Show Import Options in the Place dialog box, and because the file has multiple layers.

● **Note:** The Import Options dialog box will not appear if the image only contains a locked Background layer, even though you select Show Import Options in the Place dialog box.

4   In the Photoshop Import Options dialog box, set the following options:

    - Layer Comp: Beach (A layer comp is a snapshot of a state of the Layers panel that you create in Photoshop. In Photoshop, you can create, manage, and view multiple versions of a layout in a single Photoshop file. Any comments associated with the layer comp in Photoshop will appear in the Comments area.)

    - Show Preview: Selected (Preview displays a preview of the selected layer comp.)

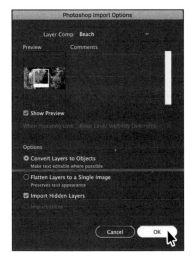

▶ **Tip:** To learn more about layer comps, see "Importing artwork from Photoshop" in Illustrator Help (Help > Illustrator Help).

    - Convert Layers To Objects: Selected (This option and the next one are available only because you deselected the Link option and chose to embed the Photoshop image.)

    - Import Hidden Layers: Selected (to import layers hidden in Photoshop)

5   Click OK.

6   Move the loaded graphics cursor into the upper-left corner of the top artboard on the right. Drag from the upper-left corner of the artboard to the lower-right corner of the artboard to place and size the image. Make sure it covers the artboard.

Rather than flatten the file, you have converted the PhotoFrame.psd Photoshop layers to layers that you can show and hide in Illustrator. When placing a Photoshop file in particular, if you had left the Link option selected (to link to the original PSD file), the only option in the Options section of the Photoshop Import Options dialog box would have been to flatten the content. Notice that, with the image still selected on the page, the Properties panel shows the word "Group" at the top. The Photoshop layers are grouped together when preserved and placed.

7 To send the image behind the content on the artboard, choose Object > Arrange > Send To Back.

8 Click the Layers panel tab in the upper-right of the application window to open the Layers panel. Drag the left edge of the Layers panel to the left to make it wider so you can read the names.

9 To reveal the image content in the Layers panel, click the Locate Object button (🔎) at the bottom of the panel.

Notice the sublayers of PhotoFrame.psd. These sublayers were layers in Photoshop and appear in the Layers panel in Illustrator because you chose not to flatten the image when you placed it.

When you place a Photoshop file with layers and you choose to convert the layers to objects in the Photoshop Import Options dialog box, Illustrator treats the layers as separate sublayers in a group. The Photoshop image has a white picture frame in it, but there was already one on the artboard, so next you'll hide the white frame that came with the Photoshop file along with one of the images.

10 In the Layers panel, click the eye icon (👁) to the left of the Pic Frame sublayer and the Beach image to hide them both. Click the visibility column for the mountains image layer (my mountain layer is named "<Background> 0") to show the image.

Placing multiple images

In Illustrator you can also place multiple image files in a single action. Next you'll place several images at once and position them.

1 Choose File > Place.

2 In the Place dialog box, in the Lessons > Lesson15 > images folder, select the Hills.jpg file. Command-click (macOS) or Ctrl-click (Windows) the image named Icon.jpg to select both image files. On macOS, click the Options button, if necessary, to reveal other options. Deselect Show Import Options, and make sure that the Link option is *not* selected.

▶ **Tip:** You could also select a range of files in the Place dialog box by pressing the Shift key.

● **Note:** The Place dialog box you see in Illustrator may show the images in a different view, like List view, and that's okay.

3 Click Place.

4 Move the loaded graphics cursor onto the left side of the artboard with the "Adventure For All" text. Press the Right or Left Arrow key (or Up and Down Arrow keys) a few times to see that you can cycle between the image thumbnails. Make sure that you see the Icon image thumbnail, then drag to place the image at a small size, like you see in the following figure.

▶ **Tip:** To discard an asset that is loaded and ready to be placed, use the arrow keys to navigate to the asset and then press the Escape key.

You can either click to place an image at 100% or click and drag to place an image and size it as you place it in the Document window. By dragging when you place an image, you are resizing the image. Resizing an image in Illustrator will most likely result in a different resolution than the original. Also, whichever thumbnail is showing in the loaded graphics cursor when you click or drag in the Document window is the image that is placed.

5 Move the loaded graphics cursor into the right, bottom artboard. Move it over the upper-left corner of the artboard and drag past the lower-right corner of the artboard to place and scale the image. Leave the image selected.

6 Click the Properties panel tab to show the panel. To arrange the image behind the other content on the artboard, click the Arrange button in the Properties panel and choose Send To Back.

7 Leave the image selected and choose File > Save.

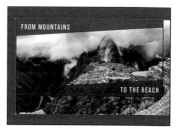

Masking images

● **Note:** You will hear people use the phrases "clipping mask," "clipping path," and "mask." Usually they mean the same thing.

To achieve certain design effects, you can apply a clipping mask (clipping path) to content. A *clipping mask* is an object whose shape masks other artwork so that only areas that lie within the shape are visible. In the first part of the figure to the right is an image with a white circle on top. In the second part of the figure, the white circle was used to mask or hide part of the image.

Image with a white circle on top.

The circle masking (hiding) part of the image.

Only vector objects can be clipping paths; however, any artwork can be masked. You can also import masks created in Photoshop files. The clipping path and the masked object are referred to as the *clipping set*.

Applying a simple mask to an image

In this section, you'll see how to let Illustrator create a simple mask for you on the Hills.jpg image so that you can hide parts of the image.

1 With the Hills.jpg image still selected, in the Properties panel, click the Mask button in the Quick Actions section.

▶ **Tip:** You can also apply a clipping mask by choosing Object > Clipping Mask > Make.

Clicking the Mask button applies a clipping mask to the image in the shape and size of the image. In this case, the image doesn't look any different.

2 Click the Layers panel tab to show it again. Click the Locate Object button (🔍) at the bottom of the panel.

Notice the <Clipping Path> and <Image> sublayers that are contained within the <Clip Group> sublayer. The <Clipping Path> object is the clipping path (mask) that was created, and the <Clip Group> is a set that contains the mask and the object that is masked (the embedded image).

Editing a clipping path (mask)

To edit a clipping path, you need to be able to select it. Illustrator offers several ways to do this. Next you'll edit the mask you just created.

1 Click the Properties panel tab to show the panel. With the Hills.jpg image still selected on the artboard, click the Edit Contents button (⊙) at the top of the Properties panel.

2 Click the Layers panel tab, and notice that the <Image> sublayer (in the <Clip Group>) is showing the selected-art indicator (small color box) to the far right of the sublayer name. That means it's selected on the artboard.

▶ **Tip:** You can also double-click a clip group (object masked with a clipping path) to enter Isolation mode. You can then either click the masked object (the image in this case) to select it or click the edge of the clipping path to select the clipping path. After you are finished editing, you can then exit Isolation mode using a variety of methods, as discussed in previous lessons (like pressing the Escape key).

3 Click the Properties panel tab and in the Properties panel, click the Edit Clipping Path button (⬚) at the top of the Properties panel. Back in the Layers panel, the <Clipping Path> will now be selected.

When an object is masked, you can edit the mask, the object that is masked, or both. Use these two buttons to select which to edit. When you first click to select an object that is masked, you will edit both the mask and the masked object.

▶ **Tip:** You can also edit a clipping path with transformation options, like Rotate, Skew, and so on, or by using the Direct Selection tool (▷).

4 With the Selection tool (▶) selected, drag the lower-right bounding point of the selected mask so it fits the artboard.

5 With the Properties panel showing, click the Edit Contents button (⬚) at the top of the Properties panel to edit the Hills.jpg image, *not* the mask.

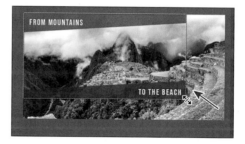

▶ **Tip:** You can also press the arrow keys on the keyboard to reposition the image.

6 With the Selection tool (▶), be careful to drag from within the bounds of the mask to reposition the image more in the center of the mask, and release the mouse button. Notice that you are moving the image and not the mask.

With the Edit Contents button (⬚) selected, you can apply many transformations to the image, including scaling, moving, rotating, and more.

7 Choose View > Fit All In Window.

8 Choose Select > Deselect and then choose File > Save.

Masking with a shape

You can also mask content with a shape that you create. In this section, you'll take a circle and mask an image to make a small image icon.

1. Select the gray circle to the left of the "Adventure For All" text and drag it on top of the Icon.jpg image.

   The circle will be behind the image.

2. To zoom in to the circle, press Command and + (macOS) or Ctrl and + (Windows) four or so times.

3. To arrange the circle on top of the image, click the Arrange button in the Properties panel and choose Bring To Front.

4. Shift-click the image to select the circle and the image. To mask the image with the circle, click the Make Clipping Mask button in the Quick Actions section of the Properties panel.

   Parts of the image that are outside the bounds of the circle are now hidden.

5. To resize and reposition the image, double-click in the circle to enter isolation mode. In isolation mode, you can edit the image and the mask (the circle) separately.

6 Move the pointer over the image and click to select it (be careful not to click the edge of the circle).

7 Shift-drag a corner of the image to make it smaller. Release the mouse button and then the key.

8 Move the pointer over the image and when the pointer looks like this: ⬐ᴴ, drag the image to reposition it.

9 Press the Escape key to exit isolation mode.

10 Click away from the masked image to deselect it, then drag the circle onto the artboard, to the left of the "Adventure For All" text.

11 Choose Select > Deselect, and then choose View > Fit All In Window to see everything again.

Masking an object with text

In this section, you'll use text as a mask for an image you placed. In this example, the text will remain editable rather than converting to outlines. Also, you'll use one of the images you previously placed as part of the Photoshop file.

1 With the Selection tool (▶) selected, click the PSD file on the top-right artboard that you placed earlier.

2 In the Layers panel, click the Locate Object button (⊘) to highlight the image content in the Layers panel.

3 Click the visibility column to the left of the Beach image to show it. Then click the Selected Art column in the Layers panel to select only that image.

4 Choose Edit > Copy and then choose Edit > Paste.

5 To paste another copy, choose Edit > Paste and drag it to an empty area.

6 In the Layers panel, click the eye icon () to the left of the Beach image in the PhotoFrame.psd group to hide it again.

7 Drag the first copy of the image on top of the large EXPLORE PARADISE text. Make sure that the image is positioned roughly as it is in the following figure.

8 Click the Properties panel tab to show the panel. Click the Arrange button in the Properties panel and choose Send To Back.

You should see the EXPLORE PARADISE text now. To create a mask from text, the text needs to be on top of the image.

9 To duplicate the image, choose Edit > Copy, and then choose Edit > Paste In Front.

10 Hide the copy by choosing Object > Hide > Selection.

11 Click the image under the text and Shift-click the EXPLORE PARADISE text to select them both.

12 In the Properties panel, click the Make Clipping Mask button.

The image should now be masked by the text.

13 In the Layers panel, click the visibility column for the hidden Beach image at the bottom of the Layers panel to show it.

14 Select the Rectangle tool (▭) in the toolbar and draw a rectangle as big as the image. Click the Fill box in the Properties panel and select a dark gray swatch.

15 Change the Opacity to **80%** in the Properties panel.

16 To send the rectangle behind the masked image, click the Arrange button and choose Send To Back. To bring it in front of the image that is not masked, click the Arrange button and choose Bring Forward.

17 Choose Select > Deselect and then choose File > Save.

Masking an object with multiple shapes

You can easily create a mask from either a single shape or multiple shapes.

- In order to create a clipping mask with multiple shapes, the shapes first need to be converted to a compound path. This can be done by selecting the shapes that will be used as the mask and choosing Object > Compound Path > Make.

- Ensure that the compound path is on top of the content to be masked and both are selected. Choose Object > Clipping Mask > Make.

Creating an opacity mask

An *opacity mask* is different from a clipping mask because it allows you to mask an object and also alter the transparency of artwork. You can make and edit an opacity mask using the Transparency panel. In this section, you'll create an opacity mask for the copied beach image, so that it fades into another image.

1 With the Selection tool (▶) selected, select the copied beach image and drag it into the position you see in the figure.

2 Select the Rectangle tool (▢) in the toolbar and drag to create a rectangle that covers most of the beach image. See the figure. This will become the mask.

3 Press the D key to set the default stroke (black, 1 pt) and fill (white) for the new rectangle to more easily select and move it.

4 Select the Selection tool (▶) and, while pressing the Shift key, click the beach image to select it as well.

5 Click the Properties panel tab to see the Properties panel again. Click the word "Opacity" to open the Transparency panel. Click the Make Mask button, and leave the artwork selected and the panel showing.

● **Note:** If you had wanted to create a mask with the same dimensions as the image, instead of drawing a shape, you could have simply clicked the Make Mask button in the Transparency panel.

After clicking the Make Mask button, the button now shows as "Release." If you were to click the button again, the image would no longer be masked.

Editing an opacity mask

Next you'll adjust the opacity mask that you just created.

1. Choose Window > Transparency to open the Transparency panel.

   By opening the Transparency panel, you will see the same panel you did when you clicked "Opacity" in the Properties panel. When you click Opacity to reveal the Transparency panel, you will need to hide the panel for the changes you make in this section to take place. In the free-floating Transparency panel, changes will happen automatically.

Tip: To disable and enable an opacity mask, you can also choose Disable Opacity Mask or Enable Opacity Mask from the Transparency panel menu.

2. In the Transparency panel, Shift-click the mask thumbnail (as indicated by the white rectangle on the black background) to disable the mask.

   Notice that a red X appears on the mask in the Transparency panel and that the entire beach image reappears in the Document window. Hiding the mask can be useful to see all of the masked object again (the image in this case) if you need to do anything with it.

3. In the Transparency panel, Shift-click the mask thumbnail to enable the mask again.

Tip: To show the mask by itself (in grayscale if the original mask had color in it) on the artboard, you can also Option-click (macOS) or Alt-click (Windows) the mask thumbnail in the Transparency panel.

4. Click to select the mask thumbnail on the right side of the Transparency panel. If the mask isn't selected on the artboard, click to select it with the Selection tool (▶).

   Clicking the opacity mask in the Transparency panel selects the mask (the rectangle) on the artboard. With the mask selected, you can't edit other artwork on the artboard. Also, notice that the document tab shows (<Opacity Mask>/Opacity Mask), indicating that you are now editing the mask.

5. Click the Layers panel tab to show the Layers panel, and click the disclosure triangle (▶) for the <Opacity Mask> layer to reveal the contents, if necessary.

6. With the mask selected in the Transparency panel and on the artboard, use the Properties panel to change the fill color to a white-to-black linear gradient, called White, Black.

You'll now see that where there is white in the mask, the beach image is showing, and where there is black, it is hidden. The gradient mask gradually reveals the image.

7   Make sure that the Fill box toward the bottom of the toolbar is selected.

8   Select the Gradient tool (▦) in the toolbar. Move the pointer to the right side of the beach image. Drag to the left, just past the left edge of the image.

Notice how the mask thumbnail in the Transparency panel now shows the gradient. Next you'll move the image but not the opacity mask. With the image thumbnail selected in the Transparency panel, the image and the mask are linked by default, so if you move the image, the mask moves as well.

9   In the Transparency panel, click the image thumbnail so you are no longer editing the mask (an arrow is pointing to it in the figure). Click the link icon (▤) between the image thumbnail and the mask thumbnail.

This allows you to move just the image or the mask, but not both.

● **Note:** You have access to the link icon only when the image thumbnail, not the mask thumbnail, is selected in the Transparency panel.

10 With the Selection tool, drag the beach image to the left. After dragging a little, release the mouse button to see where it's positioned.

● **Note:** The position of the beach image does not have to match the figure exactly.

11 In the Transparency panel, click the broken link icon () between the image thumbnail and the mask thumbnail to link the two together again.

12 Drag the beach image to the left to cover more of the mountains image.

13 Shift-click the mountains image to select it as well and, to send both behind the text on the artboard, choose Object > Arrange > Send To Back.

14 Choose Select > Deselect and then choose File > Save.

Working with image links

Note: Learn about working with links and Creative Cloud library items in Lesson 14, "Creating Artwork for a T-Shirt."

When you place images in Illustrator and either link to them or embed them, you can see a listing of these images in the Links panel. You use the Links panel to see and manage all linked or embedded artwork. The Links panel displays a small thumbnail of the artwork and uses icons to indicate the artwork's status. From the Links panel, you can view the images that have been linked to and embedded, replace a placed image, update a linked image that has been edited outside of Illustrator, or edit a linked image in the original application, such as Photoshop.

Finding link information

When you place an image, it can be helpful to see where the original image is located, what transformations have been applied to the image (such as rotation and scale), and more. Next you'll explore the Links panel to discover image information.

1 Choose Window > Workspace > Reset Essentials.

2 Choose Window > Links to open the Links panel.

Tip: You can also double-click the image in the Layers panel list to see the image information.

3 Select the Icon.jpg image in the Links panel. Click the disclosure triangle in the lower-left corner of the Links panel to reveal the link information at the bottom of the panel.

Note: The link information you see may be different than what you see in the figure, and that's okay.

Looking in the Links panel, you'll see a listing of all the images you've placed. You can tell whether an image has been embedded by the embedded icon (🖼) to the far right of the image name or thumbnail. If you don't see a name for an image listed in the Links panel, it usually means it was embedded when placing or came in with a layered PSD file that you preserved the layers for, or it was pasted into Illustrator. You'll also see information about the image, such as the fact that it's embedded (Embedded File), the resolution, transformation information, and more.

4   Click the Go To Link button (🔗) below the list of images.

The Icon.jpg image will be selected and centered in the Document window.

5   Choose Select > Deselect and then choose File > Save.

Embedding and unembedding images

As mentioned, if you choose not to link to an image when placing it, the image is embedded in the Illustrator file. That means that the image data is stored within the Illustrator document. You can choose to embed an image later, after placing and linking to it. Also, you might want to use embedded images outside of Illustrator or to edit them in an image-editing application like Photoshop. Illustrator allows you to unembed images, which saves the embedded artwork to your file system as a PSD or TIFF file (you can choose) and automatically links it to the Illustrator file. Next you will unembed an image in the document.

1   Choose View > Fit All In Window.

2   Click to select the Hills.jpg image (the mountains) on the right, lower artboard.

The Hills.jpg image was embedded when you originally placed it. With an embedded image, you may need to make an edit to that image in a program like Adobe Photoshop. You will need to unembed that image to make edits to it, which is what you'll do next to the image.

3   Click the Unembed button in the Properties panel.

▶ **Tip:** You can also choose Unembed from the Links panel menu (☰).

● **Note:** The embedded Hills.jpg image data is unembedded from the file and saved as a PSD file in the images folder. The image on the artboard is now linked to the PSD file. You can tell it's a linked graphic because of the X that appears in the bounding box when it's selected.

4 In the dialog box that appears, navigate to the Lessons > Lesson15 > images folder (if you are not already there). Make sure Photoshop (*.PSD) is chosen from the File Format menu (macOS) or the Save As Type (Windows) menu, and click Save.

If you were to edit the Hills.psd file in Photoshop, for instance, the image would be updated in Illustrator since it is linked.

5 Choose Select > Deselect.

Replacing an image

You can easily replace a linked or embedded image with another image to update the artwork. The replacement image is positioned exactly where the original image was, so no adjustment should be necessary if the new image has the same dimensions. If you scaled the image that you are replacing, you may need to resize the replacement image to match the original. Next you'll replace an image.

1 Click the Mountains2.jpg image on the artboard on the left. It was the first image you placed.

2 In the Links panel, click the Relink button (![]) below the list of images.

3 In the dialog box that opens, navigate to the Lessons > Lesson15 > images folder, and select the Mountains1.jpg image. Make sure that the Link option is selected. Click Place to replace the image.

4 Choose Select > Deselect, and then choose File > Save.

5 Choose File > Close as many times as necessary to close all open files.

Review questions

1 Describe the difference between linking and embedding in Illustrator.

2 How do you show options when importing images?

3 What kinds of objects can be used as masks?

4 How do you create an opacity mask for a placed image?

5 Describe how to replace a placed image with another image in a document.

Review answers

1 A *linked file* is a separate, external file connected to the Illustrator file by a link. A linked file does not add significantly to the size of the Illustrator file. The linked file must accompany the Illustrator file to preserve the link and to ensure that the placed file appears when you open the Illustrator file. An *embedded file* becomes part of the Illustrator file. The increased Illustrator file size reflects the addition of the embedded file. Because the embedded file is part of the Illustrator file, no link can be broken. You can update linked and embedded files using the Relink button (⬚) in the Links panel.

2 When placing an image using the File > Place command, in the Place dialog box, select the Show Import Options option. Selecting this option will open an Import Options dialog box where you can set import options before placing. In macOS, if you don't see the options in the Import Options dialog box, click the Options button.

3 A mask can be a simple or compound path, and masks (such as an opacity mask) may be imported with placed Photoshop files. You can also create layer clipping masks with any shape that is the topmost object of a group or layer.

4 You create an opacity mask by placing the object to be used as a mask on top of the object to be masked. Then you select the mask and the object(s) to be masked, and either click the Make Mask button in the Transparency panel or choose Make Opacity Mask from the Transparency panel menu.

5 To replace a placed image with a different image, select the image in the Links panel. Then click the Relink button (⬚), and locate and select the replacement image. Click Place.

16 SHARING PROJECTS

Lesson overview

In this lesson, you'll learn how to do the following:

- Package a file.

- Create a PDF.

- Create pixel perfect drawings.

- Use the Export For Screens command.

- Work with the Asset Export panel.

This lesson will take about 30 minutes to complete. To get the lesson files used in this chapter, download them from the web page for this book at www.adobepress.com/IllustratorCIB2020. For more information, see "Accessing the lesson files and Web Edition" in the Getting Started section at the beginning of this book.

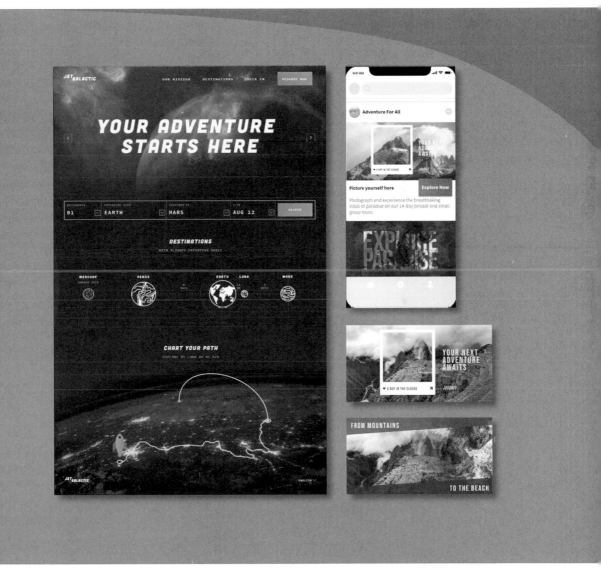

You can use various methods to share and export your projects as PDFs or to optimize your Illustrator content for use on the web, in apps, and in onscreen presentations.

Starting the lesson

Before you begin this lesson, you'll restore the default preferences for Adobe Illustrator and open the first lesson file.

● **Note:** If you have not already downloaded the project files for this lesson to your computer from your Account page, make sure to do so now. See the "Getting Started" section at the beginning of the book.

● **Note:** The projects for this lesson were designed by Meng He (www.mynameismeng.com).

1 To ensure that the tools function and the defaults are set exactly as described in this lesson, delete or deactivate (by renaming) the Adobe Illustrator preferences file. See "Restoring default preferences" in the "Getting Started" section at the beginning of the book.

2 Start Adobe Illustrator.

3 Choose File > Open. In the Open dialog box, navigate to the Lessons > Lesson16 folder. Select the L16_start1.ai file, and click Open.

4 In the warning dialog that appears, select Apply To All and then click Ignore.

There is at least one image, Ocean.jpg, linked to the Illustrator document that Illustrator can't find on your system. Instead of replacing the missing image(s) from this dialog box, you will open the Links panel so you can see which are missing, and replace them there.

5 If you skipped Lesson 15, the Missing Fonts dialog box will most likely appear. Click Activate Fonts to activate all missing fonts (your list may not match the figure). After they are activated and you see the message stating that there are no more missing fonts, click Close.

● **Note:** If you don't see Reset Essentials in the Workspace menu, choose Window > Workspace > Essentials before choosing Window > Workspace > Reset Essentials.

6 Choose Window > Workspace > Reset Essentials to ensure that the workspace is set to the default settings.

7 Choose View > Fit All In Window.

8 Choose Select > Deselect, if available.

9 To open the Links panel, choose Window > Links.

In the Links panel, you can see which linked images Illustrator cannot find on your system by the icon (◪) to the right of the name.

10 In the Links panel, select the Ocean.jpg image; it has an icon () to the right of its name. At the bottom of the panel, click the Relink button (⟨⟩) to link the missing image to the original.

11 In the dialog box that opens, navigate to the Lessons > Lesson16 > images folder, select the Ocean image, and click Place.

12 Choose Select > Deselect and then choose File > Save.

13 Close the Links panel group.

Packaging a file

When you *package* a file, you create a folder that contains a copy of the Illustrator document, any necessary fonts, copies of the linked graphics, and a report that contains information about the packaged files. This is an easy way to hand off all necessary files for an Illustrator project. Next you'll package the open file.

1 Choose File > Package. If you are asked to save the file, save it. In the Package dialog box, set the following options:

- Click the folder icon (▣), and navigate to the Lesson16 folder, if you are not already there. Click Choose (macOS) or Select Folder (Windows) to return to the Package dialog box.
- Folder name: **Social**
- Options: Leave at default settings.

The Copy Links option *duplicates* all of the linked files to the new folder it creates. The Collect Links In Separate Folder option creates a folder called Links and copies the links into it. The Relink Linked Files To Document option updates the links within the Illustrator document to link to the new copies.

2 Click Package.

Note: If the file needs to be saved, a dialog box will appear to notify you.

Note: The Create Report option, when selected, will create a package report (summary) as a .txt (text) file, which is placed in the package folder by default.

3 In the next dialog box, which discusses font licensing restrictions, click OK.

Clicking Back would allow you to deselect Copy Fonts (Except Adobe Fonts and non-Adobe CJK Fonts).

4 In the final dialog box to appear, click Show Package to see the package folder.

In the package folder there should be a copy of the Illustrator document and a folder named Links that contains all of the linked images. The L16_start1 Report text file contains information about the document contents.

5 Return to Illustrator.

Creating a PDF

Portable Document Format (PDF) is a universal file format that preserves the fonts, images, and layout of source documents created on a wide range of applications and platforms. Adobe PDF is the standard for the secure, reliable distribution and exchange of electronic documents and forms around the world. Adobe PDF files are compact and complete and can be shared, viewed, and printed by anyone with the free Adobe Acrobat Reader or other PDF-compatible software.

You can create different types of PDF files from within Illustrator. You can create multi-page PDFs, layered PDFs, and PDF/x-compliant files. Layered PDFs allow you to save one PDF with layers that can be used in different contexts. PDF/X-compliant files ease the burden of color, font, and trapping issues in printing. Next you'll save this project as a PDF so you can send it to someone else to view.

1 Choose File > Save As. In the Save As dialog box, choose Adobe PDF (pdf) from the Format menu (macOS) or Adobe PDF (*.PDF) from the Save As Type menu (Windows). Navigate to the Lessons > Lesson16 folder, if necessary. At the bottom of the dialog box, you can choose to save all of the artboards in the PDF or a range of artboards. Select All, then click Save.

When creating a PDF, to save all of the artboards to one PDF, select All, or to save a subset of the artboards to one PDF, select Range and type the range of artboards. For example, in a document with three artboards, a range can be "1-3" to save all three artboards or "1,3" to save the first and third artboards.

● **Note:** If you want to learn about the options and other presets in the Save Adobe PDF dialog box, choose Help > Illustrator Help and search for "Creating Adobe PDF files."

2 In the Save Adobe PDF dialog box, click the Adobe PDF Preset menu to see all of the different PDF presets available. Ensure that [Illustrator Default] is chosen, and click Save PDF.

There are many ways to customize the creation of a PDF. Creating a PDF using the [Illustrator Default] preset creates a PDF in which all Illustrator data is preserved. PDFs created with this preset can be reopened in Illustrator without any loss of data. If you are planning on saving a PDF for a particular purpose, such as viewing on the web or printing, you may want to choose another preset or adjust the options.

3   Choose File > Save, if necessary, and then choose File > Close to close the PDF.

● **Note:** You may notice that the file currently open is the PDF (L16_start1.pdf).

Creating pixel perfect drawings

When creating content for use on the web, in mobile apps, in onscreen presentations, and more, it's important that images saved from vector art look sharp. To enable designers to create pixel-accurate designs, you can align artwork to the pixel grid using the Snap To Pixel option. The *pixel grid* is a grid of 72 squares per inch, vertically and horizontally, that is viewable when you zoom to 600% or higher with Pixel Preview mode enabled (View > Pixel Preview).

Pixel-aligned is an object-level property that enables an object to have its vertical and horizontal paths aligned to the pixel grid. This property remains with the object when the object is modified. Any vertical or horizontal path in the object gets aligned to the pixel grid as long as the property is set for it.

Previewing artwork in Pixel Preview

When you export assets in a format such as GIF, JPEG, or PNG, any artwork that was vector is rasterized in the resulting file. Turning on Pixel Preview is a great way to be able to see what the artwork will look like when it's rasterized. First you'll view artwork with Pixel Preview on.

1 Choose File > Open. In the Open dialog box, navigate to the Lessons > Lesson16 folder. Select the L16_start2.ai file, and click Open.

2 Choose File > Document Color Mode, and you will see that RGB Color is chosen.

▶ **Tip:** After you create a document, you can change the document color mode using File > Document Color Mode. This sets the default color mode for all new colors you create and the existing swatches. RGB is the correct color mode to use when creating content for the web, for apps, or for onscreen presentations.

When designing for onscreen viewing (web, apps, etc.), RGB (Red, Green, Blue) is the preferred color mode for documents in Illustrator. When you create a new document (File > New), you can choose which color mode to use with the Color Mode option. In the New Document dialog box, choosing any document profile *except* Print sets Color Mode to RGB by default.

3 Select the Selection tool (▶), and click to select the Earth icon in the middle of the page. Press Command and + (macOS) or Ctrl and + (Windows) several times to zoom in closely to the selected artwork.

4 Choose View > Pixel Preview to preview a rasterized version of the entire design.

Preview mode

Pixel Preview mode

Aligning new artwork to the pixel grid

With Pixel Preview on, you'll be able to see the pixel grid and also align artwork to the pixel grid. When Snap To Pixel (View > Snap To Pixel) is enabled, shapes that are drawn, modified, or transformed snap to the pixel grid and appear crisp. This makes most artwork, including most Live Shapes, align to the pixel grid automatically. In this section, you'll view the pixel grid and learn how to align new content to it.

▶ **Tip:** You can turn off the pixel grid by choosing Illustrator CC > Preferences > Guides & Grid (macOS) or Edit > Preferences > Guides & Grid (Windows) and deselecting Show Pixel Grid (Above 600% Zoom).

1 Choose View > Fit Artboard In Window.

2 With the Selection tool (▶) selected, click to select the blue button shape with the text "SEARCH" on it.

3 Press Command and + (macOS) or Ctrl and + (Windows) several times until you see 600% in the View menu in the lower-left corner of the Document window (in the Status bar).

By zooming in to at least 600% and with Pixel Preview turned on, you can see a pixel grid appear. The pixel grid divides the artboard into 1-pt (1/72-inch) increments. For the next steps, you need to see the pixel grid (zoom level of 600% or greater).

4   Press Delete or Backspace to remove the rectangle.

5   Select the Rectangle tool (▭) in the toolbar. Draw a rectangle roughly the size of the one you just deleted.

● **Note:** As of this writing, the creation tools affected by Snap To Pixel are the Pen tool; the Curvature tool; shape tools, like the Ellipse tool and the Rectangle tool; the Line Segment tool; the Arc tool; the grid tools; and the Artboard tool.

You might notice that the edges of the rectangle look a little fuzzy. That's because Snap To Pixel is turned off in this document, so the straight edges of the rectangle aren't snapping (aligning) to the pixel grid by default.

6   Press Delete or Backspace to remove the rectangle.

7   Choose View > Snap To Pixel to turn on Snap To Pixel.

Now, any shapes that are drawn, modified, or transformed will snap to the pixel grid, if possible. By default, Snap To Pixel is turned on when you create a new document that uses the Web or Mobile document profile.

8   With the Rectangle tool selected, draw a simple rectangle to make the button, and notice that the edges appear cleaner.

▶ **Tip:** You can also click the Snap To Pixel option in the Properties panel with nothing selected and the Selection tool selected, or you can select the Snap To Pixel option (▣) on the right end of the Control panel (Window > Control).

The vertical and horizontal segments of the drawn artwork snap to the pixel grid. In the next section, you'll see that you can snap existing artwork to the pixel grid. In this case, I had you redraw the shape just to see the difference.

9 Click the Arrange button in the Properties panel and choose Send To Back to arrange it behind the "SEARCH" text.

Tip: You can press the arrow keys to move the selected artwork. The artwork will snap to the pixel grid.

10 Select the Selection tool, and drag the rectangle into position as you see in the figure.

As you drag, you may notice that the artwork is snapping to the pixel grid.

Aligning existing artwork to the pixel grid

You can also align existing artwork to the pixel grid in several ways, which is what you will do in this section.

Note: In this instance, the Align To Pixel Grid button in the Properties panel and the Object > Make Pixel Perfect command will do the same thing.

1 Press Command and – (macOS) or Ctrl and – (Windows) once to zoom out.

2 Select the Selection tool (▶), and click to select the blue stroked rectangle surrounding the rectangle you drew.

3 Click the Align To Pixel Grid button in the Properties panel to the right (or choose Object > Make Pixel Perfect).

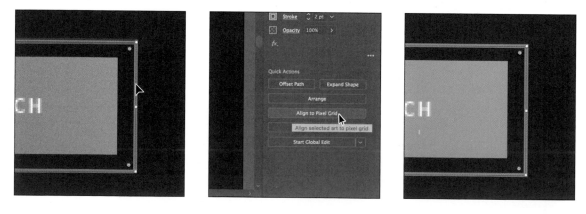

The rectangle was created when View > Snap To Pixel wasn't selected. After you aligned the rectangle to the pixel grid, the horizontal and vertical straight edges were snapped to the closest pixel grid lines. Live Shapes and Live Corners are preserved when this is done.

Objects that you pixel-align that have no straight vertical or horizontal segments are not modified to align to the pixel grid. For example, because a rotated rectangle does not have straight vertical or horizontal segments, it is not moved to produce crisp paths when the pixel-aligned property is set for it.

4   Click to select the blue "V" to the left of the button. You may need to scroll to the left. Choose Object > Make Pixel Perfect.

You will see a message in the Document window: "Selection Contains Art That Cannot Be Made Pixel Perfect." In this case, this means there are no vertical or horizontal straight edges to align.

● **Note:** The Align To Pixel Grid button does not appear in the Properties panel when an open path is selected.

5   Click the blue square surrounding the "V" (see the figure). Press Command and + (macOS) or Ctrl and + (Windows) several times to zoom in closely to the selected artwork.

6   Drag the top bounding point up to make the square a bit larger.

After dragging, notice that resizing the shape using the corner or side handles only fixes the *corresponding* edges (snaps them to the pixel grid).

7   Choose Edit > Undo Scale so it remains square.

8   Click the Align To Pixel Grid button in the Properties panel to ensure that all of the vertical or horizontal straight edges are aligned to the pixel grid.

Unfortunately, when aligning something that small, it may move. In this case, it is no longer aligned with the center of the "V." You will need to align the "V" with the square.

9   Press the Shift key, and click the "V" to select it as well. Release the Shift key, and click the edge of the square to make it the key object.

● **Note:** Moving artwork is constrained to whole pixels when transforming via the Selection tool, Direct Selection tool, Live Shape center widget, arrow keys, and Artboard tool. The Direct Selection tool snaps anchor points and handles to pixel or subpixel locations depending on the stroke settings of the path. This snap is similar to how the Pen tool snaps when you're creating artwork with it.

10 Click the Horizontal Align Center button (▦) and the Vertical Align Center button (▦) to align the "V" to the square.

11 Choose Select > Deselect (if available) and then choose File > Save.

Exporting artboards and assets

▶ **Tip:** To learn more about working with web graphics, search for "File formats for exporting artwork" in Illustrator Help (Help > Illustrator Help).

In Illustrator, using the File > Export > Export For Screens command and the Asset Export panel, you can export entire artboards, perhaps to show a design in progress, or just selected assets. The exported content can be saved in several file formats such as JPEG, SVG, PDF, and PNG. These formats are optimized for use on the web, on devices, and in onscreen presentations and are compatible with most browsers, yet each has different capabilities. Once selected, the artwork is automatically isolated from the rest of the design and saved as an individual file.

Slicing content

Before the Export For Screens command and the Asset Export panel existed, you had to isolate artwork that you wanted to export. This was done by placing the artwork on its own artboard or by slicing the content. (In Illustrator, you can create slices to define the boundaries of different web elements in your artwork.) When you save the artwork using the File > Export > Save For Web (Legacy) command, you can choose to save each slice as an independent file with its own format and settings.

It is no longer necessary to isolate artwork by slicing when using the File > Export > Export For Screens command or the Asset Export panel, since artwork is now isolated automatically.

Exporting artboards

In this section, you'll see how to export artboards in your document. This can be useful when you want to show someone a design you are working on, or to capture a design for use in a presentation, website, or app, among other uses.

1 Choose View > Pixel Preview to turn it off.

2 Choose View > Fit Artboard In Window.

3 Choose File > Export > Export For Screens.

   In the Export For Screens dialog box that appears, you can choose between exporting artboards and exporting assets. Once you decide what to export, you can set the export settings on the right side of the dialog box.

4 With the Artboards tab selected, on the right side of the dialog box, ensure that All is selected.

   You can choose to export all or a specific range of artboards. This document has only one artboard, so selecting All is the same as selecting a range of 1. Selecting Full Document will export all artwork in a single file.

5 Click the folder icon (▦) to the right of the Export To field. Navigate to the Lessons > Lesson16 folder, and click Choose (macOS) or Select Folder (Windows). Click the Format menu, and choose JPG 80.

   In the Formats section of the Export For Screens dialog box, you can set a Scale factor for the exported asset, create (or in this case edit) a suffix for the filename, and change the format. You can also export multiple versions with different scale factors and formats by clicking the + Add Scale button.

6   Click Export Artboard.

The Lesson16 folder should open, and you should see a folder named "1x" and, in that folder, the JPEG image.

7   Close the folder, and return to Illustrator.

Exporting assets

You can also quickly and easily export individual assets in file formats such as JPEG, PNG, PDF, and SVG using the Asset Export panel. The Asset Export panel lets you collect assets that you might export frequently and can be a great tool for web and mobile workflows because it allows for the export of multiple assets with a single click. In this section, you'll open the Asset Export panel and see how to collect artwork in the panel and then export it.

1   With the Selection tool (▶) selected, click to select the artwork labeled "VENUS" toward the middle of the artboard.

2   Press Command and + (macOS) or Ctrl and + (Windows) several times to zoom in to the artwork.

3   Press the Shift key, and click to select the artwork labeled "EARTH" to the right of the selected artwork.

4   With the artwork selected, choose Window > Asset Export to open the Asset Export panel.

The Asset Export panel is where you can save content for export now or later. It can work in conjunction with the Export For Screens dialog box to set export options for the selected assets, as you'll see.

5   Drag the selected artwork into the top part of the Asset Export panel. When you see a plus sign (+) appear, release the mouse button to add the artwork to the Asset Export panel.

The assets are tied to the original artwork in the document. In other words, if you update the artwork in the document, the corresponding asset is updated in the Asset Export panel. Every asset you add to the Asset Export panel is saved with the panel and will stay there until you delete it from either the document or the Asset panel.

▶ **Tip:** If you Option-drag (macOS) or Alt-drag (Windows) multiple objects into the Asset Export panel, the selected content will become a single asset in the Asset Export panel.

6 Click the name of the item in the Asset Export panel corresponding to the VENUS graphic and rename it **Venus**. Click the name of the item in the Asset Export panel corresponding to the EARTH graphic and rename it **Earth**. Press Return or Enter to accept the last name.

The asset name that appears is based on what the artwork is named in the Layers panel if you drag the asset into the panel. Also, how you name assets in the Asset Export panel is up to you. I name them so I can more easily keep track of what each asset is used for.

7 Click the Venus asset thumbnail to select it in the Asset Export panel.

As you add assets to the panel using various methods, you will need to first select the assets you'd like to export.

8 In the Export Settings area of the Asset Export panel, choose SVG from the Format menu, if necessary.

SVG is perfect for a website, but sometimes a co-worker may ask for a PNG version or other format of the same logo as well.

● **Note:** If you are creating assets for use on iOS or Android, you could click iOS or Android to display a list of scaled export presets appropriate to each platform.

● **Note:** The first part of the figure shows after clicking the + Add Scale button.

9 Click the + Add Scale button to export the artwork in another format (in this case). Choose 1x from the scale menu so the asset is exported at 100% of the size of the artwork on the artboard and ensure that Format is set to PNG.

In this case, an SVG file *and* a PNG file will be created for every selected asset in the Asset Export panel. You can also set a scale (1x, 2x, etc.) if you need multiple scaled versions of the selected assets—perhaps for Retina and non-Retina displays for raster formats like JPEG or PNG. You can also add a suffix to the exported filename. A suffix could be something like "@1x" to indicate the 100% scaled version of an exported asset.

▶ **Tip:** You can also click the Launch The Export For Screens Dialog button (▤) at the bottom of the Asset Export panel. This will open the Export For Screens dialog box, where you can adjust all the same settings, including a few more.

10 With the Venus thumbnail selected at the top of the Asset Export panel, click the Export button at the bottom of the Asset Export panel to export the selected asset. In the dialog box that appears, navigate to the Lessons > Lesson16 > Asset_Export folder, and click Choose (macOS) or Select Folder (Windows) to export the assets.

Both the SVG file (Venus.svg) and the PNG file (Venus.png) will be exported to the Asset_Export folder in separate folders.

Review questions

1 Describe what packaging an Illustrator document does.

2 Why do you align content to the pixel grid?

3 Describe how you export an artboard.

4 Name image file types that can be chosen in the Export For Screens dialog box and Asset Export panel.

5 Describe the generic process for exporting assets with the Asset Export panel.

Review answers

1 *Packaging* is used to gather all of the necessary pieces of an Illustrator document. Packaging creates a copy of the Illustrator file, the linked images, and the necessary fonts (if desired), and gathers those copies into a folder.

2 Aligning content to the pixel grid creates a crisp appearance at the edges of artwork. When Snap To Pixel is enabled for supported artwork, all the horizontal and vertical segments in the object are aligned to the pixel grid.

3 To export an artboard, choose File > Export > Export As (not covered in the lesson) or File > Export > Export For Screens. In the Export For Screens dialog box that appears, you can choose between exporting artboards and exporting assets. You can choose to export all or a specific range of artboards.

4 The image file types that can be chosen in the Export For Screens dialog box and the Asset Export panel are PNG, JPEG, SVG, and PDF.

5 To export assets using the Asset Export panel, the artwork to be exported needs to be collected in the Asset Export panel. Once it's in the panel, you can select the asset(s) to be exported, set the export settings, and then export.

INDEX

CMYK (cyan, magenta, yellow, black)
    color mode, 213
    fields, 216
    sliders, 14, 18
    tool tip, 89, 102, 169
Collect Links In Separate Folder option, 437
Color button, 24
color fill, applying, 18
color groups
    creating, 227–228
    saving edited colors as, 232
Color Guide panel, 228–231
Color Mixer, 14, 18, 23, 216
color modes, 213, 233, 440
Color Picker, 222–223
color spectrum, enlarging, 215
color stops
    applying in lines mode, 318
    copying, 309
    gradients as, 303
Color Swatches button, 223. *See also* swatches
Color Themes panel, 230, 235
colors. *See also* spot colors; tints of colors
    applying, 214–215
    applying and editing, 13
    assigning to artwork, 236
    changing number of, 234–235
    converting, 226
    customizing, 215–216
    editing in artwork, 231–234
    naming, 217
    saving as swatches, 216–217
columns of text, creating, 262
combining shapes, 127–133
Command key. *See* keyboard shortcuts
compound paths, creating, 125–126. *See also* paths
compound shape, creating and editing, 130–131
Consolidate All button, 57
Constrain icon, 160
Constrain Width And Height Proportions setting, 89
constraining paths, 190
Content Aware feature, 415

Content layer, 15
context and panel menus, 45–46
Convert Selected Anchor Points To Corner button, 180, 206, 208. *See also* anchor points
convert-point icon, 196, 198, 202. *See also* anchor points
Copy Links option, 437
copying
    appearance attributes, 227
    artwork, 109
    color stops, 309
    dashed lines, 176
    images, 424–425
    and reflecting artwork, 155
    symbol instances, 390
corner points
    converting between smooth points, 206
    converting smooth points to, 195–197, 208
    defined, 188
    icons, 173
corner tiles, using with brushes, 350
corner widgets, 12, 18, 90. *See also* Live Corners widget
corners
    creating with Curvature tool, 173–174
    rounding, 90–92
Create New Layer button, 281
Creative Cloud desktop application, 251–252
Creative Cloud libraries, 399–404. *See also* assets
cropping images, 414–416
Ctrl key. *See* keyboard shortcuts
cursors. *See* pointers
Curvature tool, 19
curved paths, 186–187, 192. *See also* paths
curves
    combining with straight lines, 197–198
    drawing with Pen tool, 193–194
cutting
    with Scissors tool, 115–116
    in straight line, 119–122
    vector artwork, 118–121

images *(continued)*

    resolution of, 414
    scaling, 414
    transforming, 413–414
importing plain-text files, 249
inches, choosing, 149, 153
iOS and Android, assets for, 447
Isolation mode
    editing groups in, 77
    entering, 421
    getting out of, 382

J

Jellyfish_poster.ai, 302
Join tool, 180–181
joining paths, 117–118
JPEG (.jpg) images, 412–413, 448

K

"Keep it Reel," 48
Keep Selected option, 338, 346
key anchor point, 73
key object, aligning, 72
keyboard shortcuts
    color fill, 18
    constraining handles, 190
    copying and reflecting, 155
    copying and rotating artwork, 157
    cutting in straight line, 120
    deselecting paths, 203
    duplicating layer content, 293
    hiding and showing panels, 43
    Layers panel, 298
    Live Corners widget, 91
    locking artwork, 404
    locking guides, 150
    locking objects, 68
    opacity masks, 428
    Pattern brushes, 353
    Presentation mode, 29
    Preview and Outline modes, 51
    reshaping shapes, 21
    Select All text, 273
    Selection tool, 35
    straight lines, 179, 181
    sublayers, 282

    Transform Align command, 176
    width points, 134
    zooming, 47, 49, 115
Knife tool, 118–121

L

Landscape orientation, 85
Launch The Export For Screens Dialog
    button, 448
launching Adobe Illustrator, 33
layer color, 279
layer comps, 417
layer content
    duplicating, 285, 293–294
    locking, 292
    showing and hiding, 279, 281–282, 284,
        297
    viewing, 287–288
layer indicator, 279
Layer Options dialog box, 281
layers
    appearance attributes, 296
    applying graphic styles, 382
    Collect For Export, 279
    creating, 279–281
    disclosure triangle, 280
    edit column, 279
    eye icon, 279
    hiding contents, 204
    Locate Object, 279
    locking and hiding, 291–293
    Make/Release Clipping Mask, 279
    moving content between, 285–286
    pasting, 294–296
    selection column, 279
    target column, 279
    Template Layer icon, 279
    visibility column, 279
    working with, 15
layers and content, reordering, 289–291
Layers panel
    finding content in, 282–284
    keyboard shortcuts, 298
    using, 24, 40
Leading value, 257–258

Round Join option, 368
rounding corners, 90–92
RTF files, 249
rubber band preview, 169
ruler intersection icon, 150
rulers and guides, 147–150

S

Save As option, 11
Save As Type option, 432
Save in Background, 7
saving
    colors as swatches, 216–217
    gradients, 305–306
    selections, 70
    shapes, 21
    workspaces, 44–45
scaling
    images, 414
    objects, 152–154
    patterns, 328
    point type, 245
    strokes and effects, 383–384
Scatter brushes, 333
Scissors tool, 115–116, 180
Select All text, 273
selecting
    and editing, 65–66
    hidden objects, 80
    with marquees, 67
    objects, 69–70, 79–80
    in Outline mode, 70–71
    paths with Pen tool, 188–190
    shapes and text, 28
    type objects, 374
Selection Indicator, 39, 283–284
Selection tool, 63–64
selections, locking, 170
selections, saving, 70
Send To Back option, 23, 79, 426
Shape Builder tool, 18–19, 21, 127–129, 176
shape modes, 130–131
Shaper tool, 38
shapes. *See also* editing paths and shapes
    circles, 94–96

combining, 127–133
deleting within marquees, 128
deselecting, 46
displaying, 80
drawing, 11
editing, 12
ellipses, 93–94
grouping, 93, 109
lines, 102–103
masking objects with, 426
masking with, 423–424
polygons, 97–99
rectangles, 87–92
reselecting, 72
reshaping, 21
selecting, 28
side widget, 98
stars, 100–101
and strokes, 116
Share Link, using with libraries, 401
shearing objects, 161–162
Shift key. *See* keyboard shortcuts
shortcuts. *See* keyboard shortcuts
Show All Layers option, 292
Show Import options, using to place
    Photoshop images, 416–418
Show Rulers button, 148
side widget, 98
Silhouettes option, 104
Simplify feature, 6
Sizes.ai file, 294
slicing content, 444
Small List View, choosing from panel menu,
    45
Smart Guides
    aligning circles, 126
    turning off, 136
    turning on, 11
    using, 63, 87, 98, 132, 389
    using with Pen tool, 190–191
    using with symbols, 396
Smooth Color blend option, 322–323
smooth points
    converting between corner points, 206
    converting to corner points, 195–197,
    208

Contributors

Brian Wood is a content developer and the author of fifteen + training books (Illustrator, InDesign, Muse, XD, and Adobe DPS), as well as training videos on Dreamweaver & CSS, InDesign, Illustrator, XD, Acrobat, Adobe Muse and others. In addition to training many clients large and small, Brian speaks regularly at national conferences, such as Adobe MAX, as well as events hosted by AIGA and other industry organizations. To learn more, check out www.youtube.com/askbrianwood or visit www.brianwoodtraining.com.

Production Notes

The *Adobe Illustrator Classroom in a Book (2020 release)* was created electronically using Adobe InDesign 2019. Art was produced using Adobe InDesign, Adobe Illustrator, and Adobe Photoshop.

References to company names, websites, or addresses in the lessons are for demonstration purposes only and are not intended to refer to any actual organization or person.

Images

Photographic images and illustrations are intended for use with the tutorials.

Typefaces used

Adobe Myriad Pro and Adobe Warnock Pro are used throughout this book. For more information about OpenType and Adobe fonts, visit www.adobe.com/type/opentype/.

Team credits

The following individuals contributed to the development of this edition of the *Adobe Illustrator Classroom in a Book (2020 release)*:

Writer: Brian Wood

Adobe Press Executive Editor: Laura Norman

Adobe Press Senior Production Editor: Tracey Croom

Copyeditor: Scout Festa

Keystroke Editors: Jean-Claude Tremblay, Victor Gavenda

Technical Editor: Victor Gavenda

Project Design: Danielle Fritz, Meng He, Trey Shively, and Brian Wood

Compositor: Brian Wood

Proofreader: Rebecca Winter

Indexer: Valerie Haynes-Perry

Cover design: Eddie Yuen

Cover illustration: Karan Singh, behance.net/madebykaran

Interior design: Mimi Heft

Lesson project credits

The following individuals contributed artwork for the lesson files for this edition of the *Adobe Illustrator Classroom in a Book (2020 release)*:

Danielle Fritz (www.behance.net/danielle_fritz): The hand lettering for "A Quick Tour of Adobe Illustrator (2020 release)," as well as lessons: 00, 1, 3, 4, 5, 7, 9, 11, 12, and 13.

Dan Stiles (www.danstiles.com): Lesson 1, "Getting to Know the Work Area," page 32.

Meng He (www.mynameismeng.com): Lessons 10, 15, and 16.

Trey Shively (@tshiv): Lesson 14.

In Chapter 3, a photo of a lemon by **Lauren Mancke** on Unsplash was used: unsplash.com/photos/sil2Hx4iupI

Throughout Chapter 10, the following is used:

Photo by **Danka & Peter** on Unsplash: unsplash.com/photos/tvicgTdh7Fg

Throughout Chapter 15 and 16, the following images are used:

Photo by **David Marcu** on Unsplash: unsplash.com/photos/f2SeKHyjqk4

Photo by **Andreas Kind** on Unsplash: unsplash.com/photos/pGdKXbqTOQ4

Photo by **Mason Panos** on Unsplash: unsplash.com/photos/8Lv4uJEoHmo

Photo by **Jeremiah Berman** on Unsplash: unsplash.com/photos/9dmycbFE7mQ

Photo by **Rodrigo Flores** on Unsplash: unsplash.com/photos/nk_JKocDkDo

Throughout Chapter 16, two photos by **NASA** (@nasa) on Unsplash.com are used:

unsplash.com/photos/rTZW4f02zY8
unsplash.com/photos/Q1p7bh3SHj8

The fastest, easiest, most comprehensive way to learn
Adobe Creative Cloud

Classroom in a Book®, the best-selling series of hands-on software training books, helps you learn the features of Adobe software quickly and easily.

The **Classroom in a Book** series offers what no other book or training program does—an official training series from Adobe Systems, developed with the support of Adobe product experts.

To see a complete list of our Classroom in a Book titles covering the 2020 release of Adobe Creative Cloud go to: www.adobepress.com/CC2020

Adobe Photoshop Classroom in a Book (2020 release)
ISBN: 9780136447993

Adobe Illustrator Classroom in a Book (2020 release)
ISBN: 9780136412670

Adobe InDesign Classroom in a Book (2020 release)
ISBN: 9780136502678

Adobe Dreamweaver Classroom in a Book (2020 release)
ISBN: 9780136412298

Adobe Premiere Pro Classroom in a Book (2020 release)
ISBN: 9780136602200

Adobe Dimension Classroom in a Book (2020 release)
ISBN: 9780136583936

Adobe XD Classroom in a Book (2020 release)
ISBN: 9780136583806

Adobe Audition CC Classroom in a Book, Second edition
ISBN: 9780135228326

Adobe After Effects Classroom in a Book (2020 release)
ISBN: 9780136411871

Adobe Animate Classroom in a Book (2020 release)
ISBN: 9780136449331

Adobe Photoshop Lightroom Classic Classroom in a Book (2020 release)
ISBN: 9780136623793

Adobe Press